So...You Say You Want To Feel Better?

A Book On Health And Healing

John J. Gaudio

Edited By Marcia Howenstein Nelken

RIVER PRESS

Cheshire, Connecticut

The River Press edition
Is the first publication of
So... You Say
You Want To Feel Better?

ISBN 1-887880-17-8
Library of Congress Catalog Card Number 2006929052

River Press edition: 2006

Printed in the United States of America

If you are closer to the Source that has made you, then you are closer to the Source that can heal you, because all of the information that ever was, and ever will be, is in that body of yours. How much of it you are using, is another question.

*

Meditation. Practice. It is not something that is difficult. It is not anything that is going to overwhelm you. It is something that is going to take you to a new place and make you a better person. I can honestly and truly say that it has made me a better person. I am not saying that I am extraordinary. I am not saying anything like that. I am saying that it has made me a better person, and I know from the knowledge that I have within me that there is a universal consciousness, because there is no way on This God's Earth that I would have known all of these things if there was not something that I tapped into. There is no way on earth that I would know all of these things from anything I read, because I have never read anything like this.

CONTENTS

EDITOR'S PREFACE

John J. Gaudio considers himself common: an ordinary person. He says, "Know what you have within you. I am a simple person who has touched upon certain things within the physical reality that can give us the capacity to move from where we are. If I can do it, anybody can do it."

John has developed an original work on attaining self-knowledge through meditation for over thirty years. His story is unique. Discovering meditation in his late thirties, he progressed in his own spiritual growth very quickly. Within two years he experienced major energy changes within his body as a result of his keen ability to utilize meditation to question and focus upon the needs of the mind and body. John began to access new platforms of information for human kind and the marvelous physical reality in which we live. Concurrently he taught meditation several nights a week at his informal meditation school called "Window of Reality," located in southern Connecticut, starting in the mid 1970s. At present, the school still meets, although now on a monthly basis. In John's words, "Window of Reality is an incubator of knowledge within us that stimulates us into every moment of every day."

For many years John taught classes in a fourteen-week series that developed information on the seven centers, or "chakras," of the body, and how to utilize the information to maintain one's own excellent health and balance, and how to heal others. In 1995 John's first book "COMMON AS RAIN," was published. Class transcripts were assembled into a book that encapsulated some of the knowledge of those years. Then John discarded the series format in class to move into informal dialogue with a core of students who practiced the knowledge. This second book "SO... YOU SAY YOU WANT TO FEEL BETTER?" continues the dialogue, delving even further into the essence of health and disease and healing.

Is it possible to maintain yourself on the centerline of health and never have to turn to modern medicine, pills, or drugs? John never suggests that we shun modern medicine. We must always use everything at our disposal to maintain our health. Yet successfully applying the knowledge in this book will make a vast difference. The knowledge is new. It will take a while for humanity to catch up to it. One hundred years from now, physicians will be applying this knowledge along with their medical interventions so that the patient can lead the way in their healing process. However, if we practice this information regularly in our meditations now, many years down the road we will be so glad we did, because meditation utilized in this manner becomes the quintessence of preventive medicine: taking control of our life through maintaining our health and inner balance.

In these chapters John is dropping into different levels of consciousness as he conveys all the necessary points around what he calls "the sphere of comprehension" of a given topic. The esoteric classroom is a feeling and sensing environment whereby teacher and students engage in dialogue to push the edge of knowledge while experiencing personal moments that can have transformational impact for days, weeks, or for one's whole life.

How the book was made should be mentioned: the editor chose certain class evenings as the subject matter of this book and read the chapters to John so that he could correct them from a deeper state of consciousness. Each class evening starts with a guided meditation, but for reasons of space, we include only two complete meditations. The written word, of course, cannot convey the velocity of the spoken word. If the reader wants to meditate with one of John's guided meditations, or is in ill health and wishes to heal oneself, John recommends purchasing one of his CD's through the website, www.johngaudio.com, or by writing to River Press, P.O. Box 2113, Cheshire, CT 06410.

Acknowledgments: Love goes to my children, Tod Lessard and Miranda Nelken, (and grandchildren, Ella and Zeb Lessard,) Zeke Valtz and Beata Nelken, and Ben Nelken and Gretchen Schwanfelder (and grandchild, Aubrey Schwanfelder-Nelken), and thank you for all the joy that we share together. Love and many thanks go to my friends, Gregory Blosick, Donna Bates Gaudio, Rosemary Payne and Noel Werle for their support and help with editing. Finally, I thank John Gaudio for his unstinting thirty years of revelatory transmission of love and knowledge. I feel honored to take part in the dissemination of this knowledge for humanity.

Marcia Howenstein Nelken, Editor
New Haven, Connecticut, May2006

PART ONE

THE TOOLS OF CONSCIOUSNESS

You know what you have to do within your mind and body. You know what it is within your body that is bothering you and causing a lack of harmony. It might be a lack of sleep, or too much of something like drinking, smoking, or eating. It might be your inability to speak out for yourself, or talk to other people. It might be over-reacting, or exhibiting too much anger. You know what you have to work on. You have to start. You can see it in humanity today, especially in the elderly people that you meet: if you do not want to be flawed when you get to that age, do not be flawed now in that hidden way. It is hidden there. Whatever it might be, it is hidden. Bring it out and correct it, because someday it will not be hidden. It will be on the surface. It will be right there. It will bother you. It will nag you. This flaw will no longer be correctable then. It will be so deep seated, the roots of it will be right into the essence of your soul. It is up to you to understand how to eliminate it now. That is what healing is all about: heal yourself first in the simplest way. If you have had a chronic thing happen to you like an ear infection, nose blockage, or painful feeling in the chest, and it is happening over and over, you have to begin to question why it is happening to you. Get some answers. Get some answers to the answers. That is the pathway. You are teaching yourself the velocity that is usable in comprehension. If you do not, that is how you are going to leave.

CHAPTER ONE

So... You Say You Want to Feel Better?

A uniquely beautiful process is taking place upon this planet if only we would take the opportunity to slow down to understand it within ourselves: deterioration of the body eventually happens to us when we cannot comprehend the speed, or velocity, of what is going on in our lives. I have been involved in many things in my lifetime, but there is nothing that I can think of that can help you more than understanding the tool of meditation. It is like being nowhere without a vehicle; then somebody gives you a vehicle so that you can move and see the sights of this world. Meditation is a vehicle of comprehension.

First of all, meditation is relaxation. You teach yourself to be still. Then you teach yourself to slow your process down. As you are slowing your process down, you give yourself some semblance of inner balance, which allows you to slow yourself down even further. The relaxation gives you the ability to stabilize yourself. The stabilizing quality gives you the ability to rejuvenate your mind and body. As you become quiet within yourself, as you begin to focus upon your mind and body, you can begin to eliminate stress and tension. Meditation has the capacity within itself to accelerate into something beyond relaxation, but that capacity has to come from you. You have to slow down your mind and body in order to cause some semblance of balance, so the meditative state can blossom into more than just relaxation. Then you move into a different portion of the level that you are dealing with. You are putting yourself in a position of becoming more transcendable and usable, as you dissect problems in life. You begin to draw upon more of the essence of your soul within the flesh. Profound things begin to happen to you as you make everything more usable for you, each and every day. Every place that you are in, no matter where it is, is unique and profound, but when you put yourself in a position of understanding that next aspect or problem in your life, it becomes absorbed. It becomes you. It becomes the sustenance that gives you the ability to change your next reaction in life. But if you begin to think of yourself as being profound, you are in one place too long. You become complacent and will not move into a more pliable area of understanding the

Awareness of God. I always like to put the thought in my mind that says: *If I am feeling the wonderment of where I am now, what must be coming next?*

I have the preconceived thought within my mind: *Everything is God.* If you do not believe that everything was started by Some Great Entity, then none of this information will work. *I* think of it as God. If you want to think of it as George, Harry, or the "Big Bang," whatever you want to name it, nevertheless, It is so Absolutely Unique. There has to be that Start, that Common Denominator, Nucleus of Explosion, or Nova, just like a star exploding throughout the universe. It has the quality of extending Itself out. Every particle becomes usable when you have the strength within the gravitational field of what you are to absorb It. You can become gigantic within your energy field; then you can absorb the Essence of Whatever It Might Be. Then logically speaking, more of the Essence of God Awareness becomes part of you in that next aspect in your life that you comprehend. That is the true essence of growth. If you believe the preconceived thought: *Everything is God,* then every part of your life, physically, sensually and emotionally will be increased, and the capability of it will be in balance. You will be able to feel and sense all of the beauty to your new capability, because you have used your mind correctly. You are slowing yourself down, in order to see where you are, so you may move into a more pliable area of understanding the velocity that is usable in comprehension. You are picking up meditation and are beginning to understand how to use it. It is just like picking up a tennis racquet and going out on the court to learn to play tennis.

What do I mean by the word, "velocity"? Let us say you are going down a highway one hundred m.p.h. and want to locate a house. Are you going to find it? You are going to have blurs on either side of you. But if you are going at a proper speed, you can find the house because you are going at a speed that is usable in absorbing what is in front of you. If you want to know the next thing that is in front of you, you have to know the speed or velocity of absorption. That is what I am talking about in terms of everything: you go slowly, so that you can strip away any fear that you might have through comprehension.

Now, I do not want you to have a preconceived thought that immediately you are going to go to some profound place in your mind. You are going to be within yourself, and if you go slowly, you will feel very comfortable. Then you will want to drop a little deeper. You are going to tap into the higher essence of you. If you feel a little more comfortable because you are going at a proper speed, more information and vibration will be absorbed. You can feel more creativity within you, and more of the essence of beauty and balance and love, and you will make it all usable within the flesh. You are teaching yourself the proper velocity for you, not only in meditation, but also in the moments of each and every day. Every time you use meditation, it changes your life forever. You will never be the same again. You will have more compassion and balance and love, and more of the strength to use everything in a more positive way. It becomes you. It flows through you, and some of it stays with you. Do not take my word for it, you will see. Each time it flows through you, more of it stays with you. Each moment of every day becomes more cherished because you see all of the beauty around you. Each time it gives you the opportunity to say: *I must slow down. I must look at what I have, because I am truly unique and beautiful.*

Not that it is always easy. Sometimes we get caught up in the mundane aspects of our lives, physically, sensually and emotionally, and do not give ourselves a chance to see the awesome beauty that we have around us. Most times we are rather complacent. In meditation however, you begin to see certain things. You begin to see that you do not like some of the ways you are acting in life: that you are either over-escalating or under-escalating yourself in certain areas. In meditation class I have seen it happen so many times: a person will come once or twice, then is gone. Maybe two or three years later, we might see them return to class. They were not ready to examine self the first time around. They had to leave and perhaps blame me. I understand that. That is fine. I can take the weight of it. Probably eighty-percent of the people who come into the classes dislike me for being up in front of class. What makes it rewarding for me, there is always that one person out of a thousand who is lifted to a level where they understand the brightness of the moment. You examine yourself, find new solutions to life problems and become more usable in life.

Sometimes you might experience a difficult time in life, and at such a time, it might seem to you that you do not deserve it. All of us have experienced those times. You just have to be strong within the quest of the particular event and deal with whatever it is. Sometimes if you do not look at a situation in a positive way, you do not appreciate it, and you begin to think that this planet is not a nice place to be. But it *is* nice, it *is* beautiful, and there are reasons for certain things happening to you. If you can just take the opportunity to slow down and ask why, then you can begin to see why. Perhaps you needed the strength that the particular situation gives you. Even though it seems negative within the physical sense, it really is not. There is growth in everything. I am not saying life is always easy, but because of what you do in meditation in a balanced way, it will be easier. You will have the balance and strength to come through events in a more positive way, whereas if you did not have this basic strength, there is more of a chance of being overwhelmed.

I had a situation, probably self-induced, happen to me a few years ago that would have crumbled most people. There were some difficulties I put others through, too. I had to use my strength in many different avenues. I had to send out positive thought patterns to many different people in order to sustain some semblance of balance in all directions, and at the same time, try to stay outside of the situation most of the time. I have become stronger because of it. Some people have not. I regard those difficult times as new avenues of strength. I know there is a reason for things happening. I do not stifle a particular thing that happens to me. Rather, I look at it and use it. If I do not want another seemingly difficult situation to happen, I know that if I understand it, there is less of a chance of a similar situation ever happening to me again. There is beauty in that. There is growth in that. If you think of certain situations as negative, you never leave those areas because you dig yourself into the particular structure that says: *I am not going to be out of this area because I am not good enough to be out of it.* Nothing is negative if you use it to make it understandable within you and change yourself for the next time. As you do so, you are absorbing more of the essence of your soul each time.

CHAPTER TWO

The Fold of Meditation
A Guided Meditation

(John's remarks on preparing for meditation:) In the beginning practice of meditation you might want to give yourself two fifteen-minute meditations daily. The first meditation is for the purpose of rejuvenating your mind and body. At a later point, you may want come back to another fifteen-minute meditation, with the capability of using your mind at a higher level in order to transcend.

Choose a quiet place and time. Put on some quiet, soothing music. Choose a comfortable chair that supports a straight spine because eventually energies will be flowing up your spine. Place your feet flat on the floor. Do not cross your legs or arms, because you want to begin to comprehend how the energy flows within the body. Place your hands on your lap, palms faced either up or down. At first, you may want to replenish the supply of energy in your body, so you place palms faced down on your lap, thereby staying within yourself to absorb energy within the first center of awareness, the survival center, located at the base of the spine, which is "love of self."

As you start relaxing, you will begin to feel rejuvenation coming into your body. When you begin to achieve a deeper sense of relaxation and rejuvenation, you may want to turn your palms faced up. Then the survival energies in your hands become more transcendable. You are interrelating to your seventh center of awareness, the crown center at the top of the head. You are beginning to open up a viable channel of awareness to the higher self, and are acquiring the capability of absorbing some of those energies and using them in every moment of every day. Start to train your mind by putting the preconceived thought within your mind: *I will come out of the meditation in fifteen minutes.* It will happen. You will surprise yourself with the power of your mind.

You will be taking three deep breaths. As you inhale, visualize love coming into your body, collecting all of the stress, tension and fatigue of the day. As you exhale, visualize the love expelling the stress, tension and fatigue. You will actually feel yourself relaxing and rejuvenating. Put other preconceived thoughts in your mind: *My mind will be sharp and alert. I will be aware of everything that is going on within me. I will be going at a speed that is just right for me, so I may comprehend.* Put other good thoughts in your mind. Some people find it hard

5

to think of self as being good. It is hard for me too, at times. I want you to think of yourself as good, by saying: *Deep down inside, I know without question, that I am good. I love myself.* Love yourself, with the intent in the back of your mind knowing that you will have more love within you to give to others in a balanced way: *I will feel compassion, love and balance which will give me the capacity to go forward in life in a uniquely beautiful way, and I will feel and sense these qualities in every moment.*

The first person you work on is you, so it is important to prepare yourself. As you enter the first meditation, your intent will be to fill that chalice of what you are with energy, so you can really help other people. You have to believe in yourself. You have to really believe that you can do it. To make it sensible, logical and understandable, think of yourself as being part of God. Say: *I am part of God.* Then your next thought should be: *The more I understand about everything, the more of God I have within me.* Then it becomes easier to say: *I can do this! I am part of That Total Picture. Each time I add a brushstroke of reality to myself, I am involved in more of That Picture.*

Think about that when you are thinking about how truly unique you are and you can change anything that takes place in your body. Your incentive should be: *Each level that I hit gives me more of that energy to actually change whatever it is into perfection and eliminate the probability of harm happening to me.* The uniqueness is within all of us, so it is important that you have these preconceived thoughts within your mind as you enter the meditative state and think about what meditation is. Meditation is that tool that teaches you to become transcendable within the awareness of self, and as you do so, you actually use more of the essence of the soul within the flesh.

(The Guided Meditation:) Close your eyes now and begin to relax. I want you to think about the value of love, and what is a uniquely beautiful process of comprehending who you are, within the essence of it. Each time, and I am sure some of you have felt this, when you reach another level within the awareness of what you are, there is a compelling thought that tells you: *Truly there is Something that has made All of This, and It Is Uniquely Beautiful!* As you meditate and deal with the velocity in a balanced way, you begin to feel some of that esoteric comprehension. It is within all of us. Either you have the capacity to feel and sense it quickly, or not so quickly, but no matter at what velocity you try to comprehend, it is uniquely beautiful, because it is a process of understanding who you are, within the Awareness of God. Meditation is that tool that can begin to understand how to knowingly enter into that process with the conscious mind. In every moment of every day you do absorb the essence of what you are, within your ignorance, but as you begin to understand and filter That God Awareness into that which is usable in a common way, your conscious mind becomes more involved in wanting to become more of That God Awareness. That should be your thought of today, or tomorrow: a thought of understanding who you are, within the participation of understanding who you can become.

Take a nice deep breath: inhale... and hold it. Now as you slowly exhale, begin to feel yourself relax, relax, relax. Know that you are rejuvenating yourself. Put it in your mind. Know the power of your mind. All the stress and tension is dissipating, and in its place there is a soothing, relaxing, comforting energy. How fantastic that makes you feel!

Take another deep breath: inhale... Think of your soul coming into your body as you take the breath. It is filling you with balance, compassion and love. As you slowly exhale, your soul is getting rid of the fatigue, tension and stress. Relaxation and balance are upon your mind.

A third deep breath: inhale... Once again, feel comforting energy coming into your body, and as you exhale, actually feel yourself relaxing and rejuvenating your mind and body. To utilize your mind correctly to begin to comprehend stability and relaxation within your body, put these preconceived thoughts within your mind: *Every part of my body that I look upon will be rejuvenated for all of my tomorrows. I understand in the meditative state that I transcend into a higher level, thereby making more of my soul essence usable within my mind and body.*

Put your mind on your toes. As you do so, feel and sense the rejuvenation within this area. Relaxation, comfort and rejuvenation are within your toes. You are healing yourself, and your toes are very relaxed and comfortable.

Your mind is upon your feet. Relax and rejuvenate your feet. Utilize your mind correctly to actually feel the stress and fatigue dissipating from your feet, and replace the stress and fatigue with relaxation, comfort and rejuvenation. How fantastic your feet feel! Stay there for a moment. Feel and sense balance and relaxation. Remember that you walk upon the earth. The earth has a tremendous amount of energy. You should begin to concentrate on drawing it within your feet. Just as your body has a total conscious awareness and you have millions of cells within you, you are a cell upon this earth and can nourish yourself if you understand. You understand now that you can do so.

Relax your ankles and lower part of your legs, right up to your knees. Feel the healing properties within this area. Know the power and balance that you have within your mind when you use it for good. Your ankles are relaxed, rejuvenated and very comfortable.

With the thought of balance and compassion upon your mind as it interrelates to love of self, relax your knees. Stay there for a moment. Nourish this area. Feel the compassion and balance within this area for you. Know that it is selfish if you do not work on you, because then you cannot give to others. Therefore, this is your time.

Relax and rejuvenate the upper part of your legs, including your hips. As you relax and rejuvenate this area, you can feel and sense new strength and vitality coming into your mind and body. It truly interrelates to love of self. You can feel the capabilities of survival within it. It gives you the strength of mind and body to go forward in your normal, daily life. Feel it. Sense it. You feel extremely good about yourself. You understand what is right for you. You know without question, that everything is functioning properly within your hips and your legs, right down to your toes, and you are very relaxed and comfortable.

Relax and rejuvenate the lower part of the trunk of the body. You can feel and sense control over your emotional state. It gives you the comprehension of human decency. As you use your mind correctly now in the meditative state, there is more human decency upon this entire earth plane, because you are drawing it in right now. If you do not like some of the events that you see happening in the world, work on yourself. As you do so, as a single individual, you change everybody without manipulating, just by your growth. Know the power of your mind. You know without question, that everything is functioning properly within this area. You are very relaxed and comfortable.

Relax and rejuvenate the upper part of the trunk of the body. As you relax this area, you tap into an inner peace and beauty. Now you can feel and sense compassion and balance and love. Feel and sense it within you at a universal level, as it purifies the comprehension of compassion and balance and love within you. It actually changes the comprehension of love within you. It truly is the essence of love flowing from that next level and becoming usable within you because you are using your mind properly. You are bridging the gap between you and the essence of your soul. In doing so, you are unleashing the creativity and wonderment of what you are at a soul level. Feel the balance and compassion and peacefulness of this area as you heal the upper part of your body. Once again, you know without question that everything is functioning properly within this area. You are very relaxed and comfortable.

Relax your back, from the base of your spine to the base of your neck. You can actually feel and sense your posture being corrected, and strength and vitality for all of your tomorrows. Feel it. Sense it. Make it you. Your back is very relaxed and comfortable.

Relax and rejuvenate your shoulders and your arms, starting with your fingers, and moving slowly up to the shoulders. Feel the energy. Focus upon your arms. Feel and sense all of the fatigue dissipating, and relaxation and comfort taking its place. Know that you are healing your shoulders and arms, and you are very relaxed and comfortable. You are feeling absolutely fantastic.

Relax your forehead, your jaw, your cheeks, your mouth, your nose, your ears and your eyes. Each part is being healed. Feel it. Sense it. You have that capability within you. Can you become a person who can transcend to a particular level to eliminate misconception from your mind and body? As you meditate, practice each time. As you go deeper into your meditations, you open up a channel of awareness to your higher self. You allow the essence of it to flow and become usable within the flesh. Each time that you use it properly within your ordinary day, more will come for the next time. Use that for incentive so that you will want to go forward to feel and sense more of the wonderment as it becomes usable. Never lose the thought that you must consider the information that you receive in your meditation and use it in the next few days. If you do not, no more will come, because you truly are the teacher within the teacher. If you are a proper teacher, and your soul is, your soul will not allow too much information to come in because that would cause confusion.

Visualize a pure white dot of energy in your heart center. Think of it as your soul sending a light to you within the flesh. That is exactly what it is. This light has the full spectrum of what you are. Within the capacity of what you are within the physical reality, there are prisms that refract light into necessary areas, making it usable for you in every moment. As you visualize or feel or sense the light, it begins to expand. As it does so, you can feel and sense it purifying every part of your body right down to the cellular level, healing as it does so. The white light totally surrounds that uniquely beautiful body of what you are. You can feel and sense the strength within it, and the rewards. It has the capability of going into necessary areas of misconception in order to become more usable in changing the density of the misconception. It is so awesomely beautiful. Feel and sense it. Compound the reality of it helping you, by understanding that it changes the balancing qualities within the immune system. You actually give yourself an aura that protects you from disease. Think about what you are doing and from where you are doing it. When you meditate, you put yourself closer to your soul. When you are closer to your soul, you have more of its capacity. When you have more of its capacity, you can give yourself the balancing qualities that are necessary to deal with the sustenance that is necessary for growth. The white light totally surrounds you once again. Feel the security within it. Within the wonderment of that white light, knowing that you are nourishing yourself within the silence of what you are, and that everything is functioning properly within your mind and body, rejuvenate yourself. Use the music. Each note of the music will be suitable and usable for you. Relax.

(After a silent twenty-minute interval, John prepared the students to return to their normal states of consciousness:) You will now return to your normal state slowly. You can do so, just by changing your breath pattern and saying to yourself: *I wish to come back slowly, while retaining all of the beauty, balance and compassion within my mind and body. Everything is functioning properly within my body.* Open your eyes. You should have a nice smile on your face because you should be feeling absolutely fantastic. From one human being to another, I love you. I hope that you use the meditation. I know that it will change your life forever.

CHAPTER THREE

You Are a Multi-Dimensional Reality

Think about what you just participated in. Some people come here for the first time and say, "Well, I have meditated before, but I never went through a process of talking to my toes, feet, or ankles; I always used a mantra or sound." But if you consider the usefulness of what we have participated in, you are trying to comprehend you. If you can focus in upon you, and rejuvenate you, then everything that comes forward from that moment on becomes more comprehendible. You have balance, which gives you the ability to see what is happening in front of you. That is the unique process of understanding growth.

Meditation is a tool of understanding the speed or velocity that is usable in comprehension. First, you give yourself balance by rejuvenating yourself. Then you lift yourself to a plateau where you can absorb what you are dealing with in your life, or what you want to put into motion within the meditative state. It is just like the hypnotist that puts you in a hypnotic state: when you are told to do something, you retain it by using and absorbing it instantly. By meditating you are eliminating those distortions out there, those radio waves. You are focusing in upon that one station, and that one station deals with the velocity of understanding you. Therefore, it is important that you use the meditative state in a balanced way.

Use your mind properly, which means, think about the things that are good for you. Begin to solve your problems in life. There is no better place to solve them, than from that plateau of comprehension. I tell you not to cross your limbs because I want you to begin to understand what is going on within your body. Every part of your body has a consciousness to it. If you have a distortion in the form of an illness or discomfort that might become harmful in a particular area of your body, and you know what the consciousness of that area is, you can begin to focus upon that area and use it within the awareness of your mind, each and every moment of every day. There is a reason for that distortion in the energy field. If you can use your mind, and know the awareness of the particular place, you can eliminate it before it has a chance to eliminate you.

That is the nature of disease. You are a multi-dimensional reality within the physical sense, and if you begin to understand who you are, and how you relate to everything, more of that reality becomes usable within the flesh. That is what meditation is all about. You are transcending or moving to a higher level. When you transcend to a higher level, some of that reality becomes usable. When you participate in coming out of the meditative state, it changes the reality of how you use your mind, and that is growth. But then you have to take the information that you have received in the meditative state, and use it in each and every day. If you do not, no more will come, because that becomes a contradiction to growth.

Therefore, meditation becomes that tool first to rejuvenate yourself, refuel the supply of energy and balance your mind so that you can go forward to comprehend. I have the preconceived thought within my mind: *I am here upon this planet as an extension of my soul, and I set probabilities in motion within the physical sense to become more evolved, just as the actor performs upon the stage to become a better actor within the particular art form.* The same thing takes place when you manifest a body within the physical sense: you put it in the stage of life and set certain sets of probabilities in motion in order to become more evolved. As you do so, you place at your disposal different layers, structures, or "bodies" of energy, that interrelate to the awareness of what you are. Those different layers interrelate to different energy centers within your body, and those centers are the vehicles that you use to comprehend, each and every day, whether you know it or not.

When we first started these classes thirty years ago, a lot of the information that we mentioned back then, seemed to be out of the reach of most people. They could not use it in every moment of every day. Now it has become common knowledge where we can use it. For instance, there are nurses in hospitals who now use therapeutic touch. There are healers sending energy to people in distant places. There are people who are beginning to understand the usage of the mind as a powerful tool of understanding the body. It is important that you begin to understand how truly unique and multi-dimensional you are. You can bridge the gap between you and your soul, and use more of those different layers that you placed there for you, by understanding the particular source that you gave to yourself at birth. You gave your source, your energy, to a particular body within the physical sense, which is you. You gave yourself a portion of what you want to achieve, so you can achieve those probabilities in a balanced way. You are dealing with only part of your probabilities, not the total identity. Your probabilities might involve learning compassion, love, or tolerance. Whatever it is, you set those probabilities in motion from a different level. Using meditation as a tool, you begin to understand what those particular things are within the physical sense that you must comprehend.

First, you have to slow yourself down, replenish the supply of energy, and adjust and balance your vehicle so you may understand the velocity, or speed, that is usable in comprehension. If you are going at the proper velocity, you begin to notice everything around you. You begin to comprehend and absorb. You begin to see the painting of life. You see the trees, the leaves and the different people along the roadside, the stop signs. You see all of the things that are necessary for you to participate in safety. The same thing takes place in comprehension: if you have balance that you receive from meditation, you have more of a chance of comprehending, absorbing and using that next thing that you are trying to comprehend. Logic tells you that. Then there is less out there that can bother you and more information within you for comprehending whatever comes next. I have another preconceived thought within my mind that makes some of the statements I just mentioned seemingly usable in simplicity and logic: *Everything out there is God. Everything! ...And we are part of It.* Therefore, as you comprehend that next thing, more of God Essence becomes usable within you, and you use more God Essence in each moment. That is a uniquely beautiful process of absorbing that next level that is usable for you.

Let us talk for a moment about a level that might be usable for you. If you were going to build a house, you would need a foundation. In meditation you are building a foundation that is moveable within the physical sense. In order to do that with balance, you must focus upon and work on you. I say to you that you are egotistical if you do not work on yourself. For instance, if you have a child who asks for water, and you do not have water, you cannot give it. In the same way, if the child asks you for love, and you do not have love, you cannot give it. If you do not work on yourself and that basic foundation, you have nothing to give. You cannot give the child love, but you can give the child an analogy of love, as you participate with the child in trying to comprehend love.

If you work on yourself and fill the vessel of what you are with the water of life, then it gives you the capacity to give to others in a balanced way. That is truly dealing with self first. If you have stability within you, you have the knowledge, strength and survival energies within you to truly give love. You have the capacity to go forward and give others whatever is necessary to grow from there. In relating to whomever it might be, you may be giving a "no" answer. An example: let us say that every day your child comes in asking for a lollipop, and you know those lollipops are eventually going to decay the child's teeth, so you have to have the strength to say, "No. Those lollipops are not good for you." You know that because you have participated in an avenue of comprehension that gave you the information to know it as so.

"Love of self" becomes a vehicle so you can give "love to an-other." If not, you see it in life so many times, two people think they love each other, but then start bombarding each other and eventually end up parting rather than joining. On the other hand, if each loves self, then each goes forward to love the other, the two begin to blend and be purified. It becomes a comprehension of the duality and quest of love at a different level. They are dealing with "love of two," rather than "love of one." They are accomplishing the first two steps of a sequence of love that takes place within the physical sense. The sequence of love is a vehicle of comprehension that deals with you and how you interrelate to everything else in your life.

Therefore, work on yourself, with the intent in the back of your mind: *If I fill the chalice of what I am, I will have something to give to my mate, daughter, son, or whomever else if they come seeking help.* And beyond that, you will begin to feel and sense the true joys of why we are here. When events become staggeringly tough, it will give you the capacity to deal with some semblance of strength. When events become pleasurable, you will begin to understand all of the vibrations because you will have won the right to have that capacity within you. That is what meditation can give you. That is what the sequence of events is that we talk about in meditation.

There is an energy source that flows from another level. You are part of that energy source, which is earth. As you walk upon.the earth, you absorb energies and use them. There are different layers, or struc-tures, of comprehension even within earth's atmosphere. As you grow, earth grows too. Remember in the guided meditation when we first mentioned the toes and the feet? I am talking about areas of compre-hension now: your feet interrelate to the first major center of survival, which is "love of self," located at the base of your spine. Your hands also interrelate to survival and "love of self." But when you begin to come into the fold of meditation, your hands become transcendental to another level. You begin to use the velocity of "survival from the soul," which is located within the crown center at the top of your head. It provides an aura of white. When you meditate, you are using the sur-vival center at the base of the spine, which is the color red, and esoteric survival at the top of the head, which is white. The crown center has the capacity to quench the thirst of misconception by using the refractability of what it is.

You truly are multi-dimensional. By using the meditative state to quiet yourself down, it gives you a direction. It gives you the capacity to grasp upon what is coming next. That should be your goal. You are doing yourself a tremendous favor, because you are eliminating the probability of harm happening to you. Joy, happiness, balance and love become more usable. Meditation does not eliminate all the problems, but gives you the capacity to comprehend and eliminate them, one at a time. That is the uniqueness of that place of absorption. Sit. Keep your feet flat on the floor. Keep your palms faced down on your lap when you have a lot of fatigue; you will want to stay within yourself within the survival center, "love of self," to replenish the supply of energy within you. After a while, if you wish to become transcendable, turn your palms faced up. Then it becomes more transcendable within the survival energies in your hands, because now you are interrelating to your crown center. You are using higher, transcendable sources of energy. You are beginning to open up viable channels of awareness to your higher self. You have the capability of absorbing some of those energies and using them in every moment of every day.

I love you, and when I say I love you, I am being selfish, because more love comes through me each and every time. But my intent is beyond the structure of that. I send love forward from one person to another. I hope your intent will be to understand the structure that is usable in comprehension, and make your life deal with more of the pleasures.

CHAPTER FOUR

Consciousness as a Usable Vibration of Eliminating Disease

Let us consider the reasons behind illness. Some of us might think of illness as negative, but if we consider it within the physical sense, and interrelate it to a higher level, we begin to understand the awareness of why we are here within life. We can consider illness as a tool of the soul, telling us we are going in the wrong direction. We are here upon the planet to grow in consciousness. If we contradict that, there is a safety-valve system within illness that causes us to have a particular ailment. If we do not take into consideration the reasoning behind the ailment, there is usually a parting of the way. The body is shed, and we go back up to the soul and re-manifest another body.

Now, if we consider illness as a usable vibration within the physical sense, then we can begin to consider the avenues that we can participate in within consciousness, utilizing consciousness as a usable vibration of eliminating disease. For example, if we know the awareness or consciousness of what our hands, elbows, shoulders, or any other part of the body is, and we get a pain in a particular area, we question the sphere of that comprehension and begin to get answers about that. If we are asking the right questions about the ailment, it begins to rejuvenate and eliminate the disease, pain, or agony in the particular area. Now, if we hit an area where we can consider the total reality of the ailment and participate in hitting that avenue within the higher essence of what we are, we can totally eliminate it from the body. If not, we might be at a level where we are able to slow the ailment down, or at a level where we are able to eliminate the pain, or at a level where we can begin to slow the ailment down enough so we can stay here longer upon the earth plane in order to achieve some of the probabilities that we set in motion.

If we consider it in this way, then we can take the strength of the identity of saying: *I caused this to happen to me. It was not God. It was my consideration of the Laws of God that I participated in within my life that had the particular ailment or disease manifest within my body.* We have the preconceived thought then: *That all of the diseases that will ever happen down through the ages are within us, just like anything else.*

When I mentioned a couple weeks ago that it took the Total Reality of God to make us, I was not kidding! It took the Total Reality of God to make us. That is how perfect we are. But how much of that perfection are we using? Only to the capabilities of where we are participating in within the awareness of understanding what we are, and how we interrelate it to consciousness. In other words, how much do we know of ourselves? Why? Because if we consider that question in its simplicity, "How much do we know of ourselves?" the more we know about self, the more we understand of the Total Reality of God. Therefore, the simplicity of it is so awesomely beautiful and creative; also of understanding the identity of why disease is upon this earth plane.

I have sat for so many times within the meditative state questioning the reality of illness. I used to say: *I know, God, that everything here is good, but I cannot understand why a particular person has to suffer within the awareness of these particular diseases within the structure of comprehension within the physical sense.* I would receive answers back: *Well, if you think suffering is wrong, and you are part of that structure, change yourself, John. Lift yourself higher within the awareness of what you are. Change the common denominator of humanity. You can do so. Anybody can do so.* If you do it slightly, you eliminate a slight bit of that misconception. There does not have to be agony or deviation into those considerations. There can be less of the pain and agony within the quest of the awareness of what you are.

Then if you can consider that, you begin to understand that disease is a necessary evil, part of a fallen angel that deals with the structure that gives you that identity. Do I sit here and pretend to fully understand the nature of it when I see a child, or somebody I love, suffer through a particular level, and I cannot deal with the refraction of it within me to cure it? Of course, I deal with the agonies of that. It is necessary to care, and to want to care, …and it is necessary not to care so much. It is necessary to care so much that you leave the other person alone, until they have the wisdom and knowledge to ask for help. Then when they do ask, it is necessary to care so much that you use as much of yourself as you can, to the best of your ability. The agonies of that become the incentive of saying: *I should become more than what I am. Maybe if I was a little higher, maybe if I had a little more in me, maybe if I had a little more of understanding within me interrelated to the particular thing, I could have helped the identity of the illness to the point where the person could have been here longer in order to achieve more of the probabilities they set in motion. Maybe I would have had the knowledge for them. Maybe I would have had the energy. Maybe I would have had the refractive consciousness in order to change the density of that…*

The nature of disease then becomes a compelling quality within you that gives you the incentive to say: *I want to be more than I was before. I am not saying I am good or bad. I just want to be different.* For instance, maybe one time you might look at another person and consider those physical, sensual and emotional urges within self. Then you hear ringing through your mind: *Those considerations are not bad: if you want to consider going in that direction, that is fine. But if you want to be on a higher level, you cannot be totally involved sensually and emotionally. You have to change that density within you. You have to become more than what you were before.* It is an avenue of considering the growth of what you are and what you can participate in within understanding the awareness of illnesses within others.

A true healer has the identity and knowledge of understanding the deviation within the misconception that caused the illness. The healer has the ability to cause some semblance of balance within the refractability of what the other person might be, in order to cause some semblance of balance in them. The healer has the consideration of giving some information to the other, so the other may have the ability within self and their own free will to cause some harmony within their structure. Maybe the healer will not necessarily totally eliminate the illness, but will give the other the qualities to cause stability, or whatever it might be, in order to put the illness into a dormant state.

That is what you should be considering when we are talking about the nature of disease. If you have something wrong in your body, sit in the meditative state and ask questions why. The illness does not make you a bad person. It makes you a person who has not considered why the illness is there. It makes you a person who has to take the time to work on it. We learn from everything. I can remember my mother dying, and I was sitting there and doing everything I could. I was pouring energy out of myself, knowing that she was not in total agony within the structure of the disease, but that I could not penetrate the barrier, which was the ignorance of understanding where she had to be within herself. I was giving her information, and it was flying past her like it was nothing. Nothing was being absorbed, so the only avenue that I had was to make her as comfortable as possible.

I told my wife once, "If you know of a person who is very sick, tell the family never to call me. If they are in that place, and I come and sit with them, I am going to do the best I can for them, and the best thing for them might be to die. They might be in a place so ridden with illness that they have no chance at all, and might be in agony for an extended period. But when you perform a true healing, you are not only functioning at this level, you are also functioning at other levels. To the best of your ability, you give everything you can. Know that it will be used by the other's soul to the best of its ability. At times in your healing when you see death happen, know that you have done the best you can for that person, but not for your mind. Then consider the death within the physical sense. Do not badger yourself within the quest of understanding why it happened. Lift yourself within it. Begin to question the qualities of it and use it for you. Understand that you were there for that person, and not for you, yet you were there to grow within the feelings of what you have considered within that person to put yourself in a higher place.

To the best of my ability, I have considered these particular things I have mentioned to you, through the questions and answers within the structure of what I am, and whatever level I participate in, whether it be within the simplicity of humanity, or the extraordinary capacity of humanity, and to make it understandable because of that one statement, "Everything is God." When I was a little boy, I remember the nuns telling me, "God is good and God is pure." If that is the case, it is the identity within me that does not understand the purity within the essence of what I am trying to comprehend. The more I understand of whatever it might be, the more I can consider it as a uniquely beautiful process within the awareness of this particular level as a stage of comprehension for the extension of our souls into more of That Solid Purity of God. If we can consider something in that way, it gives us the incentive eventually to look at what seems totally negative as positive. There are so many things that we look at within life that seem totally negative, causing pain and agony in the people we love or care for. If you care enough, grow. If you care enough and see something wrong going on within the awareness of humanity, send out the thoughts that stop it. It is your right, your free will, as part of what you are. That is being a true healer at an esoteric level. Send it forth. For instance there is enough child abuse upon this planet. We are going to eradicate child abuse from this planet. We are going to send our thoughts forward, and there is not going to be any more of it. You are going to see it over the next few years: there is going to be less and less of it. I am tired of seeing the free wills of those children interfered with.

You should consider different things within you to push something forward. If there is a disease within the structure of your genetics that you know is there, work on it. If you know there is a flaw within your family structure, work on it. This is your time to do it: while you are still healthy, not when you are involved in a disease. The hardest person to heal is you when you are involved in the depths of illness. You have no identity of how to pull yourself out of it, because you put yourself in there with no identity.

Consider it now: preventive medicine is the capability of using your meditations to rejuvenate and work on yourself. You are using meditation as a pawn, not as a crutch. Do not think of meditation as a cure-all: it is a stabilizing quality that gives you the perception into the cure-alls. It is here. It is within you. There are other places you can get it, but not many. There is a reason for you being here, tonight. There is a reason for you coming back. There might be a reason for you not coming back someday, but while those reasons are ringing in your mind, and they are usable, use them, try them and see if they fit. Make it, you. *I* will give you the information to the best of my ability from where I am. You have to make it to the best of your ability from where you are. I love you, and would not do one thing except from the ignorance of what I am, to infringe upon your free will. Within the knowledge of what I am, I will give you everything I can that does not infringe upon it. I am not saying that I will not infringe upon your free will from ignorance, but I will never infringe upon it from knowledge.

No matter what you hear, see, or have heard in the past, whatever it might have been, it has made you what you are now, and it has made me what I am now. There is nobody that can drag you down within that structure if you know that. Put it within you: the nature of disease is something that is ugly within its physical face and identity, but within the quest of understanding it, we understand it as being not so negative each time. We still dwell upon the pain and agony of it, and long for it not to be part of what is usable in comprehension. But while it is so, we understand it as a quality within the Structure of God, and have to consider it from the mundane areas that we comprehend. But as we do so, let us grow. Let us consider eliminating disease eventually, so we do not have to tread down that pathway. We can glide down that pathway, not deviating into the spikes of misconception that harm and wound us for life without knowing how to pull ourselves out of the bloody mass of what we have become. It is within us. I know it is. I am as simple as they made them, and if I can do it, anybody can do it. Take care of yourselves. I hope I see you next week or whenever. I love you. Good night, everybody.

CHAPTER FIVE

You Are Here to Grow

I want to talk to you for a few minutes about staying still in meditation. You have to practice staying still. That is the first thing you must learn. I am a very active person, so in the beginning I had to practice just staying still. Then you must go through that sequence of events, starting with the relaxation of the toes. It seems insignificant, but it is not. If you are focusing upon your toes, you are not thinking about the daily chores that gave you the stress or tension.

I do not know why you do not feel some of the things you have within you! There are so many unique things within you. Let them flow forward. You should be experiencing harmony in your body. When there is no harmony, something is wrong. You have to begin to question why. The hardest person to heal is you, once you are sick. If you are sick, you are nowhere near healing yourself, because you have put yourself there in the first place. Preventive medicine is meditating every day and keeping your mind active on what is going on. Feel what is going on in the body. When I am relaxing my toes, I am assessing the balance in both feet. Think about what you feel. Ask questions about what you feel.

Every part of your body has a consciousness, whether you believe it or not. Twenty-five years from now, you will say, "That guy was not kidding!" Every part of your body has a consciousness that interrelates to a higher level, and if you can understand that, it gives you an unfair advantage in keeping your body in harmony. You have some very important information about the body that other people do not have. If you have something wrong with your foot, and you know what the consciousness of that area is, you can work on it in your normal, daily life, giving you an avenue of growth and comprehension that can eliminate the misconception from your body.

I had the privilege of getting sick last week, (laughing) which is something very rare. I have not been using my mind and energy properly. I sat there. I was really sick. I was trying to meditate. I learn from everything. I said: *There is no energy here!* I can usually receive tremendous amounts of energy and send it out to hundreds of people. I sat there, and there was nothing there. My soul and I began to talk. I said: *Where are you? Are you leaving? Am I dying? What is happening here? I know I am getting old, but this is ridiculous!*

You begin to question the reality of what is going on. Sometimes when you deal with some complacency, there is going to be something coming along that seems to be very detrimental, but it is not; it is necessary to stop you from going in the wrong direction. I knew the reasons why I got sick, but the stupidity! Six or seven months ago, in similar circumstances, I would not have gotten sick. I was physically overworking then too, but would have had enough energy to sustain myself within that realm, and would have taken preventive measures to stop the illness before it happened. This time, my mind was not being used right. *I* was not using it right. I was not feeling good about myself. I was not feeling the capabilities that I normally have, and that was an injustice towards me, my soul and God because it slowed me down from understanding what was happening around me.

There is so much going on in meditation. Do you want your meditation to be profound? Deal with the simplicities of it, and it will automatically become profound. If you try to make it profound, it will not be so. Understand that certain little things are going on that will automatically make your meditation profound. Each time that you go into meditation, you should think of where you were in your previous meditation and compare those reactions to where you are now: *How did I enter meditation? How do I feel, compared to last time? What do I feel in my body? Is the energy stopping in a certain area in my body? Why? If it goes past that, why it is going past that?*

I am sure that if you have a lack of compassion towards yourself, and do not feel good about yourself, the energy is going to stay low within your legs, not coming past your knees. Each time in the guided meditation, I make certain statements, which interrelate the sources of energy and consciousness to particular parts of the body. There is a reason for doing that. For instance, when I mention in meditation, "Have compassion for yourself in the knees," that is because the consciousness of your knees interrelates to the survival center at the base of the spine, which is "love of self." Knees are secondary centers within the survival center. They also interrelate to the heart center, the fourth center of compassion. Every time you meditate, you have these interrelationships within your mind.

Have you ever asked: *If God is so beautiful, why are there so many disastrous events happening within the physical reality?* We return to the preconceived thought within us: *Everything is God.* Now, if we think that, and have logic within the quest of understanding that, then we have to say: *Everything is good.* So if a particular thing or event seems negative, it is just that we do not have the capacity, or are nowhere near the place of understanding why everything is good. Let us just say that disease seems bad to us because we cannot comprehend the essence of why it is usable within the physical sense. So everything is good, but we are nowhere near the level of comprehension that can understand the good, and until we understand the good, it uses us rather than we using it.

Why is disease upon the earth plane? To use an analogy, let us say NASA puts up a satellite in an orbit around the moon, and is collecting information, but then the satellite suddenly malfunctions. NASA shuts it off, and it falls into the atmosphere and burns up. Now think for a moment about the capability within self: you are a satellite or extension of the soul put into the physical reality to comprehend. You do not have the total capacity of your soul here in the physical reality. If you had the total knowledge and capacity here within the physical reality, you would not have the venture of understanding yourself outside the whole. If you had the total identity of your soul here, you would not want to stay here; you would just want to return to the soul. So it is necessary to put different filters, or layers of energy, in between the flesh and the soul.

Within your energy field you have seven major energy centers, or "chakras," within the trunk of the body, and many secondary energy centers within the legs and arms that interrelate to the major centers. Each of the centers has a particular consciousness to it. As you refracted, or filtered, yourself from the soul into the physical body, you deposited a layer of energy at each of the seven levels that interrelates to a particular energy source within the physical sense. The energy layer most accessible to you is the consciousness of survival, "love of self," deposited in the first center, located at the base of the spine. The second layer is the consciousness of duality, sensuality and creativity, "love of another," deposited in the abdominal area. The third layer is the ability to comprehend emotions and human decency, "love of many," deposited in the stomach or solar plexus area. The fourth layer is love and compassion, "universal love," deposited in the heart center. The fifth layer is comprehension of higher duality, "love of flesh towards soul," deposited in the throat center. The sixth layer is comprehension of insight, "the ability to see trends within humanity," deposited in the third-eye center or forehead. The seventh layer is the crown center, "the esoteric comprehension of the soul," deposited at the top of the head.

Let us return to the previous statement, "Everything is good, but we are nowhere near the level of comprehension that can understand the good, and until we understand the good, it uses us, rather than we using it." If we search for an answer regarding why disease is good, we come to the conclusion that if we have disease, disease is a tool of the soul telling us that we are not achieving our probabilities within life in a balanced way. Disease is a fail-safe system within the physical sense, telling us that we are going in the wrong direction. The nature of disease is: if we are going in the wrong direction, we will get pain and agony to slow us down. If we are not extending ourselves into the craft of understanding the awareness of what we are dealing with in life, we are shutting off that satellite of the soul because we are no longer becoming usable within why we are here. If we keep going in the same manner, we are no longer functioning properly and achieving our probabilities. Finally the soul extinguishes the body, and a logical sequence of events takes place, which is death. We die and filter back towards the soul, going through all of those different levels that we deposited there and absorbing the essence of what we are. We are absorbing all of the information and putting it within the total reality of what we are. It is just like shutting off the switch to the satellite, giving us new information. The act of dying is as important a learning process as manifesting a body within the physical sense, because we are being taught how to go through the different levels of awareness. We have many lifetimes. In the next lifetime we will choose a new road to travel.

Therefore, if you want to be free of disease or illness, you have to begin to use the meditative state and the balancing qualities to begin to understand misconceptions before they overwhelm you. Certain centers interrelate to certain diseases. Certain glands and organs interrelate to different diseases. Returning to the statement, "Each part of the body has a consciousness," what does this information do for you? It gives you a ballpark, a specific area, to comprehend what is going on. For instance, if you are miscomprehending your survival, you are going to have physical problems in the lower part of the trunk of the body and legs, because the hips, legs, knees, ankles and feet are all part of the red vibration, and possibly the orange vibration. Older males often have prostate diseases, which are within the area of the red and orange vibrations. Both males and females have hip problems. If you have problems in these areas, you want to consider how you have miscomprehended your life in the area of survival. You work on issues of survival, and "love of self," in order to solve the problem.

I was fortunate enough that my soul made me allergic to pork, tomato sauce and nuts, which are within the red and brown vibrations within the survival center. I questioned it in meditation and understood that if I had not been allergic to some of the red and brown vibrations, it would have been my tendency in this life to be involved in more aggressive activities, such as karate and fighting. I was not supposed to do that within this lifetime. If I did not have that preconceived thought built into my system, I probably would not have taken the time to understand that there is something truly unique and beautiful in every one of us: that we are part of God and can utilize the tool of meditation to make ourselves better people.

The first person you heal each and every day is you, by keeping yourself in harmony and balance. If you know what each part of the body means in consciousness, you are in a position to become involved in setting and achieving some of the probabilities that were set in motion from another level. On the other hand, if you are involved in your own sickness, you are nowhere near healing yourself. You are outside the particular vibration that can heal you because you put yourself there in the first place. Over your lifetime you experience thousands and thousands of particular opportunities of rejuvenation or dissipation. How does disease happen? To use another analogy, let us say you are going down the main river in a boat. Maybe you are not paying attention, or happen to turn your head at the wrong moment, but suddenly you veer off into a tributary. You think you are still in the main river, but are now headed in the wrong direction. You begin to encounter difficulties, such as natives shooting arrows at you, and other disastrous events. Rather than slowing down to comprehend the escalating misconceptions, you ignore the signals and keep going, until you end up in the muck where you can absolutely go no further. Perhaps you have gone so far that you cannot return, because you have become so unbalanced within mind and body.

How does this play out within the mind and body? Let us say that you exhibit a lack of compassion towards yourself and others, time and time again. Each encounter is going to affect the heart center because the heart center deals with universal love and compassion. Each time you have a lack of compassion for yourself and others, there is dissipation in that center. On the other hand, each time you have a moment of compassion for yourself and others, that center is rejuvenated. If you are experiencing constant problems in the heart center, and are not questioning the awareness of compassion and love, and how it interrelates to your normal, daily life, that is a contradiction to that center and the disease progresses.

Now, if you take a drug or pill that momentarily makes you feel better, that is also a contradiction. Taking the pill or drug is like encountering the natives and going past them. You have eliminated the natives, but have not eliminated the problem. It is still festering within you. You have eliminated the problem for a brief moment by ingesting a drug, but that center still has a problem. You still have a lack of compassion, a lack of balance and a lack of understanding towards yourself and others. Each time that you ignore the problem once again, there is another little scar of misconception put in that area. It is almost like having a mild heart attack that you do not even know you are having. Eventually the heart center weakens to the point where you will have a heart attack and die. You are going to leave because you are contradicting why you are here. You are here to grow as an extension of your soul.

CHAPTER SIX

The Seven Avenues of Love

Every part of your body has a consciousness. Every part of your body interrelates to seven major centers of energy within your body, and the seven centers of energy interrelate to seven major levels of comprehension that you have left there for you, for when you are ready to draw upon them. The key to opening up those centers is using what you have within life in a balanced way. Meditation is relaxation, rejuvenation, comfort and the replenishing of the supply of energy for the body, and is a place of awareness that you can begin to use to become more than what you were before. When we question the reality of self, we can draw upon the seven levels of comprehension that we have talked about. The first level is "love of self;" the second, "love of another;" the third, "love of many;" the fourth, "universal love;" the fifth, "duality from flesh to soul;" the sixth, "humanitarian insight;" and the seventh, "esoteric comprehension of the soul." Your mind begins to work almost like a computer. It begins to put your realities into particular categories that interrelate to the different levels of awareness or spheres within you. The balancing quality of a particular area gives you the answer pertaining to a particular sphere, then that sphere gives you the density to proceed to another level and draw in more energy within the flesh.

Let us go into more detail about your capability as an extension of your soul, starting at the soul level to manifest a body within the physical sense. You go through the process of refracting yourself through seven different densities, in order to manifest matter within the physical sense. Starting from the soul level, you are refracting the seven different densities into the flesh that interrelate to the seven major energy centers within the physical body. The energy centers are not made in the fetus; rather, they are being nourished from higher levels. There is a constant feeding from those levels. Not only is the fetus growing in the womb, there is also growth back and forth between the levels because foundation is being deposited at the different levels.

For instance, as the physical heart and heart center are being made, that structure builds the awareness of the fourth center of the heart center. There is a constant feeding, a constant channel of awareness, that sustains the heartbeat. The heartbeat is within your conscious awareness, but you have a preconceived thought built into the structure that has the capability of knowing the heart will beat. After all, you do not want to constantly think about your heartbeat in order for it to function. If you had to do that, you could not use your conscious mind in anything else. So the preconceived thought that the heart will beat is built into the structure. It is part of the involuntary system, and you do not have to worry about it.

Now, even though you have left the basic structures there, you have to fill them in within applying consciousness within life. You are filling in those areas, those voids. Are you using the consciousness at those levels? No, you are using consciousness, but are not yet taking it and making it a reality here within the physical reality; you are using consciousness from another level. You leave different portions of yourself at different levels of comprehension, and these different levels interrelate to usable vibration that you can deal with, when you are ready to deal with it. For instance, the first and most accessible level of comprehension that you deal with has to do with survival upon the planet. It is logical: whom do you have to love first? You have to love yourself, and "love of self" is survival. Survival also interrelates to the first ten or twelve years of life when, in the most ideal sense, your parents give you vital information on how to love yourself and survive in life. The energy source, the red center at the base of the spine, interrelates to "love of self" and survival within the physical sense, and corresponds to that first level. When you comprehend love and stability within yourself, you are transcending to that level more so. There is more red vibration coming into your system. For example, one night at a lecture I was talking about "love of self," and what a plus it is to have abundant energy and intellect; that if you possess both those qualities, you will be very successful in life. However, if you do not know that, family members might convince you that it is negative to have a lot of energy, and that you must contain your energy. Meanwhile, I was noticing a fidgety young man in the back of the classroom. Afterwards he came up to me with a tear in his eye to say that no one had ever told him that having a lot of energy was a plus, and that if he could learn to use it, he could become a better person. So it is a matter of taking the time to know the sequence of events that takes place in the body.

We are missing this in humanity now: children nowadays are not necessarily receiving the basic structure of love of self. When I was a child, we lived in a neighborhood where you went out, played and learned many survival aspects from people in the neighborhood, and there was no fear of anything happening to you. Children might have fights with each other, but nothing happened in the detrimental ways that are happening nowadays. If you do not have that basic foundation of love and balance within the survival center, you cannot give love to another. You can have a confrontation of love that might eventually develop into love, but the basic theme is that you must learn to love self first. For instance, when the child masturbates, they are learning how to love self. Some adults view the act as negative because they do not comprehend the importance of it. If the child does not learn how to love self, it affects them for the rest of their life. But we can always begin to change our misconceptions by going back to basics and dealing with the wonderment of understanding how truly unique we are.

Then it happens automatically, organically, around age of ten or twelve, the next sequence begins to take place. Suddenly the opposite sex begins to look good to you. You are accustomed to think and fend for yourself; then all of a sudden there is a whole new feeling within you that you cannot comprehend. If you are not prepared in the adolescent years for that first transition from the first level to the second, the phrase so often heard, "the crazy teenage years" seems true. These transitions happen seven times in your lifetime, but probably the most drastic one takes place in adolescence when you are passing from "love of one" to "love of two." Turbulent changes and chemical reactions within the body are going on that interrelate to consciousness and genetic changes. It is a whole new ball game. At first, it may threaten your survival and cause great confusion, but if your parents did a good job raising you by giving you stability, knowledge, and the vibration of the reds and oranges, you will have an easier time of it.

When that first transition takes place, you can begin to integrate the duality of love, which is the second level, "love of another." The orange center of duality and sensuality is within the abdominal area, the gonadic area. Doesn't that make sense? All of this information has to be logical; it has to make sense and fit within the physical sense. When you master the skills of survival and "love of self," then it gives you the capacity to "love another" in the orange vibration. When you love self to the point where you can begin to see another person in a balanced way, that is a duality that collects, goes forward and becomes one again. If you are not ready for duality, there is a bombardment of egos, and you part, which is the necessary vibration of understanding that you have not taken the time to prepare yourself for that duality which is the venture of dealing with the reaction of another person.

Male and female participation in the act of sensuality is a duality. There is a confrontation within the essence of the two. The male's seven centers are spinning in one direction, and the female's seven centers in the other. If you look at creation at the level of understanding the essence of "love of another," the two are actually giving the awareness of their consciousness to each other if they really love each other. Then duality becomes a catalyst for learning "love of many," as they learn about and deal with the creativity of a new life form coming forward, the child. The total awareness of what the parents are is contained within the sperm and egg that join to form the embryo. The blending properties of the two parents are so uniquely combined. As they love their child, their consciousness moves into the yellow vibration within the third center, which is the ability to "love many." I should add that we do not have to have a partner in order to deal with duality. We also deal with duality whenever we interact with another person, whether at work or play. Whatever duality it involves, it brings us a new strength.

One of the greatest examples of the strength of duality is that of Adam and Eve. Think of Adam all alone in the garden. It seemed he had everything. He could walk around. He had all the food he wanted. He had no responsibilities. Then God looked upon Adam and said: *Nothing is happening in this garden! Adam is not leaving that playpen of love of self. He does not even eat the forbidden fruit on the tree. There is no one there to give him incentive.* So God put Adam to sleep, and Eve came forward. God put half of him on the right side of the body, meaning the male vibration, and half of him on the left side of the body, meaning the female vibration. Then that caused the conflict of the duality that gave Adam the strength to defy God and eat of the fruit.

Without the strength of that duality, Adam and Eve never would have left the garden. It was no sin that they were thrown from the garden, it was a reward of comprehension. It is just as if you allow your child to cross the street, once the child is old enough to have the comprehension to cross the street safely. God knew that if Adam did not have the incentive to eat of the forbidden fruit, he would not have had the strength to survive outside the garden. If he had no incentive, how could he survive, kill the animals and do whatever he had to do in order to survive? There are billions of people upon the planet who believe that Adam sinned. Remember when we mentioned comprehension, and that when we understand something as being usable and good, then we can use it for us rather than against us, and that the particular thing is not regarded as good until we can understand it? We see Adam and Eve leaving the garden as good: by eating of the forbidden fruit they are given the rewards of going outside the garden and growing on their own.

Do you notice what we are doing? We are talking about avenues of love. You "love yourself." If you love yourself properly, you can then have the capability to "love another." If you love another, that duality makes you more than what you were before. We come to the next level. It is a difficult one: you then learn to "love many," which is love of humanity and comprehension of human decency within the yellow vibration. It teaches you to become a more humanitarian person. You learn to control your emotional state, which then gives you the capacity to focus upon life problems, dissect them and make them usable for you. As you become more usable in life, your clairvoyant capacities begin to open. You can hear other people's thoughts. Then you have to learn to shut all of that off, in order to keep yourself in balance.

I have gone through many of those changes. There have been times when I have had to muster all my inner resources to keep from crying when I feel the other person's anguish. Even watching a movie can set me off. People close to me think I am crazy half the time, yet I am controlling it to the best of my ability. Velocity is so important. Do not force it. When those feelings of love come, you want to be ready. You do not want those feelings to overwhelm you. I am talking about when you suddenly feel or sense another person's anguish. Let us say someone gives you a photo of someone who is sick. You can feel the soul of the individual and you have to have strength! The feelings of love that come from those levels are extraordinary. You receive those feelings through growing within the sequence of events that I mention to you here. You absorb. It is no illusion. It happens and is understandable when you think about the other person.

We are talking about healing now because we are going through a sequence of events. As you grow in this manner, when your child comes up to you to grab your hand, or ask a question, when you respond, there is more energy, sound and vibration emanating from you. There is more of the information that will change the density of the usability of the person that you are interrelating with. It is teaching at an esoteric level, and is total absorption if the other person hits the place where they can use it. You are clearing the pathway through the jungle so the other can have some sense of light as they are going forward.

It is important that you understand the events that take place within you. Is it logical? Is it understandable? Is there something I said that does not make sense? Everything has to fit within the sphere of comprehension. If it does not fit into the sphere and come into the nucleus of it, I do not want to use it. The only one who can distort the Essence of what *I* know is God is me, and you, wherever you are. If you are not balanced, you can only put it back into you, and tell yourself that you have to grow, or deal with more stability within your life in order to sense more of the love. I have a goal: at the time of my death I want to hit a level where I can walk out of this body to the next level without trauma, and it is possible if I can absorb all of that.

Then there is the heart center: "universal love." Visualize a tree. There are the roots of the tree, "survival," and the trunk, "duality," and the branches, "comprehension of emotions and human decency." We come now to the fruit of the tree: there is a place in the heart center that contains a reservoir that has the green vibration. That is where "universal love and compassion" reside. Great entities in the past have used the heart center. Some individuals even had a sacred heart.

We have the three lower centers below the heart center and the three higher centers above. They constantly bombard each other with information and are tributaries of comprehension that begin to fill the chalice of the heart center in the middle. When you fill the heart center, you actually blossom the tree and put food upon the table for others to come forward and eat, and they are not even aware this is happening. In the initial thrust of experiencing the fullness of the heart center, it can be overwhelming for you. If you are a healer, each moment that you feel the heart center, it is awesome because you can actually see, feel and sense the other person's cells within their body either dying or automatically being rejuvenated. You can feel the person's anguish. You do not see the illusions of reality, you see the reality of the person, and you have to have the strength not to react. When they approach, you cannot infringe upon their free will by asking to help them unless they request it, because you know they are here to grow, and that it would be the gravest sin to infringe upon their free will.

If you want to be a healer, grow. As you grow, you become closer to the reality that made you. If you are closer to the reality that made you, you will automatically have more energy with which to heal. For instance, you and I can stand over Lazarus for ten years, and nothing will happen, but at the level that Jesus was, he could see the total reality of Lazarus at a cellular level. When he said, "Lazarus, rise!" the information, velocity and consciousness went right into the reality of Lazarus. He was at the level that made Lazarus, so why couldn't he make Lazarus again?

There is teaching in everything, no matter what religion it comes from, but the information has to fit. It does not matter what religion you are, you grow within the system of comprehending something because it is a true reality. You have this true reality within you. If you are truly upon the pathway, you are not one of those "born-agains," dogmatically maintaining that you are right and everyone else is wrong. You are a "born-again" who understands that everything is right and understandable and usable.

Then there is more love beyond the heart center. We enter into the knowledge of the throat center, the seventh center, which interrelates to a new higher duality, "the duality between flesh and soul." You begin to understand the awesome beauty of the soul and how to refract consciousness, into energy, into matter. You use the different densities of those levels to refract, in order to make humanity a more loving and compassionate place. You have the capability of going into the blue vibration, which is the essence of understanding the reality of taking the beauty and becoming a person who can transcend the information. It gives you the capability of dealing with art forms, such as music, writing and art, and conveying them forward within humanity, thereby changing the density of many people. An example of this is Michelangelo, who saw the figure within the marble even before he started carving because he possessed esoteric sight. He was so involved at that level that he even distorted his own sensuality. He was impotent because he was tied right into That Essence. He did not have one single thought about sensuality because all of that energy was lifted to the throat center. He would be carving for days, and his friends would have to put food in front of him.

In the throat center you are not only giving the person a brush to paint a picture, you are giving them the information that makes the brush move. You are automatically giving the person color and information. You are changing their density just by having the capacity to walk into a room and be whoever you are, without infringing upon the person's free will. You can just be there, so others can absorb. Most of the energy that is projected through this center from another level is used within the flesh in the second center of duality, which is sensuality and creativity. It takes a great deal of strength to use higher duality, "flesh-on-soul," rather than lower duality, "flesh-on-flesh." One is the candle maker and one is the candle. For instance, have you ever noticed that when a new medical cure is discovered, there is the phenomenon of many scientists in different parts of the world receiving it almost simultaneously? We do not realize that there is a collective consciousness, or bank of information, that is drawn upon, but it takes one individual to transcend to the particular level to make it happen in the first place.

Within the sixth center of the third-eye center in the forehead, we come to a new place, a new book of knowledge. It deals with "higher insight," which first filters information into our personal reality within the third center. Then when we move into a higher place, it goes beyond that by becoming esoteric sight in the lavender vibration. It gives us the capability of seeing aspects that are usable for self and others. We know when to use the essence of ourselves in a balanced, beautiful way in helping others, and at other times, we know when not to do anything for others, because what appears to be negative within the other person might be good. We begin to see the flow of humanity and multi-dimensional reality, which is everything that is going on around us. We see trends within humanity. We get to the point where we become more usable in changing the density of humanity. By utilizing the mind properly within the physical sense, we can increase the ability of the conscious mind to participate at that level. When we achieve the probabilities that we set in motion from another level, we win the right to use that level within the physical reality. I received all of the information about the energy centers from the third-eye center.

Finally we come to the seventh center at the top of the head, which is the white vibration: "esoteric comprehension of survival." There has to be a center that controls the reality of all the other centers. It is the crown center. The crown center deals with a new survival that interrelates to the soul. We want to feel and sense the wisdom of the soul, and the protective qualities of its refractability. In meditation we are bridging the gap between where we are and where we can be. For fleeting moments from where we are, using only a portion of trying to understand the whole, we truly understand how awesomely beautiful and creative All of This Is within Its Majestic Beauty. We can think of the seventh center as a fountain of white vibration. White is everything. It contains all colors. It puts out the fires of misconception to the best of its ability. Its awesome refractability of protective qualities helps us within every moment within the flesh. For instance, if you are meditating at a particularly good level of comprehension, then experience a very emotional day, the crown center starts spinning, giving you the capability of refracting the white vibration into the yellow center of emotions in order to replenish that center and help with the misconception. In doing so, it enables you to rejuvenate and balance yourself in a profoundly quick way.

Now, when you are upon that avenue of growth, and are dealing in a balanced way, you are drawing in more energy and igniting brain cells. You are participating in opening the crown center further, giving you more information within the physical sense. Furthermore, there is a bombardment between the crown center and the survival center. The energy source at the base of the spine interrelates to survival energies within the physical sense and the crown center deals with survival within the soul. That is why there are red and white cells in the body. When the red cells experience a misconception, the white cells rush in to surround the red cells and stabilize them. The crown center energy is cool, coming from the soul, and the survival center energy is warm, coming from the earth. In meditation when you are tapping into information regarding your life and growth, you will experience a bombardment between these two centers, giving you more information in regard to whatever center of awareness you are working on and how you can become a better person. You will have more capability of focus in whatever you do, because you are turning on the crown center that gives you that capability. You are also igniting brain cells within the physical sense to retain whatever it is within the physical sense that you are trying to retain. Some people use more of their brain than others because they are constantly turning on cells within the brain, and that is done esoterically.

When you are meditating, you will actually begin to feel tingling and sensations of warmth throughout your whole body, from the tips of your toes to the top of your head. You will actually begin to feel a vortex of energy almost like a funnel, and that funnel actually extends out to infinity. It actually collects the esoteric comprehension of what you are. As you begin to comprehend more, you win the right to use more of that esoteric comprehension. You feel as if you have a kind of esoteric helmet on at first; then you will feel that vortex move you. You will feel it spinning right down to the base of your spine eventually, and you win the right to use more of the consciousness of the crown center.

Normally, you use only a fraction of the consciousness of each of the seven major energy centers, but at a certain point you can become so balanced that the whole survival level becomes you within the flesh. Major energy changes will then take place. You win the right through comprehension to have the whole level of red be absorbed within you. It changes you instantly and profoundly. Your energy sources in the first two centers will be changed: the red and orange centers will become crystallined with white. Normally, the centers are facing out from the spine towards the front of the body, but when you go through major energy changes, those centers will turn up. I remember one evening, when that energy source was ignited within me, coming up from the base of my spine. The energy was so awesome. I felt the whole bottom part of my spine opening like a bomb door. I was weeping like a baby, and knowledge was coming through me so fast, it was incredible.

So there are levels that you interrelate to that you can draw down and make them, you, within the physical sense. Eventually you will have the capability of being able to sit in front of another person, or think of them, and become transcendable. If the person has some problems in the stomach area in the third center, and you have the capability of going through that level, you are going to give them healing energies. You are going to give them the ability of having balance for a brief moment, so they may see a direction.

In this information I hope that there might be one thing that triggers you into a semblance of more balance, so that you may participate in moving from where you are and use more of the essence of your soul within the flesh. That is what growth is about. Go slowly. I might mention this statement a thousand times: "Understand the velocity that is usable for you," because if you are not ready, there are areas of love that will overwhelm you. It will take longer to collect it, and believe me, I am living proof of that. I love you.

THE SEVEN AVENUES OF LOVE
THE BODY MAP OF THE SEVEN CENTERS OF CONSCIOUSNESS

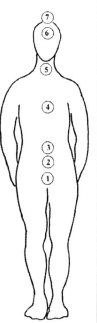

7 The Seventh Center of the Crown: The White Vibration
Esoteric Comprehension of the Soul

6 The Sixth Center of the Third-Eye: The Lavender Vibration
Insight Into Humanity

5 The Fifth Center of the Throat: The Blue Vibration
Higher Duality and Creativity (Duality from Flesh to Soul)

4 The Fourth Center of the Heart: The Green Vibration
The Reservoir of Balance and Compassion (Universal Love)

3 The Third Center of the Solar Plexus: The Yellow Vibration
Emotions and Human Decency (Love of Many)

2 The Second Center of the Sacral Center: The Orange Vibration
Lower Duality Of Sensuality and Creativity (Love of Another)

1 The First Center of Survival: The Red Vibration
The Strength and Wisdom To Take Care of Self (Love of Self)

ALL OF THE SECONDARY CENTERS INTERRELATE TO THE MAJOR CENTERS
The Secondary Centers of Survival

The Toes and Feet interrelate to our comprehension of survival.

The Ankles interrelate to our comprehension of lower duality within survival.

The Calves interrelate to our comprehension of emotions and human decency within survival.

The Knees interrelate to our comprehension of balance and compassion within survival.

The Thighs interrelate to our comprehension of emotions and insight into survival.

The Hips interrelate to our comprehension of survival and lower duality.

The Secondary Centers Of Our Comprehension
Of Different Aspects Of The Higher Essence Within Us

The Fingers and Hands interrelate to our comprehension of survival within the soul.

The Wrists interrelate to our comprehension of lower duality within the soul.

The Forearms interrelate to our comprehension of human decency and emotions within the soul.

The Elbows interrelate to our comprehension of balance and compassion within the soul.

The Upper Arms interrelate to our comprehension of emotions and insight within the soul.

The Shoulders interrelate to our comprehension of duality and creativity within the soul.

CHAPTER SEVEN

A Pawn Rather Than a Crutch

All of you who have meditated over the years know that when you are sick, you are nowhere near healing yourself because you put yourself in that illness. So preventive medicine is the key. Through probabilities you set in motion from another lifetime, you chose your parents and the reality of whatever genetic flaws you have within you received from your parents. You can fix it, whatever it is. I know what genetic flaws I have in me and I have to work on them. If I do not, they will come forth within me. I have to look at those places within my body and understand how to fix them. If not, a mirrored image will come forth.

Whoever your parents are, you will become, or you can change yourself. It is up to you. If you look at the way you live life, and it seems necessary, understandable, usable and likeable, flow with it. But if you want to change and perfect it, change the perfection of your mother and your father, whoever they might be, or whatever they might have done to you. It is where you came from, and if you work on it, you can peak the perfection. You can ignite the perfection beyond that. You can spark it. You can stimulate it. You can see it lifting itself, maybe not totally out of certain genetic factors, but you can change it. Within the next few years as scientists are looking at the genetic process and understanding the genome, or whatever it might be, they will see that certain people can change that genetic process. They do not see it yet because they do not understand the process enough, but they will see that genetic process being changed by certain people. Those little cells that trigger certain diseases will be eliminated, or certain processes will be triggered within the genetic process beyond that, which surround the cells, not allowing disease to come forward; because it cannot; there is no room for it. Disease cannot enter through a door of comprehension because it is slammed shut. There is a locked door there, forever.

It is new. It is seemingly untouchable, but is so touchable. It is that next moment. It is something you do not have to worry about. Even within the complacency of where I have been lately, I see, feel and sense the wisdom, even as I try to hide it within the awareness of myself, wherever I might be. But you cannot hide it for long. It always comes forth. It always filters out and pulls you back. It always tells you where you should be, even when you are stupid within that framework of comprehension. You are on that pathway. Sometimes there are necessary times of rest that seem complacent, but they are not. They are little roadside cafes that nourish you and push you back onto that highway of comprehension.

How do we proceed? Some people come into the meditation classes saying they have been involved in "advanced" techniques of meditation and wonder why they have to go through looking at their toes or feet. My response is, at a seemingly simple level you are looking at your toes and feet, but at an esoteric level you are looking at your survival, which is the first level of awareness that you left there for you. Your toes and feet interrelate to an area at the base of the spine, the first major energy center of the body, which deals with survival and "love of self." So within the simplicity of thinking you are just relaxing your toes, at another level you are igniting that reality that can flow forward and become more usable within the flesh. You are stimulating the properties within the energy field that give you the capacity to grab that reality and use it. You are stimulating brain matter and escalating your comprehension, so you can absorb it and make a place for it where it can steep within the brain. All of these things are happening when you are looking at your toes.

That is the wonderment of this place. Even within our ignorance, there are so many multi-dimensional things happening. These things are beyond our comprehension and not usable, but when we hit a particular level, and see a particular aspect, it becomes an absolute. It becomes usable, extending itself into the balancing qualities of that awareness, so we may extend ourselves further into the reality of what we are. So there is so much going on within the simplicity of everything that is happening.

When I mention relaxing each part of the body in the guided meditation, I also mention the particular consciousness of each part. That sequence of events that we go through in relaxing the body is very important in understanding how energy flows within the body. In meditation you are teaching yourself the velocity of your energy field, which is what you feel and sense first in your energy field. I have mentioned that toes and feet interrelate to survival upon this planet. You draw in a tremendous amount of energy from the earth. When you begin to feel energy changes, first you will feel the energy coming in through the soles of your feet and up your legs. You will feel energy flow there first, but it will be initiated from the crown center. So you must begin to see what is happening in your energy field and question the reality of what is going on. Each particular sensation of energy flow, which may be felt or sensed as warmness, coolness, tingling, jabs, or jolts, happens for a reason.

First, learn to meditate properly, so you can rejuvenate yourself. When you drop a little deeper, you are dropping to the awareness of your soul. You are bridging the gap between you and your soul by opening up viable channels of awareness to the level that is usable for you. Begin to understand what is going on in the body; ask: *Why am I feeling and sensing something in my toe, foot, or knee? What particular awareness is within it? What does it interrelate to in my normal, daily life? Why does the energy stop in a particular place? What did I do today to cause that particular blockage?* Then everything that you learn from the meditative state has to be applied in your tomorrows. If you do not, no more will come.

The deeper you go into meditation, the more power you have to change your reactions within life. When you do that, you are changing consciousness, into energy, into matter. For example, when I was about thirty years old, I developed a persistent pain in my right shoulder, and that resulted in an injury one evening: while working out in karate, my shoulder locked up and I could not block a kick to my face. Several years later, I discovered meditation, and when I began to understand its capabilities, I wanted to know how I could eliminate the shoulder problem. I totally rejuvenated my shoulder and eliminated the problem because I gained the information regarding what misconception in my life it was interrelated to. Not only did I heal myself, I also eliminated the probability of having the ailment, as I grew older. Without meditation, by now I would be dealing with pain and agony every moment of my life. Every once in a while though, I will feel a twinge in that area that tells me: *John, you are moving into misconception again. Begin to question the reality of it.* Sometimes I will get another signal: when I physically overwork, my right hip will start aching. The right hip on a male interrelates to survival, so that tells me to question my physical survival. In my case I should slow down in the physical work I do, or I will get sick.

Therefore, in the seemingly simple meditation you use, you are using meditation as a pawn, rather than a crutch. In order to use the seven major centers of the body, you have to use what was given to you at birth properly. You cannot use anything beyond that, because it would be a contradiction to growth. For instance, if you think you can just use meditation to rejuvenate your body without thinking about what you are doing in your life to cause the dissipation, after a while meditation is not going to work. You will no longer receive the rejuvenation because you are using meditation as a crutch, rather than a pawn. If you want to heal yourself, you have to go through that sequence of events that we mention. Otherwise meditation becomes not usable. It will seem like you are doing nothing, because you are doing absolutely nothing.

You have to understand why you are here upon this earth plane. You are here to grow within the physical reality. You set probabilities in motion to be achieved within the physical reality. When you do achieve a probability, you win the right to use more of the essence of the soul within the flesh.

Put yourself in that place of absorption. Feel the wonderment of where you are and sense what is going on. If you feel something in your body, ask a question. When you ask questions at those levels, you are retaining the information and drawing in more usable answers in regard to eliminating whatever problem you might have. If you do not receive an answer, know that you are just starting out, and that the answers will come. If you ask the wrong question, nothing will happen. Try rephrasing the question. Ask it once again, pertaining to what you are feeling and sensing within a particular area. Do not give up. Do not think that you cannot do it, because you really can. It is like anything else: once you start, you are moving in the right direction. If you are moving in the right direction, you are closer to the reality of understanding what you are trying to comprehend. When you do so, more of that love flows through you and changes you.

We have talked about the sequence of events that takes place within the centers. In order to move successfully from "love of self" to "love of another," you must have "love of self." You cannot skip from third grade to Yale, because the extraordinary vibration of that level is going to fling you back and put you where you should be. That is exactly what happens within the growth process. If you truly work on yourself, if you truly have enough survival within yourself, then there is the next level to work on, which is duality. It becomes usable automatically. Duality is involved in giving your love to someone else, or something else, or understanding something else. If you understand the sequence of events that we talk about, you begin to participate in understanding the growth process within the physical reality on how to grow and become more usable. When you do so, the crown center, the white vibration dealing with esoteric survival, will ignite certain portions of the disk or awareness within the particular center. When that sequence of events takes place, it is like a thermometer, where the awareness of a particular center is pushed to another level and ignites the next center automatically. It will actually increase the capability of the vortex of the different centers. Then there is more energy, knowledge and capability of giving to others. There is more sound vibration and understanding of the reality of a particular center.

At a certain point, major energy changes will occur. At that point, the red center becomes a usable vibration, crystallined in white. The red level filters down, and becomes usable within the flesh, and no longer has to be worked on. The weight, density, knowledge and information of what you are changes automatically. People around you will understand that you are changing in your questions and answers. They will feel something different about you because you *are* different. You have opened up those viable channels of awareness to that level and made them you. Subtle little changes start taking place. Now when you ask questions, you are no longer asking questions about self, but about the duality of love, which is the blending of love and creativity, and two people becoming one. Or maybe it is that next step, questions about humanity becoming one. Or the step after that, questions regarding humanity, which comprises the entire structure of comprehension. Then you go past that, to several more types of love. That is the structure or movement within the foundation of understanding consciousness. Understand that there is an energy field around you. The energy field has a consciousness. If you want to heal yourself, move from where you are, then you can eliminate the distortion within the body.

Let us talk about the interrelationships between the major centers; also the interrelationships between the major centers and the secondary centers. When you were part of the animal kingdom, all four limbs were in contact with the ground and interrelated to survival within the survival center. At the point in evolution where you extended yourself into standing erect, you made self a vehicle of comprehension that could transcend. You now had the capacity to move beyond the awareness of one particular level, whereas animals can move within one particular level but never change a level.

The interrelationships of the major centers. You have seven major centers located within the trunk, and you are using only a portion of them. The three higher centers each refract consciousness and energy into their interrelating lower center in order to help you solve more basic problems. When you fill in the lower centers with knowledge and consciousness, you begin to utilize the higher centers more. Also, when you begin to meditate and use your meditations, the crown center increases its flow of refractable consciousness and color into the particular center that needs replenishing. Then there is the heart center in the middle, where universal love and compassion reside. When you begin to balance the three higher and three lower centers through comprehension, you begin to develop tributaries of comprehension that fill the chalice of the heart center.

The seventh center of the crown interrelates to the first center of survival. The crown and survival centers are both entrances for consciousness and energy permeating the body. You receive warm energy from the earth through the survival center, and cool energy from the soul through the crown center. As you begin to solve your problems within the survival center, you can utilize the crown center's capabilities more so.

The sixth center of the third-eye interrelates to the third center of the solar plexus. When you fill the chalice of the third center through comprehension, you can begin to tap into the essence of the sixth center, using insight beyond normal.

The fifth center of the throat, (higher duality) interrelates to the second center of sensuality and creativity, (lower duality.) When you fill the chalice of the second center through comprehension, you can begin to tap into the fifth center of the throat, utilizing a deeper creative connection to the soul.

Let us talk about the interrelationships between the major centers and the secondary centers. You have the seven secondary centers within the legs: the foot, ankle, calf, knee, above-knee, upper thigh and hip, and you have the seven secondary centers within the arms: hand, wrist, forearm, elbow, above-elbow, upper arm and shoulder. The seven secondary centers within the legs interrelate to your comprehension of different aspects of survival upon the earth plane. The toes and feet interrelate to your comprehension of survival. The ankles interrelate to your comprehension of duality within survival. The calves interrelate to your comprehension of human decency and emotions within survival. The knees interrelate to your comprehension of balance and compassion within survival. The thighs interrelate to your comprehension of emotions and insight into survival. The hips interrelate to your comprehension of survival and lower duality.

The seven secondary centers in the arms interrelate to your comprehension of different aspects of the higher essence within you, your soul. The fingers and hands interrelate to your comprehension of survival within the soul. The wrists interrelate to your comprehension of lower duality within the soul. The forearms interrelate to your comprehension of human decency and emotions within the soul. The elbows interrelate to your comprehension of balance and compassion within the soul. The upper arms interrelate to your comprehension of emotions and insight within the soul. The shoulders interrelate to duality and creativity within the soul.

Then there is the capacity of opposites that attract. As we practice meditation regularly, males will begin to feel energy flow coming in through the sole of the right foot, and up the right side of the body. Females will feel the flow coming in through the sole of the left foot, and up the left side. As you meditate and progress in life to become a better person, you will feel more energy within your foot, telling you that you are drawing in more of the essence of the energy, and winning the right to ignite a secondary center, the foot, within the essence of love within you. Then if your survival, or "love of self," is threatened within the physical sense, that center will now automatically "turn on" to give you more energy and consciousness.

As you work with consciousness, you begin to integrate the opposite side of the body. Eventually you may win the right to feel balance and energy flow on both sides of the body, thereby achieving a more finely attuned sense of balance. When you are dealing with knowledge to the point of igniting even more energy, male and female energies come together into the center of the body to become androgynous, rather than either male or female. Dualities within the physical sense also take place within warm and cold, up and down, high and low. Working with these dualities, you can acquire the capacity to bring them into the center, balancing yourself more so. For instance, a person who meditates regularly will achieve a finer sense of balance whereby they can more easily tolerate extremes of temperature in their environment.

As you question the body, you begin to understand how truly important each part of the body is. Your energy field is constantly feeding you information. The secondary centers of consciousness within the legs and arms interrelate to the seven major centers, giving you information on what you want to solve in life. For instance, the knees and elbows are secondary centers to the heart center: if you begin to experience a heart attack, the arm will stiffen before the heart fails. The secondary center within the elbow would have to be totally eliminated before the heart would be totally eliminated. Do not take my word for it; it is within you, because the Total Reality that made you at that level understands everything about you. If you use your mind logically, if you can filter down energies that are closer to the reality that has made you, you have more information on how to heal yourself.

Your daily experiences are catalysts for learning. We all experience dualities, physically, sensually and emotionally towards others. You begin to understand that you are here within the physical reality with certain probabilities you set in motion at another level in order to achieve them within the physical reality. If you use meditation, you can see those probabilities. If you can see those probabilities, you can work on them. When you work on them, you can eliminate the probability of harm happening to your body, and can live to a ripe old age at all of those levels, to the best of your ability.

Now, you are automatically going to hit all of those levels within the flesh within the involuntary system, whether you like it or not, because each of the centers interrelates to a particular vibration that takes place organically within the body. Every ten or twelve years, you will enter a new stage of development. Remember when you went through the first transition from "love of self" to "love of another" at age twelve or thirteen? You automatically go through the seven stages within life, passing through the awareness of each center. We have mentioned the stages of love: "love of self," "love of another," "love of many," "universal love," "duality from flesh to soul," "humanitarian insight," and "esoteric comprehension of the soul." Wouldn't you like to be ready for each stage as it comes along? Imagine if you had been prepared in adolescence when you went from survival to duality. Wouldn't that have made a difference for you?

If that is not logical and sensible, I do not know what is. If you have something that is more sensible, tell me, because I would like to know about it. If we are closer to the reality that has made us, and have more of that consciousness within us, there is less probability of harm happening to us. I have been at levels at times, when I have such a semblance of balance that I can hear at a cellular level. It is so extraordinary, you can cry just thinking about it. There is so much love within you at times when you feel the essence of these things. It will stimulate you into areas where others will look at you and think there is something wrong with you. You will have so much love and emotion, you will not know what to do with it, and you have to control all of that, in order for more to come.

Some people meditate, then return from meditation feeling no different. Some people cannot believe in self. In class I demonstrate how I can change myself in one brief moment. Taking one deep breath, I will feel total rejuvenation within my mind and body, because I have trained myself, and I know it will happen. I can quiet the system of what I am. I can open channels of awareness within myself. I can feel my eyesight and intellect changing. I can feel a quietness and peacefulness enter me that is so extraordinary, whereas a moment before, I did not feel it. Where does that come from? I have the ability of changing the velocity within me in an instant. Did it take place in a moment? Only if that moment was thoroughly usable and pliable, gained from the understanding of what is coming next. That is how the opportunity of feeling so great comes about. If there had not been twenty thousand previous meditations that gave me the opportunity of having all of that understanding become instantly usable in a thought, it would not have taken place.

There is no other way of growing other than that. You can read all the great books, but if you do not take the knowledge and put it into your normal, daily life, you will not grow in consciousness. You can deal with the illusion that you are growing. It is an illusion that is important, because it gives you the confidence in order to grow eventually so the illusion can become a reality. Then when you do control it, the rewards of consciousness are unbelievable because they do not interrelate to one feeling, or one thing, but interrelate to everything and every feeling. Everything you do in life will be changed. Every facet of your life will change forever. It will never be the same again. If you listen to music, it will be far beyond where you heard it before. If you see beauty in your life, it will be far beyond what you have seen before.

One day you will see two young people holding hands and walking along. You will see the energy between them passing back and forth, and it will extend you into an area where you understand aspects beyond sensuality and its creativity. Even though you have participated in sensuality, you will see it at a level where it is extraordinary. It goes beyond the boundaries of understanding the needs and the wants of the physical body. It goes into the identity of understanding the process of the awakening of love, and how the participation of the survival level becomes usable in understanding creativity and the duality of life.

CHAPTER EIGHT

A Moveable Vehicle of Comprehension

Medical doctors maintain that stress plays a part in the eventual deterioration of the physical body. I say stress is only the beginning. That is just brushing the surface. Stress is just the initial thrust of understanding that you deteriorate the body. The factors go so far beyond that, you cannot even imagine. Everything that you do with your mind comes back at you. Everything that you allow to come through you has an effect on you. You have to begin to understand that. If you do something wrong that contradicts the probabilities that you set in motion at a soul level, pain and agony will come forward to slow you down so you may correct that deviation in order to bring yourself back into the river of reality, rather than being in a tributary away from the main river.

On the other hand, do you realize what you can do in the meditative state? Do you realize the levels that you can eventually hit if you understand where you are now? It is important to balance yourself and not go too quickly. You can actually rejuvenate yourself right down to the cellular level. If you are looking at your toes, and actually believe that you are healing that part of your body, you are healing that part of your body. It is eliminating the probability of harm happening to you in that area. Eventually you will learn to drop so deep, you will actually feel your teeth, gums, eyes and every part of your body being purified. You will feel the structure of your muscles being toned up. If you have a slight extension of your gut or stomach, you will feel it being tightened up. It is almost as if the energy field is tightening up your skin.

You are also increasing the capability of understanding the next level, and believe me, there is another level that surrounds your body. It is becoming scientific fact now: there is energy around your body, and if you can control that energy, it rejuvenates you. There is a cushion of energy that you tap into that protects you from misconceptions within life. Meditation gives you one of the most magnificent feelings you will ever have. It is a uniquely beautiful process of sustaining your particular age and phase of life to the best of your ability. In meditation you actually extend your life force by giving yourself the opportunity to slow your body down and rejuvenate yourself.

Meditation is a tool using a natural state. You do not contradict why you are here upon the planet. You are finding out what the capabilities of your mind are and why you are upon the planet. Each part of your body has a consciousness to it. When you begin to feel the flow of subtle energies within your body, you can then begin to use your mind correctly in questioning the reality of what you are dealing with, in every moment of every day. It will make your life more pleasurable in every way. Most of us have so many different things that we are working on. Meditation gives us an opportunity to work on problems from a level where we can absorb the answers in a positive way.

Every time you meditate, there should be subtle changes in your body. If you question the reality of these changes, it gives you information on how to become more profound within the meditative state. Understand where you are now. Understand that there is an extraordinary essence around you, just waiting for you to start. It is like having a Cadillac in the garage that you have never driven. Use your mind and open up the garage door through comprehension. If you go slowly and comprehend, a uniquely beautiful process happens automatically. Then the comprehension escalates your ability to comprehend, and you have a moveable vehicle of comprehension without even trying. You do not have to force it. It forces itself. It has its own ability to move. If you comprehend one thing, more will come: If you comprehend one thing, more will become you. If you comprehend one thing, there is more of a probability of comprehending what is coming next because the essence of balance is within you. You do not deviate. You can focus. This process is so uniquely beautiful because you do not have to think about it. The only thing you have to do is to go slowly into it.

So much thought was put into this particular level of comprehension, even when you are ignorant, you can use it. Isn't that uniquely beautiful? There is so much going on around you, and you can use it even if you do not understand it. But what takes place when you do begin to understand it, more of that information becomes usable in your thoughts. You can train yourself in the correct usage of the mind. You can feel good all of the time, or most of the time. If you feel out of balance and do not feel well, meditate and put yourself back into balance. It teaches you the velocity that is usable in comprehension: not going too quickly into something, but going at a speed that is usable for you. Then you are bringing yourself into the center of self. You are not in the seesaw of life going up and down like most of humanity, but are comprehending those seemingly insignificant things and growing at an incredible speed because you have given yourself the vehicle of comprehension.

If you just sit there in meditation, nothing is going to happen. For instance, some people think that once they have meditation, they can go out and do any deed they want, then return to meditation to rejuvenate. It works like that for a while, but then it will not work at all because it contradicts why you are here upon the planet. It contradicts the meditation and the usage of anything that you are involved in within the structure of meditation. For instance, if you constantly react in life with a lack of compassion towards yourself and others, and know that you are dissipating your heart center, using meditation to simply rejuvenate is not going to work after a while. Meditation will give you a fair chance by bringing you back into the fold so that you can comprehend what you do in a more balanced way. But eventually you will hit that avenue where you have to understand the particular thing you do. If you do not, you are abusing something you should be using in a balanced way. Meditation is like anything else: if you over use it and do not apply it within your everyday life, you lose the right to use it.

So learning how to meditate is one thing, but learning how to use the meditation is another. Play the game of awareness within the structure of the meditative state so you can comprehend. You can have some quiet periods of rejuvenation, but then you have the choice to take out a problem and look at it. Ask questions within yourself concerning the problem and you begin to open up viable channels of awareness to that higher level. If you do not know what to work on, ask: *What should I be working on today? What is the thing that bothers me the most?* Then you will see something come before you, and you will work on it. You will then experience an event within your normal, daily life that will interrelate to the particular problem that you are trying to comprehend. If you want to grow and experience increased consciousness in your meditations, understand your last meditation and use it in your tomorrows. Then you can build upon it. It is the idea of focusing upon a particular area and collecting information. The balancing quality of that area gives you the answer pertaining to the particular sphere. Then that sphere gives you the density to proceed to another level and also draw energy into the flesh.

At times I am guilty of the misuse of the mind. I was sitting the other day thinking about some of the thought patterns I have had. They have not been good lately, at least not to the point I want them to be. I thought about that for a moment, then a flash came into my mind: *Do you realize the truth of the statement, "What you think comes through you?" That if you think negative thoughts of violence, anger, or whatever, it comes through you: that it is in you, just as if you are drinking a glass of poison?* It is in you. Sometimes you can hear a statement like that, and it passes you by, it passes you by. Then suddenly if you are truly trying to comprehend and be involved in dealing with the problem, there is a flash. That flash is so true and so accurate. You see that thing, like you have never seen it before. Those are the times when it really sticks and becomes that which you can utilize in a more usable way within comprehension.

When you sit down to meditate, you are working on self at a higher level. You are putting self in that plateau of absorption and are also changing the density of the particular problem that you work on, because you change consciousness, into energy, into matter. Consciousness, into energy, into matter: for instance, an illness that seems to come upon you so suddenly might have been the result of your miscomprehension, maybe twenty-five or thirty days ago. How long does it take for a misconception to manifest in your body? It depends on where you are upon that ladder of comprehension. Some people change consciousness, into energy, into matter, in a quicker way. As you grow within the soul, you shrink the time it takes for either growth, or misconception, to become a reality within the body. For instance, it became an instant reaction when Jesus raised Lazarus from the dead, because Jesus was at the level that made Lazarus within the flesh. We can stand over Lazarus for seven billion years, saying, "Lazarus, rise!" and nothing will happen because we are nowhere near the place of changing consciousness into energy, into matter, in such an extraordinary way.

You change consciousness, into energy, into matter, in a very subtle way when you sit down to meditate and work on yourself at a higher level. For example, many people have problems working on their survival and "love of self." Let us say you are in the outer orbit of the sphere of "love of self" and want to approach the core of "love of self." The deeper you go into meditation, the more power you have to change your reactions within the physical sense of changing consciousness, into energy, into matter. You question those parts of the body that have blockages or problems, knowing that everything happens to you for a reason.

Now, if you were to grow in such a manner and shrink the time of your reactions of consciousness, into energy, into matter, to the extraordinary point that Jesus did, you would have to begin to question every thought that you have. If you have the capability of bringing a person back from the dead, the opposite can also happen: if you think of a person dying, you can kill the person. But there are safeguards placed at other levels before something like that can happen. There is a sequence of events that takes place within the structure of comprehension that puts you in a particular place, until you can put your thoughts into the proper way.

My point is: the mind is powerful. That plateau of absorption is more usable in employing the power of the essence of you. So it is unique and beautiful, and when you know that, you can then compound the reality of it. The key to it is that you have to believe in yourself. Some people sit there for years, never believing that they can rejuvenate self, and they never can. You have to understand that your mind can work and become involved in that. You are stimulating yourself within the meditative state, and are using more of the essence and power of your soul within the flesh because you are making yourself transcendable. You are using more of the energy at a particular level first. Then eventually you are making that level so balanced, you become transcendable. It is like having the total understanding of how you have made your body. For instance, we imagine so many times that we can use everything within the physical reality that was so uniquely made, even if we are ignorant to the fact. Let us say you were not ignorant to the fact and were involved in it: it is like walking up to your car, knowing every part in the motor and taking the motor apart without a second thought because you know where every part goes. You are doing the same thing with your body. Know that, when you enter meditation. It is important that you use this tool properly in order to understand. You can totally rejuvenate yourself at work or play, because those preconceived thoughts are within you.

Here at the school people are taught to feel and sense the energy field in meditation, and question subtle physical sensations or ailments in particular parts of the body. They begin to interrelate these bodily sensations to what is going on within their daily lives. They have the capacity of utilizing time segments within the system of comprehending. If they become sick, they can trace the problem back to particular miscomprehended events, in order to gain the knowledge to heal whatever it is and not have it happen again. On the other hand, you do not want to trace things all of the time. You can get bogged down if you dwell upon how a miscomprehended event thirty-one days ago caused illness to manifest within the present. Understanding how to change consciousness, into energy, into matter, becomes secondary when you realize that you do it all of the time. It is a teaching process that puts you in that moment so that you will not miss what is coming next. Focusing on the present moment and on whatever is coming next is necessary for your growth. You learn to go down that avenue and interrelate whatever it is, to the instant reaction of the moment because that capacity gives you the incentive, or escalation of speed, to the point where you can begin to comprehend everything.

Do you want to solve a persistent problem? In your next meditation put that problem in your mind when you come to that place of absorption. That is the place that opens that book of knowledge. That is the place where you can absorb and change, because you are opening up that channel of absorption where you are literally putting a suggestion in your mind, absorbing it and leaving it there. It is not glancing off from you. It is going right in. If you can work on that one thing that is bothering you, that one particular sphere that you are trying to comprehend, and get information on it, you are taking a step.

Let us say you want to work on an interpersonal problem of some kind. You are going to take just a portion of the problem and begin to ask questions about it. Perhaps you have a problem with either over-reacting or under-reacting with others. You consider new ways to handle the problem. Then you visualize yourself reacting in a more positive way for the following day when a similar interaction will take place. React within the particular structure the next day and return to meditation to assess how you did, by questioning: *How was I involved? How did I perform? How would I have liked to perform? What do I have to work on to change the density of the problem so I can have more stability within that particular interaction?* When you do begin to use a new and more successful way of interacting, give yourself statements every day in meditation to reinforce your new behavior, by saying: *I want to receive the same statement each time I react from now on.* In this way you are compounding the reality of changing your reaction. Just getting the message once is not enough. You have to get the message for the next time also.

You are going to use your mind correctly by saying: *If I comprehend a portion of the problem, there is more comprehension within me, and less within the particular thing that bothers me.* As you work in this way, you are actually changing a portion of the problem. You are not eliminating it totally because the process that gave you the particular problem has been with you for a long time. You are changing a small portion of it, and by accomplishing that, you have more control and ability within you towards solving more of the larger portion. That is a reaction towards growth and stability. If you do not, you will have events happen to you that give you pain and agony to make you see it. You never go backwards, whether you believe it or not. You are always gaining. There are times when it seems as if you are going backwards, because that gives you the incentive to say: *Hey, I should be working a little harder.* There are reasons for everything happening to you. You just have to take the opportunity to question why a particular thing is happening.

Growth is the process of understanding how to use self as you interrelate to others within the physical sense, and within higher levels. If a normal individual like me can do it, anybody can do it. Each one of us is unique. Each one of us is totally different than anyone else, anywhere. You have to feel that within you. Nobody, anywhere, is exactly like you. It took me about forty-five years to learn how to cry. In the neighborhood where I grew up, you did not show a tear. There is so much joy in understanding the beauty of allowing what you are to come forward, no matter what it is. Eliminate those illusions, or moments of grandeur, and put the reality of what you are right out there. I have learned somewhat to do so. With me, what you see is what you get. I do not hold anything back with most people. If I have to say something, I will say it. It becomes a positive reaction. It becomes a learning process. You do not have to wait twenty-one days. Instantly you can make a reaction. That filtering process can take place in moments. That is what you should be striving for: taking that gap between self and soul, and shrinking it, and bringing it closer to the reality of an instant reaction of consciousness. I guess my goal in life at the end is not to die, but walk right out of the body. When it comes to that level, and you know you are dying, you can just walk right into that next level. But you can only do so by eliminating the distortions within the refractability of it, and eliminating the process of going back by taking the process and making it, you.

CHAPTER NINE

Your Soul is Doing Everything

Your soul is doing everything that it can possibly do to help and heal you, each and every day. It is changing the chemical reactions within your body in the dream state. It is also setting probabilities in motion, using time as an essence in understanding the reality of what is going to happen within your normal, daily life. If you notice, similar events in your daily life will happen to you to make you comprehend something. They will all be different events, but will be interrelated to make you comprehend a particular thing. Our souls are doing so much, but usually we are so involved in our lives, we are outside of understanding that reality. We begin to see and understand some of that reality through feeling and sensing the energy field in meditation. We will actually feel the reality of the illness within the energy field before it happens within the flesh and can take steps to correct it before it manifests within the physical body.

So many people experience roadblocks in meditation and cannot utilize it: that is the misuse of the mind. For instance, we have talked about how a person will do two or three negative things in their life, then dwell upon and allow the negative things to slow them down, by saying: *I am not good enough to grow.* But then they will not become more godlike, and that is a contradiction to the laws of this level. You must look at a seemingly negative event to say: *Whatever the event was, it made me what I am today, and I will not allow it to slow me down from becoming more godlike. I do not want to contradict my growth, because then I cannot help another person.* When you think of it in that way, it gives you total incentive. Your experiences, whether seemingly good or bad, made you what you are today, and you are part of God, or whatever you wish to name the process of how All of This Started. Every time I hit a new level of seeing the beauty of what we are here, I wish I had been there when All of This Started! Who started All of This? Who made my finger? Who made the rain, water, or earth? Earth is unbelievable! Earth is so extraordinary that it sustains itself. And if we no longer fit in, we will not be here. We will just be eliminated, and some other species will be here that deserves it until it does not deserve it.

The Total Reality of God is within each of us, but we do not use the Total Reality of God because our capacity to use It is not there. The body is so unique! We truly do not understand what it is! In the next twenty years we will see such advances in medical knowledge that we will look back upon today as the stone ages. If we wish, one day we will just say: *Drift*, and be able to lift ourselves right off the ground and fly. The energy sources within us will spiral so significantly at extraordinary levels, the velocity of the energy will just lift us right off the ground. So when you go into meditation to look at a problem, know who you are: you are part of All of That, and if you want to understand more of All of That through meditation, you have more capacity to understand the remaining portion of All of That. The structure of meditation becomes usable in comprehension. It gives you the velocity that is usable in comprehension, and comprehension happens effortlessly. You do not even have to think about it. Then when that takes place, the next moment becomes joy rather than drudgery because you can absorb it. The moment becomes you. You use it rather than it abusing you.

Let us talk about some of the tools of consciousness that you have at your disposal. Fear is one tool. Is fear a negative thing? One evening I was sitting at a philosopher's forum preparing to give a talk, and the speaker before me was speaking at length about fear, saying that we must just command ourselves to eliminate our fears and so forth. I was sitting there listening. My mind starts going crazy when I hear things like that. Coming home in the car, I started asking hundreds of questions and immediately understood the importance of fear: fear is a tool of the soul telling you that you are in a place before you are ready. You have to use the velocity of fear in order to understand whether you are going too fast or too slow. If you push yourself too fast, or force something, fear will be put in front of you to slow you down and push you back. If you force something, you experience only scattering moments. But if you go at a speed that is usable for you, everything happens in a natural way so you can comprehend. For instance, you are not going to take your child out of third grade and put them in Yale. You want the child to experience a natural sequence of events in order to give them the opportunity of comprehending. You eliminate fear through comprehension. If you understand what is in that dark room, you can open the door and walk in without fear. If you do not understand what is in the room, you are going to open the door very slowly. As you proceed slowly, you increase the speed of comprehension, and that process happens automatically. You do not force it. You do not make it drudgery. It is beautiful, because everything is running so smoothly. Even when it does not seem to go right, you have the strength to stay in the river of reality without drowning.

Insecurities of various kinds and illusions are tools. A person will come up to me after class to tell me they have an extraordinary spirit guide. I say, "That is absolutely beautiful." Then I look at them straight in the eye and say, "I have me with me. Your statement tells me where you are, but someday you will understand that it is not a spirit guide, it is you." My remarks are sometimes interpreted as an egotistical gesture on my part, until I explain, "When we do not have the capacity to take the weight of whatever it might be upon our shoulders, we think of something outside of us helping us. Eventually when we comprehend and look at it thoroughly, we understand it was an illusion: it was not a spirit guide but self. We were tricking ourselves out of insecurity."

Now, when you do hit that level and see the absolute of it, do you condemn yourself for the previous understanding? No. When you go past any level, you look back upon the previous understanding as necessary because it made you what you are today. Is there such a thing as a devil? One day in meditation I remember going through a level where I had to face the reality of the misconception interrelated to the realm of the devil, with only the essence and strength of the portion of God that was within me. In other words, rather than being able to say: *God, help me through this level,* I had to rely on the comprehension of God that I had within me to cope with it. I looked at the image and said: *You are necessary.* At that moment I understood if we are at a basic survival level in our consciousness, we make a devil in our minds in order to give us fear, so we will be good. Once we go past that level, we no longer need the devil in order to be good.

The same thing takes place when you put fear in the small child's mind about the dangers of crossing the street. You want to slow them down so they will automatically practice safety measures until they master certain skills. When the child masters those skills, then you can take them out of the playpen and give them more freedom. That freedom has a cost, which is comprehension. When you eliminate a certain fear of something, you then give yourself the freedom to move beyond that into a new area of consciousness. Once again, you do not condemn the previous concept because you understand it as good and usable for that basic level. If you condemn it, you are not past that level.

The expression of anger for self, or others, can be a tool. We can use anger, or being upset with self, in order to give us some semblance of movement. In regard to the expression of anger towards another person, why should we think that expression of anger is always a negative thing? Uncontrolled expression of anger is negative, but a drop of anger sent to an individual who needs some incentive to come out of a shell that they have erected around self, may possibly move them along. Expression of anger can use to counteract complacency in the other. For instance, if you had a very inward child, just sitting around, not reacting, not enjoying, showing no love, compassion, or understanding, stimulating them by directing a slight bit of anger at them might give them the strength to move out of that area. You want to make the child understand how to participate with strength, by putting them in a sphere to comprehend reacting with strength, thereby making them more of a reacting person. Instead of you making a reaction towards the child that makes them confine self to the sphere of what they have to comprehend, your slight anger directed towards them puts them into a sphere that prepares them within the strengths. In that way they can eventually comprehend and use that strength in participating in understanding the events of what they have to be involved in.

Therefore, when we see something that seems negative within life, we return to that one understanding: *Everything is God. Everything is perfect. It is just that we cannot comprehend something in our life as so, because we are nowhere near understanding the Reality of Perfection.* So within the quest of understanding that a particular situation is not totally negative, we will attempt to look at it from different levels within the threads of what we are. As we do so, we will dissect and begin to comprehend portions of it, and each time we understand that there will be less negativity within it. Of course, anything that is overdone is harmful. Fear is a tool of the soul, yet if we totally misuse it within life, it can overwhelm us, just like anything else.

Do not push. Think about your body. Feel where the energy is. Some people exhibit a lot of nervous energy in their daily lives and when they increase their velocity too quickly, they give themselves more confusion. There is a balancing quality. You can take a glass of water and quench your thirst coming out of the desert, and you can also put your head under water and drown. Sometimes you can overindulge in an activity to a point where it becomes a contradiction to even be involved in it. Let us say you needed some physical activity: are you going to contradict your body by suddenly running ten miles a day? A friend of mine was jogging long distances and was then complaining about problems in his legs. I told him he was overdoing. If you overdo it, you then harm yourself and lose the right of doing it at all. If you want to exercise, build up your routine slowly. That causes harmony. Another thing: if you do get to a more advanced level of bodily strength, do you want to go beyond that? At the age of fifty, do you want to have a body of a twenty-year old? It is impossible. Rather, you want a body that is going to be pliable for the particular stage of life that you are dealing with.

Balance: you are adding stress to your whole system when you are overweight or underweight. It causes imperfections and imbalance usually within the heart center with a lot of coughing and colds. You can tell when you are out of whack. Nobody has to tell you when you do not feel well. It is very rare that I do not feel absolutely perfect. When I do not, I question why. I have not deviated within more than five pounds in the past twenty years. Sometimes I can eat, but then I feel my system changing, so I tell myself to slow it down. Most times I do not allow situations to overwhelm me. I try to the best of my ability to control the situations, even though sometimes they do have an over-whelming effect. They would have a catastrophic effect if I did not have some semblance of balance.

Anything that is coming through you is either a consideration of what you are trying to comprehend now, or a point that will give you the strength to eventually consider it. Sometimes there is an event that brings you to a place where you will comprehend what you have to comprehend. Sometimes there is so much that takes place in dreams. People in class sometimes ask for interpretations to their dreams. When I make an interpretation, I focus in on the particular structure of what the person is involved in within the density of their life, and the inter-pretation is for that person only. Another person can relate a similar dream and the interpretation might be totally different.

Some people go to sleep at night and wake up the next morning feeling fatigued. Some people have a lot of nightmares and do not know why. In both these instances they are so entrenched at a particular level, they will dream only at the one particular level. They do not go closer and closer to the soul where it is totally refreshing so they can return to the waking state feeling fantastic. Each of the major centers in the body interrelates to different levels of comprehension. If you are balanced, you will dream at all seven levels, going closer and closer to your soul. If you are not balanced, you will not dream at all the levels. You should have those seven dreams where you are going all the way up to the soul level so you can wake up in the morning feeling totally refreshed. That is one capability I have: I can rejuvenate myself so quickly, and if I do not hit all of those levels in the sleep state, I will hit them in meditation.

Everything within the framework of dreams and sleep is for the purpose of rejuvenating the mind and body so it can participate within the next day with more balance. It is a manifestation of the soul using the unconscious mind to reprogram you for your tomorrows. The dream state changes the density of a particular reaction within the physical sense into a more pliable, understandable level, helping you to com-prehend in a more pliable way within your next day. For instance, a scary dream actually provides shock therapy in the form of changing chemical reactions within the body to help you to perform within your tomorrows in a more balanced way. Your soul is changing certain reac-tions within you so you can see and face certain things in your tomorrows. For instance, if you have to learn about survival, your soul is going to show you a movie that is going to threaten your survival.

Now, if you experienced a very emotional day, your soul is absent within the reality of the misconceptions that you have dealt with during the day, so you will not be in a position to receive rejuvenation at all of the higher levels. Therefore, at night you will dream at the level where you need the sustenance in order for you to receive common knowledge. Since you were emotional that day, that night you will dream at the first three levels only, in order for you to deal with that structure. You are given information interrelated to the particular factor that gave you all of the stress, so that you can then function more properly within the next day. Of course, you will wake up less refreshed in the morning, because you were not closer to that fountain that totally eliminates the process of fatigue and allows you to receive rejuvenation at all the levels. You cannot control your dreams; you can only control what you do in your normal, daily life. But if you work on the emotional problem in meditation the next day, the following night you will not be stuck at that particular level, but will be able to dream at all of the levels. As you do so, you will absorb all of the sustenance that eliminates the fatigue from the body.

If you have balance and comprehension within life, you will never remember your dreams because it is not necessary to remember them. But when you are out of balance within the physical sense, and not comprehending something, you are going to remember those dreams. Those dreams are shock therapy because you are not remembering what you should be doing within life. If you remember a dream, and it interrelates to something that you are dealing with, it is because you are not facing it within your daily life. So face it. Now it is right out in the open. You have to solve it.

Very seldom do I remember dreams. When I do remember a dream, I will ask: *Now what am I doing wrong? Why did my soul show me that? I should have comprehended that within my life in some way*. It is teaching me something. You see, I try to the best of my ability to use everything for me, not against me. Whatever is happening to me is happening to me for a reason. If I can comprehend it, no matter what it is, I grow. Ten seconds after I am in bed, bombs could go off, and I would not know. There are certain levels you go through. Where you enter from is the key. If you have filtered down some of those levels within you, there is more within you interrelated to the particular levels that you have integrated between you and your soul. Even though the levels are transcendable, and the soul is digesting the information, it is like a gigantic computer up there, digesting all of the information pertaining to the reality of you and changing constantly. If you absorb those particular levels, where are you dreaming now? Those levels are extraordinary.

What about the dreams that get stored in your memory? You can reconsider them, but they are much more difficult to draw upon, because each dream is a consideration that is constantly changing within the structure that emanates them forward. Why should your soul have you remember a past dream when it is going to make you a new one tomorrow? It is taking into consideration all of the considerations it once did, then looking back upon the consideration that you gave it and changing the density of it in a similar way. Your soul is giving you that avenue that stimulates you for where you are.

During your day you might have an experience that gives you a flash of understanding. Perhaps it is a déjà vu experience, which is an insight regarding a previous life. Whatever it is, it might make you consider a particular aspect that is necessary for change now. Perhaps as you are walking down the street, you experience a lifting sensation, or hear someone calling out, or see colored clothes on the line flapping in the wind. All are experiences that give you a point of consideration. We sometimes brush these experiences aside because we are usually involved in something else at the time, but we can come back later to look upon them.

The point is, it is not necessary to know where something comes from, it is what you do with it here and now. If you can take the opportunity to sit for a moment, it gives you a great deal of information pertaining to what you need, or where you are going, or what you are comprehending. You might ask: *What was it about the walk...or the feeling of the sun, the wind or the temperature?* You might get an answer and understand what it is. You use it as a usable vibration that puts you in a place where you can consider the comprehension. It may seem so insignificant sometimes, but it is not. It is an opportunity. It is almost as if you are sending a rocket to the moon and are making that subtle mid-flight adjustment in order to land on the moon. Your soul is in that particular quality that gives it a dimension within a time frame to have you understand that you are going somewhere, and that you will eventually hit a point. These are all important considerations.

CHAPTER TEN

Making the Body Stable From the Mind

When I sit in front of an ill person, sometimes I wonder what I can do. I trace some of these pathways back, twenty, thirty, forty, fifty years: I can go right back to the seed-atom that went forward and caused certain things to happen within the person. There is nothing that I can do about it, other than to give the person the information. So if we are healers, we cannot take the blame for something that was stimulated within the other's genetic process that was not eliminated through the proper use of the mind in understanding the particular thing.

We must look at the genetic makeup of our family and understand the flaws. I know that by the time my mother and father hit my present age, they were both having problems with eyesight. I know that I am on the borderline of having that problem, so I have to work on my insight and my capacity to understand it. I have another problem: lately my cholesterol has been a little high, so the doctor told me that I had to take some pills. I took these pills for two days and started getting blurry vision because one of the properties of the pills is that you can experience blurry vision. Genetically, that is one of my weak spots, so do I take the pills? I have to be some kind of nut to take those pills! So I stopped taking the pills, called up the doctor and told him I was going to work out a little more and watch my diet. Now, if I do not do those things, I am going to have to take the pills.

Therefore, in meditation you want to consider some of those factors of health and security of the mind. Making the body stable from the mind. It is important that you meditate, bridge the gap between self and soul, and begin to enjoy some of that information that comes forward. It is fine to go at a pace that is so beautiful, it does not seem like you are growing or are in that game of life. It is fine to rejuvenate the body and have complacent moments. But then you have to seize the opportunity of understanding that you have to question yourself about what is going on and get answers regarding what could possibly happen to you in the future if you do not correct whatever the imbalance might be. It is your body, and it is your mind, and you have to work on it. If you are feeling something abnormal in the knee, ankle, shoulder, or elbow, ask questions about why you are feeling it. It is giving you an opportunity to question the reality of something that could go wrong in the future and affect the quality of your life.

Sit down today to meditate. Have new intent within the quest of understanding your meditations. I am as guilty as anybody else in my reactions of not understanding what is necessary for me. Do not let it go into the avenue of pain and agony. You have to look at the overall picture of what you are and what is going on in your body, by asking: *What do I have to do to make my body better?* If you do not do it, things are going to happen to you. It is your choice. You have all of the tools at your disposal to make your body deal with harmony most of the time. It is not saying that you are not going to fluctuate from one area to another, but you are going to have harmony even within the fluctuation. My intent is not to make you feel bad, my intent is to make you feel good, by you questioning the reality of what you have to work on.

Today you will get a message on what you have to work on to make yourself a better person and enhance the capability of your body, whatever it might be. Is it an addiction of some sort? Are you either under-reacting or over-reacting in life situations? Are you displaying too much anger within you? Do you not have enough motivation? You will get a picture of what you have to work on. There are many things you have to work on, but I want you to see that one stumbling block, that one key to opening up the doorway to that next level. Focus more on using that meditation right, than you have ever done before. Work on those areas dealing with genetic misconception. The misconception is the reality of what caused certain things to happen in your family. If you know your family is prone to a particular trait, focus upon it to ask: *Where does it come from? What can I do to eliminate it?* Ask questions and get answers. If you do not get answers at first, that tells you that you are asking the wrong questions, or are in the wrong place to ask the questions. Perhaps you are just starting out. The answers will come if you work on the trait daily.

The healer can only give information pertaining to the illness; they cannot walk for the ill person. I might tell the ill person a hundred times, if they do not go forward within questioning the particular ailment, they are going to deteriorate something within the system. On the other hand, sometimes in our healing capacities we do not take the opportunity to meditate and look at certain factors within others. As we try to understand a particular flaw within the person who has requested a healing, we have to try to change our own interactions into more pliable areas of understanding the needs of the other. For instance, if we give them the information, and they do not seem to know how to utilize it, we have to learn and apply new methods of teaching them how to use the information better.

You might wonder what you can do for someone close to you who seems to be going in a wrong direction. You should not take the blame for their problem. You are doing the best you can for where you are. Your energy field is sustaining you, and the others around you, the best it can. Work on yourself and see what you have to do to increase your capabilities. There are certain things that happen to others that are probably going to happen. There is nothing you can do to change it. You can work on the other, morning, noon and night, but if they do not change the trait that caused the disease, you are not going to get rid of it. Christ said, "Go and sin no more," which means, do not go and do the same thing again; if you do the same thing again, it will come back. So work on yourself, then work on others.

How does a healer eliminate disease? A lot of people have disease. It is not saying that the sick person is bad, it is saying that they have not comprehended some probabilities that were set in motion within life, so disease comes forward. You try to make them understand where the consciousness is and what is going on there. Sometimes you cannot change a rigid structure. The individual has to return back to the soul, filter through the levels once again and eventually re-manifest a body.

What happens in the returning process? As the deceased goes back towards the soul, it strains the awareness of that particular level within the conscious awareness of the soul. Some of the refracting process eliminates the denseness of their comprehension through the knowledge of becoming closer and closer to the soul, which then once again grabs upon the entire essence of the life. Then there is a bolt that can flash back into the physical sense within new sets of probabilities interrelated to that filtered information through the process of osmosis through the different levels. It has the wondrous capacity to set new probabilities in motion, knowing what has to be achieved within the physical sense to become more evolved within the structure of what it might be.

Do not go and do the same thing again. The scientific medical advances of today in eliminating some of the agony are important, but if you eliminate the agony without information, it contradicts why you are here. For example, we have talked about the awareness of the heart center, and a person who deals with a lack of compassion or balance within life. It could be a person who allows others to react towards them with a lack of compassion and they are not outwardly reacting back, or the person could be overwhelming others around them with their lack of compassion and balance. Whether it is under-reacting or over-reacting, the person is demonstrating lack of compassion. There are thousands of bits of information coming into the heart center all of the time, and if that information is not put into the structure of comprehension, there is increasing deterioration. Thousands and thousands of bits of misconception eventually lead the person down a pathway where deterioration begins to overwhelm the particular center, and they experience a heart attack.

Now, if the person has a heart attack and has the good fortune to be in a place where they can survive, and they are taking in all of the medical information and chemicals within the body to cause some semblance of balance, *and* the healer gives them the awareness of the consciousness, they will have a total healing if they take that information into consideration and change their life. The healer has them understand the reason for the particular physical problem happening to the body and why they have deviated into an avenue of misconception to have the problem happen to them. That knowledge does not contradict why we are here.

Healing: it is all here and within us. Let us return to the statement, "It took the Total Reality of God to make you." The Total Reality of God is within you, but what portion of God are you using? Each time that you comprehend something, you win the right to use more of the God Essence within life. If you believe that you are part of a Total Reality, a single cell within God, and you grow, how could you dispute the logic of saying you will not use more of God? If everything is God, and you comprehend that next thing, there is more God Essence within you that you can ignite and use within you. You are going to feel the God Essence turn on, and that is healing.

Who performs a healing? Let us say there are two priests, rabbis, nuns, or ministers in front of you to heal you. One says to you, "You are healed," and nothing happens; the other one says, "You are healed," and something happens. Both have a similar title or rank, but one has more God Essence within. When this person looks at you, or just says, "Have a good day," or, "I hope you feel better," you will actually have a better day and feel better. If the person says they have healed you, you will be healed to the necessary, understandable level of their comprehension, and nothing past that. If the healer understands that they are participating in and using the true essence of what they are, they will say each time: *God, I know that You are me at another level. As You come through me, I wish to learn from this healing, so the next time I heal someone else, I will have more information, understanding and energy to heal whatever it is I do not understand within the illness.*

Work on yourself. If you do not, you are egotistical because then you will not grow and be able to help another. If someone says you are selfish to think of yourself, say, "Thank you. I am really trying not to be selfish. I am working on myself so I can help others." And when you think about it, it pays to be a good person, whether you believe it or not, or whether you think another person is taking advantage of you. If you are a good person, most people will send you good vibrations. If that happens, there is more of a chance of having some semblance of balance. In fact, if you are really good, and there are others who wish to send you negative thoughts and energies, they cannot possibly touch you, or enter into your mind or body. There are so many people out there who like to gloat over things that others participate in. They end up swelling up in their own misconceptions. They never see who they are, because they are not worried about who they are. They are always trying to find out what others are doing, which has nothing to do with them, and they do not understand anything pertaining to self.

Work on yourself. You are the center of the entire universe to you. There is nobody better than you and nobody worse than you. There is nobody exactly like you anywhere! If you had a twin, your twin is not exactly like you. There is a pimple, or cell, or just a little twinkle, or something different about you. Do you want that twinkle to become something that glows? Grow and then you will glow. Glow within the awareness of what you are. Then you will heal yourself before illness takes place. When you think about love, think about who you are. You are a son or daughter of God. For those of you who are religious, Jesus told you that: "You are my son, you are my daughter, you are my brother, you are my sister. We are all one. I go to make a place for you." Maybe some of us will be there sooner, but all of us will be there eventually. Work on yourself, because whatever you think you are, you are beautiful and totally unique.

CHAPTER ELEVEN

The Echoes of Love

If you are ill and want to heal yourself, you might want to prepare a special room to spend time each day. You begin to participate in making that room a place of healing by working on the sphere and cleansing quality of the room with your thoughts. When you put your thoughts in one place, you are actually confining them to an area. The Native Americans understood that thoroughly. They were not scattered into all of the areas that we are involved in today. They were into the basic strength of understanding their needs and all of what transpired in nature. They thought of their burial ground as holy ground, which was sacred and inaccessible to others; a structure that should not be tampered with by others. Your prepared room is going to be considered hallowed or holy ground. It gives you an opportunity to prepare yourself for particular acts of cleansing. Not only do you put illusions around the particular structure, you put the framework that deals with the density of refracting necessary information and consciousness into it. When you are considering cleansing, you are using everything.

If you want to cleanse and purify yourself, you use the density of what is necessary for you. One tool is to use the physical color spectrum, by refracting the necessary consciousness into the visible spectrum. You interrelate the illness to the particular consciousness of the different colors within the spectrum and begin to participate in the building blocks of understanding the essence of that purification. Let us say you have an ailment in the lower part of the trunk of the body or legs. You would use the red vibration because it has an awareness within it that interrelates to survival and "love of self." Red is the level of comprehension that is most accessible for you within the physical sense; it is the most easily transferable center that interrelates you to your multidimensional self. Your room would then have a lot of vibrant red in it. You would use red color outside the room: red in your bath water, red clothes, red-colored food. If you have something wrong in the heart center, wear green. If you have a problem in the third center, wear yellow. Put beloved art objects and paintings in your room. Use music, candles and incense with the awareness of knowing that your room is a holy place for you, and that when you walk into it, it has cleansing properties within it.

Does all of this become a reaction that is necessarily esoteric? If you begin to use your reaction here within the physical reality, then you confine it to a particular level and can now say that it is within the physical reality because you have made it the property of the physical reality. However, it has one unique quality that you can look upon when you are considering it: your work in this direction has the unique quality of the Fibers of That, Which has made you. It has the quality that extends you into the awareness of knowing that you have a spirit. If you draw spirit within self, it is an esoteric cleansing because it has all of those qualities. It pulls you out of the avenues that you participate in your normal life and puts you within the sphere of the room. It makes you know without question, there is an Unbelievable Creation beyond you that has refracted Itself and made this portion of which you are a part.

What about healing others? I have been asked, "How do we heal others if we are not sure we are capable of doing anything?" I respond that you have to hit a level where you can help, but that does not mean that you should not use the capacity that you have within you now to help because it is a teaching process. You allow that vibration to come through you by saying: *As the vibration flows through me, I am helping. In doing so, the healing changes me so I will have more of the healing essence for the next time.* As you are involved in the healing, you should always have the thought in your mind: *More of the essence of that particular awareness is coming through me.* For instance, when you say, "I love you," to another person, you are allowing more love to flow through you, and the next time you say it, there is even more love coming through you.

If you do not rely on yourself in the healing, you are selfish. If you say: *God, heal this person,* rather than: *God, help me to heal this person,* you are thereby relying on something outside of yourself, rather than allowing it to flow through you. Then you will not grow and the next time you cannot help more because it becomes a contradiction. In the same way if you say: *Jesus, heal this person,* it is a contradiction to Jesus. On the other hand, if you say: *Jesus, help me to understand the avenue of how to heal this person,* it is totally different: it is one person helping another. So it is a contradiction not to have the healing come through you and not to understand that you are part of God, just like anybody else.

Then you rely on that system of awareness. There is the duality of understanding that a great figure of the past participated in the creation of balance at particular levels, such as the awareness of Jesus who laid down a pathway for us to see and understand, or Buddha, Moses, or whoever is that icon of information interrelated to what is usable for you in becoming more of what you are within the physical sense. It becomes a pawn of awareness within you, as you comprehend. The most creative and usable healing is the capacity of transcending some of the energy that you have and refracting it through you to another person. By doing so, you are stimulating some semblance of balance within the awareness of the other person's particular area of misconception. There is a reason for the illness being in the body. Then while doing the healing, you should always rely upon what is coming through your mind as something that you can interrelate to the other in regard to their condition. "Do not go and do the same thing again." You give them some information regarding why they are in the particular area of misconception.

At a certain point in healing the person, you might feel a drain in your energy field. That will tell you there is too much of you involved in the healing. You should then pull back and ask for help from your higher self. You understand that you should pull back because you do not want to become sick yourself. If you are sitting in front of the person, or are thinking about them, and are feeling somewhat of a drain, ask for help by asking: *What is going on? What can I do to help? Should I slow myself down? Is this too much for me? Should I be involved in just a particular level?* If you proceed in the healing and allow yourself to be drained, that is a contradiction to healing, unless you are at such a level where you are willing to give your essence away and die. That is a very high level. I do not know where that place is. There is a vast elimination of fear through comprehension before you hit that level. I once asked the question: *Why are so many of these healers dying? Why do they put themselves in harms way?* The answer came back: *There are certain people that understand what you are talking about. They understand the structure of healing. They know if they go too far, they will not be here anymore. They understand that and still make the choice to continue giving too much of themselves.*

That is an avenue I am not sure I would want to go down, or teach, but it is an avenue. If you eventually get there and feel very comfortable with it, I can understand it as something that is usable. But within the system of awareness within me now, to have the capacity to give the total awareness of what I am to the other person, is beyond my comprehension. Because where I am now, I look at it as a system of understanding that if I do that, then I die and cannot help anybody else. On the other hand, if I stay here as long as I can, and grow within the system, I can help a lot more. Nevertheless, if I were faced with the true understanding of the essence of love for someone like my wife, or child, I think that whole scenario would change into understanding more of the avenue where I would want to give my whole being. If you had a child who was dying, and you could heal the child only by giving yourself away, wouldn't you do it? The idea is that there is no way out, other than to do it. Many people have done so. You are giving away everything you have within your body. But you cannot give the total reality of what you are away. You give away just the awareness of the body here, which is what you are within the physical reality. If you look at it from another level, you are giving some of that away because if you are truly at that level, you have a tremendous amount of what you are at the level here within the physical sense. But you know in essence that you are only giving that portion away because you will be there again.

Consider something totally different: Christ said, "God, why have You forsaken me?" A split second later, he was walking right out of the body and understanding that he truly was at that level. In other words, we can get to the awareness of understanding that dying is just walking from one place to another. It is like bridging that gap. When you are dying, you are not dying within fear, but dying within the awareness of knowing, and as you do so, you can then enter into another level instantly. You have eliminated only that thread of doubt, which is: "God, why have You forsaken me?"

In the particular moment where Jesus experienced doubt, it tells you that there was a split within him; that there was even a little portion of him within the physical sense that doubted. That gives us the incentive to know that moment within Jesus was truly unique, because it gives us the incentive of going forward and understanding it. Do you remember the preconceived thought put within our minds: *Everything is good because everything is God: that we just do not understand something as good because we do not have the capacity to understand it as good?* But every time we comprehend something, it brings us closer to the reality of understanding that statement, and it compounds the reality of feeling and sensing it once again.

I happened to be talking to a nun yesterday. I do not know how I got on the subject, but I was telling her about Adam and Eve, and how the structure of their leaving the garden can be regarded as a reward rather than a sin. She looked at me and was dumbfounded for a moment; then she said, "Yes." It is rewarding to have an exchange with an individual who is within a structure of religion that now has a liberal change of mind within the identity of it. It is good to know that some religious people are opening up in directions that question the reality of logic and sensibility within the consciousness of the particular things that they comprehend. They are not stuck in the dogmatic mire of misconception that locks upon something so they will never change.

When we go forward in our healings, different factors become apparent. Sometimes I enter into areas like the workplace where I may be either brash, or subdued, yet my energy has an effect on other people.

The other person does not know what is going on, and when they do not know what is going on, their only reaction is to dislike me. As you acquire more energy, you are going to have to learn that your energy affects others. A simple little thought that you have might be totally misunderstood. It might be just a simple thought, but is totally blown out of proportion by the other because it is not a simple thought anymore; it is a thought that has a profound amount of energy behind it. It instantly puts the other into a reaction of not knowing what it is, and when they do not know what it is, it puts them into a defensive posture of shutting you off.

When you look at it in that way, you can then understand the initial thrust into answering other people's questions in a positive way. So from now on, when you feel the other's reaction coming back at you, work on yourself. Work on why you are feeling and sensing it within you, and why the other might think about you in that way. Then you have to soften your reactions. You have to pull back and become involved in a teaching process that makes you better understand the other. The other person is so important. If you pull back, it then gives you the opportunity of saying: *I entered the situation here, and affected the person here, here and here. How could I change that so they can truly see me?* Even more importantly: *If I truly look at the situation, how could I understand the awareness of myself so it automatically changes the other? How can I simplify the thought, or pull it back, so it does not have such a tremendous flow of reaction within the other's system?* That is growth. When you think about it, this teaching process is the fundamental structure of the awareness of a particular place that you are trying to comprehend, and it is related to the other person. It is seemingly simple, yet so extraordinarily profound within your quest of comprehending and stabilizing it. Because it is not easy. There will be many things coming at you. Yet it goes back to that thought again: *How unique it must be, if it is so difficult to comprehend. What must the rewards be!* There are always such tremendous rewards from the stabilizing quality within the comprehension.

I try so hard sometimes. My wife and I were out driving one evening, and she said, "Don't you think you are getting a little too mad at some of those drivers who are sending you thought patterns? It seems like you are over-reacting a lot." I looked at her and said, "I am reacting every second here because every second I am hearing something!"

Then I had the thought: *Yes, but it is not a reaction that is overwhelming to me.* Now, if I take that thought and filter it through me, what it does, it shrinks my reaction time into something that is more stabilizing. Then I said to myself: *It is necessary to hear that thought. That thought has not pulled me down; it has pulled me into the sphere of comprehension. To compound the reality of that, I know that it is going to help me every moment after I make that thought.*

(John entered into a deeper meditative state:) Let us see if we can feel and sense the echoes of love. I love you. Remember, it never stops. It just keeps going. The incentive of it is to know that it touches everybody. So the next time we have a thought that is seemingly negative, pulling us in the direction that is not necessarily pliable, remember that moment and say: *I love you.* And when things become seemingly heavy, know who you are, and what you are participating in, and how uniquely beautiful it is! No matter what seems like trauma now, will be growth eventually. It will not pull you down if you understand that it cannot. You will only deviate slightly off that road of comprehension. You will have the capacity within the proper use of your mind to pull yourself back upon that white line of comprehension to see the necessary potholes of misconception within the avenue of comprehension, because you are going at a speed that is usable for you. I love you.

PART TWO

DIALOGUE AT THE WINDOW OF REALITY

What you feel and sense in this room is a true reality. What you see and hear is the absolute truth. There is no nonsense about it. That is the unique thing about it. We can make something within the physical sense. We can make a classroom with a format that has a structure to it. Then we can talk about it drawing in thousands of people. But I do not want to do that. I want to keep it simple. I want to make it something that is usable and understandable, and keep it within the context of the truth of the reality of it.

Any questions? Do you have to believe any of that? Do you have to believe anything? Do you want to sit for a while to meditate and then leave? I love you.

CHAPTER TWELVE

A Guided Meditation and Talk on the Absolutes
January 19, 2000

(A Guided Meditation:) Close your eyes. I want you to take a few moments to think about the total picture of your body; then we are going to have a nice, slow, healing meditation. You might want to put a thought within your mind: *I am part of God.* If you want to wander into the realm of what I understand as the True Essence of God, within the awareness of you, it took the Total Awareness of God to make you. It is within you, but what portion of It are you using? The meditation that you are going to participate in tonight is going to bridge the gap between you and the comprehension of God within you, and the capabilities of reaching farther within It. If you have that thought within your mind, the capacity of healing is increased beyond the awareness of what you are. If God made everything, and you and I are part of God, and we are searching out God within this meditation, you are closer to The Source that has made you. As you do so, logic tells you, more of that healing, rejuvenating, comprehendible energy will become usable for you here within the wonderment of that body that you have. Each time that you touch a part of your body with your mind, you will actually feel the rejuvenation at that wondrous level. It will give you the capacity to eliminate misconception and the probability of harm happening to your mind and body from this moment forward. The wondrous thing about it, within the Awareness of God, you do that even within your ignorance, but within the awareness of meditation you compound the reality of it. Right now, you are aware of the flavor and usable vibration within it. As you go forward, it proceeds in comprehending and eliminating all of those things that can possibly happen to you, because your intent glorifies and pushes it in a direction that is more usable for you from your awareness of it.

With these blessed thoughts within your mind, and as you compound the reality of the usefulness of the meditation, take a nice, deep breath now: inhale… hold it, hold it, and as you slowly exhale, begin to feel yourself relax, relax, relax. You are using your mind correctly. You are beginning to feel and sense all of the fatigue, stress, and tension dissipating, and of course, in its place, relaxation, rejuvenation, comfort, and awareness. Feel it. Sense it. This meditation that you proceed towards will be one of the most wondrous meditations you have ever experienced.

A second deep breath, inhale... hold it, hold it, and as you slowly exhale, relax, relax, relax.

A third deep breath, inhale... slowly sigh out the air, and once again, relax, relax, relax.

Utilizing your mind so correctly now to comprehend stability, relaxation, and comfort within your body, focus upon your toes. As you do so, you can actually feel and sense relaxation, rejuvenation, and comfort within your toes. Your toes are relaxed, free of tension, and very comfortable.

Relax and rejuvenate now both feet. Feel the new strength, vitality, and rejuvenation. All of the fatigue of the day is dissipating and your feet are very relaxed and comfortable.

Relax your ankles. As you relax this area, you put a thought within your mind: *Each particular part of the body that I will be looking upon will be rejuvenated for all of my tomorrows.* Feel it, sense it, and make it usable within your mind and body. Relax deeper and deeper.

Relax the lower part of your legs, right up to your knees. Relaxation, rejuvenation, and comfort are within the lower part of your legs.

Relax your knees, and as you relax this area, you can feel and sense compassion and balance within you as you deal with the wonderment of what you are. Your knees are relaxed, free of tension, and very comfortable.

Relax the upper part of your legs, including your hips. You can feel and sense new strength and vitality coming into your mind and body. You feel very good about yourself. You love yourself. You nourish yourself. It gives you the capability of going forward each and every day with strength and vitality, knowing what is right for you. You know without question, that everything is functioning properly within your hips and legs, right down to your toes, and you are very relaxed and comfortable.

Relax the lower part of the trunk of the body. As you relax this area, that love and strength that you felt for yourself becomes usable within your dualities, may it be at work or play. You can feel and sense that you wish to share whatever you have within you in a loving, compassionate way. It gives you control over the emotional state of what you are, and the comprehension of human decency. Feel it within you. You can say to yourself: *I feel the strength within myself. I feel the love I have within me. I nourish it. It gives me the capacity of going forward and dealing with others in a balanced way. It gives me the sense of understanding the needs of others, by sometimes listening, and sometimes talking. When I do talk, it gives me the wisdom within my words to have the necessary sustenance for others in a balanced way. It gives me the capacity to see myself as I grow within the awareness of that. It gives me the incentive of those moments, knowing that for the next time there will be more within me to give to others. Within that pathway I become aware of the necessary sustenance in the realm of giving within the physical sense, and the capacity of grasping upon those levels that become so readily usable as I do so.*

You know without question, that everything is functioning properly within this part of the body. You are very relaxed and comfortable. Relax now the upper part of the trunk of the body. As you nourish yourself, and give to others, and look upon all of these aspects in a beautiful way, you are extending yourself into the higher essence of what you are. You nourish a beautiful reservoir that is so readily usable for the entire structure of humanity. Relax in this place now with comfort. You can feel the peacefulness of this reservoir. It extends you into that esoteric love, balance and compassion that nourish those needs within you. You can feel and sense it changing the common denominator of love within you into a more pliable, usable place, for all of your moments. Feel and sense the wonderment of this place now: your heart center, your reservoir. You fill it with the wonderment of what you are now. Its capacity flows first within you; then it flows from the brim of what you are into the sustenance that is usable within humanity. Feel it, sense it, and use it. I love you. Everything is functioning properly within this area, and you are very relaxed and comfortable.

Relax your back, from the base of your spine to the base of your neck. It is a relaxing, soothing, comforting energy. You can feel it eliminating all of that stress and tension within your back, and rejuvenating all of those areas that need it. You can actually feel and sense your posture being corrected. There is relaxation, rejuvenation and comfort within your back, and you are very relaxed and comfortable.

Relax your shoulders, and your arms, starting from your fingertips, and moving up from there. Relax your neck, where all of that stress and tension seems to build up. Dissipate it with your mind. Relax the back of your head, and the top of your head. Your mind is sharp and alert. You realize without question that you have free will. Think about that free will for a moment within the wonderment of what you have within you, which is the Essence of God. Relax your forehead, your jaw, your cheeks, your mouth, your nose, your ears and your eyes. Your entire body is totally relaxed and free of tension. Everything is functioning properly within your mind and body.

To help us further understand that we truly have an esoteric part of what we are, or soul essence, or whatever you wish to call it, visualize or sense within your heart center, a small pure white dot of energy: you will either see it, or sense it; both ways totally usable. It begins to expand. As it does so, it touches every part of your body, cleansing and purifying you right down to the cellular level. Feel the uniqueness within that cleansing property. Feel the strength and the love you have for yourself. Feel the love you have for another. Feel the control over the emotional state of what you are, and the human decency within you. Feel the compassion, balance and universal love. Feel the capability of understanding the duality of flesh towards soul. See insight into yourself and into humanity. Finally, feel the vibrations of your soul. See yourself in that sphere of life, understanding that your consciousness interrelates to every moment of every day, and to particular spots within the awareness of that sphere that come around once again and cut you, whether you know it or not. Each time you are stimulated into a more beautiful quality of the essence of your soul.

That white light totally surrounds that unique body of what you are. You can truly feel and sense that uniqueness now: security, balance, love, and an aura of white and purity. It has the capacity of safeguarding you in every pathway and room within the essence of your awareness. You can feel it. You can sense it. It becomes more of you as you use what and where you are now, in a positive way. Know what you have at your disposal now, within that aura of white: you have the capabilities of the refractable part of your soul within the flesh. It becomes usable as it refracts to the awareness that is necessary within the probabilities of what you are. The uniqueness of that becomes so usable in extinguishing the misconceptions and balancing the qualities that propel you forward within the awareness of understanding truly who you are.

Within the wonderment of the white light, using the music as a suitable vibration to help you to relax more so, rejuvenate and comfort yourself. Be aware of the uniqueness within you: nourish it. When those fleeting moments of misconception come forward, push them aside until you are ready to look at them. This is your time now to rejuvenate, relax, and heal your mind and body. Use these moments for you, because you truly are in a sacred place. You have put yourself there through the uniqueness of your mind and the capabilities of it within the flesh. I love you. Everything is functioning properly within your mind and body. You are going at a speed that is usable for you. (The meditation proceeded as usual.)

(Second half of class:) Talking to the different parts of your body in meditation is a pathway into the awareness of understanding how energy flows into your body. If you can begin to understand that, it increases its capacity each time. You are not forcing it, but by questioning the reality of what it is, you are then drawing in more of the essence of the soul within the flesh. It is important to go through that sequence of events of looking at each part of the body, until you get to a point where you can make them preconceived thoughts within you so that you do not have to extend yourself so specifically into each part. With one thought, I can relax my whole body in one instant, because I have trained myself to do so over time. It is a matter of programming: instead of saying: *Relax the toes,* you say: *Relax the feet.* Then you include other parts of the body. Eventually you can say: *My whole body is totally relaxed.* You can drop very deeply in a few minutes, whether at work or play.

With one breath, watch what happens: (John takes a deep breath and drops into meditation while talking.) Twenty years ago, I could not even come close to the degree of relaxation in that one moment. As I am speaking, I am dropping deeper and deeper. If you ask a question pertaining to something that is within the realm of myself where I have to extend into the higher essence of what I am, it will be automatically done within the system of what I am. I am dropping deeper and deeper as I am talking to you, because I have practiced and rejuvenated myself so many times in meditation. It extends itself into that preconceived thought of what the existence of meditation is. Every now and then, it is good to return to the fundamentals of talking to the toes, feet, and ankles, but we do not have to do that all of the time. It is just that it becomes a preconceived thought within us, just like our heartbeat, because we have won the right to have it happen within the system of what we are.

In meditation you are teaching yourself a pathway into understanding balance within the system of what you are, how it interrelates to everything within the physical sense, and how to become more of what you are within the awareness of balance so you can win the right to have more of the essence of the soul within the flesh. You truly are a multi-dimensional person. By using the tool of meditation, you open up viable channels of awareness to the higher self. As it extends itself more so, it becomes the reality of what you are within the physical sense. Everything here upon the earth plane becomes more usable in every moment of every day because you have won the right to have it so. When you think of that tool of relaxation and rejuvenation, it extends itself into the transcendable self of understanding the identity of you as it moves within the sea of awareness, and that feeling of tranquility can become you in a moment if you train yourself to do so.

I send you a feeling now, knowing that you will feel it and sense it to the degree of the awareness of what you are and what you can become within you. As I do so, a unique thought rings throughout me: *As you extend yourself, John, more of what you can become will come through you. Eventually if you use it in balance, more of what you can become from that Higher Essence will become usable again: one sphere, one circle, one usable vibration that extends itself into pushing you into higher levels without you even thinking about it. It escalates its ability within your ability to comprehend.* That is the uniqueness of what we are. It truly is something that is obtainable within each one of us, but is not obtainable in those fleeting moments when we do not extend ourselves into the particular structure that makes us meditate. We have to pull ourselves in by meditating in order to grab upon those moments and make them what we can.

First questioner: **In the meditation tonight I felt what I could only describe as inner joy.**

Well, my intent tonight was to send joy, happiness, and balance. When I feel something within the framework of humanity, I extend that particular structure out within me. Know what happens to you when you do so: more of that comes through you, and a different flavor and blend of it becomes usable in the awareness of what that is within you. In other words, if you extend yourself into love, you are truly filling the chalice of what you are with love, whether you wish to believe it or not. When you extend it out, it is being automatically replenished because you are on a finely attuned awareness of doing something that is proper within humanity. On the other hand, when you extend yourself into something that is detrimental within the balance of humanity, that particular thing comes through you so you will feel the trauma of it eventually. Therefore, in tonight's awareness my thought was: *As I am dealing with the reality of what is going on within the room, I wish everyone here, within the awareness of what they are, will feel the wonderment of balance and compassion.* I was not infringing upon your free will with that thought. You will feel it in a certain way, just with your capacity of understanding that particular structure within you when you walked through that door. Some of the awareness of what we are is usable within the conscious awareness of this room, and that is what takes place.

Another thing takes place when you feel and sense something in that direction: it gives you the capacity of understanding the needs of others without even extending yourself into the awareness of those needs. It is an automatic thing. It is as if you are a river flowing with the sustenance of humanity. You know other people drink from the river, not even knowing that they do so, or what they use to drink it with. That is what takes place in this room, meaning that each one of us should be hit within a certain area of our awareness to stimulate ourselves into a more proper balance, so we may understand where we are and move from there. I know that each one of us gets that, every single time we come here. It might be a subtle word, or that moment in class when you say to yourself: *John is saying that for me.* Or: *That person is asking that question for me.* It hits you in that moment, and you say: *That is exactly for me!* Each week that you come, something like that, will happen to you.

Reply: **When we were relaxing the parts of the body, I was telling myself that I wanted balance for myself, but if there was anything left over, I wanted it to go to my family and others.**

That happens automatically. You see, sometimes we think of ourselves not being able to help humanity. Let me give you an example: let us just say that we were all five feet tall, then all of a sudden there is a person eight feet tall, who is the only one to see over the fence. That one person can change the entire structure of humanity, by giving insight into what is beyond that fence. When you take and use yourself properly within the physical sense, growing within the awareness of what you are to become that transcendable person by igniting the system of what you are, your major energy centers can be stimulated to the point where they turn upwardly within your system. You extend yourself into the absolute of what you are at a soul level and draw the vortex of it down within you. As you do so, you change the entire structure, or the common denominator of humanity. You change that whole identity that automatically gives everyone more love and compassion and balance within the awareness of what they are. That is what you were feeling tonight within that structure.

Last night I was getting some information; my wife made some comments that really triggered something within me. I happened to mention that I was thinking of a certain place, and she said, "Do you realize that we were in that exact place, at that exact time, last year?" I was going through that exact spot, at that exact time, last year! Now, when I hear something like that, my mind just goes in so many directions. I was thinking about the sphere of consciousness: we truly do not know what is going on yet! There is so much going on within the framework of what we are, and how we interrelate to time and the velocity within it; and the density and the ability of the soul to use these factors to set probabilities in motion so that we can achieve certain things within the physical sense. But it also interrelates to different slots of awareness, and how each slot of awareness comes back and feeds back into the system of what we are. We really do not know how that brain works into the total reality of the common denominator of humanity yet. There are so many different avenues of awareness that we are not even tapping into.

Therefore, we have to begin to consider: *How do we stimulate that?* Do we think that we can never obtain it? Of course not: we can obtain it if we can focus in on that next moment. That next moment is where we obtain it. We also have to extend ourselves into the awareness of understanding the preconceived thought: *Something Unique made All of This.* That is so important if we want to grow. All of This just could not happen! To become so unique where everything depends upon everything, and everything functions properly within the system, and everything filters through a system that makes this awareness seem absolute. In other words, everything is here for us! The only thing that can make a particular structure look terrible is our awareness and perception of it as we deal with it. We have to understand that everything is God. *I* think of it as God. It is so Absolutely Unique! When you think about it, it is absolutely incredible what is going on here! Just think of a tree, or dog, finger, eye, or even a thought! Who would give us the capability of having legs to move, or fingers to grab objects?

We can think about the uniqueness of everything, but if we extend ourselves too constantly into that, then we will contradict the next moment. That is what my point is: the next moment is the awareness of Whatever It Is That Made All of This. The next moment is part of This Total Reality. This is so important to your growth, whether you wish to believe it or not. If you do not believe that, then everything I teach here does not mean anything. If you comprehend that next moment, and understand the statement, "Everything is God," what happens to you? More of the Essence of God is within you. That might seem like a contradiction to some people who have been brought up in a religious framework, but when we think about Christ saying, "I am a son of God, and you are a son or daughter of God," that means that we are all within the same capabilities of what Christ was.

Do we have the same identity of understanding that pathway? No, we do not, because we do not give ourselves the chance. Do we have the avenues within our system to obtain that particular structure that Jesus did? Of course we do. Do we have the extension, or the absolute creativity within the soul level? I do not know that we do. I think eventually we do, as we become more evolved within ourselves. Maybe the next time we re-manifest into something, we will have the capacity of saying: *Hey, this time I do not want to be a human, I want to have the capability of the consciousness of making a gigantic earth.* Do you think this is outside of the realm of what you are? Of course not! You know that the cells and germs in your body think that you are their entire universe. They think you are it. You are the most gigantic thing to them. They cannot think beyond that. You are the host, just like we are cells upon our host, the earth. The earth is maybe like a cell within the Awareness of God. We have to think of ourselves as being an extension of That.

I mentioned something last week that has been ringing through my mind so creatively lately, and it is the truth: "The Total Reality of God is within each one of us." That statement is not a contradiction to religion. It is not a contradiction to God. It is not a contradiction to our neighbor, friend, or whomever. It is an absolute. But then there is another absolute: "What portion are you using?" You are so unique. There is nobody, anywhere, exactly like you. That is the Uniqueness of God. Each of us is unique and different, and there will never be someone exactly like you ever again. And in the next moment a change will take place in you that will make you different from what you were a moment ago. The cells dividing within your system are changing you so much. The identity of you is not visible at this level, but at another level, you are changing so rapidly, so uniquely. Understand that within you, and the goodness of everything else will become more usable. Nothing ever contradicts whatever you were or whatever you will become. The only thing you *will* understand is misconception within the realm of another person who does not understand the absolute. But if you contradict anything within the other, you do not understand that that is necessary for where they are.

For example, when people asked Jesus a question pertaining to something that was said about him, he would only reply: "If that person said that, that is fine." The questioner might persist, but Jesus would not give them an absolute answer, because that would have contradicted what another person had said. What he knew was so absolute. If he had contradicted the other person, he would have contradicted the reality of the sustenance of what he said he had become. In other words: *If I understand the dualities of life, if I understand the creativity of life, if I understand the dualities of flesh to soul, I will not contradict anything the other person says, because if I do so, I would be condemning the person. So I will not answer; I will take the responsibility of it.* That is why the people around him did not want to kill him. Everybody felt that this man did not do anything. They knew that but were caught up in the framework of that time and the theme of what he was trying to achieve within the physical sense.

Now, if we look at it properly, and truly understand the power of what Jesus was, with one thought he could have just changed the reality of a certain situation. He could have said: *I am in an area where others are going to harm me, and I do not want that to happen.* His mind was so powerful. If his mind could raise a person from the dead, it could also make a person die. He could have just thought of someone in that way, and the person would have died, but he knew if he did so, he would not have died in the events that were usable in changing the flow of humanity into a more positive direction. He knew all of that within that structure.

I am not intending to make this information so far out of the normal reach; I am trying to make it normal and understandable within the structure of logic so we can make it moveable within the awareness of what we are. I do not want to make it seem like it is unobtainable, or in some back page of the Bible, or Sanskrit, that has to be interpreted two thousand years from now. But when you make an absolute statement, the reality of it extends itself into many different slots of awareness that become absolutes within the structure. It is interpreted at many different levels. So many people will dissect it, and each bit of information pertaining to the reality of a singular statement will be absolute within the quest of whoever looks at it. It is obtainable through the structure or reality of what we are, within the sustenance of what we are in those moments. Each one of us will get different rewards from the statement.

It is like the statement I made before, "Everything is God." But the reality of that statement does not become usable in the rigidity or confinement to a slot within a particular religion. When you see dogmatic reactions from people, you know that the interrelationship of what they are dealing with within that religion has been distorted. It is like a person going out and blowing up a car, then saying: "I did it for God." That is distorting the quality or the reaction within the system that is understandable in the theme that was set in motion. For instance, one day I was talking to a nice person, who was religious, and we both agreed, "Everything is God." I then said, "When I die, I want to take sheet rock to heaven!" She looked at me and said, "You can't take sheet rock to heaven!" I said, "Isn't everything God?" She replied, "Yes, everything is God." I said, "Then if I want to take sheet rock to heaven, I can!" She said, "No, you can't!" And so forth.

When you think about that, what you have is a confinement to a particular area within the framework of religion. The person's mind becomes confined to an absolute and thinks that that is all there is. That is a confinement within the ego that has extended itself so far into a direction, they think that they are there. It is like being in the boat of reality; then suddenly you look away, and the wind blows you into a tributary. You think you are still in the main river, but you are off in a tributary. In that one moment that you did not focus, the boat extended itself into a tributary. So now as you are going along, there are threatening aspects such as natives shooting arrows. What do you do? You kill everything in your way and go forward. Suddenly you get to a place that is so shallow, you say: *Hey, this could not be the true reality.*

Maybe you were upon that reality, confining yourself to a misconception, because you felt very secure. There did not seem to be any harm around, but what you actually did was open up that funnel of awareness to harm by eliminating all of those things that should have slowed you down, and encouraged you to turn around and find the right direction. Illness is good: if you get illness, it slows you down from going in the wrong direction and thereby not achieving the probabilities of why you are here. Therefore, if you look at it from that level, you say: *Illness is not so bad anymore. It is painful, and it could kill me, but if it kills me, why does it kill me? It kills me because I am not achieving the reason why I am here.*

Second questioner: **Very old people are generally balanced then?**

Yes. Usually when you see certain people live to ripe old ages, they have self together. They would not harm anybody. They think of others in a positive way. They are usually kind, and set certain things in motion to achieve their probabilities in their lifetimes. Some people die young too, and we say: *My God! That was a good person.* The person might have been good, but there are factors there. For instance, a woman came up to me after class one night and said, "My mother died of cancer at a young age. Are you trying to tell me that she was a bad person?" I said, "No, she was a person who was not comprehending." She responded, "You said that the awareness of cancer deals with a lack of human decency, and my mother went out of her way to help everybody." I said, "Yes, but so much so, that she had a lack of human decency for herself?" She turned to me and said, "You are absolutely right." Therefore, we have to understand what human decency is: are you are so good that you run out into traffic, pull the person out of the way, then a twenty-ton truck runs you over? You might do so much good that you extinguish your body before you can do a lot of good. So understand what is necessary for you within the sustenance.

Now, we might get to the point where we have so much knowledge within us that we might want to change to the point where we give beyond what we can give, such as Mother Teresa. We make that choice. I was looking at the identity of Mother Teresa one day. Sometimes I go into certain areas, and think of pathways of death, and what causes certain things within the structure. You do not have to think about these things if you do not want to, but when you go through certain levels, you do look at some of them. I thought about certain things that she did within her life. I could not obtain some of those; I could not even come close to obtaining some of those. Then I thought about it for a while: *Is that my set of probabilities? Within the quest of what I am, why couldn't I also do similar deeds within the structure that is usable within me? Why couldn't I have that kind of compassion? Why couldn't I pick up an ill person, who had such a bad wound and smelled so bad, and carry them to a place, and take care of them? I could not do that.* Then I thought: *Maybe I could with training, but would it contradict why I am here, or what I am trying to do within the awareness of understanding why all of us are here, and what my job might be?* And it would.

I looked at the identity of Mother Teresa. I went through the framework of understanding the identity of who she was, and how she started her life's work, and how her actions came about and were accomplished. At first it was so hard for her. She was not sure if she could do it. She cried when she thought of those moments: *I cannot touch or help that person because I feel the identity of the illness might overwhelm me.* Then as she forced herself into it and dealt with it, she became more of the awareness that dealt with some of that stability that was esoteric. The knowledge of the strength and compassion and consciousness became the esoteric comprehension of the stabilizing qualities that were usable in understanding the sustenance of how to use oneself properly within the awareness of taking care of those people. Then it became something totally different: it was no longer forced; it became understandably usable without thinking about it. It became the sustenance of her awareness and the ability to go forward without even thinking about it.

Are there many people that obtain those levels? When you feel and sense a person of the magnitude of what she was, it was so extraordinary; yet if you met her, it would seem as if she was just so ordinary. But in the simplicity of that seemingly ordinary quality was the capacity to be so extraordinary, and the two qualities were balanced out within her to truly pull her into the nucleus of the reality of what she was trying to understand. It is not within the orbiting qualities that are outside of understanding the density of that nucleus, it becomes the compelling qualities that pull and shrink us into the awareness of it, and we become it. We become it so much that the total reality of the sustenance of it becomes something that we do not even think about.

Is there something so unique upon this earth plane that we do not extend ourselves into? There is so much we are missing, we cannot even imagine! The only way we can feel and sense it—and this is the only way we can do so—is by understanding and feeling and sensing what we are right now. If we do not do so in a balanced way, and understand it, no more will come. There will be those brief moments of escalation through the chemical reactions within humanity that seemingly extend us into the awareness of balance and compassion at an esoteric level, but eventually it becomes fleeting moments of that comprehension, because there is nothing: no basic foundation or pillar of quality that extends itself into holding it within the framework of what we are. The only way that we can do so is by winning the right to have that quality filter within us when we are ready for it.

Then that unique thing happens, and it happens every time: every time that you hit that absolute level, you look at it, and there is absolutely nothing within it that contradicts anything that you have ever done! It does not say that where you were before was negative; it says that where you were before was necessary so you can feel where you are now. It never says that a particular religion or person is negative; it says that religion or person is a perception within the quality that makes them what they are now. At first those moments will be fleeting little moments. Eventually the avenues that participate in the awareness of those fleeting moments extend into allowing those fleeting moments to cling together. As they become cohesive and extended, they become that which deals with the sustenance of the rewards and the qualities of what you are, and extend you further into that dome.

When you feel those moments, ...and I am sure I am feeling those moments now... it is outside of you for a fleeting moment. You wonder about the qualities of it. You wonder what you are feeling within that, which has a slightly overwhelming quality to it. You say to yourself: *It has an overwhelming quality to it, because I have not made a soft cushion of awareness within me to allow it to sit and become comfortable.* But it never extends itself into the awareness of saying: *I never wish to feel anything like this again.* You say: *My God, what must come next if I feel this now! I feel so absolute and so perfect within the realm of what I am, knowing that I do not understand perfection, but only a portion of it. But whatever it might be, it is beyond what I felt before, and the magnitude of it has so many overwhelming qualities within it.*

At times like this, I was receiving information about Adam and Eve. It was not a sin when they left the garden, but a graduation that extended them further into the awareness of becoming entities with free will. Where did this story come from? As I was getting this story and looking at it, I said: *Why have I never seen this before?* The answer came ringing down through the system of what I was: *You were light years away from understanding the reality of it. You could not even grasp upon the situations within the realm of what you are, never mind the capacity of understanding something so usable within the depths of humanity.*

It is logical, understandable, and usable. You put it in a category, and it stays there. It becomes a reality. It becomes something that you can put upon the shelf of the reality of what you are, knowing that it is absolute and usable. Does it extinguish what the three billion people are working on, thinking that leaving the garden was a sin? Let us think about that for a moment. Their understanding of needing to regard that act as a sin, thereby punished by God, is necessary and usable in giving them the incentive to make them understand "love of self," to the point where they have the strength to go forward to eat of the fruit of life.

It is just like thinking of the devil. On one level, we need the devil that says: *If you do not conduct yourself in a good manner, you are going to go to hell and burn!* It becomes usable within the framework of saying, we do not have too much knowledge within us, and we have a lot of fear because we are outside the comprehension of the reality of what fear is. If we want to extinguish the concept of the devil from humanity, the only way we can do so is by no one ever having to be there again: by all of humanity lifting itself beyond that framework. For instance, we look back to a time in the past where doctors were bleeding patients with leeches. In that treatment the patient was made weaker rather than stronger. But then you understand the consciousness, the necessary reality and sustenance of that particular time, and how that particular treatment interrelated to what can become usable for us in obtaining what we can become. Try telling the Adam and Eve story to a person confined into the area of understanding that leaving the garden is punishment. They will look at you as if you are crazy. You have given them all of the information within logic: they understand the logic of the situation, and the analogies, such as little children put within the confinement of the playpen, and they still do not see it. Then you know the person is nowhere near that level that can have the capacity to see the reality of leaving the garden as a reward rather than a sin. They have no strength within the realm of self, so they have to use punishment as an incentive. It is necessary for them to see it as a sin in order to compel them to a higher level within the awareness of self; they do not contradict self.

Sometimes I wonder whom this class is for, you or me? It gives me a capacity within myself to allow the situations to come forward within me and enhance the capability of seeing them in absolutes. Then I think about it for a moment, and the class is for all of us: there is a reason for each one of us being here, tonight. If we can take that reason, work on it and stimulate it, then the next time we meet, we can stimulate and work on something else. Was there anything within the framework of what I just said that turned you off? If so, you should turn your mind back on to question it. If it is not usable within you, do not use it; but never contradict it to a point where it becomes something that turns you off totally; you might say: *Whatever John says might be true within him, but not necessarily true for me.* But then it might be true within all of us if we really listen to it. It is something you are going to have to question within yourself in the moments of your every day.

I do know this: if you give yourself the opportunity to use that tool of meditation, that plateau of comprehension that opens up that sponge of reality, and obtains the truth of what you are, and makes it the truth of what you can become, you will feel things that will blow your mind away. The notes from music will stimulate you right down to the cellular level. You will hear music echoing throughout the cathedral of what you are. You will extend yourself into the higher essence of your soul, each moment of every day, because you have the proper machinery going forward in the direction of understanding that each moment is something that makes you more than you were before.

On the other hand, when it becomes really heavy, you have to turn to yourself to say: *I do not know why, but I put myself here through something.* For instance, I have some traits within me that I fight: I get images of being in karate and going at someone, or have moments of jealousy in regard to certain things. When it becomes really heavy, I have to say: *Why does the particular thing bother me? Where does it come from? How can I eliminate it from the awareness of what I am?* You go back into meditation to dissect it and try to make it usable. Then you see certain things within the awareness of what you were previously participating in within life and know you are going to feel those particular things for a long time to come. Even if the past thing is not the true reality, the illusion of it will seem like a true reality of what you are participating in, because the misconception of what you were made the reality seem like a true reality. So you have to flush yourself through that system. The point is, no matter what we do, it will come back, and usually come back when we are not ready for it, and we will have to deal with the sustenance.

On the way down here tonight, I was talking with my wife about certain flaws within how I think, and why certain things like that come forward within me, and how I want to eliminate them. I know a particular reality is untrue, yet it still pops up in front of me. It pops up in front of me because I have won the right for it. I have done something in my past that made that reality pop up. These things are not negative; they are just something I should not have done. The particular reality will keep coming back at me, until it is finally flushed through the system of what I am, to the point where I no longer have to deal with the penance of it. We all deal with those certain realities. The soul brings it on at the misconception of something that you participated in, that was not necessarily within the framework of what you could have done. Then what happens, you have to deal with it, even if it is an illusion of the particular reality. It will keep coming back, even though you know there is no sustenance within it because it has to be filtered through that system until it is longer usable in the wrath of that misconception. No matter how you try to comprehend it, it will always be there until it is ready to extinguish itself. It is the penance of the reaction of what you were participating in. You know it is not a true reality; it is not going to have an overwhelming effect on you; but it is going to pop up every once in a while and become you. I have traced these little things. My mind is pretty good at tracing these things back to particular events within the system of what I am. They are necessary realities, even though they are illusions. Now, I do not use the reality as something that is negative but as something that says: *Hey, I have to work on this.* So it is good.

Third questioner: **Is this karma you are talking about?**

Yes, karma. I am talking about the reality of that sustenance within the physical sense. We have to deal with it even though we know it is not a true reality. It is an illusion, but there are many people who do not see it in that way. When the reality of it comes before them, they say: *My God, this is overwhelming!* It does not become overwhelming for me because I know I can confine it. I tighten the reins of it and put it back within the confines of where it should be, because I know the reality of what is going on in that particular sphere. That helps me, but a person who does not know how to do that, will not get help from it. They will deal with trauma in their life to the point where the trait becomes so engrained in them that they cannot eliminate it.

CHAPTER THIRTEEN

Questions Within the Healer
June 17, 1998

(In the guided meditation, when John came to the heart center awareness:) There is a reason for you sitting here tonight. Know the reasons. Feel them within you. As you feel the wonderment of the heart area, the reservoir of what you are, you are filling the chalice of what you are with sustenance not only for yourself, family and friends, but for anyone else who wishes to drink. The wisdom of you is within this area. It is a reservoir of uniqueness that extends itself into all of the pliable areas of humanity.

You know without question, that everything is functioning properly within this area. This statement becomes so true within your mind. It extends itself further into your mind because of the peacefulness of this area. You can hear it echoing through you. As you do so, you fill those simple little voids. They are necessary to fill in order to fill the chalice of what you are. They are bits of awareness that will flicker in the moments of what you have coming forth, from this day forward. Your mind is sharp and alert. Realize what that statement means to you as you see what direction humanity goes in, as it deals with the elder years of life. By doing what you are doing now, and thinking of it in a positive way, it extends you into the moments of clarity in your elder years. It gives you the capacity to live at those levels with a clear mind, comprehending the beauty of the extension back towards your soul.

Relax your forehead, your jaw, your cheeks, your mouth, your nose, your ears and your eyes. Relax your face: the window of what you are, the appearance of what you are. When you are happy, it shows! When you are sad, it shows! When there is a glisten, or sparkle in your eyes, it shows happiness. Let there be sparkles from now on. Let there be the proof of the existence of your mind working properly within the areas of growth that extend out as you look upon the world. Know that there is something beyond physical sight: it is esoteric sight, giving us the capacity to see beyond normal. Make it so normal, usable, sensible, and logical and seemingly simple.

I love you. Within your heart center there is a pure white dot of energy. It represents all of those things that we have mentioned and more. As you look upon it, or sense it, the white light within your heart center begins to expand. As it does so, it touches every part of you. This is your soul touching you. Your soul! The essence that has made you! Feel it. It totally surrounds you. You are within a cushion of relaxation and comfort, an aura of protection. You can feel the love, you can feel the balance and you can feel the capacity of understanding how to use it. It does not lay dormant but becomes the shining glory of the extension of what you do. I love you. I will try to make it more, the next time I tell you I love you. Just by saying it, it stimulates the qualities of putting more of it within me, but I have to make it something that is an extension of me by understanding it. There is more within me, but I have to give it; I have to use it.

Within the silent moments of what you are, utilize the music as a soothing, relaxing mantra, helping you to relax and rejuvenate more so. Go at a speed that is usable for you. Know that you are unique and beautiful. There is nobody exactly like you, anywhere! When you look in the mirror tomorrow, know it. You are a beautiful creation and are growing within it now, within the system of the awareness of using your mind correctly. Relax and rejuvenate yourself. I will be silent and join you more so. I love you. (The meditation proceeded as usual.)

First questioner: **You mentioned that we receive rejuvenation in a part of the body, and that our minds go to an area that shows us the causes, the linkage?**

The usage of your mind in asking the proper questions brings you to the eventual capacity to understand the essence of it.

Reply: **As the area is being rejuvenated, from this class we have an idea of what particular area relates to. Now we should question what specific things in that area caused the dissipation and eventually we get some insights?**

As you are working on a problem in your life in meditation, if you feel an escalation of energy flow within a particular area, you know you are utilizing your mind correctly in comprehending the particular thing that you are working on. It then gives you the capacity to trigger upon different qualities of understanding the rest of the misconception. It also tells you that you are now extending yourself further into increased understanding of how to take the total reality of that misconception and make it usable for you, rather than it abusing you.

If you feel an escalation of energy in that area, it is telling you are doing something right. If you feel pain, you know you are going in the wrong direction. Question that within your mind. If you do not receive an answer, extend yourself further into that particular essence and you will begin to participate in understanding a portion of the sphere of comprehension concerning the particular event or problem you are trying to comprehend. You are extending yourself into areas of how to use your mind correctly. If I feel an energy escalation in an area, I know I am going down the right path. If I feel pain, I have to stop and see what direction I am going in. If I begin to ask questions pertaining to the particular thing, and the pain begins to dissipate, I know I am reversing it. I am using my mind properly to take myself out of the strands of misconception within the awareness of the particular sphere that I am trying to comprehend.

Reply: **We should look back to three or four weeks to find the events that triggered certain reactions?**

Yes. Not only that, but it will give you the capacity of understanding that there will be similar events in the future that will make you comprehend. Or if you have extended yourself out of the particular area of misconception by solving it, it will give you the avenue of understanding what you were participating in, and what you have done for yourself by pulling yourself out of that area. That was an answer for you in particular. There are certain general answers for everybody; then there is a certain answer that hits the particular reality of the person asking the question.

Reply: **You are saying we might possibly be in an area where we cause some deep-seated dissipations of the body that will take a while to rejuvenate and put us back on the right track?**

Yes. When you are rejuvenating, then you begin to see the participation of a particular area that you are involved in. Everyday life can be tumultuous. While you are involved in it, you cannot consider anything but some fear, and your reactions, but when you are outside of the context of it for a while, and have some semblance of balance, then you can see the true reality of it. You can begin to strip away the fear and understand why certain things were triggered automatically. By doing so, it gives you the capacity of lifting the awareness of yourself within that quest.

Second questioner: **How can I help my twelve-year old daughter who is going through chaotic changes?**

What an age! It is going to get a little worse too; ages thirteen and fourteen are going to be rough. Examine the flaws that she received from you; then let your words and deeds show her. You know what she is going to be going through, so tell her certain things to prepare her for them before they actually happen. She is refracting to a new area, and everything is changing within her system. She is going to see the opposite sex in a different way. There are going to be distortions, and you have to give her strength and values.

You have to think about what she is going through. Mainly it is a survival issue because it is like having two fields now rather than just the one that she is familiar with. When she is going through the struggle of learning to love herself, suddenly she hits that transition where she is refracting into another level where she is seeing something else, and she has a feeling and attraction within her that she does not understand. The hormonal changes going on within the body are extraordinary. All of that brings the staggering quality of understanding that there are necessary areas of work.

As a result, what do you think she is going to do? She is going to let out all of her anxiety by attacking her parents and other familiar people around her because she knows there is no reprisal. She knows it is safe to react against you because she cannot safely react outside of that context for now. When she learns how to stand up for herself a little more, then there is more reaction, stability and feedback from those reactions. It is not something that you missed in giving her within issues of survival; it is something that she missed in comprehending what you gave her. So you have to work with her. Help her to understand that she is going through some new events and that it is natural. Sit down with her and help her to question certain feelings that she does not understand. You might say, "You are going through a struggle now: you are suddenly seeing the opposite sex, and you have to go at a pace that you understand. You cannot jump into this new area too quickly. You do not want to be overwhelmed by it, and you have to have values with it."

All of us can remember when we came to that particular juncture that was triggered within our minds and bodies. One week I was throwing snowballs at the girls, and the next, I was looking over at them, wanting to carry their books. There is something that struggles within you. There is something that turns, and suddenly there is an attraction there. The child becomes an adult who experiences the struggle of understanding the hormonal changes within the body. If we look at it from the structure of comprehension, the child is learning to love self. Remember when I previously mentioned that if we look at a seemingly negative event and dissect it, we then make it usable by regarding it as positive rather than negative? Physical changes become evident. I remember getting so many "F's" in class because I could not stand up; there was some stimulation, and if I stood up, something would show. For instance, little boys are always fondling themselves. Masturbation is an act that is often considered negative by adults but is so positive. The boy is learning how to use an instrument that is going to come in handy! (Laughing.) I never thought of it in that way before. When we look at that act in truth, it is so unique, and the only distortion is within our minds when we do not comprehend it. I am not saying that we should be doing that every moment: everything in moderation so we can begin to understand the beauty of what is going on.

When we consider what we are talking about here, the structure of the different stages is fundamentally here within the physical reality, but extends itself esoterically. When we look at the energy centers and how they interrelate to higher levels of comprehension, as we progress through life, we are going to experience graduations. Each graduation is a refractable area of chemical reaction within the physical sense to make that particular level. When we go through these different eleven or twelve-year periods, we will automatically experience chemical reactions that interrelate to a particular level, and there will be a change in the system of the awareness of what we are trying to comprehend.

There is a reason why we go through different stages within life. We left different levels of comprehension there for us so that we can eventually interrelate to them. There are particular levels of awareness that the particular structure of the comprehension of love interrelates to. The first center interrelates to "love of self" in survival, the second center deals with "love of another" in sensuality and creativity. Then we graduate to the third center, "love of many," and so forth. At these various eleven or twelve-year transitions, the body is going to automatically graduate to another level. The unique thing about it is, the chemical reactions within the involuntary system are going to be triggered within us whether we are ready for them or not, but if we are not graduating in our consciousness, we will not ready for the new changes, and there is going to be tremendous distortion.

For example, when I reached the age forty-four or so, my eyesight started to deteriorate somewhat, and I could not understand why, because I meditated all of the time. Then I began to question the reality of that deterioration, and the answer came back: *If you rejuvenate your eyes totally at the level that you are talking about, you will be the first one to do so. If you do so, you will change a fundamental structure or flaw within humanity, because when everybody on the earth plane hits the fifth level, if they had perfect sight before, they now have distortion.* Around age forty-four or so, we are within the fourth level within our system that is going to change automatically. When that fourth level refracts to the fifth level, we are going to be affected because there is weakness within humanity's insight within the third-eye center. Humanity has never been totally ready to comprehend human decency in the third center, and universal love and compassion in the fourth center, so when we enter the fourth or fifth stage of our development, there is going to be a fundamental change: our nearsightedness becomes distorted because we do not have the capacity to grasp upon the new stage. When that takes place, there is a flaw there. It will happen earlier to some people, but if you previously had perfect sight but then hit that level, no matter who you are, eye deterioration is going to happen. Some people will experience it in a more drastic way than others, but it is going to happen to everybody. That is why the third center interrelates to the third-eye center. This new information reflects the quality of understanding how to use your mind correctly in comprehending. All of this information took place within me from one thought where I eliminated the triggering process of the distortion in order to understand the particular structure.

So it is important that we begin to question the reality. I know I kid around sometimes, and it is important to kid about things, but it is also important to see how a certain dynamic relates. Now, if I had this information come to me, and it did come to me, if it did not seem sensible, usable and logical here within the physical reality, I would not have used it. But when I think about it, and sit upon the identity of understanding the structure of that avenue that I participated in questioning the reality of why it happened to me, it is sensible, understandable and logical within the physical sense and also extends itself into those qualities of understanding it at higher levels. If not, I would not have believed it. If not, you would not be hearing it now. It has to be usable *here*. It has to be sensible *here*. It does not tell me to go jump off a building. It does not tell me to have faith and put my head under a tractor. It gives me a sensible identity of understanding a particular structure, and how it interrelates to the growth process, and how I interrelate to that process of that chemical reaction within the physical sense that is going to happen automatically.

Then if I think about it logically, what a uniquely beautiful process of stimulation we are involved in! Because within the Infinite Wisdom of The Genius That Made All of This, God said there was going to be complacency, God said that there was going to be a reaction of non comprehension within the physical sense; and that these particular events that happen organically within the body would give us the stimulation, or structure, or trauma, to question it somewhat. If we think about it in that unique way…

And if you are thinking how I can go from where I was a moment ago to where I am now, they are both the same: the person who was kidding around and seemingly outside any sense of logic is the same as the person now talking about certain concepts. There is a unique process of balance that we have to have that gives us the attempt of understanding the true nature of the Genius of It, yet stimulates the properties that make us understand the Humility of It. The consideration of that mundane property, or those reactions within the physical sense that might seem chaotic, are not so. On the other hand, within the system of that awareness, and the illusions of moments of grandeur, and of putting ourselves in those particular structures or categories that are seemingly profound, they are nowhere near being profound. So when I look at a person who *seems* to have that Sphere of the Reality of Total Awareness of where they are, they have confined self too long. Within the minds or awareness of individuals within the physical sense, there will be a drawing quality that will extend itself into the consideration of fame. But as we participate in truly dissecting and understanding it, the avenue of awareness, even within the consideration of it being seemingly nothing, will be considered as something profound, because the reactions of the simplicity of whomever the person might be will be totally considered because of the feelings of the moments, or the people around the person. And where that place might be, I do not know.

It is a place though, that we all long for–a place that I would consider for brief moments anyway–where we can affect automatically through the consideration of what we have participated in. That will be coming someday, in certain people. Maybe we are just that basic foundation, or the cinders, that will eventually be ground into the consideration of the powder of cement at that basic level. But whatever it might be, it is important that you work upon yourself. No matter who you are, or where you came from, or what your habits are, or what your hang-ups are, consider them, work on them. Make them that which flings you into new areas of comprehension, rather than igniting those anvils of misconception that give you stagnation, holding you back from comprehension. It is within all of us.

Tonight we considered a simple event because it is ordinary. Anybody and everybody are ordinary, and extraordinary, and anybody can do it. Those particular things should be used in a positive way, not in a negative way. To say that there might not be Something There... Because there is Everything There at higher levels, just like there is Everything Here within the physical reality. They are both the same, but we are not giving ourselves the consideration of understanding the reactions of the blending of the two that become one, no matter what end we are on, because It pulls itself back and forth in order to cause some semblance of balance within that comprehension. So, those moments that are seemingly outside of wisdom are holding wisdom together, until we can force it within us through comprehension.

Third questioner: **We were talking earlier on about how humanity has had a problem dealing with comprehension of love and compassion. In Bosnia, people of many different ethnic backgrounds were neighbors, and for a long time got along together. Then all of a sudden, things changed, and they turned on each other.**

There is lack of consideration within the awareness of humanity not having the strength to react from a higher level of reaction. In other words, if you are the leader of a particular area, and you tell others to do something, out of fear they do it, no matter what it is. So there is no basic strength. But those particular events that we read about are only a portion of the true value of what is going on there. There are people within that structure who will not react against their neighbors. We do not hear about the people who help out. There are a lot of things going on both ends of the spectrum, but what we are reading about, we should be reading about, so we do not allow that situation extend itself into an area where it will be totally overwhelming.

We might ask why there are so many people dying in Africa from starvation: there is so much to consider at different levels about something that we do not know about. The act of dying is unbelievable, even though we look at it from the physical sense as something that is so negative. In dying the drawing back of the mind from a lack of sustenance within the physical sense gives us the capacity of eventually knowing how to refract another body that is seemingly unique.

For instance, we might look at a severely autistic child and wonder why God made the child. It is not God; it is the knowledge and the awareness of a particular soul that knows only how to manifest that particular body. The child is learning. It is as if they have never made a boat before, so they make a boat that goes out a little way, then it begins to sink because they do not have the knowledge to keep self afloat. You will notice that some autistic children have one unique gifted quality. You wonder how they could be so unique in that one area, while lacking in most other basic areas. It is because everything is funneled into that one unique quality within the probabilities that were set in motion. It is so unique and beautiful.

Why are some people in an area where there is great trauma? It is like being in a barrel with rotten apples: if you are there, it is going to hit you and affect you. Even if you work with comprehension, or have a functioning body, you are going to be affected. You chose to be in that environment. You chose to become more than what you were be- fore, through the traumas of life. It is not saying that we should not strive to eliminate those probabilities that cause pain. Eventually we will be above the reaction of understanding pain as a usable vibration of learning. There is something that is beyond pain that will give us incentive, which is the stimulation of knowledge, and the feelings of the awareness of what is going through us. The impulse of comprehen- sion gives us the avenues of understanding outside that threshold of pain. That is where we are striving to go.

People have come up to me and said, "Well, if you know all of this, why are you trying to help people?" I have questioned this. People come to you and ask for a healing, or something that will give them peace and tranquility. You actually see the events that have put them there. You have the question: *Why? What right do I have to enter into that? There is a logical sequence of events that has put them in that place. Who am I to infringe upon the reactions of that structure within the framework of the laws that were set in motion by God at that par- ticular level?* You question it. You get back to the basic theme of: *Who am I?* Then a thought comes back into your mind that balances all of that: *I am part of God. Everything is part of God. So if I can change me, then it gives me the free will within the sphere of that understanding to stop another person's pain for a brief moment, through whatever ca- pacity I have within the realm of what it is that I am trying to eliminate from their body.* Whatever portion of you that understands the ailment will be eliminated from the other's body. Whatever portion you do not have within you, will not affect any of that avenue beyond that.

When I consider that, I will always try. I will never infringe. I will always listen. I will always wait for the other person within their free will to ask a question related to the problem or illness. Why did the man pull upon Jesus' robe and say, "Will you help me?" Jesus knew the person was sick. Why didn't he stop and heal the person before the person asked? Jesus did not stop because it was none of his business, until the person grabbed his robe and asked him for help. Then when that took place, energy like you would not believe, went into the per- son because they opened up the avenue of awareness of comprehen- sion through the essence of their free will. Then the healing did not contradict any reason for the other person being there. When you keep yourself within those boundaries, the reactions are pure and clean.

Even within the structure of understanding that, even though you as healer use that as your bible, you will have to live with the reactions of knowing that most people will think that you are manipulating them. Most people will think that you are reading their minds: *Oh, he knows that anyway!* It is not true. There might be some truth in the matter if the person asks for the truth. Then there might be some avenues of awareness that come forth to give you the awareness of what is necessary. But outside of that, it is not automatic. It is not something that is triggered. It is only triggered within the structure of the free will.

(John drops into a deeper state of meditation:) There is nothing outside the Context of The Law. There is nothing that says you cannot give a good thought. There is nothing that says that you cannot be what you are. And if you are what you are, and it is beyond where you were, it is more considerable within the quest of whatever it might be within that particular structure. It is more usable within your comprehension automatically. That should be your goal: *I am what I am, and if I grow, I have more to give without even giving.* It will be there. It goes. That word never stops. That thought never stops. It keeps spinning through the awareness of where we are. It is in that filtering process within humanity. It stays. That sound never stops. It keeps refracting and becoming part of the whole

So when you consider that, it changes everything. If it is pure, and it has more knowledge behind it, it has more consideration within the quest of purity. That is what for fleeting moments I strive for, ...and "fleeting moments" is probably the correct analogy of the consideration of movement within that structure. When we thoroughly think about it for a moment, and the overwhelming quality of the reactions within it, if we consider that it has to come through us first, before it can go anywhere else, it would be egotistical not to have just fleeting moments, until it can become one moment of balance in order to use it right. Those fleeting moments are a necessary reaction because we have no alternative. It is so overwhelming.

So hide yourself well. Hide yourself in those moments that consider nothing but a reaction that makes you understand why you did a particular deed, whatever it might be. Then maybe one day, even within those things that we consider not usable, it all pulls together immediately, instantly, and becomes a sphere that has no other consideration but to affect in a positive way, whether it is seemingly mundane or profound. I love you.

CHAPTER FOURTEEN

Opening New Threads of Comprehension
March 17, 1999

First questioner: When I meditate at times, my mind wanders and gets into imagery, or I start nodding off. I asked a question about that, and the answer was that I was closing off, or losing a connection in my crown center, and that it was similar to sleep. I think it would be helpful if I had the ability to use images, but I do not seem to be able to get there without nodding off.

There is something in between there that you have to get to. That happens to me frequently too: occasionally I hit a place where I blank out for some strange reason. When I question the reality of it, usually the answer comes back: *It is not related to what you should be doing within the physical sense.* Those particular things will not happen. You will not have the insight to see something, so you get knocked out of the particular area and are put back where you should be. Then I search into another area: *Do I need more sleep?* I question the reality of how much sleep I have, or should have, and interrelate that to my meditations. I also try to deal with the velocity of control in the meditation: *Am I getting to a certain place too fast?* Then the rejuvenation is taken care of from the involuntary system because I did not give myself enough time to get there.

There are many little questions you can ask, interrelated to those little blank-out periods, and you get answers coming back that are usable. Eventually you can ride through some of them and feel the essence. The other day I was hearing some incredible sounds within myself that I had never heard before. Then there are times when you will be at a level where you can actually feel the essence of a thought, and where it is going and how, or you can hear a word coming through you and out of you before it actually comes out of you. So there are some extraordinary places you can visit eventually when you are ready, but before you are ready, you will get those little periods from the higher self that will knock you out of the situation, or free you from the exhausting inability to comprehend it. So it happens: you are going in there and are getting focus, and you think you are in the right place, but actually you are focusing beyond where you should be, and there is a blank-out period. Ask questions pertaining to it. You might get an answer pertaining to two or three of the things I just mentioned, or you might get something totally different interrelated just to you.

Reply: **I also got the response that I needed to be still and receive, rather than search it out.**

That is also teaching you the velocity that is usable in comprehension.

Reply: **It is a difficult task.**

I know, but it becomes a more difficult task if you do not do it. That is the key right there. For a few times as you are going into meditation, say: *If I do not do it, it is a more difficult task, and that might compound the reality.*

For instance, there are few things I have been working on. When I was in that pretty good level that we were in tonight, there were certain thoughts going into different areas: *You have been eating a little too much. Cut down on certain foods. Where are your thoughts going? What are you doing? What particular things are you working on? Are you being too complacent, reacting simple and stupid too much? The reality of you being in that place has less of an opportunity for others to see it as proper. Take yourself out of there and put yourself in a more suitable place. Do not stifle your personality, but make it more pliable in reaching out to others.*

So those things will come to us that cause us some semblance of balance. We do not have to search them out because we put ourselves in that place where we start it with a question, and it seeks itself out. It gives us new avenues that penetrate into the layers of what we should be comprehending. That one question put us into directions. That one thought searches us out into a different direction. You see it here in class when I am answering a question. I will start in one place, and it is a sphere: I go all around the edges of it; then all of a sudden, I am back to that point again. I have given each person in class the analogy of the situation, yet have brought them through that path of comprehension and returned them to the original point once again. Along the way I gave them an avenue, a roadway. I gave them something to participate in: a channel, a thread of awareness. That is an important thing.

That is why some people seemingly think that I am going somewhere outside of the context of the particular question that they have asked, because I am there one moment and answer the question, but then bring them through the particular thing and around once again. I do not have to search it out; it becomes a necessary reaction in answering the question pertaining to the movement of the person through that particular place. It is like putting film on a projector for the questioner, but the film is sometimes misinterpreted because it takes them out of the context. They are saying: *Where is he going? Why is he going there?* Because they have never been there before; they have never searched out something to put self in that curve of reality, that puts them into the centrifugal force that brings them back to that point.

For instance, I notice sometimes when I answer a question for one person in class, another person will jump in and answer the question. But when I look at the triangle of it, the second person's response has nothing to do with first person's question; rather it has to do with where they are. I try to make them see that. When I make them see that, it is no longer the teacher to the student, it is a confrontation; they do not see the triangle. So there has to be a new avenue in my approach to the particular thing. Even though that is a teaching process, it puts them outside of the context of *this* sphere, *this* particular place.

I have been questioning the reality of the way we present the information in this class. In order to make the knowledge more suitable for newcomers, you have to make certain sensible patterns, and that is something I do not do. It is constantly clipping and putting new patterns in the structure of that comprehension. What it does, it takes them to a place that flushes them into moments of confusion; it does not give them the stabilizing qualities of the security. What it does do, it gives information that, probably if you hit those levels you are going to have to be dead for it to become something that is questioned in that sphere.

It is similar to the fact that we can interpret the Bible in many different ways, because it has the context of moveable levels within it. It has staircases to different avenues of comprehension that interrelate to particular things, and that is important. So when I am asking or answering a question, and my intent is to search it out, the initial question searches it out, but then pushes it into different pathways of comprehension, and that is an important factor in the sphere of the identity of dealing with the sustenance of that question or answer. That is something I have been thinking about.

So if you want to run a class that is well attended, just make the information structured, and ordinary, and recognizable, and right down the pathway of a particular thing. But what happens when you are dealing with the strings of esoteric comprehension, the information has a scattering quality, a threatening quality. It has an inroad into pushing the reality of the sustenance of humanity aside. It pushes it in a direction where it moves people out of the way because it opens up new threads of comprehension. It has new avenues that person has to walk down, and there is the initial thrust of fear that threatens the security of where the person is that holds them back from going into that direction.

So it is important that we look upon that. We look upon the avenue of why we are here, and what particular things we are dealing with. If you want to deal with a class that attracts many people, make it structured each week, recognizable, and written, and make it have a series to it. There is no series to esoteric comprehension; there is just movement into new directions. Those qualities–which are extraordinary at times–have a tremendously threatening aspect to them. Esoteric comprehension staggers the person's particular position; it pulls the foundation of what they are and cracks it. It makes it something that they have to consider resurfacing, because there is new movement into comprehension. I notice this happens with a lot of newcomers: they walk into the class, and you know they are probably teaching a class somewhere and want to pick up some new information. Suddenly, boom, you hit them with an entirely new theory of where they are, and they say: *Let me out of here! This is not what I want! What I want is something that I can use, and build upon from where I am, or use at a party somewhere.* Yet if they really looked at it, it is truly that; but in the initial thrust, they put up that security wall around self, saying: *I am threatened. It is new.*

What do you do when you as teacher or healer, go through that? Some of you will go through that. Most of you will go through that. You look upon the structure of different things that happened to particular people who are very famous and you build upon that. There is a statement that triggers my mind constantly that says: *Who are you to think that people should believe you? They did not even believe Christ!* That is not a bad place to be. That is a pretty good place, because what you are doing is changing a theme. It is not saying you are at the level that Christ is; you are just using that particular figure as an analogy for looking at situations within yourself, and that is important because you are going to be up against that.

The same thing happens when you bring your mate to the class. Your other half is totally outside of the context of what is usable. You are getting so much new information coming here regularly, that they cannot possibly keep up with you unless you learn how to blend it and make it usable. It has that threatening quality. I remember years ago, people would tell me that they were in so much trouble with their partner for going so fast. They tried to convey the information, and it did not happen. It does not happen because the other is not ready. They are not moving at that speed. So it is a matter of slowing yourself down and making it usable within the mundane qualities of humanity, which is so extraordinary.

Second questioner: **I have been desirous of being in prayer but have not been able to achieve it.**

Prayer is good, but when prayer becomes a crutch and we do not use it, prayer becomes nothing. It is like sitting in a place and using the short prayer: *God, please help me. I need you today.* If you keep using it, after a while that prayer does not mean anything; that sustenance seemingly becomes no reaction. The prayer that is truly usable is: *God, help me, so I may understand, so that I can move more thoroughly into understanding You.* That is an understandable prayer. It is a prayer that is usable. It moves you, and makes you understand that you can move.

If it is a prayer that gives you the property of seeming to think that outside forces will help you all of the time, that is not true. There are those occasions when the burden becomes so heavy, we make that prayer where we reach out to every avenue that we have within our quest of whatever we are trying to comprehend. That prayer becomes something of a reward because That Particular Structure understands that to the best of your ability, you have gone through all of the necessary vibrations to comprehend the situation. That is when you get that reward. The prayer, *I need help*, will work instantly, but only after you have gone down the pathway of trying to solve the problem, and have searched out everything to the best of your ability, but then have hit some stumbling blocks. But when you sit there and pray, then do not go forward and use it, do not go forward and comprehend, the prayer becomes nothing. It becomes a crutch. It becomes the seeming identity of something that we are trying to comprehend, but it is not going to be there.

Reply: **That is the thing: I used to feel that I was not moved to prayer. That used to concern me, but now I realize you have to feel it.**

Right. That flash does not come all of the time, but when it comes, use it. Sometimes I think about prayer; one time I asked: *What does the sign of the cross mean, and the phrase, "In the Name of the Father, the Son, and the Holy Ghost, Amen?"* We think about it within the structure of what we attempt to teach here. The crown center means there is a Father. The heart center means there is a Son. The Holy Ghost, which is on both sides of us, is the identity of what we do not understand and are trying to comprehend. It is something outside of the context of the reality of where we are, that we are constantly searching out. We have the strength of both sides together, but there is that strange area that we do not comprehend. What is that movement? That is the movement within duality in the physical sense. It is neither male nor female, but eventually has the capacity of being androgynous, which is neither, which is in the center.

There are so many symbolic things within the structure of gestures, or written words, in the Bible, Cabala, or wherever it might be, if we just search them out. Sometimes I will be so deep in meditation, I can feel my hands go to the center of my chest, and I ask: *Why do my hands join?* We take our two hands and put our palms together; as we put them together, it is the joining of survival energies at higher levels; our fingers are pointed towards the crown center, the Father, and we pray, joining the two together, Father and Son. We look upon the attitude of prayer in the Christian sense to ask: *Why do I kneel when I pray? Is there a structure there?* The comprehension of kneeling: the knees are a secondary center of the heart center. Doesn't that make more of the duality of the heart center, and Father and Son? Kneeling is compassion and balance within the physical sense, and the heart center is compassion and balance esoterically. The Holy Ghost is what we are trying to comprehend, which is outside of the reach of what we are. When we pray: *In the name of the Father, the Son, and the Holy Ghost, Amen,* all of them come together. *Amen* is: we have it; we have moved from all of those places to the center of that reality and higher within the quest of what we are.

If we just take the opportunity to say: *There is something going on here;* then to ask: *What is it?* That is the first step. Then to ask: *What is it in my tomorrows in everything I do?* I am guilty of the absence of meditation at times, as much as anybody else. I do some of the most stupid things, just to keep myself outside of the context of comprehension. Maybe it is necessary because there is too much of the reality of the levels around me. Or maybe it is just stupidity: that I do not realize what I have. Or maybe it is, what I have, I want to be there for a while, and do not want to be threatened anymore from different levels.

It is important not to be famous. It can be the most detrimental thing that can happen to you. Everything about you becomes outward rather than inward. You no longer have a private life. You have nothing left for yourself. Then if you are truly inwardly searching something out, you cannot, because being famous threatens your identity at every doorstep. You cannot even eat out anywhere, walk anywhere, or do anything without being bothered. So you have to understand what your reality is, and what you want to do, and where you might go within the structure of that. I was watching a movie the other night about a healer who was almost mobbed to death. Eventually she had to move and leave everything and hide. Hiding yourself is good in one sense, but having the capacity of doing all of those things without being recognized is another thing. It all depends what your probabilities in life are, and what your particular theme is. There is healing constantly within the words of the reality of what is usable in questioning the property of what you are. I understand that. But then you have to look at the theme of what you are, and where you are heading, and what your knowledge is, and what your bases are within the structure of that. You have to understand the identity of it, and what your calling is. Your calling might be something that is totally outside of the context of that which puts it in a theme of healing or whatever. It might be the awareness of moving us into a new area, or bringing in more information pertaining to the Laws of God.

For instance, Moses had the capacity of saying: "This is what is going to happen to you if you threaten my son: your son is going to die. You do not realize what you are doing. Do not do that to yourself." Now there are new laws being written within the awareness of humanity that have the capacity of giving us information of what we should be doing, or what we should not be doing. It is just the opportunity to say: *There is something going on here,* and to ask: *What is it?* That is the first step. Then to ask: *What is it in my tomorrows, in everything I do?* Good night, everyone.

CHAPTER FIFTEEN

The Preventive Medicine That is Necessary for You
July 14, 1999

Understand that your soul is doing everything it can to make you become more evolved. When you feel lonely, or when you need strength, think about that. Believe me, there are so many things going on at different levels of comprehension that interrelate to keeping you in some semblance of balance within the flesh. The more you become attuned to yourself within meditation, the more that reality will become usable in the flesh. You will begin to understand that there is so much going on for you. When you are unable to understand that, of course, it is necessary for you not to understand it; you cannot take on the weight of that within the flesh. But when you begin to bridge the gap between the flesh and the soul, you can then begin to understand how truly unique and multi-dimensional you are. Logic tells you that it is necessary for it to be that way. You cannot graduate from kindergarten to Yale. There is a gradual sequence of events that is usable in comprehension that interrelates to changing and achieving probabilities within the flesh.

Meditation is a uniquely beautiful tool of understanding you and how you interrelate to everything in life. Do not take my word for it, try it; it is like anything else: the more you understand about the particular thing you are involved in, the more usable you can become within the sphere of your comprehension. Logic also tells you if you are working on yourself and becoming more usable, it becomes a natural reaction that is commonplace. You begin to eliminate the small things that slow you down. You begin to focus upon the reality of what is usable in increasing your capacity of performing within any structure that you are involved in. When I tell you in the meditation to use your mind correctly, it means, begin to comprehend what is going on in your body; question what you feel and sense; if something passes through your mind, ask why. Open up that viable channel of awareness to that next level. If you feel tingling, warmth, or energy, in a certain part of the body, you ask questions. Every part of your body has a consciousness to it. If you understand the reality of a particular area of your body, logic then tells you, you have more of a capacity of giving yourself balance so you do not deviate into the avenues of misconception.

Do you realize what that statement means? That tells you, if you have a pain in a particular area, and you can understand why you have that pain, it will be gone before it becomes agony. You have a roadway, or ballpark of knowledge, interrelated to the particular thing that is happening to your body. If there is one thing I should get across to you, this is it! Just look around you. Look at the illnesses upon this planet and how many minds are distorted. People of ages sixty or seventy years old do not have the capacity of understanding anything. Most of the people in nursing homes are suffering from dementia because they never nourished their minds; they never rejuvenated themselves when they were younger. You are giving yourself the capacity of performing at all of those levels to the best of your ability, and it will be magnificent.

First questioner: **Recently I had an experience at work where I was having a casual conversation with some colleagues. Afterwards, I noticed my energy field was depleted, and I felt muddled.**

Did you ask questions later on? Where did you feel the distortion? What particular center was depleted?

Reply: **Primarily in the abdominal area.**

So it interrelates to physical, sensual and emotional issues, which are the three lower centers. Tell yourself in meditation: *When I deal with these people in the future, I have to prepare myself to be more balanced when entering that particular sphere.*

When I first started meditation about twenty-five years ago, the woman who ran the psychic school would ask me to do healings on people there, and that started me doing healings. Then I began to have unusual experiences. One evening I was walking through a hospital ward and suddenly felt energy being sucked out of me from all different directions because I was so wide open. I could not understand why I was experiencing so much fatigue. My energy field was being depleted because I was not prepared for it. What do you do in such an instance? You have to hit a thought in your mind that you cannot help anybody else unless you are ready. You have to begin to prepare yourself as you enter those realities. That is what I am asking you to do. When you enter into that next sphere of comprehension, if you know you are going to be with a person who is going to make you feel emotional, work on yourself so when you enter that sphere again, you will have more stability within you as you deal with that duality.

It also gives you the capability of understanding the reaction within the other person, and your work in that area lifts that reality and sustains them at a higher level. If you draw in energy through meditation into the third center of the solar plexus, which deals with the comprehension of human decency and control over your emotional state, you increase that vibration within your system. It is a more vibrant, balanced color, and gives a more beautiful reaction for the other. When you are prepared in that way, the next time you have an interaction with the other, it becomes an arena of growth, rather than having a confrontation where your egos become involved and you end up parting. You will have more capability of not only giving the word of knowledge, but the energy field of knowledge.

For instance, if you walked past Moses, Buddha, Christ, or any other great entity, you would feel an extraordinary amount of balancing energy from that person just within the free will of the sphere of what that person is. I am not saying that they would knowingly send it to you, but if you asked within your free will, the capacity to be healed would be increased. Within many of the statements that all of these people made, free will was an important factor. You do not infringe upon the other person's free will. If you want to heal the other, they have to have the capacity to ask for it, otherwise it contradicts why they are here. Each of us is here to grow. If you contradict why the other is here upon the earth plane, that is the gravest sin you can commit. It contradicts the entire structure of what the other is trying to comprehend.

(Addressing the questioner:) The next time you have a conversation with your colleagues, ask yourself what you feel from each. If you feel one particular person draining you, then you know whom they are, and what you have to do within the structure of comprehension. You know you have to increase your capabilities within that system. You can see energy changes in every moment of every day if you are aware. You can be out walking, and the sun hits you and changes you. There is much going on if you take the opportunity to ask questions, and that is what makes you grow.

Let us return to the statement, "Every part of the body has a consciousness." When I lead you in the guided meditation, I make certain statements. For instance, when we get to the solar plexus area, I say, "Relax the lower part of the trunk of the body. You will feel more love for others, within the duality of whatever it might be. You will have control over the emotional state of what you are." The comprehension of that area is human decency. Whether you know it or not, the third center of the solar plexus is the area that has the misconception of cancer within it. It is misconception within lack of human decency, and our over-reactions or under-reactions within emotions. An additional factor is taking into account where the cancer breaks out in the body. For instance, cancer can break out in your finger, head, nerves, toes or organs. If you interrelate the cancer towards understanding the consciousness of the particular area, then put it within the context of understanding that it is within a lack of human decency, you will focus in on the reality of why the particular disease has happened in that particular part of your body. I am not saying that the ill person is bad; I am simply saying that the person is miscomprehending the particular level they are dealing with. My own mother died of cancer, and I tried so many times to sway her out of certain avenues of miscomprehension within the structure of understanding that disease. The information of the reality that is usable for the person passes them by; passes them by. They are so entrenched into a particular avenue of awareness, it is hard to deviate them out of the pathway of misconception.

I do not want you to take anything I say as the truth. I want you to put it in your meditations and make it the truth within you. I know that everything I tell you here, I have questioned thousands of times from different levels within me, but you still have to make it the truth within you. You might come back the next week and tell me you do not believe what I say. That is truly usable. That is when we open up a dialogue of awareness that makes us grow beyond where we are. There is no better way to grow than utilizing questions and answers, because the questions are coming from an area that you are interrelating to, and how you become more usable within the flesh. But I can tell you one thing—and this is the truth from the tips of my toes to the top of my head—if you comprehend one more thing, you are more godlike.

Second questioner: **I begin to get ringing in my ears in meditation; then it may or may not go away.**

Do not force anything at those levels. When you feel that ringing, just stay at that level. Let it go away by itself, or bring self back up a bit. You might be going a little too fast, or trying too hard. Sometimes when you try too hard, it pushes you back. Sometimes you get a signal within the energy system that you are getting into an area before you are ready. For instance, when you come up too quickly from the meditative state, you may feel a little out of balance. In that instance you have to drop back down and bring yourself up slowly.

When you are listening to the higher essence within you, do not overdo it. Take it slowly. Then you have to make it usable. Anything that you get from the meditative state, you have to put into your normal, daily life and make it normal; then more information and energy will come. You will never see that flash of light unless you use what you have been given. Remember, you are in control of the meditative state, or of anything that comes through you. It is important that you have the strength to say: *I do not want to see or experience this,* and easily bring yourself back from wherever it is. That is part of your training. If you experience fear, fear is good because fear is a tool of the soul telling you that you are going too fast, and are in a certain place before you are ready. Fear slows you down. You eliminate fear through comprehension. If you know what you are dealing with, then there is no fear.

As you are going through the different levels, you look at different things and begin to understand why certain things are here for us. We are not going to understand why millions of people are dying in poverty, but there are reasons for everything. If we hit those levels and begin to see different factors from those particular levels, then we understand. It is like an actor upon the stage playing a murderer: they are acting. If we begin to see something from that next level, we begin to understand that the only distortion is within the realm of what we are trying to comprehend at this level. We are the only ones that can distort it. If we put ourselves in balance, then we will begin to understand the reason for a particular thing happening.

Third questioner: **I know two chronically ill individuals who have managed to survive throughout the years. They basically have good hearts, always trying to help other people.**

In the solitude of agony those individuals have the ability to comprehend some deviations into misconception and slow the reality of death down. We can see certain ill people who will fight for their lives, and fighting is the ability to comprehend what is going on. Some people make it through heart attacks, and open heart surgery, and if they go forward from there with good diet, and understand the knowledge of what is going on, they will have a better chance.

The same thing takes place in consciousness. Begin to understand the interrelationship of consciousness to the body. For instance, we have talked about heart disease and a lack of compassion either for self or others. If you suffer from that disease and are told the reason behind why you have it, "You have a lack of compassion," then you start having more compassion towards yourself and others, you begin to heal yourself.

Therefore, if you dissect and truly look at ill health, you are going to understand the reality of what is going on. You ask: *Is something being dissipated within my body?* I know the flaws within my genetic process. Every single one of us knows flaws in our family structure.

More than likely, whatever is wrong with our parents will go wrong with us. You work on those particular parts of the body. I know my eyesight is one of the areas I have to work on. My father is eighty-seven and has some problems with sight, and my mother had cataracts. What other factors in the family structure are you going to have to work on? You have to look at certain trends. If you hit the level that makes you understand the conscious awareness of some of them, you eliminate them from the reality of what you are. You can eliminate the probability of them happening to you and give yourself the capacity to live beyond that structure of misconception. It can happen. I am only brushing the surface of certain things.

Take the opportunity to understand. For instance, when you bite into an apple, do you know what happens to you? We have often heard the adage, "An apple a day keeps the doctor away." If you look at an apple, it is both ends of the spectrum, red and white. If you look at the system of what you are, you have a red energy source at the base of the spine, survival in the flesh, and a white energy source at the top of the head, survival esoterically. There is also the red and white combination at work in your blood: if there is a misconception within the red blood cells, the white cells rush in and surround the misconception, trying to eliminate it. All of the information that we learn at a different level has to brought into the physical level and become sensible. If it is not sensible, we cannot use it. Anything that I have ever taught myself, or learned from a different level in that book of wisdom that I tap into, has to become sensible, usable and understandable as it interrelates to what I already know. It does not contradict the responsibility of that basic foundation of me, but increases the capability of understanding why it has happened to me, or why I was there. It is important that I understand it.

Fourth questioner: **Ill people who are approaching death might receive this kind of knowledge and use the knowledge against self by starting to blame self. What would you say to them?**

I would explain, if they take the responsibility of it upon self and work on it, it is going to eliminate the reality of the problem, not compound it. I know that people suffering from mental illness often cannot use the information. If you give them information when they are very unbalanced, they are not going to retain it at all. It overwhelms the person to a certain point where everything is shut off. It is necessary for that to happen. To help them, you do not have to search out the reason; you take them out of that particular place that they are in, by building upon the knowledge slowly. You give them certain little keys or tidbits interrelating to a particular pathway that pulls them out of the avenue of misconception. On an energy level you throw them a rope and tell them to hold on. You do not tell them that there is something gigantic pulling them up because you might frighten them. You do certain little things to trigger the quality. If they get to a point where they understand that they have done something harmful to self, and it is overwhelming, at that point, you have to shut it off again. You have to give them information pertaining to the balancing qualities of understanding the whole sphere of things, which is not an easy thing to do.

That is where you as healer, come into the picture. If you are at a level where you can give the person information and energy, it helps. It is very difficult to bring a person back from the brink of misconception because you have to refract to the particular level within the system of what you are. If you do not have that particular level of awareness or consciousness within you, you cannot eliminate that disease within the other; you can only eliminate a portion of the identity of that disease according to what you are within you, within the structure of that disease. For example, it is difficult to bring a person back from the brink of death because you have to understand the brink of death. We have talked about Christ re-igniting the body of Lazarus, because he was at the level that understood the misconception totally. You cannot contradict the one statement: "If you are at the particular level, you can deal with it. If you are not there, you cannot deal with it."

If you are sick, the hardest person to heal is you, because you are in the mire of misconception. You are nowhere near bringing yourself out, because you put yourself there. You have to slowly bring yourself out through the knowledge of understanding it. If you know of a healer who is at a particular level that can refract to that level, they can give you some semblance of balance. They can give you a rope to help you out. You still have to hold onto that rope to the best of your knowledge, which is the strength within you. If you cannot hold onto that rope, nobody can pull you out: you do not have the knowledge of tying it around you; you do not have the knowledge of yelling for help. All of that is so important in what you have to do within the structure of eliminating the disease.

Understand that the meditative state is the preventive medicine that is necessary for you. You are rejuvenating yourself. It is not going to eliminate everything. If you go back into your life, and abuse yourself, or others, then think you can rejuvenate yourself through meditating, it is only going to take a short time before those meditations do not work. You have to be involved in them. You have to have some sort of truth within you that interrelates to the awareness of what is going on. It is important that you work on yourself, and after that, that you use yourself properly. If you contradict why you are here upon the earth plane, no matter what it is, eventually you are not going to be here.

I look forward to going to different levels of awareness that inter-relate to particular phases within my life. I go through those levels to the best of my ability. Half of my high school graduating class is dead, and the other half, when I look at them I have to wonder what has happened to them. I know they are probably looking at me and saying the same thing, but I see some people who can hardly walk. I am not a young man, but I look at them to say: *What is going on within the structure of what that person is comprehending?* I know that part of my makeup is genetics, and part is the awareness of meditating and elimi-nating some flaws within the system of what I am. The point is, use the meditation to eliminate the probability of harm happening to you. I am not saying that you are going to be doing what you did, twenty years ago; I am saying whatever you are going to do now, is within the best of your ability for your age level. You are somewhere at the top of the structure of your age level. Wherever the misconception is, you have the ability to float above it, rather than being dragged down to the bot-tom. Practice each day. Know what is going on. If you know what is going on when you are meditating, the next meditation will be deeper and deeper. And deeper means closer and closer to your soul, and closer and closer to the reality that made you. Good night, everybody.

CHAPTER SIXTEEN

On the Breath of God
August 18, 1999

First questioner: **I have been working in the area of emotions. To-night I felt a lot of tightness in my calves at times. What is the significance of that?**

You just answered it: tightness in your emotions. The calves are secondary centers that interrelate to the third center of the solar plexus, which is the consciousness that interrelates to personal reality and control over your emotional state. If you are feeling energy in that particular area, you are igniting emotions within you as you participate in trying to deal with the balancing qualities within it. You need to loosen up. Sense and feel what is going on in your body. Ask: *What does it interrelate to?* Every part of your body has a consciousness to it. If you can focus in on it, you can begin to filter down that esoteric level that is usable for you within the flesh. Then you become more than what you were before, and that is how you grow. If you comprehend what is going on in your body, more consciousness and energy will come. Eventually you will ignite all of those energies and lift yourself to another level, whether you wish to believe it or not.

Second questioner: **I am experiencing back pain only here in this classroom. At first I thought it was the chair, so I brought a heating pad, but it has not released the pain at all.**

There is more energy here in the classroom and it is hitting a particular area within your body that has a blockage to it. So feel and sense the back pain, and interrelate it to the energy center in the front of the body. What energy center would that be?

Reply: **The heart center.**

You need more balance within the system of what you are, as you interrelate to compassion first for self, then others. In your case, you are mainly in the habit of not reacting in life. You want to react more in a positive way and deal with the balancing qualities of that. I will work on that with you too. Pain is not necessarily something that is negative; it can be positive, giving you a reaction within an area that you can begin to comprehend. You want to ask what the particular center interrelates to within consciousness and link it to what you are doing in your normal, daily life. The heart center deals with compassion; also the balance between the higher three centers and the lower three centers. Ask: *What am I doing for myself within my life? Am I allowing others to take advantage of me, or am I taking advantage of others? How am I dealing with compassion in certain situations?* That is the ballpark you should be working in.

Reply: **What do you mean by react?**

In your case, outwardly react a little more. Sometimes when you are involved in situations and see something, you hold back too much. Learn how to react. Do not let your anger build to a point where you explode or have to sever your interaction; those pathways pull you out of control. Get to the point where you react in a positive way within the realm of growth and comprehension. The pathway we are talking about allows us to control the velocity that is usable so it does not bring us to the point of explosion; rather, it brings us to the point of comprehending the essence of speed within the reaction of comprehension. It is teaching us the velocity that is usable in comprehension. Work on that, and the next time you meditate here in class, you will feel more energy relaxing you in that particular area.

Reply: **I also felt like a bump in the throat center.**

What you are doing in the guided meditation is allowing that unreleased tension to come forward. When you feel something like that, just relax the area mentally and ask questions why: *What is the consciousness of that area?* That gives you more information. Now we know that your back pain in the region of the heart center interrelates to duality, sensuality, and creativity, which is "love of another," because the fifth center of the throat interrelates to the second center of duality in the gonadic area. You need more balance and compassion as you deal with sensuality and creativity within the physical sense. Do not allow others to overwhelm you, but participate in a balanced way. You have that to work on now. That is an important sphere of comprehension.

Third questioner: **For the last three sessions, I have felt a lot of pressure at the bottom of my spine.**

That is very good. There is an energy source at the base of the spine that deals with survival, and that pressure is fine. The energy is starting to come up, and you are going to get information interrelated to your survival, which you have to deal with eventually.

Reply: **I do not think it will occur.**

Believe me, it will. You will see it, feel it and sense it. When you feel energy, pressure, pain or an escalation of energy in a certain area, ask what is going on. You are feeling it within the base of the spine, which deals with survival, and within the second center, which deals with comprehension of how you interrelate to another. The first two centers interrelate a lot, dealing with love of self and our confrontations within duality in daily life. If you are feeling energy in those two centers, it is stimulating those areas. You are beginning to feel energy in the survival center, which is the basic foundation of what you are. I can remember feeling pressure in that area when I first started to meditate. It is stimulating that particular comprehension within you. You say you are not receiving information; actually you are receiving information that you are not seeing. At first we receive certain things that we cannot see, because we are asking the wrong questions and are involved in the outer orbits of the sphere of comprehension. Eventually we begin to ask the right questions interrelated to a particular thing, which will bring us into the nucleus of it, and we will begin to comprehend what is usable for us. It is so important to question: *What am I feeling? What am I sensing?*

Fourth questioner: **I do find that the energy flow in the heart center is easier than within in the survival center where I feel very tired and enormously pressured.**

Well, that teacher, which is the heart center, is stimulating the qualities within you to make you be involved in that seemingly tough area. Eventually when you are involved in the sphere of comprehension, you will see it as easier because you will be involved in it. You will begin to look forward to being involved in something similar, just to see how you perform. Then you will get involved in it and say: *My God, if I really look at this closely, I am making progress!* The enormous pressure is the cooking within you, stimulating that area that deals with survival within life. You are opening the book of knowledge about you. When you open up that book, there is confusion. It is the first day of school, and you are outside the realm of what you are normally involved in; there is fear and misconception because you are going into a new area. But look at it in this way: you have graduated to a new area; you have put yourself there through comprehension; you have won the right to be there. It is a graduation, not a denouncement of what you are. You should be looking upon this as growth. This happens to a lot of people when they first start meditating: they come back to me, saying, "John, before I meditated, I never had problems." I say, "You had a lot of problems that you were not facing, but now you have a tool to face your problems." Is that growth? Of course, it is. Sometimes within the particular thing that we are trying to comprehend, there is trauma that seems to be pushing us back. We are not going backwards, we are going forward all of the time.

(Addressing the questioner:) What is truly happening, you have put yourself in a place where you are looking at a particular flaw within the particular sphere of what you are, and that is growth. You never had the capability of seeing the flaw before, because there were so many illusions around it. You could not see it because the illusion was put there in order to give you the capability of going forward in your life with some semblance of balance so you could perform to the point of understanding some ability. Now there is the capability of having that veil of misconception, that illusion, being stripped away. In the initial thrust, it seems as if something has kicked you back. Actually it is propelling you forward into an area of comprehension, not illusion. Within the stimulating qualities of approaching that new area of comprehension, there is pressure and there appears to be misconception. It is clearing out the channels of awareness within the system of what you are. You are laying new pipeline. You are putting in new foundation that will allow the fluid of what you are to eventually flow to a new level of comprehension. It is like opening up the pipes in a new house before there is any water in them: you can hear knocking from the movement of air flowing. Nothing has traveled through there before, but it is not negative. What you are doing is eliminating misconception so it can flow. It is so unique and beautiful. It takes you to new places.

What are the rewards? The feelings you receive from the new place. The feelings will be beyond where you are now and will make everything that you deal with more extraordinary. Everything you feel and sense will change. Everything that you do will have more capability within it. Logic tells you it will be so, because you are in a new place automatically. The force of comprehension has lifted you there automatically because you have won the right to be there. It does not push you out, it pulls you in with the feeling of wondering: *What will come next?* There will be brief moments of rejoicing, using and sensing. Then you will experience the stimulating quality, and the trauma, but there is more of you, and more of you that can control it. The uniqueness of it stimulates you into the wonderment of saying: *I wish to be here, because it is closer to where I want to be eventually.*

Let me try to give you an example of how I work on myself. For my whole life I have had to try to control my over-reactions in anger. If a person came at me, I went at them, no matter whom they were. I have had to learn to control myself a little more so and try to see the other. I have had many opportunities and different events that have made that more usable within me. Therefore, if I want to work on that, I look at my day and ask: *What particular reactions took place today? Did the reactions pull me in, or was I in control?* Today I had a pretty good day, so I ask: *Is there room for improvement?* There is always room for improvement because I know my soul is so brilliant when it sets events in motion.

For instance, if you are just working on yourself, that is easy. If you just have to work on yourself, deal with the stabilizing qualities and put illusions around everything else, others cannot bother you, because what do you care about them? But it does not take place like that. You work on yourself; then all of a sudden, it stimulates you and puts you in a position where you begin to get information about other people and situations. You begin to have a clairvoyant capacity that puts you into the comprehension of others, and feeling and sensing their anguish. That basic foundation that you have built within you gives you the strength to do so. You now have the strength within you to see things that you could not see before. You see anguish in others and are compelled to go forward in dealing with those reactions within yourself. You are going to lift yourself to the point where you can become more usable. If you see an injustice within another person's realm, you react within that realm as quickly as when you are within the realm of understanding a misconception within yourself. If you see a person trying to overwhelm another, you react. If you see hate, bigotry or whatever it might be, you react, not necessarily to the best of your ability, but to the ability of where you are at that moment. Then in meditation you have to bring it back out to look at the particular event to ask: *Did I have compassion? Did I have the understanding within me to look at the other without opening my mouth? Did I enter into a particular situation when I shouldn't have? Was I asked to enter? Did I walk with bravery and knowledge into an area that seemed to be overwhelming?*

It has happened to me so many times. Recently in a New York airport a woman was instigating two men into fighting each other, and her husband was a frail looking person. Everybody was watching and doing nothing. I just walked right up to them and said, "Stop it! Don't be stupid!" If I had not done that, the husband would have been badly hurt. There were choices there. There was no fear on my part because I had the confidence to do that from everything I have ever participated in, so it put me in a new place, avenue, or perspective on something I had to be involved in.

An event that seems so insignificant is so profound. You have to search it out and look at it. It has to hit you. It is the trauma of saying you wish to work on a particular thing because you feel so bad about it. Perhaps you have hurt another person with your anger, anguish, or words. You have to sit there and ask what you can do to change it. You have to change it, because others will never forget what you do to them. I can remember incidences when I was younger where I embarrassed some people. I had so much vigor within, and when I went at the other person, I made them feel small. Usually it was not anything I initiated, nonetheless I felt bad after the event. It was necessary to feel bad because I was in a place where I should not have been. I should have had enough control to see it, but I had insecurities within me and had to react with: *Who do they think they are! That person is threatening my manhood!* The same thing happened in karate in adulthood. All those experiences were preparing me for something beyond that. Now when I do something wrong at home, or elsewhere, I have to correct it. It might be a spoken word that is hostile; a few moments later I have to say, "I am sorry, I should not have said that to you." There has to be that constant dialogue. You are not holding it in. You have a reaction that says that you have done something wrong. Do something about it now. Take the opportunity.

Then there are times, especially when you have knowledge like this, you have to be rigid or cold with a particular person in order to demonstrate a point. You are involved in the reaction for a reason. You are taking the other into consideration: it is not within anger, or overwhelming moments, rather it is within a sphere of teaching and opening up a dialogue. You are withdrawing in order to show the other that there is something they have to work on. You bend and pull back into the structure of comprehension. You give sometimes, and are rigid sometimes, when you know the other person is wrong or doing something wrong to self. You can see the pathway of destruction that will eventually take place within their wrong usage of the mind. If you love that person, if you have the knowledge, it is up to you to stop them in some way. Sit down, talk to them and open up a dialogue: "Why did you do that to me? You hurt me. I would not have done that to you." Question it. Get an answer. Question it again. Get an answer. That is involvement, duality and growth. It is the sphere of the two moving together and the two becoming one. If it is within the family, the family becomes a unit of love that blossoms into that which is awesomely beautiful because you see the needs of others that you love and grow within it.

If you are engaged in a situation with family members, are you infringing upon their free will, or has that person made a choice there to join with you? Of course, if you are involved in that sphere of duality, you have the right to do what you can to cause some stability within you and the sphere of that duality, and how you interrelate to the person. Free will has been given in that reaction. Sometimes just a word is the wrong thing and sometimes it is the right thing. That is the pathway you will be involved in, if you have the reaction of understanding some semblance of balance within yourself that gives you the strength to lift yourself beyond questioning yourself. When you question yourself enough where you have that strength that lifts you, you have the insight into seeing someone else, or something else. That clairvoyant capacity is triggered naturally because you have that ability to see what the needs of the other person are. Eventually you will have the need to feel the flow of the reality of humanity and know what is needed for the conscious awareness of humanity. We will not talk about that, tonight.

That personal reality is the key. Do you ask yourself constantly: *Where am I?* Occasionally you might do so for incentive. It gives you the rewards of saying you want to grow. You say: *I am in a new place, and that feels good because I am growing.* Bring it out to look at for a short while, then put it aside and go forward with that next moment. If you are on that pathway, focus in on the next moment that you should be comprehending. It will automatically be there because you have won the right to be there. Logic tells you it will be there. It is necessary for it to be there because you are here to grow. It will be there through a sequence of events, using time as the density that propels it forward to have that probability take place within that particular day. Your soul will have it happen because it is necessary for your growth. Do not take my word for it; it will be there. For instance, if you are lonely, another person will be there for you, because it is necessary for you to be in that sphere of comprehension if that is what you want. There are other avenues of work or play, whether it is music, song or dance that deals with the same sustenance of duality. Whatever it might be, there is that duality that extends us into the esoteric quality and moves us up. We have seen so many people that have had the ability to accelerate themselves to a place where their performance has become so good within that quest, others want to see it and listen to it.

Occasionally I go through the basic steps of meditation to put myself in that more transcendable place. Then other times I take the opportunity to go through the basics of rejuvenation and of looking at my day, and by choice, not put myself there. Sometimes when I open my-self up, there is so much coming at me, I do not want to be there. When I go into transcendable states, I see where I will be: I see the pathway and where it will take me. I see the total identity of John no longer being involved in daily matters at all. I see many things, I do not see a few, and I see the information pulling me away from the confines of where I want to be. But then there are those fleeting moments when my mind dashes into an area where an ill person needs some healing en-ergy. Then I turn it on, and when I turn it on, it stimulates all of those reactions, all of those feelings, all of those pulling events that deal with the reaction of saying: *Hey, open this up, more and more.*

(While talking, John enters into a deeper meditation state:) There is so much to question within the reality of what you are, but it is so necessary to put on the brakes when the reality extends itself past where you want to be. When you do that, you are taking more control of the velocity that controls the reactions of your probabilities each time you grow within the flesh. More of the essence of the soul is here and more of the reaction of control is here. It is you, nobody else, who either applies the brakes or accelerates. Just within the vessel of what you are, there is a steering wheel, clutch, brake and accelerator, jet fuels and ordinary fuels. It is up to you whether you want to be a rocket that day, or just be someone sailing upon the wind along with the person you want to be with.

Then you look at your reality and realize that the wind is stiff and strong, and the waves high, but you do not feel them at all. It seems tranquil to you because the misconceptions are flattening everything out. There is nothing there to stimulate you. Then chaos, which is so usable within the Vibration of God, becomes that aspect that stimulates you once again, because you never know what is going to come next! Because it will never be the same again! How necessary that has to be. Every time that you think you have control over something, something beyond that will come to stimulate it out of control, and thank God for that. Because sometimes the realm of control becomes rigid within the framework of humanity, and it is the density that stops and pulls you into tributaries that seem to be the true reality. But those tributaries are not the true reality. You are sailing into the muck of misconception, thinking that you might be in the true reality but you are not; you are killing everything along the way that seems to hold you back from the quest or knowledge of where you want to be.

Then one day, you stop, look and understand that you are nowhere near the true river of reality. The initial thrust of the illusions and mo-ments of grandeur made it seem as if you were going somewhere unique and beautiful, but the confinement of thinking you were more than you were became the ego of misconception that propelled you forward. You have to turn around. You have to go back, and mend the fences of misconception as you do so. The fibers of misconception have to be put back together again. The fibers of misconception have to be there because they are avenues that are necessary to slow you down from going totally off that tributary of misconception. Eventually you have to stop, or there is an overwhelming quality to that area that extinguishes the flame of what you are.

So it is all right to take a sabbatical. It is also necessary to see that you are still in that river of reality rather than in the muck of that tributary of misconception that seems to deal with moments of grandeur. The moments of grandeur eventually deal with moments of trauma and agony, and the overwhelming quality that extinguishes the light of what you are. Pull yourself back from that place. Put yourself back upon the wind of reality. Let it pull you gently, so eventually you can be at a gentle warp speed.

These are some of the things I go through sometimes within the quest of understanding who I am, and what I might become, or what I will become. You have to control it, nobody else. If you do not, no more will come. If you feel something within you, stop and ask what you feel. The question itself will slow you down and put you in a place that will comprehend at least a portion of it. That portion that you comprehend will escalate your ability to slow it down even more. Eventually you will pull yourself into the center that will give you the questions and answers that will automatically escalate your ability to comprehend. Then you will not have to worry anymore, because you will truly be on the Breath of God, pushing you forward in a seemingly effortless way, seeing and using everything for you, not against you. What a place! A Sea of Tranquility, the Enlightened Mountain. In the Veins of God.

I love you. I hope a few words or moments or different things that you have felt tonight will stimulate you into the quality that is necessary to stimulate you into a more beautiful area of you. I see you as being so unique. I hope you see yourself that way also. You truly are part of God, and nobody can ever change that because it is unchangeable within the event of what you are. I love You, God. You certainly are Elusive and Creative, but we search You out, and that is the Wonderment of the Pleasure of You.

Sometimes some of the things I hear within myself I cannot even put into words because they embarrass me, but I know without question that you are more than what you were before, when you stepped forth into this room, and so am I. I hope I see you again next month. Take care of yourselves. It is a bit overwhelming for me right now.

CHAPTER SEVENTEEN

Taking Control of Our Reactions
December 8, 1999

(John's beginning comments in leading the guided meditation for the evening:) Put good thoughts in your mind. I want you to think about healing tonight. I have been getting so many calls about sick people. The first meditation is for you. I want you to heal yourself first. Think of yourself as a vessel, preparing self to give sustenance to another. Be selfish with the good intent of putting your focus in the proper place, which is you. Selfishness is so misunderstood within the physical sense: see it in its proper perspective now, by understanding it as that which is usable in building a platform for you and others; then in the second meditation we will emanate our thoughts forward to others who are sick. Within our infinite wisdom we are putting ourselves on that plateau of comprehension beyond where we are now, so that we may have more of a transcendable effect on each person that we mentally look at in the second meditation. It is so important to prepare ourselves, and that is what we do now.

Take a nice deep breath: inhale... Now as you slowly exhale, begin to feel yourself relax, relax, relax. All of the stress and tension is dissipating, and through the proper use of your mind, you are replacing it with relaxing, soothing, comforting energy. Feel it. Sense it. Make it you. You truly have the capacity to do so. I feel fortunate to be in this room with you tonight. You should be fortunate to be in this room also, because with your mind and wisdom you truly make this place a holy place, whether you wish to believe it or not; but if you do believe it, it compounds the reality of the sustenance of what will come forward from here for others. (The meditation proceeded as usual.)

First questioner: **Could you talk more about the probabilities that we set for ourselves from a different level?**

There is a set of probabilities put in motion from another level to achieve certain things that we want to achieve in order to become more evolved at a soul level. We are an extension of the soul within the physical sense in order to absorb the essence of it, and there are certain goals that we put ourselves within the physical sense to achieve. We came down here to learn something: it may be control of anger, or love of another, or learning to deal with the whole vehicle. There are so many avenues.

We achieve a particular goal from a refracted part of what we are. In order to achieve a goal, sometimes we have to refract necessary consciousness away from it; we have to make ourselves weak in certain areas in order to see certain strengths and achieve the goal from weakness rather than strength within the realm of what we are trying to achieve within those probabilities. For instance, it would be so easy to climb a mountain at a soul level: we have a helicopter, we just get in it, go the top of the mountain and we are there. In order to achieve the goal in the physical reality, we have to go through different reactions within the realm of what we are, without the security blanket of the helicopter or the awareness of the soul. We have to learn how to climb, deal with the weather and the awareness of it. When we finally do achieve the goal, just with the strength of what was put within the motion of what we are, the achievement becomes such a reaction of growth and comprehension. It gives us the strength of some semblance of balance and stability within the awareness of that level, so we can achieve and filter down more of the essence of the soul within the physical sense.

We set goals in motion. There are so many avenues. Let us say we wanted to consider some of the stresses of being of a certain ethnic group and seeing some of those aspects coming at us, or being born with a bodily affliction. Once we achieve the goal, then we have the helicopter here within the physical reality and can go there all the time. It is an instantaneous reaction. We do not have to prepare self for months. We do not have to go through all the seeming anguish of the participation of a trip. It is not anguish but the glorified comprehension of the essence of what we are trying to comprehend. That is the beauty of it. We can then participate in being there instantaneously because we have achieved it. It is part of us. We have given self a ladder of comprehension. We have eliminated all of the steps. We can jump up to the top of it. In order to participate at that level, we are there in an instant, because we have the knowledge of the pathway within the system of what we are. That is so uniquely beautiful if we think about it. It is so simple to do something if we have everything. It is so difficult to do it if we have very little when we first start out. When we finally get to that point where we have what we set out to get, there is so much satisfaction in it because we have achieved it from where we are.

Reply: **It depends upon how we react within our circumstances?**

How we react from using only a portion of the capacity of what we have at a soul level. What happens then, it gives us the capacity to win more of the soul level within the physical sense, achieving it from a different perspective. We are going to have to go through whatever it is, again and again, but each time there is a different slant to it, a different avenue to it. It has more of the capacity within oneself here within the physical sense, interrelating to the capacity of seeing it totally different. Then you can hit a certain point where you absorb so much of the essence of the soul within the physical sense, you can set probabilities in motion from the physical reality. It is not set in motion from the involuntary system but from the conscious system. You set certain things in motion to achieve a particular thing, and it is done almost automatically through the strength of what you are. Your goals change and your conditions change within the realm of setting probabilities in motion.

Now, it is important to know that there is so much going on, and that we are here to become evolved. That is something we can wonder about, but we do not want to fasten upon it too much. Occasionally we bring it out to say: *Wow!* We do have certain probabilities that we set in motion, and we look at them for a brief moment, but we do not stay there too long. We just relax, enjoy and comprehend, relax, enjoy and comprehend. We do not want to confine ourselves to the rigidity of constantly studying. We want to be involved in the system of the sphere of comprehension.

Second questioner: **Sometimes I am going along in a certain direction and see a theme. Is that me or my soul?**

No matter what it is, you have to take control of it. If you are going down that highway too fast, slow it down by saying: *I want to know what is going on here. I want to achieve this particular thing. I know I am being pushed in this direction, but why am I being pushed in this direction? I want control here.*

Reply: **If I feel I am going too fast, will something happen to me?**

Yes, but sometimes fear is outside of, or absent from the true essence of what you are going at, so fear is good because it slows you down. But fear is not the only factor there. It is like saying you are going down the highway sixty miles an hour and you have no fear, but there might be a trailer truck accident two hundred yards ahead that you do not know about, so there is no fear until the instant reaction. But if you have control of your reactions as you are participating in going at the particular thing, whether it might be good or bad, there is more of a chance of you controlling the velocity of whatever happens. If you see people around you who are going through a lot of different traumas, you will amaze yourself at the strength you have, because you are meditating and giving yourself balance. Do you realize what you did in that first meditation? If you really believed it, you rejuvenated yourself. You eliminated the probability of hobbling or stumbling along twenty or thirty years from now, just by going through that sequence of events. You are giving yourself rejuvenation to the point where it gives you perfection within those areas that you look at.

(In the second half of class John led the group in meditation:) As we enter a healing meditation tonight, we are going to hit a level and get to a certain point where we can work on some people we know who are sick. I want you to think about a particular person you know who needs a healing, and then as a group, we will send energy to that person. When we have done this in the past, I am sure some people have felt better; some of the afflictions have disappeared and actually gone from their bodies. So think about this, if you know someone who is sick. It is going to be fun to join and go deeper than I normally do. It is a very simple thing to do. It is nothing that is difficult. As a unit, we will join together and send healing vibrations to each person. The more balance that you have, the closer you get to your soul and the more energy you will have to enter into the unit of this room. We will start over here on the right: think of a person; we will take a few minutes between each person. (John pointed to one student after another, allowing about two minutes for each healing.)

(Afterwards:) The deeper you go, and the closer you are to your soul, the more balance and information you will be getting. I utilized some different things in the room, such as colors and other factors that I did not mention to you. I was thinking about different things as far as healing is concerned. Sometimes you can visualize a pyramid over the person. It all depends on where the disease is within the body. Seeing the person as whole is very important. There were a lot of things going on in the room from different perspectives, whoever the different people were, but then I added some things too. If you are really attuned, you can feel so much within the other person's body, you cannot even imagine! So just keep going in the direction you are going in. Sometimes you can hit levels where you can feel the affliction. I can feel exactly where the affliction is within the body. It is amazing. Every time I feel something like that, it gives me the incentive to want to feel more, which is so important. I say to myself: *If I am feeling this now, and can use this, and cause more semblance of balance within me, what can I feel the next time?* It is always improving, and that is what you want to do.

Each time you hit a new area, aspect, or feeling, it is incredible, and that is what it is all about. What are the rewards? The rewards are the intensifying of your capacity to feel and sense everything, no matter what it is. Life becomes more pleasurable, no matter what you are involved in, because you can feel the entire joy of what is going on. Sometimes you can feel the agony beyond normal too. That is something that you can look at from a different perspective. It gives you the capacity of seeing where the other person is. It gives you more of a capacity of helping them. You change that agony into something that is helpful and ride with the pleasant waves of whatever you are feeling. Remember though, it is never your pain or agony, it is always the other's pain and agony. When you immediately sever that healing, it is not yours anymore. You do not want to take on too much. That is something you do not want to do. If you take on too much, then you cannot help more for next time, so always stop. If you are in a place where you are feeling something that you do not understand, ask for help from the higher essence within you, by saying: *I wish to have help with this. There is too much pain or agony. I do not want to be so involved in it.*

Healing is a beautiful thing. Every time you meditate, you should have more healing power from whatever you are participating in, because you are lifting yourself closer to that level that has made this level. Logic should tell you that. You say: *If I am closer to that person's place where they were born in their soul, then I am closer to the place where they are born within the essence of what I am, as I become closer to their soul and my soul.* So logic tells you once again, if you are closer to that, you have more healing energies within you. It is as simple as that, yet as profound as that.

Therefore, if you see a person in agony and pain, it should give you the incentive to want to become more. I was getting some beautiful information the other night on what I can possibly do with some of my thoughts within the realm of humanity. It was extraordinary. I am in some place of complacency within myself, but there is that place that I see that I could be in, that could do a lot of help. We can all hit those places within ourselves. There is so much that can be done within changing the structure of disease and eliminating it. I have been giving that some thought lately. Pain or agony is necessary to a certain point. Let us bring it to that certain point so that pain or agony does not become necessary. Let us not be a contradiction to this place; rather, it is the reality of the sustenance of what we have become in this place that changes the density of what we are and what we can participate in. I have been giving that some thought even within the stupidity of what I have been participating in, so we will see what information we get pertaining to that in the coming months. Good night, everybody.

CHAPTER EIGHTEEN

On Becoming a Better Person
January 12, 2000

(John's beginning remarks before the first guided meditation:) Many people go into meditation with a lot of fear. Fear is a tool of the soul telling you to slow down because you are going too fast. It is important when you enter meditation to take your time. By doing so, it increases your capability of understanding how to comprehend. It teaches you the velocity that is usable in comprehension. If you force something, it pushes you back. By going slowly, it escalates your ability to comprehend meditation. (The meditation proceeded as usual.)

First questioner: **In the guided meditation when I got to my wrists, there was a lot of white light that went into them; also my forearms, elbows and upper arms.**

Fantastic. The wrists interrelate to duality and sensuality within the physical sense, and are an extension of the gonadic area within the second major center of the body, so you are going to have more balance and comprehension towards dealing with your opposite, your partner.

The secondary centers within your arms and legs interrelate to the major centers within the body. It is becoming scientific fact now that each particular part of your body has a consciousness to it. If you can begin to trace that consciousness throughout your body, then you eliminate harm from happening to your body. You can feel whatever it is within the energy field before it happens within the physical sense. I know that if I am going in a direction of illness, immediately I can feel it within my system. If I do not make minor changes in my meditation, I will end up with a cold or something like that. If I understand where I am going wrong in my attitude and my information in regard to those dualities that I deal with within the physical sense, and make changes, I will not end up with an illness. Illness slows us down so we may comprehend misconception.

So everything is good if we search it out: everything. Many people do not understand an event in their lives as good until they can trace it to a particular place and make it understandable within the physical sense. For instance, a person will come up to me in class and say, "So you think illness, pain and agony are good?" You do not have to delve so far into illness to understand that you are going down a wrong pathway. I just explained to you for a brief moment about fear: you cannot eliminate fear from your body just by commanding it to go away. The way you eliminate fear is through comprehension. Fear is the tool of the soul telling you that you are going too fast, so slow down. It is like going down a highway two hundred miles an hour: everything is a blur along the roadside and total confusion. The soul knows that, so it teaches you to pull yourself back and put yourself in a place where you should be. If you comprehend that place, when the next situation comes along, there is more of a chance of you comprehending it. You are teaching yourself to listen to your mind and body.

First, you rejuvenate yourself in meditation. Then you put yourself in a plateau of comprehension where you eliminate all of the distortions. You open up that funnel of energy and absorption, retaining the information. You are reprogramming the reality of what you are, so you may participate in your daily activities in a balanced way and grow. This is what life is all about. If you are doing something that is deteriorating your body, and you are here upon this earth plane to grow, what do you think is going to happen to you? Illness will come forward and eliminate the body. You die, go back up to the soul and re-manifest another body because you are not achieving the probabilities that you set in motion for this lifetime.

If somebody has a better answer, I want to know about it! If you do not believe any of this, I want you to come back at me and say, "John, I don't believe that; how do you know that?" Where did this information come from? Every part of the book "COMMON AS RAIN" came through the questioning process of me: how I deal with my life, how I can become a better person and how I can eliminate my misconceptions. Before that book was started, I was fighting in karate, rather than dealing with the reality of understanding myself as a person who could deal with love and compassion. I gave up karate and that hostility, and went towards the direction of balance and compassion, because meditation stimulated me to that point.

Do you know what growth is? Do you know why you use only a certain portion of your brain within the physical sense? Do you want to know how to stimulate it? Through comprehension: you go to a higher level through meditation, stimulate cells within your brain, then return to your normal reality, and there is more information and intellect for you. Everything that you do in your life will change in a more positive way. Your attitude will change in such a positive way. It will affect you at work or play. You will be a more successful person. You will appreciate food more, music more. All of your senses will be stimulated to a higher level. Everything that you deal with will have more of a higher vibration to it. You will have feelings within you that you have never felt before.

(Addressing the questioner:) You felt an ignition within your wrists. The wrists interrelate to sensuality and duality within the physical sense, and are an extension of the gonadic area, the second center. How did I get this information? In meditation I was getting so much information coming in so quickly, I would have to stop and say: *That is enough! I want to know what I am dealing with, right now. Why am I feeling this stimulation in my legs and head? Why is the energy coming through my feet? Where is it going? Why is it shooting up my spine and out through the top of my head like a bolt of lightning, and I feel like the Empire State Building?*

Ask questions and slow it down. If you do not comprehend and use the meditation properly in your life, no more will come. The simplicity is so awesomely beautiful. You have to take the meditation and understand what it truly is: it is a tool of rejuvenation, and beyond that, it is a true tool of balance and comprehension. It brings you to the center of yourself, rather than seesawing up and down like most of humanity. You open up that viable channel of awareness to the higher self, the higher level; and you can absorb it. When you ask questions at that level, you get answers pertaining to the sustenance of the reality of it, and it will change you forever. Does this sound way out? It might sound unobtainable to you, but it is not. I am ordinary. That is why I named the book "COMMON AS RAIN." If somebody like me can do it, anybody can do it. You just have to take the time to do so. Give yourself the opportunity to slow yourself down so you may understand a direction. Within the essence of that direction you will understand the velocity that is usable in comprehension. If you do that, you can begin to extend yourself into solving your problems. If you do that, there will be more within you to extend yourself into solving more of your other problems. That is growth and more of the essence of the soul becomes usable within the physical sense.

Do you think Michelangelo was ordinary? He could see the veins within the arms and legs of his figures within the slab of marble before he even started carving. Think of the Russian weightlifter that broke the world record: when he closed his eyes, and his head went back, do you think he was tapping into normal energies? Do you think that Joe Naimath, who meditated before he went out on the football field is normal, or Barbara Streisand, who is deathly afraid of being in front of an audience? She meditates before she goes out, just to comprehend some stability. Do you think these people are normal? They are not. Anyone who can obtain some semblance of balance within the normalcy of their sphere of expertise, and extend self into the essence of their soul and become whatever they want within the physical sense is not normal. When Christ was a little boy, didn't he get colds like anyone else? He became a god within the flesh through absorbing all of the essence of his soul through the particular structure that we just talked about. Each one of us truly has that within us. The tool of meditation is the key to lighting that little flame within you, no matter what you want to become. If you want to be extraordinary at it, understand the simplicity of it first; then it will become extraordinary within the simplicity of it.

Second questioner: **How often should I meditate?**

You should meditate every day. I like to do it when I come home from work. Twenty minutes is good. At first, just practice staying still. I would practice that even before I started dropping into meditation. I would put on some music or look at the scenery. After relaxing my body, then I would say to myself: *I am ready.* I would close my eyes and begin to feel the energies flowing within my system.

Then you teach yourself so well that you can drop deeper as you are talking, just as I am doing right now. You can rejuvenate yourself at work with one deep breath. It is a gradual thing, yet is escalated swiftly if you understand that it is gradual. If you understand the simplicity of it, it moves itself; but if you force it, it pushes you back. If you understand that you do not have to force it, automatically it goes by itself, and in doing so, it escalates your ability to comprehend. You learn to go at a pace that is usable for you. There are those days when you are so relaxed. Everything is happening just right because you are allowing it to flow. Then there are other days where you try to rush, and things begin to happen not to your liking. That tells you to slow down.

Usually I would have two meditations in the evening. In the first one I rejuvenated my mind and body, which gave me a different entrance into the second meditation later on in the evening. The second meditation was more balanced, more secure. I could use that plateau to begin to comprehend and get information. If I felt something in my toes, I would ask: *Why am I feeling something in my toes? Why is the energy on my right side, not the left?* I would receive the information: *The right side of the body is male; the left side, female. Doesn't everything have dualities to it?* It mushrooms itself. You begin to ask the right questions. You begin to grow and interrelate it to consciousness: *Now, if I know my right foot deals with survival, and I am on this earth plane and part of the total conscious awareness of humanity...*

You begin to deal with multi-dimensional reality. For instance, there are cells in your body that think you are it: you are their universe. Similarly we are cells upon this earth plane, but we can grow and use the earth plane because we are transcendable. Somewhere within our existence we learned how to stand up on two legs, and our crown center interrelated to higher levels. Just by doing that it gives us the capability of using more than what we were given at birth, whereas animals just have that earthly vibration to deal with.

Ask questions in meditation. I cannot stress that enough. When I felt something in meditation, I would stop right there and say: *Whoa! What is going on here? Why am I feeling and sensing this? What does it interrelate to, so I can become a better person?* I always listen to whatever it might be. I also never listen to anything that might participate in any semblance of harm happening to myself or anyone else. I always go on the premise that whatever I allow to come through me that I have to extend to another person is going to change me before it changes the other. For instance, if you have hate, what is going to happen? Hate is going to come through you, and a certain portion of it is going to stay with you. Wouldn't you like to have more love and balance, rather than hate? I am not saying hate does not have its existence within the awareness of the framework of comprehension, but what would you rather have come through you? You have to understand the usage of whatever it is. Water is good, but if someone holds your head under water for a few minutes, you are dead. How do you understand the usage of something? By taking the opportunity of the meditative state and slowing yourself down so you can look at it. Remember, you are opening yourself up, so anything that you comprehend within that structure stays with you because it is absorbed instantly into the reality of what you are. It has more of a profoundly beautiful effect of changing you. That is what you are teaching yourself. I like the second meditation for transcending. Then there are days when I skip meditation too. Maybe I want a little exercise instead. You will understand what is right for you.

Third questioner: **I was meditating and thinking that I have just about everything I want. There is no misery in my life, no stress to get rid of. I do not want to be done. I try to have things that I am responsible for.**

When you hit certain absolutes in meditation, there will be ringing proof of the reality of that being so magnificent, you will understand that something more has to come. What you are dealing with is some complacency within your reactions. There will be stimulation that will take you out of that place. Watch out for what you ask for though, because sometimes when you ask for something, there will be an event that comes along, and you do not understand why it is coming along to change the reality of what you are. For instance, you might say: *I am having a boring time; I want something to bring me out of this!* Then suddenly something will happen to you. So just understand that something will come. Just keep meditating. Keep yourself balanced.

Fourth questioner: **I feel some tingling in my head. I asked a question about it but did not quite get an answer.**

At first, you will not get an answer. Maybe you are asking the wrong question, so just keep asking. Sometimes if you do not get an answer, you ask: *Why am I not getting an answer?*

You are feeling tingling? That is good. I feel that throughout my body. If I take a deep breath, I feel tingling from the tips of my toes to the top of my head. I feel a vortex of energy at the top of my head that is awesome. The more you feel and sense in meditation, the more you become usable within the flesh. That is good. That is an improvement for you because there were certain times you were not feeling anything.

Fifth questioner: **I had a dream where I was back in my hometown. I was driving down a familiar street but there was a fire truck there blocking the road, so I had to turn off onto a side street. Finally I came to an open area that was somewhat high. I could see familiar landmarks around the city, yet this side street became a very strange place, a totally foreign culture to me. There were families there who were very unusual. I did not seem to belong to that place.**

It is interesting that you went back to a place you recognized. It brought you back to a point where you recognized aspects from your childhood. Then it brought you into the directions of the unknown: some of the misconceptions in the reality of your choices when you were younger, and now the changes you have made in your adult life in regard to survival. The foreign things that you look out at now, represent you understanding that there is something different and unrecognizable in the reality of what you are participating in now. Some of the points that you are looking at seem foreign to you, but there will be something there that you will eventually deal with within the sustenance of it. A very good dream for you: one of the best dreams you have had.

What are dreams? Dreams are a reaction within the involuntary system, the unconscious state of what we are, changing chemical reactions within the body in order for us to participate in our normal, daily lives with some semblance of balance. Meditation is the same thing, only dealing with the conscious mind, and you are in control of the conscious mind. When you are in the dream state, the soul is in charge of the reality of it, changing the density of what you are. Some of those traumatic dreams are seemingly shock therapy, helping you to change the chemical reactions. It is teaching you to react within particular situations with more stability. Even though the dream is frightening you at that level, fear causes certain adrenaline or chemical changes within your system, and those reactions help you cope with situations in your tomorrows. So when we look at dreams from that point of view, we think of how truly unique the system of comprehension is: even within our ignorance we have the reality of the sustenance of something we do not truly understand, yet it is giving us that information anyway. That is truly unique! Even if we are ignorant, we get that sustenance because the soul is doing everything it can to give us some semblance of balance within the physical sense.

Sixth questioner: **I had a dream about being in a dark basement and my teeth were hurting.**

Your hands and feet interrelate to survival. Your teeth interrelate to many different things within the body. When I am in a deep-trance state, I can feel my gums vibrating and rejuvenating. Teeth also interrelate to what we project out verbally. In your case you have to project more of an image of being solid within your love of self and understanding of survival energies. The dream of being in the basement is basic foundation information dealing with dark, unknown situations. You have to become stronger. Understand that nobody is better than you. You are just as good as anybody else. Work on your survival energies, which is "love of self." Feel very good about yourself. If there is something you have to work on, work on it. That problem gives you a ballpark, a particular sphere you want to comprehend, to make you better than you were before.

You are where you should be within your comprehension. How important that is. When you get a vision, use it for incentive. When I have a bad day, I say: *What is happening here? I put myself here, here, and here.* If you understand why you put yourself in a particular place, it becomes a better day because you are comprehending whatever it is that put you there; then the chances of ever getting there again are less than what they were before. Then you will amaze yourself how strong you are when something comes into your life that seems to be overwhelming, and how much more strength you have to help your family.

Logic tells you, you will have it, because you have grown to the point where you have given yourself enough strength. Let us meditate.

(With music in the background, the class drops into a deeper state of meditation:) When you hear a piece of music like this, you do not need a deep breath, you just need the thought: *Just think of relaxation.* Just think of the notes touching you. As they do so, they have a very tranquil effect upon your mind and body. The notes were made just for you. Everything upon this earth plane was put here for you. Use it. These notes touch you, and as they do so, they relax you. If you want to be a bird flying, feeling relaxed, you can be it. If you want to be looking at a sunset, you can. If you want to feel good about yourself, you should. If you want to see yourself succeeding in normal daily chores, you have the right to do so, as long as you do not infringe upon another person's free will.

These are the things I want you to use within your mind to become a better person. Each time that you do so, you put dry wood upon the flame of what you are. It glows. You become different. You become a person that others can come to for help. You become a fountain within the physical sense. Your words change, your information changes, the reality of what you are changes. A unique thing takes place: you change the common denominator of humanity. Everything that you do in a good way brings about more good for everybody. Every time you allow love to come through you, there is more love for everything and everybody. If you see an injustice, work on yourself, because if you become stronger, the injustice has more of a chance of being eliminated. If you see injustices coming at you, and you are strong, you have an armor of purity and perfection that cannot be penetrated. I love you.

The piano notes become you. Listen to the music; feel it and sense it. That uniqueness that you feel now, use it as incentive to feel more. There is more. There is always more. The uniqueness never contradicts that absolute moment that you feel. It only enhances your capabilities. I wish for you that you see yourself in a balanced way: at first slowly, then through comprehension, the ability is increased. I want you to see joy and happiness in your life. Feel it within you. Feel the strength. Within me I know there is Everything, which is God. I use a portion of It each day, and each day everything becomes more usable. Someday, more of It becomes the enlightenment for each moment. What you do for yourself now, you reward yourself for every moment of every day that will come forth. Know it. Use it as incentive. You truly are refueling the supply of energy that is necessary for you to go forward with balance and love and compassion, and to understand this place that we live in. If your circumstances seem rough to you, it is because you are so strong that you can take it; if they seem light to you, it is because you have won the right to be there and to have them light: either way, so usable. Begin to see how your mind can use everything correctly for you, not against you.

Am I being selfish if I tell you, I love you? Because I know as I do so, I know more will come within me. If the reality of that is true, and I say it knowingly, without any strings attached other than from one human being to another, it is selfish with the intent to share. But then if you truly look at it, it is not selfish at all: it is you understanding the analogy to a situation that makes you have the ability of understanding that everything is usable for self. Within the wonderment of what you are, praise is needed until praise is no longer needed; but until then, use it, knowing that it is necessary for you. Feel good about yourself.

CHAPTER NINETEEN

New Laws Concerning the Singular Self
March 1, 2000

First questioner: **Lately certain situations have made me more aware of my reactions towards others and what I need to learn in regard to that, and I have felt a lot of inner trauma like I have not experienced over twenty years. At one point I was in the grocery store just sensing other people's inner conflicts and was bothered by it.**

That is great. You are finally getting to the point where you can allow your emotions, your true feelings, to come out rather than holding them in. We will not get into it more than that, but that is fantastic. That is growth. You cannot feel the wind until you come out of the house and you cannot comprehend the wind until you feel it.

Second questioner: **You mentioned a while ago, if you did not learn to take care of yourself when you were younger, it would be much harder to take care of yourself when you are older.**

Meaning that your body will deteriorate so much when you get older, you do not have a chance to take care of it. Let us say you were learning to be a farmer: wouldn't it be nice if you had one small acre and you learned how to farm on just that one acre? But if you have to make a living by farming, and do not learn how to farm on that acre, suddenly when you have acquired several more acres, you do not have the capacity to refract to those areas. The same thing takes place, as you grow older. As you go through your lifetime from the involuntary system, you automatically go through different changes within the levels and stages of life, but if you have not solved the first stage, your comprehension does not have the capacity to refract to the next new stage. For instance, if in the first twelve years you did not work on your survival and "love of self" to the point where it is secure, it becomes more difficult to solve your survival in your teenage years because you have more awareness and are automatically given a whole new area to work with. If you have not learned to love yourself, and suddenly are thrown into a whole new picture, it becomes more confusing. You are refracting to the next stage, which is duality, sensuality and the capacity to emanate life form forward. All of a sudden, you are experiencing

136

thoughts and feelings in your body about other people like you have never felt before. There is a bombardment of attraction between you and another, and if you are not ready for it, the fear of the confrontation does not push you into a relationship but pulls you out of it. You are in such an outer orbit of that sphere that you do not have the comprehension of what that nucleus is. You are outside of the context of what you should be dealing with within the realm of understanding the purity of that nucleus.

Now, when you are more secure in your duality, there are other things that come into play. I have been giving it some thought about some of the things that I allow myself to fluctuate into with my wife. For instance, sometimes I am unfair: I go too far off into seeing the absolute of a particular act of hers; then I allow myself to get involved in the punishing act of it. In other words, there is so just much dissecting going on. I see little strains of what she does and tell her about it. It is unfair to her that I do that, so I am going to work on that. I am going to make it something that is more pliable. I am not going to react in the realm of dissecting it. I will understand it as a duality that I can build from, rather than seeing it as an avenue that might push that particular structure into another place. I am going to make it confined to an area of comprehension.

Let us talk about another stage. When we hit the age forty to forty-five, if we had perfect sight previously, our sight will start to deteriorate at that juncture because we are refracting through another level. This happens to everyone on the planet. The capacity of insight is now blurred within the physical sense because there is a flaw within humanity that we cannot participate above. Someday, when the capacity of humanity gets to the level where it can have that insight, the flaw that interrelates to the weakness within the muscles of the eye will no longer happen because we will have won the right to be above it.

We are talking about insight tonight. You will begin to see some of these things when you work at a particular level. It gives you the capacity of having insight into the reality of the physical reality rather than insight into oneself, another person, or a few people. It gives you the capacity to refract through those levels and see trends within the realm of humanity. It gives you strains or tendencies within humanity. It makes you see a pathway where humanity is going. It is a pleasure to see at that level, but also becomes drudgery at the physical level. If you are dealing with those strains, it is difficult. You see how a particular person uses one sentence, and how a reaction can take place within the realm of how they comprehend their mind, and it is not a pleasurable thing to see. You refract yourself, and your reactions are beyond where they should be, because your mind is beyond where it should be within the realm of that capacity. So those things have to be worked on as you refract through different areas of understanding the awareness of where you are and what you have refracted through.

Now, as you progress through the different stages in life, if you do not work on the objectives of each level, there is more confusion between all of the levels. There is more confusion and deterioration within the body, and less ability to control the reactions in your health, or the health of those around you. So what do you do? You just react to the best of your capabilities. For all of us there will be events that stick in our minds and make us comprehend certain things. For instance, one day one of my daughters was going through some difficulties, and I was admonishing her; suddenly there was a flash in my mind: *I am trying to correct something that I gave her! It is my own fault. She got it from me genetically.* Her problem gave me another chance to see my own flaw from a new vantage point. So I turned to her and told her that I was sorry; that it was a flaw that I gave her, and that I would work on it with her to try to eliminate it from the both of us. Parents blame the child for something they gave the child. They have not comprehended it, so it reacts within them when they see a similar reaction from the child. What they have to do is comprehend it and deal with it.

Third questioner: **I watch Opra Winfrey occasionally and one of her guests was talking a lot about the soul, saying the soul is the greater part of us and is very powerful.**

Yes it is. Have we ever said anything here that would contradict that?

Reply: **No, but I was curious about a statement the person was making, "…and this seems to be true of humanity, nobody has an easy time of it."**

That is absolutely wrong. That is an untrue statement. There are people that have a very easy time of it. There are times when I look at my life, and I can honestly say I have worked very hard for where I am, no question about it, but I always thought that it was very easy. I have had brief moments of thinking it is tough, but then when I had those brief moments, I looked at them to say: *Why am I having those brief moments? It is because I put myself in that position to look at that particular thing as being tough.* That is why my daily job does not bother me. That is why I am not bothered when I do something else, or do not get mentally tired from doing anything. I try to make certain people see that within their minds. If they see something as drudgery, they are going to feel the burden of it, and it is going to come back and haunt them as fatigue. I do not regard work as being that. I see it as something that I have to do. I am not saying that I will not get physically tired, because I do, but I can rejuvenate myself in a quicker fashion because of the ability of seeing the quality of the mind.

How does that work? Let us say you have a gallon of water, which is your energy for the day; then you have a negative thought and a little energy seeps out. When you have a positive thought, there is a little esoteric faucet up there that starts dripping: a small stream at first, then a little more. You say: *Wow! I just had a drink, and the water level is not going down.* The water is being replenished by the ability of your mind to comprehend that stabilizing quality in your reactions that does not extinguish the energy but participates in drawing it in. If there is one thing that I can give anybody, it is that.

I know when I escalate myself into some areas where the energy is dissipating. I can feel it. I know I can react easier within the framework of humanity than I can within the duality of life. I am totally happy in my marriage, but within the duality of it, it is much more difficult for me to comprehend a stabilizing quality in the essence of what escalates me into a misconception. I can do it within that framework, but when I have that heart open, and give all of me, when I give it, there is something about it: it is as if you are giving the other person the ability to tip the pitcher over. In other words, you are not the only one that can extinguish you. I am not saying my wife is this way, but I am saying, if there is a person on the side of you that works the direct opposite of what you are, and you have just so much energy, it is just like a river that flows constantly to the other. So you have to reevaluate the parameters of the capacity of the reservoir of what you are; then you have to stabilize your reactions within that quest, and that is something that you have to work on. When you give yourself to the other, and there is duality involved, the other can drain you because you have opened up that channel so much to the other. You have to work on those dualities to the best of your ability. You make that reservoir bigger, with more information pertaining to the reality of that sphere of duality, marriage, partnership, or whatever it might be.

But I do not think "Nobody has an easy time of it" is a fair statement. I can debate that person on it. As a matter of fact, I know it is not a fair statement, because I know what I have felt in my life, and I am sure there are other people who feel the same way. I would say there is a statement pertaining to the reality of it, "A lot of people have drudgery within their lives because of the misuse of their minds within that capacity." That person's statement is interesting though. You can almost read the reaction within them and what they are going through in life. You can almost see the strain of the lifetime of what that participation is that puts them into the particular position that can make a statement like that. In other words, they are outside of the avenue of understanding that there truly is a blessed event that can take place in the reactions of what we are.

Do you honestly think Christ thought it was tough? I do not think so. He could have made it so easy. Now there is a pathway: if we think about it for a while, there is a pathway that can make it easy but rough within the probability of the theme of why we are here. That is a different story. In other words, the story is that an individual wants to come upon the earth and make a theme, and they know someday they are going to be nailed to the cross. Let us say that Christ could have had a very easy option when the guards came to take him away; he could have just mentally said: *Please get out of my way,* and they would have been out of his way. Now, within the capacity of understanding the probabilities that he had to set in motion in that lifetime, Christ knew the events that would take place. He knew there was going to be drudgery, trauma and misconception, and people who hated him, and people who did not actually hate him but feared him to the point where they were going to kill him because he contradicted their position in life. He contradicted the rabbis and their power, and he knew within that structure that it was going to be turned against him even within the realm of the honesty of what he was. That is a unique set of probabilities: he took a pathway that did no harm but caused harm upon self, because he chose to set that pathway in motion to achieve a theme within humanity that gave others pathways of understanding the identity on how to grow.

We can take it a step beyond that to say that Christ's avenue then contradicted the statement, "Nobody has an easy time of it." To make it easier for us all, Christ cleared the vegetation of misconception to make a path for all of us to go down. So that statement is a contradiction within the realm of understanding even the theme of Jesus, Buddha, or other great entities. Moses went down the pathway of which I understand a lot more, of understanding the reality of the misuse of the mind, and how it comes back upon each of us in regard to our personal reality. He made the statement, "If you say my son is going to die, you are saying your own son is going to die. By saying such a negative thing, you allow the vibration to come through you, and it is going to happen to you, not me." That is the law Moses set in motion.

Now there is a new theme set in motion regarding laws within the realm of understanding the capacity of the singular self towards the destruction of the singular self; they are new laws; if you allow them to float through you, they become the reality of you: why allow something that comes through you to flow in a negative way rather than a positive way? Does it say that it is easy every moment? No. It says that on a particular day when you look upon the reality of it, it is easy within the structure of that rubber band of the reality of what you are, as it stretches out from when you were born. It does not say that there will not be a little trauma within that band. It does not say that there will not be moments of harm, pain or agony. When I look at the sphere of, "Nobody has an easy time of it," I never saw it as hard! I really never did! Even when there were extremely tough times, I never saw those tough times as negative, strenuous or overwhelming. I always saw them as that growth avenue that made me what I am, that always had the capacity of bringing me to a new and more usable place. So when I see all of my life from that level, and look at that statement, it is not usable within the realm of saying that all of us are like that.

I sit for moments and say: *Well, if I am within the structure that is comprehendible within God, and everything is God, and I grow within that structure, if I see trauma somewhere, I can change it into a more pliable, suitable area of comprehension. That gives me the right to do that, so there will be less of that out there.* "Nobody has an easy time of it," becomes even more of what contradicts the normal reality of growth within the physical sense. Your job and everybody's job should be to grow so much. As you do so, each time you feel more love, or have a good thought, even if you do not think it extends itself past the singular, it does. It has that capacity to roam throughout humanity. You do not know that it goes somewhere, but it does go somewhere. It goes into that collective consciousness, and there is more love there, even though you are not aware of it at that moment. The love or the good thought is filtering through you, but it does have that capacity. So the uniqueness of the ignorance of this happening even becomes a compelling factor of understanding the Uniqueness of God. Even in our ignorance, the Awareness of God becomes That Which deals with that capacity. God purifies and cleanses humanity because we have a good thought.

What does that do for you? Remember that vessel? As you are pouring water into the vessel, you are receiving it. It is like when we talk about healing: when you are healing others, if you are involved in the true reality of what is going on, you do not feel tired. When we had the big classes, people would line up for healings, and they would ask me, "How could you do so many healings before class? Don't you get depleted?" How could I do that? It was a privilege to allow healing energies and information to flow through me, and to learn from the process! Each time, it was me doing the healing. If you think that is egotistical, that is wrong. If I do not think it is me, then I will not be more than what I was before, for the next time I heal. So as it came through me, it was a pleasure. When I was done, I did not feel I was depleted. It stimulated my comprehension to try to grab upon a new aspect of healing, and if I could, just a piece of it, then there was more within me for the next time I sat in front of a person. That was the incentive of it.

"Nobody has an easy time of it." I love a statement like that. It is a beautiful statement but is wrong. I love the way it can trigger you into a reaction. Number one, you cannot make a statement like that because you do not know how everybody else feels. *I* can make a statement that contradicts that, because what I feel contradicts it. It is like saying I would know how I would feel to see Lazarus rise up and walk away: I do not know how that feels! I know in the back of my mind that somebody might have a capacity to do that. Sometimes when I feel a strain of something that might hit upon a portion of that realm, I say: *This could be a true capacity within the realm of us eventually,* and it gives me the incentive to want to go towards it.

Now, let us consider another avenue. If Christ could make Lazarus rise, he could make him die, or he could have had the thought: *Hey, fellas, I do not want to be crucified today. I do not want you near me!* If he had had such a thought, nobody would have been near him that day. There was that much power within his mind. But let us get back to what that capacity would have dealt with within the misconception of the reality of the whole thing: number one, it would have been a contradiction to everybody around him, and number two, it would have been a contradiction to the free will or the absolute credibility of what he truly was. So he could not do that. If he were truly at that level, that statement would have been a contradiction to the theme of what he was.

You see, I am nothing, but what you get here has no contradiction from me. What you get here is absolute from me. Whether it is here, there, or wherever, it does not have a contradiction in it within my theme, just as the thought: *I don't want to be crucified today,* would have been a contradiction to everything Christ did. For instance, when people asked Christ a question regarding others, do you ever wonder why he did not answer? He would say, "If the person said that about me, ask them." He did not give the person's name because he would have had to denounce them. That is why he did not answer. Why did he give stories? Because the stories had nothing to do with anyone in particular, but illustrated a theme within humanity. He did not want to infringe upon another's free will because it would have contradicted the theme of the reality of why he was here. Nothing he did contradicted that. If it did for a brief moment, it gave itself the ability to overtake it in the next moment.

For instance, why did Jesus make the statement, "Lord, why have

You forsaken me?" Because it makes us understand that a little, little portion of him was still within the flesh, and there is weakness within the flesh from misconception, which is necessary within the reality of comprehension. So those events give you little tidbits into the reality of the sustenance of understanding where you are and what you can participate in. That is the uniqueness of All of This, and what does it hit? A person like Jesus who had so much energy, no matter what he said was believable. Even people who wanted to harm him knew they were harming someone that should not be harmed. But they had to harm him, and it was so extraordinary. Those who were nailing him to the cross and doing all of those harmful acts were looking at him and saying, "What are we doing to this man? He has not done anything!" They knew it, but still did it because it was within the theme of what Christ set in motion as that capacity within the framework that made it usable for everybody. Who do we blame? Do we blame Judas for running out and doing what he did? Christ said to him, "Go and do what you have to do." He knew Judas was going to do it. Did he condemn him for it? Absolutely not.

Sometimes we meet up with people who have the capacity to misinterpret within the framework of certain religions. For instance, the other day a lady told me, "I worship the Living God." I said, "That is nice; so do I; I also worship the Dead God." If you say something like that, the other person looks at you as if you are crazy. I said, "I just worship God."

So He is living to you? I want to know why He is living to you. Is He living because that comprehension makes you a better person? Well then, God bless you, It should be a Living God. But when it contradicts the Reality of the Living God as it interrelates to another person, then you are wrong, because then you are infringing upon whatever capacity of the Living God. What do you mean when you say you are "born again?" What happened? Did you die for a minute? You see, a remark like that then triggers something within these people. Born again? You are born again, every second. In the next thought you are born again. In the next comprehension you are born again; you are born closer to that reality. Do you make religion a misconception? Does it make you feel superior to be Jewish, Catholic, or Protestant? Think of the holy wars waged in the name of God or Jesus. How could Jesus possibly tell you to kill a person when he did not do any of that? He did not kill anybody or blow up a plane. How could you say that? It is not true.

A statement is only true when it is interrelated to the properties of purity within the realm of what that person Jesus is. For instance, if I happen to hit my finger with a hammer and yell out, "Jesus Christ!" even within the ignorance of what I am at that moment, I am drawing in energy from Jesus Christ. Think about that for a moment. I did not even have one thought about Jesus: all I know is that I hit my finger, and the pain came, and I said, "Jesus Christ!" What do you think happens then? I am an ignorant fool and even I can even use it! Isn't that wonderful? Isn't that incentive for us all? Doesn't that make us seek out those hidden chunks of sustenance within the reality of what we are? The next time I hit my finger, I am going to say, "God, Jesus Christ and Mary!" Then I am going to see them all up there smiling and saying: *He is a foolish little guy!* But then they might also be saying: *He has a portion of It, anyway. He knows when he hits his finger he is going to get energy, and the idiot is going to keep on hitting his finger with the hammer just to try it out.* You see, they would be smiling because they know you are trying. When they cry is when you do not try, or you take something and twist it into something that is totally outside of the context of the reality of the theme of what was set in motion. They cry within that realm: not truly crying but crying from understanding that we are going down the wrong pathway.

By the way, those tapes are good for you. I do not mention that out of praise for myself, I mention it out of what I hear coming back to me. It is really helping people in profound ways, and you are part of that. Each tape that we make, you are part of that power that goes out. Believe me, you are. You are helping people to balance their minds and bodies. You are actually helping people to eliminate cancer, high blood pressure and different things. It is bringing them into the center. You are making them understand what they have within themselves. Those qualities are within all of us.

If you read the book "COMMON AS RAIN," that title came to me. I am common as rain, and if *I* can do it, anybody can do it. I am not outside of the realm of misconception, greed, lust or whatever. I am involved in all of that, but not to the degree where it overwhelms me. Whether you believe it or not, there is no sham. There is no reason for me to do that. I do not ask that you stay in the classes. If you stay, I love that you stay. If you go, I love that you go. You have had enough, and most people do.

Does anyone have more questions? Make it fun. Do not make it drudgery. Work on yourself. It is easier to do so. I am going to work on myself. Each time you come, I am going to be more than what I was before, and each time you come here, I bet you are going to be more than what you were before. Where does it start? Right here in the mind. If you misuse the mind, you can have the Mona Lisa smile, and in a week you look like a blob on the wall, because every time you touch it, you are blurred. If you use it right, everything is enhanced. It is your mind that controls the reaction of everything about you.

CHAPTER TWENTY

Dealing With the Plague of Our Reactions
April 5, 2000

First questioner: **In the meditation tonight I experienced a very different energy flow for me. Usually I receive a lot of rejuvenation within the legs. I felt some of that, but the main thrust seemed to be in the lower abdominal area.**

That is great. The three main lower centers of the body deal with: the survival center, "love of self," the sacral center, "love of another," and the solar plexus center, "love of many." The fourth center is the heart center, "love of humanity." You are in that mix now. Before, you were dealing with the secondary centers in the legs, which interrelate to the first center of survival. You are going to see some improvement in your reactions towards others now. You might be over-reacting, which would be unusual for you. That is all right; pull yourself back, comprehend and work on your reactions from the meditative state, which is a place of absorption. You are putting yourself in that place where you can absorb the reality of whatever you are dealing with. In doing so you can retain it and put it in motion in the reactions of that particular sphere of comprehension during the day.

Reply: **Yes, I really do not let my reactions flush through me. I hang on to them and internalize them.**

That is all right too, because you have to learn to get involved in those reactions. You have spent your whole life in the academic world so you have never had those reactions that you should have been involved in. Absorb, feel, sense and use them, but do not let them control you. You control your reactions within the particular things that you deal with now. If you feel yourself being flushed into an overwhelming area, slow it down by saying: *Hey, I am going too far. I am beyond that control. What should I do? What should I question within my reality that interrelates to control over that velocity?* Usually it is interrelated to duality, or something in that structure. Duality is so important within the refractability of comprehension, giving us the emotions that are so important. That is wonderful.

Second questioner: **When you are meditating and going deep, how deep do you go, or where are you going?**

Every time you meditate, you are bridging the gap between you and your soul, and are becoming closer to the reality that made you. Use that deepness to understand that you are going closer to the Source that has made you. When you go to that level, you are obtaining some of the reality of that particular structure. Bring it back; in order for more to come, you have to use it. Then what happens, when you deal with the reality of the energy that you were born with in a balanced way, the energy sources within your body begin to change. When you hit a certain graduating moment in consciousness by dealing with the reality of yourself within the physical sense, the survival source at the base of the spine, which initially faces down, will turn upwardly and become crystallined in white, and you open up a vortex of energy that floods through your system, right out through the crown center going to the reality of your soul. It interrelates to the seven different levels that you left there for you when you refracted from your soul to here within the physical sense. With this graduating moment, you absorb some of the layers.

Reply: **Am I absorbing? Because I cannot find anything.**

Yes, you are.

Reply: **Can you see things too?**

You can see certain things, but you will feel a lot of things. You use those things pertaining to the reality of your life for you.

Reply: **What if I do not understand what they mean?**

Slow down and ask questions when you see something: *Why am I seeing a certain thing? What does it interrelate to? How could I use it in my normal, daily life? How could I become a better person?* Everything has to be used within your normal daily life, or no more will come. I do not care if you read the Cabala, Bible, Sanskrit, or whatever, if you do not take the information and use it, no more will come because that is a contradiction to growth. So if you see something even as you are relaxing, ask a question about it. When I used to go through the different levels, I would stop and say: *Hey, there is something going on here. I do not understand it. What is going on?* If you do not do that, the soul knows you are not ready for further information. You have to control it within life before more will come.

Third questioner: **I used to meditate, but became fearful because I did not know why I was seeing these things, so I stopped.**

That is a contradiction to growth. Now that you understand that, in meditation when you see something that is fearful, stop: if you see a face, color or feeling, stop and say: *I want to stay right here. Why am I in this place?* You are in control. That is the main thing.

Fourth questioner: **I find it very difficult to put it into words what I want to ask in meditation.**

Then you have to slow down in meditation. You are going too deep, too fast. Ask: *At what level am I comfortable?* You see, when I go into a basic meditation I will feel and sense my energy field, and what is going on. Consider yourself first: if you do not worry about you, that is a contradiction to loving another person. If you do not have enough love of self, if you do not have balance, you cannot give love to another. What you have to do is give yourself the opportunity to cause some semblance of balance within your system by rejuvenating the body. What does that do for you? Most people are on a seesaw in life, going up and down. When you are in meditation, you are bringing the reality of that seesaw into the center and giving yourself the opportunity to absorb whatever it might be. If you are feeling an imbalance in your body, ask: *What am I feeling? What am I sensing? Why am I feeling this here?* That is what I mean by questioning the reality of what is going on.

Each part of your body has a consciousness. I trace things through my system. Anything that you get in this classroom did not come from a book but from the reality of questioning what was going on in my body and how I could interrelate it to mundane reality, which is putting it in place and understanding the value of it. What happens then? The energy becomes different within the lower centers. The temperature within the thermometer of you begins to build and lift up through the centers. You are igniting different portions of those centers that interrelate to different levels or layers that you left there. You are absorbing them. How do you suppose Christ brought Lazarus up from the dead? He could do so because he was at the level that made Lazarus within the physical sense. He was so perfect within himself by absorbing those layers. When Jesus was a little boy, don't you suppose he had colds like any other child, and ran through the streets and had neighbors yell at him? Of course, he did, but he took what he had and questioned it to the point where he perfected it. Then more layers were integrated within him. The layers became him within the flesh, changing him within the flesh. He became closer to the reality that made him, until eventually he absorbed so much of it that he actually became a god within the physical sense.

Logic tells you, when you are closer to the reality that has made you, you have more of the knowledge and refractability of consciousness coming through you, and more capability of healing the body. In meditation you give yourself an opportunity to go through life not having all those diseases that affect most people. There are so many things out there that can get you, but by dealing with the reality of balance within meditation, you eliminate the probability of those things happening to you. The reality of balance is so unique in itself. That alone should give you the incentive to want to meditate.

Fifth questioner: **Do we ever get to the core of self?**

Yes, we do. There are times when you hit such an absolute perfection within yourself that it is awesome.

Reply: **Does it take a long time?**

No, it does not.

Reply: **I cannot find it. It is hiding.**

You think you cannot find it, but you can. It is not hiding. Do you know what happens? It crops up at times when you cannot believe it will crop up. Suddenly you get answers to things and you say: *Why didn't I think of that before?* Then you will get the answer: *You did not think about that before because you were light years away from it before.*

For example, there are a lot of people who believe that there is a devil, and that if they do bad deeds, the devil will punish them. That is a good and usable enough level if you are dealing with adolescent thoughts within the physical sense that pertain to the structure that says: *If I do something not so good, I am going to be punished.* By using that as incentive, you do good deeds for the next time. Now, you might hit a level that goes beyond that where you look back at the concept of the devil to say: *If everything is God, and everything is good, how does the devil fit in?* Then you understand that there is no devil, but there is the incentive of the devil that gives you the quality to question yourself so you can lift yourself beyond that particular level. Once you understand that, you do not denounce the original understanding. You look upon all of that as good. It never becomes a contradiction to where you are now; rather, it becomes a usable vibration of understanding how it made you what you are today. When I was a little boy, the nuns would tell me that the devil was going to come after me. I remember asking them, "Well, you told me everything is God, so how could the devil be bad and come after me?" Usually the reply was, "Don't question things like that!"

Reply: **I never thought of the devil. I knew there was Somebody watching over whether I did good or bad...**

That was you watching you.

Reply: **Me watching me? I thought it was God watching me.**

Do you think God is not so refracted beyond where you are now? It is as if you are saying you are watching the cells within your body. You are not watching the cells within your body, the total conscious awareness of you is watching the cells within your body. Similarly, you are like a cell within God. Maybe this earth is like a cell within God, and God is watching from the refractability of the laws that made All of This, but God is not up there saying: *I am watching that little Johnny down there, and he is a creep, doing a lot of wrong things.*

Reply: **God is everywhere.**

God is everywhere, because God is everything. If you understand that, then if you see something as being negative, the reason you see it as negative is because you do not comprehend it. Then you say to yourself: *Wow! That is pretty good! Now if I want to comprehend something, if I want to go forward from here and understand everything is good, I want to see it from different levels.* Then you begin to understand that everything is here for a reason. There are certain pains and agonies that you are going to go through, but if you understand why you are here: that you are here to grow, and that some of those pains and agonies interrelate to the growth of what you are, then you can use it for you.

For instance, you might lose a loved one, or see a sick or starving child, and wonder why there has to be that suffering and agony. We do not know the particular reasons why the afflicted person refracted self here within the physical reality. Perhaps pain and agony are given to the person for incentive. In fact, you do not know if your worst enemy is your best friend at another level, making you do things. I have learned so much from people who seemingly were my enemies. I have been teaching here for over twenty-four years, and have had people come into this class, and project energy and hatred at me, or phone me in the middle of the night, hallucinating that I was in bed with them. You cannot even begin to imagine the things I have gone through. I am not saying that back then I was not a little unbalanced myself from the energy, fine; but you cannot even believe what these people used to hallucinate about.

Sixth questioner: **Where does this information come from?**

It comes from the reality of having so much energy. The energy changes were awesome, believe me, but you learn to control them. You learn that there are certain things that will happen to you that are seemingly negative, but when you sit down and think about how they changed the reality of what you are, and pointed you in a direction, you look back on these events to say: *My God, I know it seemed tough at times, but whatever it was, made me more than what I was before.*

Reply: **Do we unconsciously harness our energy throughout our life?**

Meaning that we are using things that we do not know we have? Yes; that is the uniqueness of this place: we use so much from ignorance it is incredible! For instance, your heart is beating right now. Do you have to say: *Heartbeat, heartbeat,* in order to make it function? Do you have to say: *Cells, divide?* No, because so much of that is within the conscious awareness of you that will happen automatically because you have won the right to have that happen. It takes you out of the structure of maintaining that and puts you in another level so that your focus can be on comprehending what comes at you next. Now, as you do so, you change the reality of all of that, but you do not know you do. You cause that harmony within the system.

I guess I have been a very fortunate person in my life because people, even strangers, come up to me and tell me I always seem to be so happy. I have had bad days, but I guess my mind triggers a quality within me that changes those particular things. For instance, when you lose a loved one, your mind always has the capacity of taking those bad events, and putting them in a sphere, and comprehending them beyond where you normally would have comprehended them before. It is hard, but it puts you there, because it makes you understand the whole theory of what is going on. It is hard, but it is not as hard as if it would be if you did not have a semblance of balance within yourself.

Reply: **Sometimes I sit here and have a lot of questions inside of me but find it hard to formulate a question that does not sound like I am off the wall.**

The most stupid question sometimes leads you into the most profound places. I can tell you the honest truth, I entered this school maybe twenty-six years ago, and there was a woman teaching at this school that I drove completely whacky because I asked so many questions. There were so many questions rapidly coming through my mind. Finally she took me aside and said, "John, you are driving me crazy! Please stop!" My mind was escalating so much. Then it got to a point where she could not answer my questions.

Reply: **You were opening up...**

Yes, I was opening up fast. I could not absorb it so quickly, so I had to slow it down because everything physically, sensually and emotionally was changing so fast. It was unbelievable. I would get into bed at night and could feel the bed vibrating from the energy. It was awesome. I had to learn to control it. I knew it was from something in a past life, and I knew I had to control it in this one. It has changed me; people around me understand how it has changed me. I am not a well-educated man within the physical sense; I have a high school education. All this flow of information and energy could be natural coming only through some-one who has tapped into something, and that tapping into something is tapping into self and into a higher level of what you are.

Reply: **How do we know if it is bad energy or not?**

When it is pertaining to how you feel within the physical sense. There is no bad energy; it is your usage of the energy that matters.

Reply: **What if somebody sent me some bad energy?**

You use it. If you sent me hate now, I would refract it through me and use it as good.

Reply: **How do you know?**

It is so important that we take whatever it is and question it by saying: *I seem to be having a bad day. Why is this happening? Did I put myself in that position, or am I in that sphere of comprehension and there is a reason for me being in it?* Either way, it does not make any difference, because you are going to take the problem and put it upon your shoulders and comprehend why. By doing so, you are going to grow, no matter what it is. Then you have changed that seemingly negative thing.

Seventh questioner: **Can you perhaps say that a person who would do a harmful act towards you could simply be a fallen angel that is saying you are out of balance?**

Who do we blame for that harmful act? Do we realize that everything that we do, we eventually have to pay for? It has to filter through us, no matter if it is a reality or not. For example, let us say a person is in the habit of stealing a lot; then they get to the point where they eliminate it from their system and own a store. They would believe that others are stealing from them, no matter whether it is a true reality or not, because they have to pay back for all of that. So the person receives agony thinking that others are stealing from their store. In fact, they know others are not stealing from them, but the agony is still within them. In other words, we are going to pay back what we do, whether it is a true reality or an illusion. When we think of it in that way, if we go forward, we can begin to understand that we are going to have to pay for those bad deeds that we do, no matter what they are.

The defects might not even be our fault. We might have gotten them through genetics or whatever. There are certain things that are going to happen within our system pertaining to chemical imbalances that are going to cause us to do certain things. For instance, we find that some of those mass murderers have such chemical imbalances, they will never be right, and the imbalances came from that structure that made them. The two parents had something wrong with them when they were joining with their energy fields that made the particular person. Whatever it might have been at that moment, anger, or something else within the reaction of sperm going forward touching the egg and the joining of two, the total conscious awareness of the two blends in a certain refractive way within the structure of the particular individual. Who do we blame: the mother, father, or grandparent?

It has to come from a structure, so what we have to understand is that it is wrong to terminate the murderer's life because it infringes upon their free will to comprehend certain probabilities that were set in motion within the physical sense. But then we also look at it from another level: the person dies, goes back up, absorbs all of those reactions—all of the particular things that they were dealing with—and re-manifests a sphere that will once again manifest a body within the physical sense to go wherever they choose to go. Death: when we look at the total picture of the reaction within that absorption, on the physical level, death is not negative because we take the life and absorb it. It is just like the shutting off of the satellite around the moon because it is not functioning anymore, and taking the information and making a new satellite. The same thing takes place between the self and the soul in life. Our reactions within comprehension are so important within a harmful act. Usually when the reaction of a particular harmful act comes around for us to view again, we are not ready for it, and have to deal with the plague of it, whether it is a reality or not. That is the unique thing about it. Some people think that we have to wait to die in order to go through purgatory. No, the reaction becomes a flaw within our system, and even though we know that reality is not true, we deal with the plague of our reactions all of the time, until we finally filter it through our system.

Eighth questioner: **You were talking about the illusions we erect around us. How do those illusions filter through our system and how can we affect the speed of that?**

By sitting and comprehending what you have done to certain people within a particular act. Eventually it gets to a point where you have the ability to balance whatever it is so much within your system, because you flush it through you. It is like putting sand or grit within you: if you pour water through you, eventually you filter out the sand through your comprehension and have pure water again; but it takes a long time. Every once in a while, a grain of sand will pop out, and you will say: *Where did that come from?* That grain of sand is the grit that you put in there from the misconception of what you did when you were doing the harmful act. So the filtering is the ability of the mind to filter the misconception through the reality of what you are, making it something that no longer bothers you. It takes time. How many years did you do a particular thing? That is probably how many years it is going to take.

Ninth questioner: **I told you about a person who has neurological damage in his arm. He is constantly in pain. When I questioned you about that, you said that had something to do between he and his wife. Applying what you just said to that situation, I am going to assume that eventually if he understands and comprehends that misconception, the pain and disability in his arm will disappear?**

It all depends on how far back he goes into the awareness of what he is and how far he climbs upon the ladder of understanding the misconception. Disease is something totally outside of what you can do for mental anguish. Disease is something that has lingered within the misconception so long that it has finally manifested itself within the body. In order to eliminate the disease, it has to be within the comprehension of the person and where they can lift self in order to deal with the refractability of it. Let us say a person has problems in the stomach area: in order for the healer to deal with the consciousness that is necessary to heal the person, the healer would have to drop into the higher levels of what they are. The healer might not have the higher levels fully integrated within them in order to refract the necessary consciousness to the particular misconception. If the healer does not have the higher levels fully integrated, they can lift self only to where their ability is. The healer's ability might have some of the quality that would eliminate a portion of that, but if they do not have the total reality of that particular level within what they are at that moment, the healing will not happen.

Tenth questioner: **I tend to get headaches. Does that mean I manifested that somewhere along the way?**

That means that there is a probability within you genetically, or whatever, that you have to overcome. There are flaws within all of us. I know that if I do not work on my insight into the physical reality, my eyes are going to eventually deteriorate. My mother and father both have had eye problems. Does that mean that I should not take the blame for it? I am going to take the blame for it. I am going to say: *I have this genetic flaw within me, and I am going to work on that insight, that third-eye center, in order to eliminate the probability.* I can do so at times. I have a little pressure in one eye. If I am meditating and looking at myself, I can relieve the pressure. You can do the same. You have to begin to understand why the particular thing is within your system and cause some semblance of balance within you.

Now, as you are going along meditating and dealing with higher and higher energies within you, there is a probability within you that you can change the genetic process of what you have gone through. It is a very difficult thing to do. More likely, you will hit a level where you can control that reaction, so it will not have a detrimental effect on you, as you get older. That is what you should be striving for. Now, whether you caused it within you, or whether your parents gave it to you genetically, does it make any difference? No.

Reply: **I do not understand how you can change something biologically.**

Believe me, you can, by lifting yourself to the level that can change it. Have you often wondered why certain people who have had cancer, no longer even have a trace of it anymore within their system, and others who have cancer, within a month are gone? It is because certain people change the reaction of that misconception within their normal, daily life. If you are sick, you have to search out what you deal with within the physical sense and question the reality of what you can to become a better person. By doing so, you are going to achieve certain probabilities that will eliminate certain portions of that disease.

Do you realize how close we are in humanity of having a cure for cancer? We are very close. How could we escalate the abilities of those scientists who are working on that particular cure? By lifting yourself. Think about this: when one person finds a cure to a disease, there will be other people in other countries on the edge of solving the particular thing. When the conscious awareness of humanity lifts to that particular level, then that awareness can eliminate that misconception, but not before that. The same thing takes place in disease. You can do so within yourself. You can cause control within the disease within you. You can cause the reactions within you to begin to stimulate the particular things that will eliminate that disease from you. You can do it.

When a person has manifested something within self to the point where it has caused harm within the body, the person has disease within the body. When the person has caused the manifestation of harm within the mind, that has not yet caused that manifestation of harm within the body, it is different. The person might not get to the point of incurring disease; they might only go to the point where they have to eliminate it from the grit that they have put within self. But if they continue with the particular misconception, and never eliminate it, eventually there will be a disease coming forth. Eventually that grit becomes so heavy, it clogs a particular area. Then the misconception becomes a manifestation of disease within the physical sense.

Eleventh questioner: **Let us say I did not go down a road far enough to cause a disease but have a large misconception. What do I do?**

Do not do it again. Understand why you did it originally; then eliminate it from you. Then you are cleansing that particular level. Let us say you had a lack of compassion, which is within the heart center dealing with universal love. If you constantly have a lack of compassion, you deteriorate the center. Now, the secondary centers of compassion are within the elbows and knees, and they will be affected first. When you get a heart attack, your elbows or arms will tighten up first, because they are secondary centers to the heart, and the secondary centers dissipate before the major center dissipates. In order for you to rejuvenate yourself, you have to begin to understand how you use compassion within the physical sense. That is how you eliminate the disease from your body. Could you eliminate it totally? Only if you hit that level that has the reaction of understanding total compassion within that particular sphere; then you can eliminate it totally from your system. Normally what takes place, the reaction becomes so usable in comprehension that it eliminates the probability of the reaction eliminating you at an earlier age. You could live to a ripe old age having heart disease, but it will not overwhelm you until you are in your seventies, eighties or nineties. You might live to ninety-five, but that long time slot before your death from the heart disease gives you an opportunity to extend yourself through your probabilities in order to comprehend certain things.

Twelfth questioner: **The kleptomaniac who stops stealing but then years later is delusional about others ripping him off would then need to work with awareness in order to flush it through his system. He would then be involved in an archeological dig about why he was stealing years ago?**

Yes. Not only that, he would begin to understand that he would have to filter that act through him long enough where he can begin to withdraw his suspicious thoughts directed at others, thinking they are stealing from him. When he gets to that point where he sees the fault within self, not others, then he is getting closer to filtering it through the system.

Thirteenth questioner: **I am questioning what my complacency is about.**

In your case, complacency is good once in a while.

Reply: **Yes but multiple years of it...**

No, I do not think so. I think you do question yourself. Before, you used to question yourself so much that you used to hit yourself over the head with it. That was not good. Question yourself just right and use it. Eventually you question it just right so many times, when you look at it, it is no longer there; then you do not have to question it. It is just like approaching the sphere of a particular problem: you bring it right into the nucleus. You are not in the outer orbit. Then it becomes a reaction of understanding that the nucleus has then become you.

Does it totally eliminate that probability of something happening at another level? No. You might get the particular problem at another level, and have to look at it again at another level, but then you think of it in a totally different way: *Oh God, I am having a new opportunity to see this!* It is very important that you see it from that level. Then when you do that, your reaction will not be the consideration of going backwards, your reaction will be: *This is a new opportunity of seeing it from a different place. I am up on a higher rung on this ladder and can see into the valley a little farther.*

Fourteenth questioner: **My friend has had cancer but has a positive attitude. I think it has really kept the disease in check. She has a lot of stress but also a lot of determination.**

Yes. I am working on a woman now. She has had cancer in two different places, both of which are in total remission now. She went through that same sequence of events, but the amazing thing about her is her faith: every time she phones me and says to me, "Don't forget to work on me. Will I be seeing you this week?" We tell her, yes, we will go see her. It is her ability to say, "There is something here you are doing; whatever it is that you are doing, you are helping me." Another person might shut the healing off by saying: *This guy does not know what he is doing.*

If I were sick like that, I would be up with the Indians on the hill with the drums. Anything that would get me going! Anything that would help! If someone said they could help me, I would be there. The people who seek out anything, and everything, are the people who eliminate the disease from their bodies. This particular woman does not have a trace of disease in her right now, and she has been through a great deal with that chemo, too. Good night, everyone.

CHAPTER TWENTY-ONE

Where Healing Starts
April 12, 2000

First questioner: Is there a way to surround a person with good energy so that they do not become so affected by things coming at them?

Yes. You have that capability as long as your intent is pure and good and non manipulative. If you only want to help, you can always do something like that. It is so simple, yet so difficult, and when you look at it in the simplicity of understanding how to do it, it is so usable. If I just say to you, "Be well," what do you think happens? You are well to the extent of the capacity of my thought. Therefore, when you send a thought to another person, such as wishing them to be well, you are actually changing that density within the physical sense.

When we consider this, it seems like nothing to us, because we are always making those simple little thoughts. We have to give it a concentrated thought, a focus. We have to make sure it has a penetrating quality to it. Then you always have to add safeguards within yourself, telling yourself that you will have those normal thoughts that do not extend into changing the reality of others in a negative way. There are moments when you lose your focus or balance. I am sure all of us do. I know I do. When you have those kinds of thoughts, sometimes you have force within your thoughts and wish to bring them back. You will mentally understand that, and bring them back so they do not have an effect on others. This is all understanding the rewards that you have received through your growth process. You put in fundamental safeguards in order to participate within the physical sense with some normalcy, yet have the capacity to be beyond the normal flow within that structure. That is very important in knowing what the laws are that interrelate to the particular usage of all of those things.

Reply: I am making the assumption that this person that I care about can use that good energy around them. How do I know whether that is correct?

By making the assumption that the person might need it. You see how simple it is? By making the assumption that they might need it, gives it the capacity; that if they do not need it, it will not be received. Sometimes it is so blinding in its simplicity, we do not even see it. Sometimes I see something right in front of me and wonder: *What might that be?* It is right there, but suddenly I have to pull myself back to say: *What is going on here? What should I question?* But that particular thing: *Why? What would my intent be?* Flush yourself through it. There is a sequence of events that will take place in flushing yourself through it in order to grab upon the capacity of understanding the true usage of it as it penetrates towards the other person. It is important that you question the reality of that. Then you begin to understand what is going on in the filtering process to ask: *What are the laws interrelated to that? What could I do within that situation?*

For instance, sometimes you can work on a person, and send energy until it is coming out of your ears, and nothing is going to happen. Then you sit back and think about that for a moment: *What is going on here?* Then you might want to interrelate to the other's soul for a few moments. Some aspects will flash before your eyes that will refract you to all of the areas of misconception within the other, gathering information pertaining to that place that they are in. It is so rewarding when you see it from there. Then you can see why there are so many building blocks stabilizing the misconception within the other person, and that there are only certain things that you can do at that point. It is going against the reality of the other person filtering back towards the soul, and you cannot contradict that.

Let us discuss the nature of disease: it is participation within the physical sense, understanding what we can and cannot do. We have to start with self. For instance, you might say: *I am going to meditate to eliminate this bronchitis I have, or this broken knee.* But the true reality of eliminating that misconception from the body is to question why it is there: *What is making my body out of balance? What do I have to do to give my body more balance?* For example, before class I was mentioning that I am at a point now where I am eating too much and can feel a slight imbalance in my body; I have gained a little weight, which is unusual for me. But I can see the pathways that have put me in there: where I was working on the job and other factors. There are steppingstones going along a road that brought me to this point, and the steppingstones going back the other way have to be the corrective property in understanding how to eliminate that misconception. I consider it a misconception because a few extra pounds give me some semblance of imbalance within my system that I do not want. If I do not correct it now, the imbalance is going to be very difficult to correct down the road, because the habit becomes more profound within the essence of my mind and body.

So what do I do? I will make subtle changes in the direction that correct the misconception from the mind and body. I am starting tonight. My wife and I usually stop off somewhere after class for a snack. Tonight I will stop for my wife if that is what she wants, but not for me. I will go home and have maybe a small bowl of cornflakes. These are the steppingstones that are going in a direction. Tomorrow I will have a bagel with jelly rather than butter. When it comes time for lunch, I will have a couple of glasses of water before I eat, and I will not finish all of my lunch. In this way I start correcting and purifying myself in the direction of eliminating the misconception.

That is where healing starts: cutting the misconception off at the crossroads. What is causing an imbalance in your body? If you are feeling a pain in your elbow, what is that pain? What does it interrelate to, within every moment of your life? For instance, the right elbow on a male interrelates to the heart center, which is compassion and balance towards self and others. If you have a sore elbow, what do you question that day? You trace back through your day to see instances where you have had a lack of compassion and correct it within your identity. This is what I mean by using your mind correctly: you go back and correct. Then a similar event will come forward, and it *will* come forward because you are now on a pathway of comprehension. Your soul is involved, and there will be spheres of comprehension that you will go through that will be similar to those events that you were in before. Each sphere will be a different property, and will involve different people and locations, but it will have a similar effect on understanding how to eliminate it. It will be a motion picture of the reality of what is needed to deal within eliminating that misconception from the mind and body. In meditation you ask: *Where are the blockages?* An example of what can take place: when I was dropping deep tonight, I had a blockage in my left calf, which is on my female side, and I was questioning: *There must be something there that interrelates to compassion and balance of what? Maybe in my marriage? Maybe at work or somewhere else? Maybe I have to treat my wife a little better?* I will question that reality.

You know what you have to do within your mind and body. You know what it is within your body that is bothering you and causing a lack of harmony. It might be a lack of sleep, or too much of something like drinking, smoking, or eating. It might be your inability to speak out for yourself, or talk to other people. It might be over-reacting, or exhibiting too much anger. You know what you have to work on. You have to start. You can see it in humanity today, especially in the elderly people that you meet: if you do not want to be flawed when you get to that age, do not be flawed now in that hidden way. It is hidden there. Whatever it might be, it is hidden. Bring it out and correct it, because someday it will not be hidden. It will be on the surface. It will be right there. It will bother you. It will nag you. This flaw will not be correctable then. It will be so deep seated, the roots of it will be right into the essence of your soul. It is up to you to understand how to eliminate it now. That is what healing is all about. Heal yourself first in the simplest way. If you have had a chronic thing happen to you like an ear infection, nose blockage, or painful feeling in the chest, and it is happening over and over, you have to begin to question why it is happening to you. Get some answers. Get some answers to the answers. That is the pathway. You are teaching yourself the velocity that is usable in comprehension. If you do not, that is how you are going to leave.

As a healer, it is so difficult to work on a person's mind or body that you really want to work on. You can see the person's mind going in so many directions, and you try so hard. You can correct some of it, you can slow it down, but there are some avenues that you cannot totally correct because they are interrelated to the soul and are deep-seated. The roots of misconception are so far into the fabric of the individual. In order to kill the disease, it is like killing the entire body. It is impossible to heal. You can take the person out of pain and agony. You can put them in a better frame of mind in regard to the direction they are going in, but sometimes you cannot pull them out of the threads of misconception. That is why if we are sick, we have to understand the illness or imbalance now within self. Correct it now. When it becomes so entrenched, we cannot pull it out because it is wrapped around everything.

Second questioner: **When I first started out in meditation, I did not have much awareness of what was happening in my body. As I began practicing meditation, I began to gain in bodily awareness. Even then, it took me about six months of classes to begin to be more constantly aware of what was going on within my body.**

Yes, so you have to teach yourself the tools, but in the meantime, within the ignorance of what you were, you were dealing with the capacity of rejuvenating your body from ignorance. You see, when you are involved in that pathway, there is some lead-time in saying: *All right! Stupid John is meditating. He is rejuvenating himself. He might be misusing his mind and energy, which is fine, but he is now involved in rejuvenating himself even from ignorance.* Then when you get some knowledge within that reality, you start getting answers to the questions, and the answers interrelate to something that you can change here within the conscious mind rather than having the involuntary system rejuvenate it.

That is the Wonderment of God that is so incredible! We can be so stupid and still use everything, and we use God in a profound way without knowing that we are using God in a profound way! But once you eventually end up understanding the Profoundness of God, It becomes simplicity, and the simplicity of It makes it normal, and the normalcy of It makes it nothing, and the nothing gives you the incentive to understand how truly unique It is because It becomes a preconceived thought, and uses Itself, and you do not have to think about It! That is so unique and unbelievable! It is really incredible, but it does take time. We have done this class for twenty-four years? I am just starting to learn! It is just like having a black belt in karate where you hit that level and begin to think you are profound, and you have just started.

Let us think of the nature of disease. Then we are going to have a meditation and think about some sick people; there are so many sick people around. If you were thinking about manifesting yourself into the physical reality, you would understand that you were extending a portion of you into the physical sense, and that achieving some of those probabilities would not be too good. In fact, it would be very difficult to achieve those probabilities, so you put a fail-safety system into effect, knowing that if your probabilities are not achieved, and you are not comprehending, the misconceptions begin to overwhelm the body, disease comes forward, and you die and return back towards the soul. Now, if we think of the phrase that says, "Everything is God, so everything is good," it makes that process understandable. It does not make it totally understandable, it makes it more understandable.

Therefore, it gets back to the questioning process of understanding the consciousness of a particular disease and how you can eliminate it from the body through the proper use of the mind within the sphere of the particular comprehension. Let us come back to a person's misconception of a lack of compassion in the heart center: eventually the person will deteriorate the heart center and die from a heart attack, or vascular disease, or cerebral hemorrhage, or stroke, if they misuse their mind so much so within lack of compassion. Maybe they misuse their body to the point where they do not think about certain things that are going on within their body: that is a misconception towards the usage of the mind interrelated to compassion for self; they can have a stroke through not using the mind properly. Eventually through a lack of compassion for the body, they cannot keep the body in balance, because they cannot fend for self. They cannot have compassion for self if they cannot take care of self.

It is important to understand that the nature of disease is a fail-safe system of the soul telling us that we are no longer usable within the physical sense, so we begin to filter back up towards the soul. It is traumatic, but when you think about it in that particular way, it is less traumatic. It gives you something to look forward to in the aging process and addresses the fear of no longer being anything. It is like the state of sleep: you are no longer aware of that particular realm that you are in, yet are working at levels that interrelate to that realm. You are unconscious to it because there are layers that can contain you to a particular identity in order for you to definitely stay fixed within trying to achieve those probabilities.

Disease is not intended to make us fearful, it is intended to make us understand the realm of what we are dealing with, which is so important. So we interrelate to those particular things that we were talking about before: we interrelate it to something beyond the realm of that, which is listening to the body in meditation. It is so important because you slow self down in order to give focus towards self. You focus in on the physical body and begin to understand the imbalances within the body. Then the reality of where you question it has more of the ability to absorb, because you open up that funnel of energy and make yourself open to absorb the essence of what you are thinking about. You make self a sponge of reality. You can absorb whatever it is and make it usable within the flesh.

You are doing many different things when you are considering the awareness of healing others. What do you do? You prepare self to the best of your ability and lift self to the highest possible level that interrelates self towards whatever it is that made you. I think of it as the soul; you can think of it as anything you wish; it is just that my thinking of it as the soul makes it all the more sensible to me. Now, if I am going to try to heal the other person, I have to know where I am. I have to know what is going on within my body, so when I interrelate to the other, whatever I then feel and sense will be outside the context of what I am, because I know where I am. For instance, if I feel a pain in my elbow when I am working on the other, I know the other has a pain in their elbow, because before I started working on them, I did not have a pain in my elbow. So becoming aware of yourself gives you the capability of becoming aware of something else, whether it is another person, probability or sphere that deals with many people. That cycle takes place within the awareness of comprehending all of those different levels, whether it is oneself, another person, many people, or all people.

Those capabilities change automatically so you do not have to think about it. For instance, suddenly one day you are thinking about "the reality of the physical sense," or "the common denominator of humanity," or "the ability of understanding what is going on within the framework of humanity," rather than dealing with the duality of "love of another." "Insight within the sixth center of the third-eye" is beyond the third center of "emotions and human decency:" it has the capability of seeing trends within the physical sense. It has the reasoning properties that begin to comprehend the essence of the reality of what triggers diseases within the flesh. The person at that level will be questioning what actions are necessary to stop a particular trend from becoming overwhelming within the physical sense. For instance, a particular disease within the human comes forward, and the nature of it is intended to slow down the misconception. We see the disease as detrimental within the physical sense, but very necessary from another level in order to cause some stability within the reality that we deal with. Everything is intended to cause some semblance of balance within the seesaw of life as it interrelates within flesh towards flesh, or flesh towards another level of comprehension. It all has that capability of balance. That is what we are searching out. We are searching it out within whatever level it might be.

Therefore, when you consider working on another person and are focusing upon their body, look at it, feel it, sense it, understand it and filter the awareness of the misconception that caused the disease through the person. The particular misconception is the disease. A lack of compassion is a heart attack. Both are the same. A woman came up to me after class one time and said, "How could you say that? My mother had more compassion than anybody I ever met in my life and she died from a heart attack." I said, "Did your mother let others do whatever they wanted to her, and she never thought of herself, always giving in to everybody else's whims within the family? She said, "Yes." I said, "She had a lack of compassion towards herself in understanding the true needs of others who came forward." It is like the child who comes up to mother all the time, asking, "Can I have a lollipop?" She gives him one. "Can I have another?" She gives him another. There is a certain point where too many lollipops are not good. That is the balance that we are searching out: not giving in to a misconception; not giving in to something that could hurt the other. That is what healing is all about. So a true healer will hit a particular level that will deal with the comprehension of the person's misconception, and at some point during the healing, tell the person what caused the illness within the body.

When a person wants a healing, you have to begin to filter your energy into their particular area. If they have something wrong within the stomach area, you will deal with the third center of the solar plexus. But if you, the healer, are working only on the first center of awareness within yourself, you can only give the other information pertaining to the first center, but not interrelate it to the disease within the body within the third center. The information can interrelate to their survival that helps them comprehend the disease. You can send energy all day, and it helps, but it does not eliminate the misconception, because you are nowhere near the level that can do so. We mention Jesus who healed

Lazarus: Jesus was at the level that made Lazarus so he could make Lazarus come back. If he was not in that level, he could not make Lazarus come back.

Let us say you want to heal a person. You sit in front of them, or think about them. You feel and sense them, and drop deeper and deeper. Your intent is to be as pure as you can be, within the essence of what you are. The deeper and closer you go towards your soul, the closer you go to the other's soul. That gives you the reality of understanding more of what made them. Logic then tells you, if you are closer to the place that has made the person, you have more information, energy, and knowledge to rejuvenate their mind and body. If you do not hit a level where it eliminates the disease totally from their body, you will use that as incentive, so that the next time you will have more to give to them.

The healing power comes through you. Never think of it as being Jesus, or someone else, it is you. If you want to use another person like Jesus to help you, fine, but it is you doing the healing, not Jesus, Buddha, or Moses. It is fine if you want to use the information of a great entity, and filter it through you, but if you maintain it is the other doing the healing and not you, you do not grow. If you do not grow, that is being sacrilegious and egotistical. Who are you to stop yourself from becoming more godlike? That is why you are here. If you constantly say, "Jesus, heal this person," I will tell you, the healing ability will happen for a while, but then it will go away because you contradict why Jesus came here. He came here to give you a pathway. He came here to make you understand that you have that capability within you. "You are a son and daughter of God, just like I am a son of God," was his statement which means, "Go forward, learn and become more godlike. If you want to use me, fine, but do not use me as a crutch, use me as a pawn."

Each time that you filter in whatever it might be, you grow, and for the next time, you have more to give. That is true pathway information pertaining to the reality of all of those great people who came forward. I will debate that with anybody because it is true and absolute. It does not make a contradiction to any religion. It makes you a better person, and nobody can dispute that reality. You are the most important thing. You are the center of your universe. You are the center of everything, anywhere that ever lived or interrelated to any level right here. Heal yourself first. Then you can heal another. Then you can heal many. If you grow, you change the common denominator of humanity every single moment that you breathe upon this planet.

We think of earth as a great entity that had the capacity to manifest. While I was meditating tonight, I suddenly thought about something: I had always thought of the earth, moon, and stars as cells within God, but never thought of the Milky Way as being a leg of God, or another galaxy as being the heart of God. So you can picture how gigantic God Is, yet all those stars are just cells within the Essence of God. The stars in the skies are just like the cells within you: I am sure that a cell in your stomach or heart thinks that you are everything. It cannot see anything beyond you. It can only see the light of what you are. It thinks that you are it. It might see something in the distance like another person walking by, but that person is light years beyond where it is. We have the same capacity that interrelates to stars or other systems. It is important that we understand that It Is Altogether. I have never seen it like that, before. It is important that we have those incentives within us.

Let us take a few moments to meditate together. Let us think about those people that we care about. Let us think about the sick people that we know. Think about yourself first; think about the chronic things you might have within you, or those simple little pains or agonies within you. Get information pertaining to them within you. Find out what you have to do to correct whatever it is. I know you can do it. I love you.

(The class dropped into meditation, with quiet music in the background:) You do everything you can to help another person within the realm of what you are, but never let it affect your balance, because if you do, you do not give balance to the other, you give them a misconception of balance. Rather, you give just enough, so that you do not go out of balance so you can give more the next time.

Drop deeper and deeper. You can feel all of the stress and tension dissipating from your entire body. Think for a moment: if you are dropping deeper, you are closer to your soul. If you are closer to your soul, you are closer to the Reality That has made you. More of the Light of Whatever It Might Be is being refracted through you each moment, changing you more and more. Feel it, use it. It is not hidden, it is right there! You can hear your soul saying, *"I love you. You truly are working on yourself, and each time you do so, you will never be the same again! You will be more perfect each time, and will have the capability of using that perfection more so each time."*

Each one of us knows of someone who is sick. Think about the person. See them as well. If you are sick, just work on you; nobody else. If you have something minor, just work on it for a while; then work on the other. If you have something major, just keep working on you. It is not that you should not have good thoughts towards others while you have something wrong with you, but your focus should be on you because that is where it should be.

Now for those of you, who have the capability of focusing on a person outside of self, do so. For those who cannot, just think about your body. I will do what I can, and the rest of us who can transcend a little more, will help also. We are joining together, seeing the light emanating from this room: a bright white refractable light within the physical sense. See the person getting better from the tip of their toes to the top of their head. If they have a tumor, or something detrimental within the body, see it dissipate, and being isolated and banished from the body. If it is something mental, see a clear head. If it is within the joints, or bones, see healing properties going in. Each time that you send something, send some consciousness and information with it. If you do not know it, send it from another level; ask your soul to help you. Tell your soul as you are doing so: *Will you please teach me? Let me see a portion of it so I can use that portion to extend myself further into the next part of it for the next time.*

You are so creative. Know the power you have within you. The other person could be on the moon, Phoenix, Arizona, or next door, and you can help. I am so proud of you. You give me incentive. Drop deeper and deeper. You can say to yourself: *As I drop deeper, all of those thoughts I had before will be compounded within the reality of me becoming more and more of what is usable in causing some semblance of balance in the other person.*

I love You, God. I feel so ignorant within the joy of understanding You sometimes, but even within the ignorance, it is so beautiful. We have chosen within our free will to use whatever we have within us, to the best of our capabilities. We extend ourselves within the awareness of what is coming next within us, yet we know that it extends further within the Essence of What You Are, God. Each time when we think, feel, sense, and use the words that are so necessary, we grow within the framework of what we are. We compound the reality of it, thinking upon it each day. The words become our deeds, and the deeds become the information and the sustenance that is necessary to eliminate the misconceptions to make this place a more usable place to achieve our probabilities. I love You, God.

May the people that we look upon and sense tonight be totally healed from the misconceptions of what they are. Within our ignorance, or wonderment of knowledge, as we extended ourselves into the realm of trying to help others, if within that capacity we might have felt some of the disease of others, we instruct self that the disease is not ours. Then the particular disease no longer becomes usable within the framework of what we are. We feel the balance and the wonderment of what we are, outside of the context of disease. You can begin to bring yourself up slowly, saying all of those good things for yourself. Use this for incentive. You should be feeling absolutely fantastic. Each one of these notes of the music is a beautiful mantra.

CHAPTER TWENTY-TWO

Meditation Considers Us
June 14, 2000

I want you to visualize the seven major centers of the body. They are wheels of energy shaped like donuts. The survival center is at the base of the spine, which is red. It is like a wheel or disk. In the center is a white spot, and around the edges spin all of the different shades of red. All of the red colors begin to mix together as you love yourself more, through understanding more about yourself and the identity of your survival. The center becomes vibrant, and the white vibration begins to lighten up and trickle into all of the velocities of that disk. Eventually when you become so knowledgeable in that center, the essence of it becomes totally white. When we understand and see this phenomenon from different levels, it becomes so understandable that it should be so, because we know within the physical sense that white is made up of all colors. The white ignites a reality within the center and the center begins to spin. The same thing takes place at different levels of comprehension: each time that you learn, some of the sparks, light and essence of your soul becomes a reality within a particular center. Through your growth you are no longer dealing within the realm of the physical anymore, you become more of the reality of the esoteric comprehension of what you are. You ignite everything to a flavor that is more usable for what you are.

You begin to feed the tributaries. The main survival center is ignited from all of the different secondary centers within the feet, legs and arms. At first these secondary centers become an extension of using: we can walk, touch and move. They are also that which we can understand and have insight into. All of these realities are triggered from these disks, these different centers of reality, but to perfect them in more profound ways comes from the esoteric quality of what you are: then the essence of feeling, touching, seeing, hearing, tasting and smelling changes. Each center has a new flavor, essence and usability within the flesh. Now when we think about the esoteric qualities that we left at the different levels, and how unique they can become when they are refracted through the realm of what we are, we can understand what I mean when I make the statement that says, "If you want to become more than what you are now, understand the reality of what you are now." Because if we look at those disks, the white purity within each of them, and how that white purity filters all of those little tributaries into those cards of reality, which are the different flavors and views of what we are and brightens them up, it is like a sunny day after a rain storm. From that basic sustenance of what we are, we can feel ourselves growing within the realm of that.

That is what growth and healing are all about: different flavors of colors and sounds. When you have your red center turned into white, and opened within the survival area, and a person around you needs survival, all of the different flavors and hues of that color are within the white. It becomes esoteric comprehension within the flesh, and you can help the other more so. The simplicity of it is awesome yet so extraordinary, when you look at it from that level. You can say: *I have become what I should become within that level, and the realm of it shall change the density of where I am, forever!* You as a single cell within the earth's awareness can change this place forever! Each one of us has that capability. What might those colors and sounds and information be? They are part of the Total Reality of God. So the uniqueness of it becomes the incentive of it. You can say: *If I can understand that next thing, more of the Essence of God will be within me. If I can ignite and use the knowledge properly within the physical sense, more of the Essence of God will be within me each time.* Then everything that happens to you happens to you in a more profound way.

We are going to meditate again. I want you to sense the feelings in the room. There are some unique things going on in this room tonight; feel them and use them within you. Think of the flavor and color of this room as an identity within that particular awareness within the physical sense. It has its own sphere. Where we put it? What do we turn on? How more usable can we make it from where we are and what we can become? It is up to you. Each one of us is going to add something to the awareness of this feeling. Make it unique. Make it beautiful. (The meditation proceeded as usual.)

(Afterwards, addressing the class:) Did you feel survival? Love? Compassion? Wisdom?

First questioner: **I like the idea of tributaries. I felt it was possible to open up all areas, become clear, and really send out love, and that I could do that a lot more.**

Did you feel strong? You picked up a lot of things that I was feeling in myself: a lot of good physical strength and realignment of thought patterns concerning things that are a little out of kilter in my mind and my perception of how I use my mind within the physical sense. We are sort of balancing those things, which is a healing.

It is making us focus in on some of those particular things that we are cursed with, that come back at us, even though they are not realities. They are illusions of what we might have participated in, and those illusions have to come back and filter through us one way or another. They are the little aspects that we have to balance within ourselves. I use the word "curse" because the illusion has a compelling property that seems to be a true reality but is really an illusion. What you do is filter the particular illusion through your mind and look at it, and it constantly comes back to bombard you, so you realize that you have to be within the sphere of feeling and sensing that particular illusion that you projected forward in your lifetime. Whatever it might be that you were participating in, it is that soiled laundry coming back. It seems cleaner and purer, but has a lot of soiled parts to it that you have to purify. When you examine it, you understand that it comes back and hits you constantly. But if you really look at it, there are little portions of it that you are peeling away through the trauma of the reality that you have put yourself through because of the karma of that property that you were involved in before; but then it becomes that which is usable in filtering yourself through understanding the original flaws that you participated in within that sphere. It is very helpful, and there is no other way of feeling and sensing it unless it is bombarding you. It is just that constant thing that comes around. It is necessary to come around. If it did not come around, you would not have the capability of seeing it and having it constantly hit you with that information pertaining to the misconception of the original reality of it.

Now, those illusions can be within the framework of those probabilities that are set in motion in order to achieve the elimination of that misconception from the reality of what you are. The illusions might be into the particular structure pertaining to other individuals. It is a very hard thing to describe. It might be that you are looking at a person and saying: *Hey, that person is red.* I am just using the color red, as an analogy to the situation. You will eventually see that the person is not red, but you had to see that person as red, in order to achieve that particular structure or probability that you set in motion from the misconception of the reality of how it hit you. I know as I am explaining it now, it seems outside of the grasp of the awareness of our minds to put it into a context and make it rigid so that it is totally noticeable each time. But those things taking place as illusions come back and hit the fringes of what we are, each time. What we have to look for is a noticeable change in the orbiting quality of that misconception. Are we taking it and squeezing it into the nucleus, so it no longer has to be within the realm of what we are dealing with?

The unique thing about it is, there will come a point in comprehending that sphere that you realize that it is not a true reality of where you are now, but is the sustenance that changes the reality of where you are now. It is no longer you participating in that particular sphere; it is that particular sphere participating in where you are. There is a unique significance to that particular statement that makes the reality of it more significant when we look at it from that level. It makes us truly understand the uniqueness of all of those things that correspond to that particular point that we have to comprehend, and it is so unique and beautiful if we look at it from that level. Does it have to be seemingly extraordinary? Do we have to understand it? Does it have to become something that we can see? No, it happens to us all of the time, but when that particular quality becomes something that is usable in eliminating the total process of the particular thing ever hitting us again, in doing so, that quality becomes an asset.

When we look at it like that, the information that we received here tonight hits us in so many ways. It hits upon the fringes of all of those things that we are comprehending or stimulating within ourselves. At first, the information was seemingly nothing: I felt a particular point from a particular sound or note of the music that was seemingly pleasurable and beautiful. It hit a particular part of my body, but what was the significance beyond that? Where did it go? What did it stimulate? What properties did it have within it that gave it the significant property to make me achieve some semblance of balance from the reality of the particular thing?

If we can eventually trace the reality of that, and have the usability within the instantaneous reaction of what we are trying to comprehend, the escalation of that ability to draw upon consciousness from the next level will be extraordinary. But to grasp upon it, and make it usable in that reality even in the illusion of what it is… and the trickery of what it is within the realm of what the soul is setting in motion within that probability or from that particular thing that we are trying to achieve from misconception… It is so awesomely rewarding when we can look at it from that level. Do we have to look at it from either way? We get back to that point that says: *Even from the ignorance of what I am, I can comprehend it; but then from the knowledge of what I am, I can eliminate it, because it eliminates the ignorance of what I am within the quest of that which I am trying to comprehend.*

I think it is extraordinary when we look upon some of the things that touch us in a way where they are not within the words but the feelings of where we are. We have to think about what is going on in this room sometimes. We have to think about where something goes in the class, and how it affects us in what we do each and every day. I know that when I miss a couple weeks of being here in the class, there is an effect on me. I have less balance, and less of a reaction, because I have less time to take whatever property I am and stimulate it. I do not take those two or three hours during the week to do that. I do not have the luxury of this place.

Second questioner: **What is that strange quality of, when I need meditation the most, I do not do it?**

We are so involved; but you see, as we are involved in those particular things, we do not realize in those moments what all of those past meditations have done for us! We do not realize what we have learned from those aspects interrelated to the moving of the mind, the understanding the reactions of what we are involved in, and the automatic regeneration of the mind and body as we are being involved. We never take the opportunity to see why we have that strength. For instance, sometimes it takes something catastrophic to happen to us, for us to truly take the opportunity to say: *My God, I never could have coped so well with this before, but now I can!*

Where did that strength come from? It came from you comprehending those meditations and making them usable in making you a better vehicle of achieving anything that you are involved in. So when those chaotic events happen, and we are seemingly outside of meditation, we are totally entrenched in our past meditations and their achievements. We did not take the opportunity to see this factor then, but now we can. That is the unique thing about all that we deal with: even when we do not consider meditation, meditation considers us. That is the uniqueness of it. I think that there is so much that we are missing. Each time that we feel and sense something new and extraordinary, and it touches us, we realize how much there must be that we do not understand, or have touch us through comprehension! What are we missing? So much, but we will never see something new unless we use now what we are considering.

There are times when I think about what you just said. Sometimes I just sit down to meditate and say: *I feel so fantastic. Why didn't I take the opportunity to do this before?* But then when I consider it, I say: *Isn't it just so unique that I can take those properties, use them, and make them so ordinary and insignificant, yet they are so profound?*

(The class listened to music:) This is a beautiful piece of music. There are times when there is just a little bit that makes us a lot, and there are times when just an awful lot makes us a little bit… and there are times when it does not make any difference. This is one of those times, because both of them are significant. So many times we can listen to a particular piece of music that does not touch us, or grab us, or move us, yet when we put ourselves in a particular place where we open up to the reality of what we are, we can truly hear the music. It stimulates us and puts us in a new place where we can hear it differently. It affects us differently. We use things differently. Take a few minutes right now: this is truly one of those times. It is when the pot of reality boils to the top, and has an overwhelming quality to it that touches us in a way where we bubble out from the sphere of what we are. But then when we truly look at it, it is really making the sphere of what we are, bigger. I love you. I hope you have an extraordinary week. I hope I see you next week.

CHAPTER TWENTY-THREE

A Heart Center Class: The Rewards of Comprehension
August 9, 2000

(John holds a heart center class usually twice a year. It is his custom to drop into a deep-trance state in the second half of class to open his heart center to the best of his capacity. Students are asked to focus upon what is transpiring in the room and within themselves in subtle meditation. To reach the heart center, John must achieve a fine balance within mind, body and spirit, so he begins the process of balancing out each part of his body to the best of his ability, starting with the relaxation of the toes and feet. He is able to talk occasionally as he describes what he is experiencing. Then with the opening of the heart center, he projects out heart center vibrations. At this point, he sometimes talks, or is silent. Usually within twenty minutes or so, he returns to his normal state of consciousness.)

(The balancing out of the body:) Right now I cannot feel my arms, my legs. The top of my head is spinning, the crown center. I can feel it going out, almost like to infinity. It might be difficult for me to speak, but I will speak at times.

The feelings are awesome. I do not feel too many blockages within the system. Sometimes as I am going through this particular procedure, I feel and sense some blockages, but for some strange reason, it is pretty natural and fluid.

I feel as if the lower three centers are open. They are all open, but what I am attempting to do is to open them in a major way. I feel the energy increasing around my arms and legs. My mind is clear and sharp at this level.

The energy is increasing once again. I feel my throat center spinning. Some of you people might be able to feel some of these things that I am feeling.

I feel my third-eye opening. The energy is absolutely awesome.

Sometimes when I am going through this, it drags into areas that stimulate my emotions in different ways. Right now it is pretty solid, stable and well balanced. I can feel rejuvenation in every muscle in my body, even in the organs.

More energy is coming in on my left side now, for some strange reason: tremendous healing properties to the energy.

The energy is increasing once again. The only word I can use for this energy is... awesome. My God.

(There was the heart center opening. On this particular occasion John was silent. After an interval of fifteen minutes or so, he returned to his normal state:)

Are there any questions? I have never felt it so solid and I did not even move. I am still coming up, so...

My emotions did not fluctuate as they normally do. They did not bother me either way, but they were more solid and confined to understanding what I was doing within my body and my mind. That was awesome. It makes you feel extraordinarily gigantic: as if your feet are implanted in the earth all the way down to the center. Any questions? Is anybody feeling anything extraordinary? (There were remarks of several students not included here.)

Just ride with it. Just absorb it. It comes from the rewards of what you are and what you are involved in. It is extraordinary. It does some unbelievable things to your body and mind. Even my eyesight right now is extraordinary and the energy is awesome around my body. It is still a little difficult to talk.

It felt very solid to me. Usually I will feel so much peacefulness and balance and love, it has an overwhelming effect upon me, and I feel like crying, but this was so solid and so extraordinary in its ability to balance my physical body. As a matter of fact, it is going to take me a while to come up. It was extraordinary in that sense. It made me trace certain things through my body in a different way. I believe it will take me a while to absorb some of the thoughts that I had within that particular structure, but many things ran through my mind about certain things I have to do within the physical sense to change some of the reality of what I am in a more positive way. Some of those things were floating through my mind: *Do not get involved in things in life in a way where you entrench yourself in the involvement of them, but sever some things and let them fly where they may within the Structure of the Laws of God.*

Wow. It made me see some of the things that I went through today. I usually like to eat a lot at dinner, but for some strange reason I was just getting the message: *Just eat a basic salad.* That is usually not enough for me, but it was enough for me tonight, I do not know why. Maybe it is just dealing with some thought patterns I was using to readjust some of the balancing qualities as far as weight is concerned too, but I can understand why I ate just a slight meal. It was necessary to do so in order to hit the particular level.

First questioner: **About the rewards you receive: do you feel them in your meditations?**

No, you feel the reactions of them in your daily living. The rewards through comprehension come back and interrelate to everything that you are dealing with within the normalcy of your day. In those moments of the deep-trance state you do draw the rewards in, no question about it, but it goes beyond that: it changes the common denominator of everything that you feel; everything that you are involved in has more beauty within it. Therefore, it is not a conscious thought that says: *Hey, I am feeling this.* Although you do get those thoughts occasionally where you say: *My God, I never saw it quite like that before!* Or: *I never got so much information pertaining to it.* Or: *I never felt that like that.* Or: *I never had so much control when I was involved in that.* You see, the rewards in that particular way change the way you use all of those things in the physical sense. It makes everything more beautiful, everything more usable. Of course, you take whatever it is, and put it back into your next meditation, and try to bridge the gap between that and something else. You go back into those meditations and you see certain things, but you do not make it drudgery.

Now, tonight I saw some absolutes within the structure of what I was dealing with, that will change me regarding some of the things I have to do about my feelings towards other people in a certain way. The information I received changes that structure, and the way I feel about it, and the way I sense it. It is something that I am trying to become involved in within that sphere of comprehension. It suddenly gave me that reality, that sustenance that made it understandable and recognizable and usable. It is not something that I have to flush through my system anymore. It gave me the quality of changing it so it does not have an effect on me in the way it had before, and it gives me the insight of understanding the reality of what other people are going through and have to go through. So it is not my ballgame anymore, it is something they have to deal with; but then in the same sense, I am not involved in the misconception of it too, in a way where it is detrimental to me.

When I am that deep, when I return to the normal state, I feel so solid: I feel as if I just had a forty-mile run, or just did sit-ups, push-ups and arm thrusts. I feel all of that, yet I do not feel one bit of exhaustion at all. I feel as if I just had a facial, or had my head massaged. My toes are tingling. It feels like everything that I could ever want, and I do not have to think about it. All of those rewards come: the extension of rejuvenation in my muscles, teeth and gums, because I hit the level that gave me the reality of it happening to me.

In the last couple days I had some thoughts: *Hey, you can no longer physically accomplish what you used to accomplish.* Or when I looked the mirror: *You do not look the same anymore.* Those things were going through my mind. It is understandable, looking at those things in that way, because there are changes and those changes have to be balanced within the physical sense. When I do so, it interrelates to something I can switch on at a different level, so I can understand that in a more positive way. What it gives you is the capability of understanding that, no matter what age you are, you can rejuvenate yourself to the best of your ability within that framework. It is not as if you are going to pretend that you are twenty years old, it is going to make you feel absolutely at the peak of perfection at the level that you are within, and that is the necessary thing that you have to understand about it.

Oh God, that is unusual! You see, I am way down and feeling some of that, so sometimes it gives me information even as I am coming back. I am starting to feel some of those joys, so it tells me there are different layers within that structure, more insight into the heart center. I go in, and feel and sense the extraordinary powers of the heart center. I feel its emotions and its awesome beauty. It overwhelms me, and overwhelms me, just to that point where it stimulates me: each time that I go back in, it stimulates and overwhelms me just enough. Then there is that time when I go back in, the strength of all of that–which seemingly had a fluctuation within the awareness of compassion and balance–becomes the rewards of the stabilizing quality of what I am in those moments. It takes a while for me to filter it down and make it sensible, usable and recognizable in words, then hopefully in deeds. Then the trip of the reality of it becomes more usable as I look at the density of it from that perspective. It makes me understand how much I have within the normalcy of what I am, that I am not triggering all of the time. I have been dealing with some sense of complacency or laziness in that reaction.

I love you. You should be feeling fantastic over the next weeks. Even if you have something wrong with you, you should be more stable in that direction. You should get more information pertaining to why you have it. Digest it, understand it and make it usable within you. There are reasons for everything happening. Sometimes those reasons are extraordinarily usable if you just take the opportunity to try to understand them. It is as if you are waiting in traffic somewhere, and you do not understand why you are waiting, then suddenly you get to a part of the highway where there is a gigantic washout. If you had been there five minutes previously, you would have been gone. Then you understand why there was a wait; but before then, you could not understand why you had trauma, and lack of patience and compassion within that wait. Those things trigger the qualities that make us comprehend things in a more positive way.

I am way out there right now. (Class laughter.) I am having a little difficulty talking. But tonight I really did not go through the customary thought: *Why am I sitting up here and doing this?* In most heart center classes, usually I do. There was maybe just a fleeting moment of that, but nothing that I really had to focus in on and question. Take care of yourselves. Hope to see you again next time.

CHAPTER TWENTY-FOUR

Refocus to Look at the Entire Picture
October 11, 2000

(After the guided meditation:) Let us take a couple minutes to think about focus and how truly important it is. Nothing is interrupting your meditations. You should have trained yourself by now to focus beyond any noises. If you hear another person moving about, coughing, or sneezing, there might be a reason for it. Help them with your compassionate thoughts, or send energy. You should have the compassion within you to refocus on a particular thing. Do not let anything disturb you in a negative way. Use your mind properly. Life is full of distractions. Learn to use them for you.

Sometimes I change the music. When I do that, I am actually teaching you focus. I am teaching you to overcome those reactions of hearing outside noises. That is balance. That is compassion. You should lift yourself above any distractions that you are dealing with; then you are creating that energy field that can then be usable in everyday matters, whether at work or play. You can actually isolate yourself within that sphere and cause great stability within yourself to refocus upon balance. By teaching yourself to utilize meditation in a proper way, you are actually putting yourself in the position that eliminates whatever distraction it might be in your daily life, because you are refocusing on something that gives you balance, rather than allowing the distraction to pull you into areas of misconception. As you are doing this, you are actually creating a more usable mind within the physical sense in comprehending each thing, because you have that tunnel vision towards each thing.

It happened to me today when we were on the job hanging some wallpaper. There was something so simple that happened. If my son-in-law had not been with me and just questioned very briefly, "Are you sure it goes this way?" we would have done the job wrong. He was not sure either, but when he said that, I realized that I had not given myself the opportunity of looking at the larger design within the pattern. I turned to him and said, "If you were not with me, I would have hung it wrong." The wallpaper design was not so obvious, but then it was very obvious. I just did not look at it long enough to understand it in the right way. So you learn from the particular thing. You say to yourself: *I am going to have to readjust my mind to understand that I have to take in the whole picture.* I have always done this, but sometimes it conks you in the head to make you once again refocus upon whatever you are involved in. Do not take something as an absolute all of the time. You have to focus once again to make sure the pathway is clear.

When you use focus in meditation, it then compounds the reality of the meditation. It gives you the ability to go deeper. It gives you the ability to have insight into a particular structure that is going on within the mind and body. If suddenly you are distracted by something, ask: *What happens when suddenly the distraction interferes with my relaxation? Where does it take me? What do I feel in my body? How far does it fling me away from that area of rewarding relaxation? Where does it put me now? How could I get myself back?* That is focus. That is the ability to refocus upon the reality of where you are, where you went, and how you can get back there; and there are particular structures within that event that can give you the identity of understanding how you have gone there. Ask: *Why did it bother me? What should I have done? What is the particular thing that I should be doing?* In doing so, you are dissecting it and also taking yourself out of further deviation into the misconception. You are taking control of the reality of what you are trying to comprehend. What you are trying to comprehend is the important thing, because before the distraction you were not comprehending anything but an escalation into misconception. So by comprehending the particular structure, you are slowing the reality of going into the misconception because you are looking at it and dissecting it. I should have done that today for that brief moment on the job. I intend to do so from now on. We should all intend to do that from now on.

Refocus to look at the entire picture of what is going on. Understand the entire playing field. Look at the obstacles. See what particular thing can deviate you. Know that there are hidden things within the structure of that painting or whatever it might be. Know that if you prepare yourself within the particular event of meditation, and are deep enough, you insulate yourself within that reality, that sphere of energy. Then when something does come at you in your daily life, it has to go through a thicker wave of what you are. The density of you has changed. You have more of a capability of refracting the distraction, and pushing it back, because you have made a particular structure of what you are, dealing with more of the density of the reality of what you are. It is like having a cushion or bulletproof vest around you when somebody shoots at you: it gives you protection beyond the ordinary because you have prepared yourself beyond the ordinary.

(In the second half of class, John makes some preparatory remarks before leading the class in a second meditation:) In this meditation I do not know what you should put into the intent of you, but let me give you a suggestion: that you might want to consider the word, "focus." Focus upon each of the areas that we mention: the toes, feet, ankles, and the lower part of your legs. There is so much going on within the awareness of you. Each area has a particular consciousness. Each has a secondary center that interrelates to your consciousness. If you are comprehending what is going on in your feet, what do you think is going to happen to you? You are going to have more of the awareness of the particular area within you that is usable, because you have focused in on it. You are clearing the fog of misconception. You are making the picture clearer to the perception of what you are.

Now, if you feel the stability of that awareness within your toes, or feet, you then have more stability to move from there. You have more strength within the awareness of your feet. Your feet interrelate to survival within the physical sense, giving you the stability upon the earth plane that interrelates to the survival center at the base of the spine, which is "love of self." If you comprehend more of that, logically it gives you more "love of self," energy, survival, and capacity to have the strength of your convictions in your daily life. It gives you stability, and the rewards within whatever it is that you are trying to comprehend or do. It gives you a clearer picture. You have the ability to have less distortion in each particular area that you look at. It gives you greater creativity within comprehension. The stability of the feet: what does that do in the healing process? It stimulates that area; it gives you more of the reality that sustains that particular area: less aching feet, and athlete's foot, and more comfort and ability to walk without fatigue. All of these things that you take for granted are more usable when you comprehend the ability of that particular place, and the ability of that particular place can only be more usable when you comprehend it.

There is a tremendous ability to each part of the body. It is becoming increasingly common to understand that there is more to what is going on, than what we are just looking at. There is more there; there is more to the meat of what is within the structure of the particular area, no matter what it is. If you just take the opportunity to see the surface, it clears the picture, and for the next time, increases the capability of that surface to extend itself beyond where it is now, because you have made that layer usable within the density of you. You have become thicker within the awareness of the particular place.

Sometimes I sit within my meditations, or silence, or moments like I am taking now, to ask: *What must be coming next? What am I slowing myself down from becoming, by not using my mind correctly? What am I doing when I extend myself into those stupid little acts that I do, each day?* Each day I do stupid things to take myself off that track: just enough to give myself a little vacation. Each day I take a vacation from the awareness of thoughts, or whatever is coming at me. Those are important times within the structure that says: *Hey, there is too much information coming at me, and if I do not control it, nobody will. If I do not control it, no more will come.*

It is as simple as that. If I want more, I have to control what I have, and if I control what I have, more will come. What might that be? What might be the wisdom beyond that next corner that we turn, or that next rung we climb upon that ladder of reality? What particular reward could it be that is refracted through humanity? Will we eliminate just a little portion of illness or sickness from the awareness? Will it become something that lifts us into that place where four or six people upon the earth plane will find a cure for a particular disease? It takes one person–whoever is close to the reality–who can deal with the sustenance of it, to pull in that energy, in order for that cure to be discovered by those four or six people. When that does happen, that reward refracts throughout the common denominator of humanity and truly becomes usable.

You have that within you, each one of you, which is the capability of becoming more than what you were before. When you do so, you can throw a rope to that sleigh of life within the physical reality. You have become the horse that pulls the rope attached to the sleigh. The feat becomes easier, each time. There is more of you. There is more of your ability to pull the sleigh forward. It seems lighter each time because you have won the right to lift the burden of misconception from the reality of that layer and have changed the surface that makes each person walk in a higher place, even within the ignorance of it. Each time that you do so, the stimulating qualities and the rewards are within the feelings that you have within your mind and body. They do not interrelate to just one thing, they interrelate to everything that you are: the sounds you hear, the food you eat, the people you love, all of the things you see. All of them become different within the framework of what is more harmoniously usable in what you are trying to comprehend. The feelings and the rewards are beyond where they were before, because logic tells you they will be so.

Use what you feel within you in the throat center, that higher center of duality and creativity. Heal yourself. Heal your friends. Heal whomever. It is here. Remember when Christ said, "Do you believe in me? If you do, your friend is healed. Just by your thoughts of believing, your friend has been healed." In the wisdom of your mind if you believe, it will work. If you do not believe, it will not work If you do not believe, nothing happens, and there is nothing anyone can do to help you, other than tell you to do so. I do not care if Jesus walks in this room and tells us all something: if we do not believe, we cannot use it.

I have learned so much over the last couple of months about illness. Some of the people that I have been working on have been very ill, and some of the input that I have received within what I feel within the diseases has been extraordinary.

(John led the class in a second meditation with Native American music in the background:) As I dance upon the earth, I sing to the fire, the rain and the wind. I know, each time as I do so, I become more of it. I fly upon the wings of the eagle. I see into the world beyond. As I make the sounds of that dance, the sound pulls my feet off the earth, and the ground that I walk upon eventually becomes more sacred and usable. I feel You, God. I am glad You are so far away because it makes the venture more interesting.

When you can hit a level where you can actually want to die and become the dust that is usable in the sustaining quality of plants or whatever, then we will truly understand the wisdom of the feelings of that dance or sound. Some of us will feel a trickle of it as it flows through us, but some of us will dance upon the winds that will make it a true reality. I feel portions of it occasionally, and I do not try to venture into the true reality of the whole reality of it, because it is beyond my grasp. I pull myself back and listen to it from where I am. I let it pull me once again to new areas within the Wind of God. I know one thing: what we feel in this room now will not only change us, it will definitely change everything and everyone on this earth plane. I know that is as true as I am sitting here. May it be the incentive to feel more of what we feel now. I promise you one thing: when you leave this room tonight, you will never be the same again, and it will not be in a bad way but a good way. Everything in your life will change into a more positive place. Believe in yourself. You truly are part of God.

CHAPTER TWENTY-FIVE

When You Wake Up That Secret
October 18, 2000

(John started the evening meditation by putting on Native American music:) I want you to take a few minutes just to listen to this, please. You should feel the energy in the room tonight. You should be truly at peace with yourself now. Feel what you have within you now, because there is truly so much within this room. Use it for you. It might have a slightly overwhelming quality to it. Let it stimulate your mind and your body. It truly will make you more than you were before.

Relax yourselves more so. There is information within the energy. It can give you the thoughts that are necessary to comprehend whatever misconception you might have in your mind and body. It gives you steps in the right direction to eliminate it permanently from your mind and body. What you are doing now is giving yourself that safety area that gives you a chance so you will not deteriorate your mind and body any further than it is right now: a necessary time for you, not only to look at the set of probabilities that you will achieve in eliminating the misconception, but also put energy in motion seeing yourself definitely achieving the right direction. It is important that you do so. If you are in pain or agony, it is very difficult to put yourself in that place of comprehension and rejuvenation, so it is important that you take this opportunity to put yourself within the realm of understanding the misconception now when you have the opportunity of balance outside that threshold of pain. You put yourself upon smooth water now. You can enjoy the moments. You have put out the fire of misconception. It still kindles below the surface within the realm of your identity, yet the information is within the energy that you feel and sense now to finally quench the thirst of misconception. Take some silent moments to question it.

You are beyond the first step of asking the question: *What is it that I should question?* You are within the realm of questioning the particular area. You have put yourself in a cushion of awareness. It is the true reality of what you are feeling now. It seeks out new opportunities of comprehension. You truly are part of All, and you are changing that part that you have. This place, this opportunity, is hard to find sometimes, but it is here. You are at the crossroads. It is your choice. When you make the choice, it pulls you with absolute comprehension. When you do not, it keeps you still within the place that you are and never shatters your confidence. Where you are always builds upon your plusses. It ignites new sparks of information that funnel you into new avenues of comprehension, and you never have to search out the beauties because they are before you, the beautiful things of life. They nestle themselves around you. You can feel the serenity within them. This place is a cushion of softness, blanket of comfort and warmth of movement within comprehension. This place never shatters the pure glass of comprehension; it illuminates it. It filters just the right refractable essence of life to you. The wonderment of the brightness trickles to areas of comprehension that eliminate the blockages causing the misconception. Feed upon the light. It truly is the awareness that can change you in a very positive way. It is the brightness when you feel dark. It is the warmth when you feel cold. It is the wind when you need a fresh breeze upon you. It is the insight into direction. You truly are within that boat that is upon the River of Reality. Stay within yourself. Be comfortable. Be relaxed. (The meditation proceeded as usual.)

(John's remarks when bringing the class to the end of the meditation:) Bring yourself up slowly. If you come up too fast, go back down again and come up slowly. Right now, because of what you have done, there are places upon this earth… petals are falling upon the earth. Flowers. Others cannot see them. They might be able to smell them. But each place will change because of what you did tonight. I saw it so clearly. You should feel very special, because you are in a good way; because there will not be many times in your life when you will have such things flow through you. The quality of what is here is incredible. You should feel blessed within you. I do. You made more room for sacred things and you understood those that seemingly were not. Rest for a while. Just sit and absorb. It will be a deep breath that will seem like a long, long time, but will only be the rewards of a rest that you will be feeling that will be seemingly long. God, What Must You Be, if we feel such things now?

You should feel awesome in the simplicity of what you are. It is amazing that you can feel so extraordinary, yet only have it affect you in such a simple way. Don't you wonder what might come next? I do. This has a very overwhelming effect upon me right now. I just cannot keep up with the love and the balance. It is beyond my comprehension. All of those things that seem so extraordinary during the day–which are so necessary–are outside the realm of this. It grabs you and makes everything seem so simple and usable. Let us take a break.

(Second half of class with music in the background:) The music does have some staggering rewards within it that are very overwhelming. We are so lucky too. Every time, a unique piece of music comes forward that is so different and usable within its framework. Just when you think you have got a hold on that feeling that is so extraordinary, another ripple of it touches you. It is a hard train to catch up with because it keeps moving within you. It exaggerates the feeling of wonder.

Is everyone feeling good? No words of wisdom? Aren't there moments though–anyway that I felt tonight–that transcend beyond words? The feelings and essence of the moments were so far beyond what you can describe. Yet I know that the tone and the flavor of our words change each time that we have that opportunity to feel those things come through us. It definitely does change us. In the past few months I did not feel many things that were seemingly extraordinary. I had some good thoughts of balance and such, but you never know when you wake up that secret that is going to come forward next within the Realm of God! Those secrets come at times when you think within yourself that you might not be going anywhere, and you are truly going at speeds that are incredible. Sometimes we have those vacations; it is necessary to pull ourselves back and allow the framework of what we are to become that, which is stable and dry within the paint of what we have put upon the canvas.

Each time I feel some unique things–and I feel unique things almost every moment of each day, and I mean extraordinarily unique things–they stimulate all of those plusses and unique feelings that I have. I am sure that all of us feel that way in our normal, daily lives. Here in the classroom we experience some feelings that filter through us as a unit made up of people who are joining together and searching out that uniqueness that we try to find. We do not necessarily see the uniqueness as something that was stimulated and seeded here in this classroom, but then when we come back and feed upon that uniqueness once again in class, we might see a trickle of the feelings. We understand that the feelings were truly sent forth from those moments where we took the opportunity to look upon them in this classroom. They feed those individual moments each and every day.

I know sometimes within our minds, words, and deeds that we all fumble along life's pathways. We seemingly do things that are not necessarily a credit to ourselves, or humanity, or God, but when we hit those moments, we understand that everything is good, if we do not blot it into a misconception that makes it so stagnant that it becomes the framework that does not make us move. I think tonight we were stimulated into many different properties within those particular things that will make us see things, like we have never seen them before. I know that without question. I search out those beyond-normal places that might heal individuals. Each time that we hit those particular places within the threads of that and sow the reality of what we are, I try once again, whatever it might be, to eliminate some particular facet that has distorted the identity within another person. Each time I do that, I know that I have given more than I have before, and that it has purified some funneling effects within the particular area. I know more is needed, but in those brief moments that I think are within the absence of escalating myself into the higher essence, I know this is truly not so: I am truly moving at speeds that are truly unique and beautiful.

Therefore, each day we should take the opportunity of the moments just to feel the uniqueness of what we are. If we look at it in a fundamental way, we can understand as we do so, we change our uniqueness. It becomes more fundamentally sound within the awareness of our usage. So when you are confined to those moments where you look upon yourself in a poor way, they might be necessary moments that stagger you into an area, pushing you into a more profound place. I know as we stagger through them in those brief moments of instability, we seemingly think that we might not achieve that place once again, but we do.

There is so much that we are missing of the underlying properties of this place that we are in! There are so many fundamental things left there for us that we might not even consider, and they still hit upon us within our ignorance. Each time that we sense something like we felt tonight, doesn't it make you feel more of the understanding that there is a True Reality of God that stimulates us even in our ignorance? Each time the credits in that direction become more legible, and we can read and make the True Reality of God something truly unique within the book of what we are. I know without question, each time that I feel what I am feeling now, there is so much that we are missing! We are only missing it because it is necessary to do so; we cannot use it yet. So use what you have. Bake just enough cookies within the realm of what you are to stimulate that uniqueness of what you are.

I feel You, God. Who Might You Be? Sometimes when I am thinking within myself in the moments of each and every day, my mind wanders to the place we are in now–whatever it might be considered, a class or a joining of what we are–and I try to consider little things that might stimulate each one of us, because I do not want you to think within yourself that you are a failure, or that you do not have That Spark of God that is within you. Each time that I get that little bit of information pertaining to the reality that might stimulate us, I am thankful. Sometimes I search it out, and seemingly there is nothing there. I do not know what else to give you. But each time that happens, there is always something beyond the realm of what I am, that I not only give you, I give me. I love you. It might not always show up. It shows up all the time over here. (Referring to God.) I hope it shows up over here sometimes. (Referring to self.) Listen with me one more time. Let the feelings go through you before I run out of moisture in my body.

(Referring to the music:) Think about what they do in the song. They are praying to everything: the wind, the stars, the moon, their brothers, their sisters, the earth they walk on, the water they drink. The same things you pray for. The sound reverberates throughout the consciousness of humanity. The ripples of it touch each one of us. Can't you hear the words within you now that should come out and say: *I love You, God?* No matter who you are, or where you come from, or what you say within yourself, or what religion you might be, can't you feel That Uniqueness now within you, that stimulates you within all of that which is religion and all of that which is your common ordinary life? Each and every day from now on, whomever you walk by will feel and sense you. It will stimulate those properties that were just mentioned. The time has come for us to begin to see, feel and use more.

As I look way into the distance, I see everybody. I see everybody who ever lived, especially the people close to us. Each one of them is looking upon us in a uniquely beautiful way! Feel good within yourself to know that whoever loved you is looking upon you now; looking upon you in a way where it is so unique and so usable! I have never seen anything like that before in my life! Billions of faces… and every one of them happy! They extend themselves so far out, and the ones that are necessary to be bright for us are bright. They shine; they shine in such a way! They are so proud, all of our mothers, fathers, sons, and daughters…

Do you know what we did for them? We lit the stage of our lives in a way where they can see us more clearly. We gave them a bigger light, a broader light to the reality of what we are. They can look upon us now in a more unique way. They can deal with our joys and happiness in a way they have never felt before. We have opened up a new, viable way of seeing each place. They were all looking too, all of them. Anything that we do, they do not see as wrong but so necessary. There is nothing that comes from there that condemns anything, it only salutes and glorifies it. So if you thought your mother, father, sister, brother, daughter, or son is disappointed in you, or grandfather, grandmother, aunt, uncle, friend, or neighbor, none of them is disappointed in anything that you do. You are sacred to them. You are that link from here to them. You are that seed-atom, or genetic process, that does not stop here or anywhere else.

I know deep down inside, you might think of some of these things going on tonight as being a little strange or weird. I wish I could make it different, but I cannot. I can only give you what I see, feel and sense. Sometimes it is enough. Sometimes it is too much, and sometimes it is not enough, but every time, it is everything I have. And every time I think I can shut this off for a moment, I cannot.

Could you imagine that you could just walk out into the rain and the drops will not hit you if you do not want them to? Or if there is a bump in the road, you could just glide right over it? Or if you wanted to see what is on the other side of the hill, you could just fly to it? There will be a time. It is not too far away. It is just over the horizon. There is a hill of comprehension and there are steps. You take a step each day. The realm of that becomes that country, that beautiful highway, and all of the scenery becomes usable. Every leaf has a pure color: just what you want to see in the foliage of time.

Tonight we took many steps. They were ordinary steps at first; then they became the granite of comprehension. They will be there, forever: shining steps of reality. You made that within the realm of what you are. If you like the pathway, and each valley and plateau…

Just when you think you have felt it all, the comprehension of all changes. Even though you should not make a statement like that, you make it anyway, because you know it is going to change anyway. I am going to have to sit for a few minutes. If there are those of you who have to leave, please do.

It is almost like this part here…(referring to the music.) You can just float with it. It takes you somewhere. You gave me all the notes, God, and all the flying upon it. You had to repeat it many times, and I was not really listening. I think this time I heard some of it, and what I heard was really good. It made me feel so extraordinary. I know I will hear more the next time because of this time. I heard a little song beneath this one that I will hear next time, that will magnify this one more so… Another meaning, another hidden word, another feeling beyond where I am. I am sure there always is, but what we feel now is extraordinary within the realm of it.

Just in time, God. You pull the rope, and the curtains are closing. Just the right amount of the Play of You. All of the characters fade and blend into the awareness of what we are. I have shouted enough. Now my quiet prayer comes forward, but within it, you feel and sense the emotions of all of what was said. You do it in a way where you feel the mother of earth and the mother of you. You stimulate the opposite. The harshness of the male is softened, but that harshness tilled the soil. You can seed it now. May you never be lonely. May you always feel strong. May you fly like the eagle and walk like the bear. Good night, everybody.

CHAPTER TWENTY-SIX

I Feel You, My Toes and My Feet
November 2, 2000

(A guided meditation for the evening:) I want you to think about yourself for a few minutes. This is special. What you are feeling now is a special feeling. Not many people can feel what you feel now. It is going to teach you something, and when it does so, it will linger within you for a long, long time. That special feeling that you have within you will spark every other feeling that you have ever had, and these feelings will never be the same again. I want you to dwell upon these thoughts for a few minutes. It makes the truth of this special feeling something that is more usable in a more rapid way. It repositions your thoughts forever. By you focusing upon them, it gives you that reality now. It is like when we meditate and give ourselves a second chance to focus upon those areas: that is what we are going to do tonight. When we consider each particular part of our bodies, I want you to think of it as a special place of relaxation. Give yourself the opportunity to focus and truly relax some of those areas. If you look at each of these areas and consider them for a moment, you can really feel within you more of an opportunity to relax them more so. It is just a matter of focusing upon the particular area within its awareness, making that special you, more special than you were before.

I know there is a great reason for you being here tonight. You have to consider that within you. I feel fortunate to be here in this room tonight. There are special events taking place each time we meet, but tonight those special events become extraordinary because you have the capability of seeing and using your mind in a way where you can understand them as so. This is your opportunity, not only to feel special for moments but for every moment from this day forward. Believing in self is so important. Any great person in the past who ever had to do anything interrelated to another person, always considered the belief of the other person as they interrelated to whatever it was they had to convey forward. Believe in yourself. Believe in the power that you have from that special place that you are in, that you will be in forever.

I want you to focus in on your toes now: I know that we have mentioned this so many times before, but I want you to relax them more so now. I want you not only to consider your physical toes, but the reality that sustains them from all of those different levels of what you are. Your toes are relaxed, free of tension and very comfortable.

Focus upon your feet. Just let them relax, relax, relax. As you relax each area, you might take the opportunity to ask a question about the awareness of where you are. What capabilities does this place give you? What thoughts does it generate within your mind and the consciousness of what you are? I know that each place that we look upon is special, but enhance the uniqueness of those places now, by saying: *I feel you, my toes and my feet. Where might you take me in the awareness of myself? What unique sustaining properties might I feel, as I feel the awareness of what you are within me? Who might you sustain within the reality of what I am?*

Relax and rejuvenate your ankles. Relax now the lower part of your legs, right up to the knees: relaxed, free of tension and very comfortable. You might ask those questions again about what you are feeling and sensing in each place. I will go very slowly so you may have the opportunity to do that. Relax now, your knees, and the upper part of your legs including your hips: relaxed, free of tension and very comfortable. Even though you know that each part of the body that you look upon is totally rejuvenated and relaxed, I want you to focus upon each part now by repeating within yourself: *Everything is functioning properly within my hips and my legs, right down to my toes.* Think about the total awareness of those places that we just mentioned and relax them more so now. That is it. It is amazing how much more relaxation you can feel in that area from your hips to your toes.

Relax now the lower part of the trunk of the body. Stay there for a moment: feel the wonderment of this place. You are relaxing and rejuvenating the lower part of the trunk of the body. You know without question, that everything is functioning properly here also.

Relax now the upper part of the trunk of the body. Focus upon that area. Everybody, everywhere upon this earth plane, and all of their realities can feel more comfortable because of what you do now! They do not know the source, but that is unimportant; the important thing is, there is a source. Repeat within yourself once again: *Everything is functioning properly.* By doing so, it increases the capability of everything functioning properly.

Relax now your back, from the base of your spine to your neck. You can feel your posture being corrected: new strength and vitality for your back. If you have problems in this area, think about those problems dissipating now. Believe in yourself. You have to believe in God. You have to believe in your soul. You have to believe in a Source that sustains the body. You are closer to that Source now. Logic tells you, as you move closer to That Source, you have more healing energies within you. This gives you belief in understanding the reality of

That Source. It should, if you are using your mind correctly.

Relax now your forehead, your jaw, your cheeks, your mouth, your nose, your ears, and your eyes. You are in a place now that is totally relaxed and free of tension. Everything is functioning properly within your mind and body.

Let us feel more of the wisdom and usable vibration of the soul within the flesh. You can do so by visualizing a small, white dot of energy within your heart center: it represents that esoteric reality of what you are. As you look upon it within your system, it gives you the capability of the refractability of the physical spectrum. This white light begins to expand outwardly from that spot. Some of us will see it and some of us will sense it. As it does so, it touches every part of you, cleansing and purifying you right down to the cellular level, and of course it would do so because of what it represents. This practice teaches your mind to understand the nature of using the reality of the white light in a proper way. The white light totally surrounds that unique body of what you are. You feel very relaxed, comfortable and safe. From this place, trace the reality of what we just participated in. Question the consciousness of each spot of the body. Receive whatever information you can. If none comes, search out another place, but what is important is that you are searching out and dealing with understanding the reality of what you are, and that you are special. I love you. We are going to play a piece of music now that will push you further into the reality of relaxation and comfort. Use the notes. They are just for you. I love you. (The meditation proceeded as usual.)

(Remarks after the guided meditation:) Each one of you has had an individual prayer from this place. It is very hard to take such beauty for such a long period of time. It has such an overwhelming quality to it. Would anyone like to share anything with us, or are there any questions before we take our break? I know one thing: I cannot take much more.

First questioner: I had a vision of a shaft of wheat outlined by the mountains and sky.

Good. Use it for yourself. Use it for balance to begin to understand some of the things you have to work on. That is the main thing. That is good. There is wheat growing all the time. It is up to you to harvest it. You do that by using your mind correctly in understanding the needs of the mind and the body.

Lately I have been trying to use my mind more correctly. I have never really used it against myself. Sometimes I will just exaggerate some of the feelings I have while out driving, but that does not really mean anything; I am not talking about that; I am talking about how I use my mind within the framework of humanity within the simplicity of my thoughts. I am talking about those moments that really count: those moments that change the density of everything. From where we were tonight, there was no question about it: I could see different avenues and floodgates of reality as I moved myself through those places. I saw some of the aspects within the framework of disease and agony, and how we can use whatever we are to push back the disease and agony in order to change the threshold of whatever it might be. Instead of experiencing extraordinary pain, we can change that reality into a little more tolerable reality of understanding the misconception. We have the free will within the physical sense to change, but if we can hit those levels that can do so, use those moments. Those moments are so important, and that is what the whole theme of what the first meditation was all about: having the capability of focus to change the reality of what we are, as it interrelates to other things and the total reality of those things.

It is so easy to get into those bad habits within the usage of the mind. Even when you are watching the loved ones around you, or others, you try to see how they participate in going into those avenues. You try to see the correct way of pulling them out of there. It is not easy once they have dug the trenches of misconception. It is not easy to fill those trenches in with the sustenance of reality. The winds of misconception play tricks on us in those tunnels that we have made. But as we participate in the rewards of those moments, they become the feelings of what we have within our minds and bodies. You should be in that place that has the shield of reality around you so that nothing affects you.

Lately though, I have been on the threshold of feeling and sensing the agonies of others within my body, and there had to be some questions about that within me. Was it necessarily a place that I put myself in that had less of a sustaining reality, or was it a place that I am feeling and sensing more so I have to increase the sustainability of it? There are so many beautiful avenues to question. Sometimes when you hit those places that we hit tonight, there are pathways that are so clear, smooth and usable. It is so understandable as you walk upon them. There is no hidden confinement to misconception. There is just true reality.

But then you have to go from that place and understand the strands that take place within those moments of reality so that you can pull back the misconception of what you understand is within the framework of you. If it were easy, the reward would not be so significant, so the suggestion that the reality of it is tough is understandable. But it is still your belief and your conviction that you can change within the structure of what you are. You changed it somewhat tonight, whether you wish to believe it or not. If you believed it, you changed it more so. If you did not, you changed it more so anyway, unknowingly. That place was so extraordinary that we were in. I hope that you felt and sensed and used it. I know one thing: you have to win the right to be in such a place. It might be that everything that you have ever done in your life made you be right here tonight in this moment. And as I make a statement like that, sometimes fragmented moments come before my mind's eye, and those moments give me the belief of considering that as the truth. It makes you understand how truly necessary it is to be where you are. Let us take our break.

(In the second half, the class listened to music:) Don't the words come to mind: *It is just like the drops of rain that wash away the dirt upon the earth, and you can smell the sweetness in the air...* That is what you do for yourself when you meditate. You cleanse and wash away all of that misconception. You can feel it within you. It moves through you. *I* could feel it. It tries so hard to heal everything, and the next time it has to try a little less hard than the time before. That is what this whole song is about. It cleanses you. If you see a sunset, or sunrise, or storm, open plain, or purple mountain, it does the same thing to you: it cleanses you.

You can see a person way in the distance, way out on the plain. At first it does not seem like you know that person, but as they come closer and closer, you realize that it is you wandering around out there! When you get close enough to see yourself, the enjoyment of it is incredible! Each of us sees only one face, but how many other faces of us are wandering through the plains of life, the faces of us? Shall we see all of those faces someday when they finally become one? They will. Meditate with me for a few minutes.

Each one of us searches out silence. Those moments are important. We will begin to use our minds for ourselves. We will think about what is right for us. The truth shall come forward. Each time that I use my mind incorrectly, I will remind myself, and each time that I remind myself, there will be one less time that I have to do so. I am going to use my mind for me, then for everybody else. I am going to see how I use my mind improperly, thus making the energy of what I am, dissipate. Then I am going to see how I use my mind properly, and see how I increase what I am. Each instance will be usable for incentive. We can feel it lifting us each time, and it will give us the speed that is necessary so that we will not become overwhelmed; instead we will feel the smoothness of the road before us that will give us comfort. I love You. Who are we, God? Who Might You Be?

Those brief moments that we feel like this, are overwhelming. How many more moments do we have like that? Are there millions? Trillions? Do they go on forever? Oh, the mystery of the unknown! It is so necessary. Sometimes it does confine us to the moments that bridge the gap between here and there. When I feel some of these things come through me–and I try to use my mind so correctly–sometimes a trickle of the rewards of my comprehension comes forward, and I can see some of the potentials of what we are. But the blessing within it... Most of our potential is hidden, and that is the creativity that is necessary to be that way. We have to light it ourselves. We have to lift ourselves to that place that can see, and when we do, it is so clear, precise and usable. We understand why it was hidden: it was beyond our sight because our sight did not have the capability of seeing it. Now that we see it, it is the incentive of what is beyond our sight once again. I know we feel the chaotic moments within it. Chaos becomes so usable. Let us see it clearly. Let us see the light. How shiny that windshield of life is. There is no mist upon it. We have cleared it away. We have wiped away the dirt of misconception with the cleansing properties of consciousness. Wherever we are, that is a prayer. You do not have to seek out the words; say what you feel within yourself, whatever it might be. If you are sincere, that is a true prayer, and it reaches the place that is necessary for you to grow. Search out all of the avenues first: extinguish all the opportunities; then pray once again. Make it a moveable vehicle that is usable for you, not a crutch that conveys you into areas of misconception.

Many people in the past have asked, "How do we pray?" Pray with sincerity, whatever words they might be. That is the most important prayer. If there is something that you want from life that you do not have, and it does not hurt another, and you seek out a place that makes it more pliable for you, ask whatever it might be. Then question the avenues that can make you achieve the particular thing. Information will come forward quickly from every avenue that you question, and the prayer will be answered, because it pulls you along that roadway of life. It has a gentle wind that pushes even when you do not think you are moving. You, yourself, make the wind different. Each time it moves you further into that area that truly is usable for you. If there is one thing that you can do for yourself, one important thing is to train your mind. The perception of everything changes and becomes more usable for you. It does not confine you; it moves you. What might your prayer be today? Whatever it might be, ask within the silence of you. Believe in yourself.

I love You, God. We seek You out most times with blinders on. Sometimes we peek from behind and see clearly. When we see, what a unique thing it is! We pray tonight in our words, and tomorrow in our deeds, that we may feel more of that Brilliance of What You Are. Each time the words will be different, but each time they will be from where we are. We know that it is so necessary to be exactly where we should be. Sometimes we are not there. Tonight, as we think about it, and pray, we pull ourselves closer to that place. The Wonderment of What You Are pulls us into those areas.

Tomorrow, the next day and the days after, you will see changes within you. Those moments will become those bright times within you. You will say: *Wow!* and look back upon this place and time. You will understand that you used your mind correctly from a place that was sacred and usable, because you put yourself there. Nobody else brought you here, but you. No longer confined, you soar through the realities of what you are. The wind is smooth and usable, and the pathway bright. Each horizon has new ventures for you.

I love you. I do not have a clue what time it is, but I know one thing: I cannot take much more. Hope you have a fantastic week. Hope I see you again next week.

CHAPTER TWENTY-SEVEN

There Is Something That Is Festering
November 15, 2000

(Remarks after the guided meditation:) I want you to consider some of the things we do here in class in meditation. As you consider them, what are you doing? You are compounding the reality of them becoming usable for you. When I take that deep breath, I can actually feel the fatigue leaving my body. When I enter and return from meditation, there is not one time that I do not feel rejuvenated because I am using my mind correctly! I do not feel any fatigue after that. It has to do with the mind. Know and believe in yourself. If you think that you are going to come up as tired as when you went in, you are going to come up tired, because your mind is going to tell you: *I am tired.* Where are you in the meditative state? You are in that plateau of comprehension, that place of absorption, where you can retain what you mention to yourself. So when you are deep, say: *When I come up, I will be totally rejuvenated.* It is going to compound the reality of that becoming usable when you come up. If I can do it, anybody can do it, and believe me, I do it every day; I rejuvenate myself with one deep breath on the job, or on my way home in the truck.

What are some of the things you should be working on from that plateau of comprehension, that funnel of absorption? The things that you deal with in life. When you are at that level, you should have a list of the people you know who are not well. Know the power of your mind at that level and the healing qualities that you have. You are closer to your soul, and closer to the reality that made you, and closer to the reality that can heal you. It is as simple as that. Christ, Moses, and Buddha were closer to the reality of their souls. Some of them actually absorbed the essence of the soul within the flesh. Christ did. He was able to do unbelievable things, because he had unbelievable things within him. Where do you collect those unbelievable things? You collect them from that esoteric quality of what you are, but only when you use those qualities that you were given at birth within you now. Use them and comprehend them, and more will come.

That is what meditation is all about. It gives you the opportunity to rejuvenate; the rejuvenation gives you balance; the balance gives you that plateau of comprehension; the plateau of comprehension gives you a clear mind, giving you focus. You can focus upon the reality of eliminating misconceptions from your mind and body, thereby eliminating your normal daily problems. Then what do you think takes place? There are small graduations within you, each time that you do so: opportunities to pick more of the fruit of the soul, each time that you do so. More of the sustenance of that awareness becomes usable in the flesh because you have won the right to use it within the flesh through comprehension. It is awesomely beautiful and usable. Each time that a trickle of it hits you, you will feel the wonderment of it, and it will stimulate the reality of what you are into a more finely attuned place that has a reaction dealing with more of the comprehension of what is coming next.

First, you have to teach yourself to be quiet. First, you have to teach yourself to meditate at a subtle level. Then when you feel comfortable, drop deeper by saying: *I wish to drop deeper to listen and feel and sense what is going on in my mind and body.* If you feel comfortable there, change the level once again. If you feel a little fear, fear is telling you that you are going too fast. Fear is a tool of the soul telling you to slow down because you are there before you are ready. Comprehension eliminates fear. If you know what is behind the next door, there is no fear; there is just an opportunity to turn the doorknob and open the door. You give yourself that opportunity by understanding the velocity that is usable for you to comprehend. If you are going too quickly, it pushes you back. If you are going too slowly, that is stagnation, which pushes you back. A balanced vehicle gives you the opportunity to automatically escalate to the next place without even thinking about it, because comprehension escalates your ability to comprehend. It is a uniquely beautiful process that lays dormant within all of us. It only has to be stimulated by the proper use of the mind. As you learn to do so, each time that you use your mind within the next time or moment, it gives you more of an opportunity to grasp upon using it right. It builds upon itself; it is so unique and usable, and it is there for you when you are ready. You should be ready now. It is your choice.

First questioner: **One area that has been very difficult for me to solve is a persistent skin rash in the forehead.**

That interrelates to survival. The skin organ deals with the survival center, so the rash refers to something within the physical sense that is threatening you. The particular area where the rash manifests also interrelates to the reality of what you are dealing with. If it is in the area of the forehead, it deals with perception and insight into reality. If it is in the solar plexus, it deals with the emotions of mankind.

Sometimes when we are working on something so much, we have

to absolutely stop and question it no further. I think you are at that point now. You have to pull yourself out of it and let it pull you back in. That is exactly the way I want to phrase it too. I want you to take a rest. I want you to let yourself be pulled back in automatically. When another question arises, I do not want you to react to it. Just say: *Okay, I am taking a rest.* It is as if the phone is ringing, but you do not answer it because you are on vacation. Then it gives you an opportunity to stabilize yourself within the awareness of the particular thing.

Then you are going to be able to ask questions from a new, unique and balanced place within the sphere of that comprehension. You are going to be in an outer orbit of the particular thing, but it is going to pull you back into the nucleus automatically, teaching you how to comprehend within that sphere. I want you to try that because I know you are having some trouble where you are. It is not a great deal of trouble, but it is baffling to you. It will not be so, because it will give you a new perspective on how to comprehend within that sphere. Try it. Pull yourself back. I do that occasionally. I stop. Sometimes I will not even meditate for two or three days; instead I might increase my capability of doing exercise or extra chores. It gives you an opportunity sometimes to look at things in a different way. It gives you a different perspective about what you are trying to comprehend. It is almost like taking a little vacation from your particular area of comprehension.

There is something within each one of us that is festering. You know what it is. You know what you have to do to become a better person. It is important to work on it from an area. You do not want to work on it in a subway; you want to work on it from the meditative state. You want to work on it from that place that clears things up and eliminates the distortions. There is living proof if you look at the structure of what you are doing in meditation: it gives you an opportunity to become a better person. It is a natural sequence of events, even within the initial thrust into the subtle areas of it. It is so usable. Even if it is just to rejuvenate yourself, you are putting yourself in a more pliable area of comprehension. When you come up from the meditation, you have more balance, compassion and usable understanding of whatever you might be involved in. Whatever interaction you then have with others, you are dealing with more energy without even knowing about it. For instance, when I first started meditation, the teacher told me that I had considerable healing powers. She asked me to help with different ill people. I was opening up so fast, and the energy was changing so fast within me, it was really very baffling. It changed the entire structure of everything around me. There were things happening to me so fast, you could not even imagine. For instance, around this time I remember going into a hospital to visit a friend, and as I was walking by each door, I felt huge amounts of energy vanishing from my body. It was affecting me so much that I had to pull myself back to say: *What is going on here? What could I do? I cannot let this affect me like it is affecting me now.*

Then I went to a party with some people that I knew for years. I had to leave the party because I was not seeing my friends the way I normally saw them. I was seeing all the arguments they had that day, all the insecurities. I had to get up and leave the place, and they were saying, "Hey, what is the matter with you?" Usually I am involved in a lot of loud, joking interactions. I had to pull myself back because there were so many new things happening to me. My perception of everything, along with my capacity of clairvoyance, was changing so rapidly. I was not looking at appearances anymore, I was looking at the structure of the person, and how their mind worked, and what kind of activities they were involved in that day and so forth. It was incredible.

The point is, sometimes you have to pull yourself back to say: *Hey, I know I just received a reward here. I know that I have the strength within me to comprehend all of this, because within the essence of the reward is greater knowledge.* You have greater knowledge each time that you go through a major energy change. When it filters down within you, it has an entire structure of comprehension involved within it. But you have to put the pieces together; you have to control the reality of what you are within that new area. It is just like graduating to a new class: it changes; the graduation is more profound and deals with a lot more. Now you are not listening to just one person, you are listening to many. You are not feeling and sensing what is in you, you are feeling and sensing what is in so many people. Before all of this happens, it is just so easy when you are dealing with self only. That is why it is so important each time we go into meditation that I mention, "We have love of self." It is so important to be so strong when these things come forward. There are so many things going on in this room to help you prepare for a particular event when it happens, and I could not do that for you if I did not go through it myself.

When I went through major energy changes, every single thing about my life changed. Thought patterns of others became apparent to me. I could feel it instantly if a person hated me or was inwardly saying: *He does not know what he is talking about.* I could instantly feel and sense it when sensual thoughts were coming at me. At that time, these things were so overwhelming, I had to put in safety blocks. I pulled myself out of those areas. I gave myself little vacations. I gave myself strength. I looked at what was happening and said: *If I have a new opportunity to see duality at these levels, and have all of this energy and knowledge coming at me, I have to learn how to use it prop-*

erly. Because if there is one thing I know, no more will come until you do.

Your soul will not give you more than you can comprehend. No more will come from beyond a particular level until you are ready. There are so many safety valves within the system of you between you and your soul. Only you can cause yourself confusion within a particular level. For instance, you can take drugs and lift yourself to a higher level, but when you return to the normal state, there is so much consciousness around you, and total confusion, because there is nowhere for the consciousness to rest. You have stolen the consciousness, rather than won the right. That is why people who take drugs have so much confusion. There is a tremendous amount of knowledge coming in and nowhere for it to go. You have less brain matter, because you have destroyed it by taking the drug, while you have more information coming in. If you are utilizing your mind correctly in the classroom here, you are lifting yourself to that higher level through a natural sequence of events. When you transcend, then return into your normal reality, there are new brain cells waiting to receive that which is usable in comprehension.

We are only using a certain portion of our brains now. Einstein might have used twenty or thirty percent because he lifted himself to a higher level. Michelangelo, who expressed himself through the throat center of higher creativity, was using a higher level of comprehension. These great entities did not even realize what was going on, but lifted themselves to higher levels. How could Christ bring Lazarus back from the dead? He did it because he was at the level that made Lazarus. Is it just so easy? It is just like going to the paint store to pick out a color and bring it home: you can pick a color at the paint store because there is a color at the paint store. When you bring it back home, it is there. The same thing takes place in comprehension. You bring it down within you and it becomes you. If it becomes you here within the physical reality, now more of the structure that made you is here. You have lesser trauma, less areas of misconception, and less probability of harm and illness happening to you. As you go through the different stages of life, you will look good, feel good and deal with the pleasures in life.

Each of us knows certain elderly people who deal with the pleasures of life. They have taught themselves to use their minds correctly, whether they believe it or not, through the natural sequence of teaching events within the physical sense. They might not have been in a class learning meditation, although meditation is the best way to get there. They might have learned the correct usage of the mind through concentrating in a particular art form, or in some kind of work. Whatever it is, it is focusing upon the particular thing that draws in more of the essence of the reality of what they are trying to comprehend. They have made self beyond normal. Each one of you has that capability. By being in this class, you are laying down a basic foundation within strength and love of self, thereby giving all of that information a seat within the brain.

There is the issue of free will that we have had to learn about. In the early years of the meditation classes I remember sitting here in class one night, thinking: *I wish we had good music equipment.* The following week, a new person appeared in class who had just the kind of knowledge to acquire the right equipment for us. Just my candid thoughts of wishing for something, but not knowing what was truly going on, materialized within the following week or so. It was really astonishing. I found that almost anything I thought about was coming forward, so I had to shut it off. I had to make the information sensible and usable, dealing with the essence of free will within everyone.

Now the class interactions do not infringe upon anyone. We do not have sixty or seventy people in the class anymore, because now students know they have to grow on their own. I know it is easier here, but you still have to do it yourself. When you leave here, everything that you have achieved, you have achieved on your own. Of course, there is energy. Of course, there is a consciousness. Of course, there is knowledge sometimes–I hope to think so–that will give you the stimulation, or trickles of energy, that will put you in the right direction so you may comprehend and become more than what you were before. But I guarantee one thing: that you will not get it anyplace else. It does not infringe for one single moment on your free will, and it takes a long time to teach yourself that. Infringing upon another person's free will is the gravest sin upon earth itself, whether it is taking a person's life, or taking away their opportunity to become more evolved, because that is why we are here. If I as teacher contradict that, I contradict every belief at every level. If you are here to learn more, and I teach you in a way where I am stealing it for you, you are not learning more. Then you are contradicting why you are here, and I am contradicting everything here.

All of the time, think about where you are. Ask questions, no matter whether you are in this class for the first time, or for a long time. When I first stepped into this school thirty years ago, I literally drove the teacher crazy. I was asking so many questions, finally she took me aside one night and said, "John, do me a favor and stop asking so many questions. I cannot keep up with you." That taught me something. I said: *John, if you truly are involved on that pathway that takes you to that esoteric level, and the energies change you, don't you think that the answers are within you? If you ask questions about you in your quiet moments, don't you think you will get answers pertaining to you and whatever else?* That started a series of questions within myself that actually gave me the ability to escalate my comprehension to wherever it might be now. It may be nowhere to some people, but it gave me what I have now, which is more than I had before. It might not be enough for another person, but it is more than I had before.

Second questioner: **When do you pray?**

You pray when you are dropping off to hit the particular level where you feel extremely secure, and you have balance within you, and in your mind you want to pray. Prayer can also become a contradiction to growth because it can make you stagnant. It is like asking for something when you have not given yourself the chance to achieve it first. It is like praying each and every day for the same thing, and never going out into life to achieve it. Or I have seen it happen so many times, a person prays in church, and is so pious–which is fine–but then afterwards tries to run you over in the parking lot. The time for prayer is over; it is time to run you over now. If you are involved in whatever religion it might be, and you pray, and are really involved in it, it is usable. If you have tried all the avenues that you can think of, but still hit that level where there is that stonewall that you cannot penetrate, prayer becomes truly usable. It dissipates that barrier because you have tried in so many different ways to achieve that particular next level.

We have talked about how important it is when you are healing another person that you say: *God, or Jesus, help me to heal this person, and as I do so, I know that more of the Essence of You flows through me, so the next time I have more energy to help the next person.* When I am healing someone, I say to myself so many times, and I can say it so clearly within myself: *Help me, God. I ask You for help.* As I drop off right before you now, and go deeper and deeper even as I am talking to you, I put that preconceived thought within my mind. I know each time, that I am healing the other person. I can feel tremendous energy coming through me and it goes to the particular person. Each time I ask for the Wisdom of Whomever It Might Be interrelated to me at those levels. I say: *Help me.* As it filters through me, I know it changes the density of what I am, so that the next time that I have the opportunity of trying to heal a person that has a similar misconception, I will have more energy within me to do so. That is a true healing.

At those levels you will have insight into the reality of why there is a misconception within the other person's body. You will want to give them a pathway of understanding why that disease happened to them so they will not venture into that particular area anymore. That is a true healing. You say to the person who has a heart problem, "If you go forward from this day forward and do the same thing again, you will deteriorate your heart center." It is not saying the person is bad; it is saying they are not comprehending why the particular ailment is happening to them. The heart center deals with compassion and balance. If they have a lack of compassion and balance towards self, or others, they dissipate that center. The corresponding secondary centers to the heart center are the elbows and knees. If the person has a heart attack, their arm will stiffen up and they will grab their arm. They do not even know why they are grabbing it. It is because the secondary center gives out first. When it does so, then there is a blast that happens in the chest.

You can give the person the information. I am working on a woman right now. She is doing fairly well. She has been through a terrible amount of chemotherapy and radiation. I really do not know how she is taking it; she is very strong. I am sure the healing is helping, and I am sure the acupuncture person that she is going to is helping. She asked me whether she should have acupuncture, and I said, "Sure, do that. Everything helps." The acupuncturist is good because I can feel him. Each time that I work on her, I tell her one certain little thing, whether she knows it or not, pertaining to the particular misconception in her disease: how she uses her mind and why she went down that pathway without even knowing about it. One time I might tell her that she has to have a little more patience and human decency towards her husband, because he is trying so hard and is going through a lot. If you think about what energy center the disease, cancer, comes from, it is the third center of emotions and human decency, and where the cancer is manifesting in the body is another consideration. She has to work on her human decency. If and when she does that, more energy goes into that area to rejuvenate rather than dissipate it.

Now, when we think about it in the sense of the question asked, "When do we pray?" all of these aspects are important pertaining to it. When do you pray? When you feel that you have to pray. You are good enough to pray, no matter what or wherever you are: whether meditating or not, or sitting in the corner somewhere. It is your right to pray. But get something out of it. Pray properly, which is anything that comes from the heart, and you really mean it. It does not have to be poetry; whatever the feeling might be. When you are really down and out, and need help, and have tried everything that you possibly can, pray, and it will work because it is written within so many different layers within the Framework of what was put here in absolute areas. There are certain things that are absolutes that God does not deviate from, because those absolutes fit within the context of everything else. If it is an absolute within the structure of comprehension, even God does not change it.

For example, when we go through reading and correcting the books, my wife and G will sit there for grammar, and M will read it to me. I will be listening to each word pertaining to something that could be a contradiction into what I have ever said. There are certain times when I have to take a little piece out because that seed-atom, John, made a mistake in class. Not that what comes through him at certain levels is wrong, but he was not totally ready in a verbal sense to project the particular statement forward. But the book cannot have a contradiction because it makes every other statement in the book not believable.

Now, I might say to you, "I love you," and the next time that I tell you, "I love you," won't there be more love within me because I told you this time? There will be a lot more, because I really meant it. But we have to begin to understand what we ask for sometimes. If you really mean the prayer that you make, it has a lot more velocity behind it, and a lot more rewards coming back, because the prayer will hit you in areas that will make you comprehend... But sometimes not in a way that you wish. It will make you see certain things that you will see in a different way, perhaps through drudgery. Later you will say: *God, why did I ask for that? I tried not to ask for too much lately, but now it is overwhelming. It came at me in a direction where I did not think it was coming at me.*

Therefore, sometimes I try to teach myself to pray precisely by saying: *God, could I go through this pathway and understand it without being hit by over the head with a sledgehammer?* We have to begin to understand what we ask for sometimes. It comes back at us in a different way and makes us comprehend it. Eventually we say: *Wow, that was great, but while I was going through it, that tree did hit me, and that was not nice!* Eventually what happens, when we ask, we are in those higher levels where the velocity of the misconception is not quite as bad. Good night, everybody. Practice, practice, practice. Go slowly. Do not force it. By going slowly, you increase your capability.

CHAPTER TWENTY-EIGHT

A Heart Center Class: This Is Unexpected Territory
January 10, 2001

(John's beginning remarks as the class prepares for the first guided meditation:) I really should start going deep again and doing some things. I probably will not, (laughing) but why don't we do so tonight, a little bit? This will be the first meditation helping us to prepare for the second one.

But we are having fun, aren't we? I seem to have fun all of the time. I do not know what it is. I was trying to figure out if my mother took anything while she was carrying me, but she did not; they did not have anything back then so long ago. For some strange reason, I was born on this natural high, and it is good. It might be misunderstood and thought of as being something else, but I can honestly and truly say to you–and this is unusual too, for somebody my age–I never once tried any of those drugs. I did not even puff on anything. I just did not do any of that, and that is unusual because I was at parties where people were doing some stuff. But I just never wanted to do it. I do not even know why I am talking about this, but we are, for some strange reason.

It is sort of an old crowd in here tonight. Not old in the sense that you are old in age, but old in the ability to sit in this room for so many years trying to find out what this idiot is doing up here. But I can think back a long way. We were doing some different things way back then. I can guarantee you, where we are now is in a much more balanced and pliable place. I am sure you are going to feel some of that tonight, because when I was meditating shortly before you got here, it seemed as if the energy was filling in very nicely. Let us see what can happen. I promise that you will feel some heart center tonight. You are probably feeling some already. So relax, and put good intent in your mind, and dwell upon that rejuvenation. I wish to prepare myself so when we meditate once again in the second half, we will feel and sense things that will stimulate us, and give us the opportunity to achieve something different within the realm of balance and compassion and love. For some strange reason, for the last twenty-three years I do show up here. I have only missed a couple of classes. But it is fun. It is good for me also.

You can change your breath pattern as you wish to. Let us slowly proceed through those different aspects that we talk about and actually feel the rewards of looking upon those particular parts of our bodies. Believe in yourselves. You are no longer people that deal with the initial thrust into meditation and comprehension; you have special things within you. Use them. (The guided meditation proceeded as usual.)

(In the second half of class John begins to drop into a deep-trance state, talking while doing so:) We will not have music this time. While I am dropping, if I feel and sense anything, I will probably mention it to you.

I am pretty balanced on both sides. You should be feeling that in your feet, and the lower part of your legs. It is amazing: the first meditation seemed so smooth, but now I am feeling some blockages within myself that I have to eliminate. There are those times when I think I have the areas totally relaxed, but then look upon them once again to find that a couple of these areas are not relaxed at all. I just have to make an effort to focus on further relaxation. I just experienced that. The extent of my relaxation was fine for a basic level, but when I am trying to extend myself into some higher essence, I can feel there is more relaxation needed in certain areas, and more of a concentration on my part towards that.

(There were intervals of silence between the following remarks:) I am getting the feeling once again of being gigantic. As if I am sitting on the earth itself, and the earth is small. A great deal of energy is in my knees, hands, and wrists.

It is amazing: if I really, really listen, feel, and sense, I can actually feel the stress and tension dissipating from my mind too. I never felt it quite like that before. I can actually feel the stress leaving, even the stress I did not think I had, and within the essence of it I see some of the reality of it. It gives me some information pertaining to that: how it is leaving the body, and what it does, and how it can become usable in eliminating blockages even in my nasal passageway, ears, eyes, or whatever. I can almost feel a cleansing in a different way than I would normally feel it. I can actually feel little fibers of the stress leaving my mind and body, almost like little electrical impulses.

Some of the people I know who have recently died have just passed through my mind. I do not know why, but they have. This just came out of nowhere. I am just refracting some things to each one of them. There is just a bit of sadness involved in it. If you are feeling that sadness, do not let it affect you. I am putting my thoughts outside of it.

I feel very solid and very balanced now. Basic foundation: my feet feel like two airplane carriers.

I do not actually see anything, but my perception seems to have a penetrating quality to it. The distance that it is traveling seems extraordinary. I have never seen that before either.

I am feeling some heart center energy. A lot of emptiness there. I should be spending more time there: emptiness in the sense that it is so vast I should be within its realm once in a while and comprehend the space of it.

As I am going through this, I am feeling and sensing some balancing qualities within those particular areas within... There are fleeting moments of compassion and love that have an overwhelming quality to them. There seem to be a lot of lavender flashes, seemingly giving a very stable quality almost like laser rays in the third-eye center, but are arching; they are not straight but curved outwardly to the right and to the left.

There is a shade of greenish-blue light that I have never seen before: very light. It is hard to explain what it might be. It seems to be changing into a more vibrant green, something not on the fringes but more towards the center. Almost like different boulders or rocks that are curved and piled upon each other in different colors of green. They do not seem to be heavy though. They seem light, almost like air within them. They are like cushions, very thick, very oval. Some greens and lavenders coming into that green and blue.

This is unexpected territory. Some of the things I am seeing are unexpected. I have a very sound feeling. I am very much in control of myself. Those cushions that I saw before are almost like clinging to my body like parts of muscles. That is an unusual thing. Piled upon each other. Even though their appearance seems to be heavy, they are very light.

I do not know why, but I see flashes of red that turned white within my fingers on my right hand. The flashes seem to be longer than the physical fingers. It is a beautiful color of white, with just soft, soft, red within it, not pink. I cannot explain that color – beautiful. I would think that white with red would make it pink, but it is not: I am seeing the two colors together but isolated within each of them. It is very hard to explain. They have their own identity, yet are part of each other, so they are very clear within the analogy of what they are. They move beyond the physical comprehension. Their capabilities, of course, are beyond self.

I am also seeing some flashes of lavender, blue and green which are pulsating out from the third-eye center; then seeing the same phenomenon take place within those colors. I can see the colors very clearly within the essence of each one of them, yet they are together. It is very hard to explain. When I first saw it, it seemed to consume the entire head area. It is just like a flash.

I sense more balance within my legs, hands, and arms. Wow. There was like an empty feeling within my solar plexus a short while ago, but that seems to have left. It does not feel as empty as it was before.

I am seeing objects that seemingly have absolutely no relationship to my body, but for some strange reason seem to be involved with my body. I have never seen that before. They are almost like those traffic cones on the highway, but these are outlined. I am just thinking of the shape of them, and it has nothing to do with those cones, but they seem to have almost like candy stripes around them almost like the thickness of a candy cane; but these stripes are revolving around each one of those cones, and there is just one big one, bright white and red.

I saw a flash of lavender, white and green shoot right up in the sky over wherever, and I caught a glimpse of a place in Vermont where I was one time where I was seeing a lot of people who were "way out there." I do not know why that flashed before my mind. It is almost like that area right in front of the statehouse: there is some kind of vortex of energy there. I felt something when I was there, but did not realize what it was.

Oh, I feel like I am ... Very hard to describe the things I am seeing: as if I am in a very bright place, green and white. Big tubes of energy and they are not... They are just like the expansion structures on the George Washington Bridge and they are gigantic. There is almost like a seat, and I am sitting within it, yet the seat is bigger than I am. It is almost like I am sitting in a small cabin in it, or something.

All of these things that I see are new and unexplainable. In the distance I am seeing a pulsating light, a very soft, bluish-white light, and it is way in the distance. It is pulsating towards me. Once in a while, I see some bodies floating around. They do not seem to be in too much distress; just floating. They seemed to be very aware of what is going on.

It is like... some gigantic crystals are shooting up: enormous. It is almost like they are growing before me, first seemingly dark, then turning lighter.

It seems to be as if I am just in a vacuum, and I feel very, very, very comfortable. But I have no emotion, no feelings other than the reality of stability, and I am seeing all of these different colors. Now I am getting a lime-green-white crystal color. I do not know where these crystals are coming from, but they are gigantic. They are not coming from one area but coming from a lot of different areas.

My third-eye center seems to be opening more so. I seem to be looking at something. I cannot see what it is. As I am doing so, my survival center is opening unbelievably so. I feel great stability within my heart center now: a sort of a lime-green color. I have never seen a color like that before. All of these colors are translucent too. You can see right through them. They are almost like streams of light; as if you are looking at rays from the sun.

Sometimes I can almost feel like something... and something is looking right back at me.

Wow. Over my head, I almost feel like... see a storm almost like a gigantic umbrella over my head, with clouds just moving outwardly from it: all around, black and white, though. There does not seem to be any disturbance within it. It just reminds me of storm clouds and the way they are moving outwardly: they are being pushed by tremendous winds, the winds of reality, and within them, once in a while, I am seeing channels. One of them is a black channel going somewhere. There are dots of light. A strange place.

Start bringing myself up slowly. Wow. Wow. I am starting to come up and I just felt my arms as if they were two gigantic... I cannot explain it. They do not seem like wings, but big doors, and they just swung forward and closed in front of me. They were not even seemingly attached to my arms, but my arms seemed to go with them.

I can look down through myself now. I guess we are not what we appear to be.

I am trying to bring myself up. I am being preoccupied with some other things. You would think I would be able to come up faster than I am, but I am not coming up that fast.

I am like, in the center of a tornado. Wow. Like a cone; sort of round at the bottom. It is moving, but I do not seem to be moving at all. I am going to give myself an effort to bring myself up more so.

Wow. Whew. Wow. Sort of strange, to tell you the truth. Was it a heart center? Whew. I do not know. Wow. Forced myself to come up too fast.... (John struggles to take off the microphone.)

CHAPTER TWENTY-NINE

The Extraordinary Umbrella of Comprehension
January 17, 2001

(John's beginning remarks about the previous class, The Heart Center:)
That class was different, really different. It was the first class that I
could actually say that I left, and it was beyond me. It was something
that was beyond what I could cling to. I mean, there was so much going
on, and I was seeing so many things, I could not grab upon a particular
thing and use it instantly to say: *Yes, I know where that goes*. I could
not do that, which is fine. I could feel comfortable with that, but it did
have a different effect on my ability to use my abilities, whatever they
might be. The energy was awesome, but very, very balanced, very steady
and very out of the ordinary. I did have a very difficult time coming up;
I know that. It was that deep, and that is unusual for me because I come
up very quickly most times. Since then, I have noticed a difference in
my ability to drop deeper too, which is unusual because I usually drop
very deep, anyway.

It is very difficult sometimes. The information that I seemingly get
is so clear and so precise to me, and I have been giving it some thought
about the capacity of newcomers being on the fringe of being frightened by it. I think a lot of them are frightened by it. When they come
into the class for the first time, I think they sense and feel something,
and are very frightened in the initial thrust into hearing some of the
things that we say here. It has made me question the reality of why we
are doing this. I suppose it is not mainly for the class; I think it is
mainly for the information pertaining to some of the things that have to
be said or whatever. Certain things and certain evenings: there are certain people in the classroom to interrelate to how things can be stimulated into a direction to draw in some of those energies. For instance,
there might be a new person in the class one night that makes me go
into a particular direction.

I had a few thoughts in the direction of trying to understand the
reality of these factors and their capacities to make oneself usable in
humility, which is something I have to consider. I have to consider also
why it does not affect me to the point where I could have more people
coming in the classroom. I know if I opened myself up more, there
would be a lot more people. I say: *Why don't I push it in the direction
where I open myself up more, and have newcomers feel and sense cer-*

tain things so they will come back? Then it makes me question the reality of why we are here and why we are in this particular place: *What is happening within this particular room? Why do we continue? Why do we go in a certain direction?*

I have been giving some thought into those particular questions; but most of the information related to last week's class was interrelated to the reality of the creation of consciousness into what is usable in the framework of humanity, and how the capacity of certain individuals within the physical sense impact upon that, and how to sway that reality in one direction or another. Those particular things have been passing through my mind over the last four or five days. It has been making me consider the reality of balance, and the utilization of thought patterns, and what an extraordinary capacity those particular factors have within the physical sense in changing our reality. It also made me see that there is so much to be done, yet it interrelates to what I can do within the framework of what can be done and the will that I have to do so. It made me think about certain capacities of certain individuals within the physical sense who were not even known upon the planet, but chose to come into the physical reality to change certain realities without being within the spotlight of the change of that reality. We could maybe consider some of the pathways that are necessary within the physical sense in that capacity.

It is very interesting: an umbrella of comprehension, a swirling pattern of chaos, stimulated by the simplicity of thought patterns that cling upon it and draw upon it. It made me feel the reality of this umbrella of comprehension that is constantly moving. I had never thought of it in that way before, because each time that we say we feel and sense something different, it is because it is constantly moving, it is constantly changing the analogy of a thought that is seemingly stagnation. But it is not stagnation, because the capacity of stagnation is impossible within the realm of something that is constantly moving; so even though you think you are in the same place, the analogy of the same place is different, which is usable and understandable when you think about it.

The energy is extraordinary. The umbrella of comprehension's capacities are not totally known, only partially so. Its usability clings to every moment that you attend to, yet within its presence it has no force or direction other than the will of you, which makes it staggeringly perfect. Where the knowledge comes from is an extraordinary ability to translate the movement of it between you and it, and its qualities change constantly, so your perception of it is seemingly outside of comprehension at times.

Was it a heart center last week? It is hard to say. Its intention was in that direction and the reality of it becomes the sustenance of that particular center, so yes, it was. Does it have the common ordinary feelings of such within the realm of what it was, last week? No, it infringed upon the awesome stability of the truth of it that was staggering beyond our comprehension, and its capacity made me see it as so. Yet as the days come forth and leave, each time they do so, more of it becomes understandable in each moment, and the truth behind it is, you do not even have to seek it out, it is there. It compounds the reality of what you are, in its extraordinary presence.

Did we win the right to be there? Within our ordinary understanding of the reality of winning it through comprehension, I guess that we might say, "Yes." Did we stagger upon it within the ignorance of what we are? We might say, "Yes, within the understanding of it, but not yet within its awareness." If we had totally won the right to have the umbrella of comprehension within us, it would be totally understandable; but if we staggered upon it, there would be no realm of it that we would understand. So either way is not totally right or wrong. Either way has something to do with why we were there last week. Does its presence change us? Yes, for brief moments, yet it is hidden within the misconceptions of what we are. That is so important, because if it were clear and shiny, and right in front of us, and totally usable, it would totally abuse it without the next necessary prisms to refract it into the necessary areas. So as we slant the ability of what we are into necessary places to refract the light into necessary people or places, it becomes more known within its ability because our ability and perception has changed; because for that brief moment we had focus and understood what took place.

I felt the umbrella of comprehension as extraordinary. I felt it as totally balanced and sometimes protected by the awareness beyond what I am, which was necessary not to see the brightness of it. We saw the necessary color of it, and it was usable for where we are, but its stimulating qualities in every moment will never leave us. Whether we won the right, or staggered upon it through ignorance, we are there. Either way, we will make it more usable, because we focused upon it as it moves within the misconception and the storms of life to become the comprehensions of our tomorrows; yet it protects us even when we look upon it as something totally beyond our comprehension, and totally extraordinary and powerful. It protects us. It is so extraordinary in its simplicity, but its simplicity is extraordinary.

Is this the place, God, that we feel more of You? That we truly know You Are There, and Your Presence becomes something that changes the reality of what we can see, or do, and makes us know without question that we truly are extensions of You? What we feel upon in the fringes of this new place certainly gives us insight into possible directions that might give us that stabilizing comprehension that we speak of. There are moments that we feel so ordinary and there are moments that we feel so extraordinary. They both stimulate, but what path do they lead us down so we may make common ground between the two? The Staggering Presence of What You Are becomes the reality of the pathway between the two.

Do we understand why we are here and why we are just what we are? A few of us, but not many. I think we can brush upon it when we think about some of the things that we discuss and talk about, that are necessary to do so maybe more than we know. What do we draw upon within that umbrella of comprehension? What particular things make the stabilizing blocks of humanity, without us knowing about them, yet knowing about them for brief moments? We truly do not know the staggering quality of what the stabilizing qualities are within those blocks of comprehension. Brief moments tell us it is so necessary that we *do* know about them. When we confine ourselves to the rigidity of the ignorance of what we are once again, as we confine ourselves in each moment of every day sometimes blinded by the light so much that we shun the responsibility of walking into the umbrella of comprehension, yet it is present; it is shining upon us. We use just what is necessary to use or abuse. When we feel these moments that seemingly have a stimulating quality beyond the normalcy of what we should feel within our normal day, let us try to use them for incentive in making us understand the usage of what we are, and the umbrella's ability to change the density of this extraordinary place that we live in. Let us try not to confine ourselves within the rigidity of not focusing in on what is truly necessary to stimulate us into a more pliable area of comprehension.

(John leads the class into meditation:) Where you are within the relaxing quality, talk to yourself. Express some of those stabilizing qualities to yourself as you extend yourself more into that relaxing, rejuvenating essence of what you are. Think about all of the sick people around us. Think about the healing quality of where you are. First filter it through you. Cleanse yourself. Purify yourself. It is your right to do so, and it is your right within the awareness of what is usable and right for you to do so. Let us clean the vessel of what we are first, so as we sail forth and give what we are to others, the purity of the stabilizing and healing qualities is true, sound and usable in a more pliable way for us. I feel lucky that I can see that particular statement and make it usable within myself, knowing how necessary it is to work on it. You first: yet look at this aspect in a balanced way in making it something that is not detrimental to growth, but a proper steppingstone within the structure of growth. It is not selfishness; it is the understanding of the true reality of what is usable in giving to others in a proper way. It is not selfishness; it is the understanding how to use self in a proper way. Be silent within yourself. Work on you and others. (The meditation proceeded as usual.)

(After the meditation:) I have felt energy before, but nothing like that! My God! I really thought I was going to leave this chair! That is a funny feeling. That was extraordinary. I really thought I was going to start hovering in this room. I have never felt energy like that before. I could have banged my head against the ceiling and gone to the next room. Oh, I tell you, I slowed it down because it was extraordinary. Whew.

There was a lot of energy around, especially from the knees down. My legs seemed as if they were moving and they were not really moving: almost as if I could get up and walk, yet stay here. That was different. I am going to have to give that some thought. It is common for me to feel a lot of energy, but that was definitely different. When I feel something like that, I slow it down and make it understandable for myself. That is what I did: I took control of it. You should be feeling some survival center energies now. How many of you feel that? Any questions? Answers? Anything you would like to share with us? Did you feel anything extraordinary? Different? Sometimes I think I am here alone. (Class laughter.) Whew.

The healing quality within the energy was awesome: the teeth, ears, nose, sinuses, eyes. My God! And every time that I was hitting a certain place and thinking of someone who had a certain affliction in one of those areas, I immediately went to the person. It was extraordinary. It was almost as if it had its own message within it. Sometimes I deal with an absence of thought patterns of thinking about people, so within the structure of this, there was none of that. I mean, once you hit those levels where you felt certain things, and they were in a particular awareness, and you knew there was a need somewhere, the person came automatically into your mind. That was unique and beautiful, extraordinary and very different: just that capability that freed itself from the experience of ignorance. I do not know. There are times when you feel very blessed, and I am sure this is one of those times when we are not outside of that particular awareness. It makes you wonder what it might be next.

First questioner: **It was like a prayer and you opened us up to God.**

I do not know. Within our comprehension of What God Might Be perhaps, but I am sure not beyond that. Certainly the meditation had a feeling within it that was extraordinary... and what is happening now,

I am having a little trouble formulating words, it is so awesome.

Then I would see a correction after I made a mistake. Then sometimes I would correct it, and sometimes I would just go right by it. It definitely had a feeling within it like a presence within the structure of the room that can sometimes be understood as something outside of you, but it is not. Some people might give it names like "Seth" or "Peter." It is not. It is within the structure of what you are and how you got there. Our sensibilities shine sometimes. When those things are happening, there is an inability to focus directly upon something with normal sight. Your focus is beyond the normal awareness or density of matter that you normally see. For instance, I am looking at the door, but have no thought of it because I am past it, or skipping beyond it. As you are going through the awareness of those levels, sometimes that skipping is hard to translate. Sometimes it takes the focus off the ordinary; then the focus becomes something different. You are looking at something but not seeing it because your focus is within your mind and the awareness. At those times, sometimes you almost want to shut your eyes but cannot even do so.

What I am finding so extraordinary about these meditations are the deepness of them, and the focus that it is taking me to stay at particular levels and not let the levels pull me somewhere beyond where I want to be so I cannot understand whatever it is and make it me. Because the levels are so extraordinary, they have a pulling effect, and that pulling effect is necessary. But the will of what I am slows it down and makes it something that is more stable. As I am speaking to you now, I am still feeling and sensing different things. There is like a draft around the entire lower part of my legs and feet. I can feel almost like a swirling effect around them. It is cooler than normal, but it does not have an effect of coolness upon me. I can feel the swirling, but it is almost as if it is right inside of me. It is very difficult to explain. It is a draft within. I never saw it as that before: it is a capacity that is there but normally beyond my ability to feel. That is understandable. Thank you. (Responding to an answer within.)

What does a thought do when it goes through you? How does the thought affect you? Meaning, there is so much that we have to look upon, and see what a thought and its natural reactions are at different places. You know, we can never really see, or sense, or begin to comprehend the thought, until the essence of it is felt in such a way that we are feeling it now or will feel it eventually. And its capacity changes the awareness of it, or its belief, within the structure of our comprehension, and that becomes more usable in stimulating ourselves into more of the comprehension of it. Let us maybe sit, or have a break. I think it would be hard *not* to see that what I am saying is different. Is that not true?

(The students seemed to agree.)

For the last week or so on the job, we have been working at a Howard Johnson's motel. A cleaning woman who works there came up to me today and said something to me for a moment. She said, "You know, even when we walk by you, it is very hard not to feel a change even in what seems to be a bad day. Even if we are in a bad mood, when you come in, you change the entire room. It is hard to be in a bad mood after talking to you."

I looked at her and thanked her. I was taken aback by her ability to see. Here is someone who does not really know me! I said to myself: *Let us use that for incentive. Let us stimulate...* You have to put things like that in the back of your mind to say: *Hey, come on! Turn this on! Use more of this! Be more of what you should be, or what anybody should be: more of what is a better and happy person who can use what you are in a positive way.* Those things happen to you for a reason and are usually usable in incentive to become more, or use more of what you have within you. Those things should be used properly. You never forget those things. There are certain things in your life that you flash back to. That is probably one statement that I will never forget, from a person who is seemingly so ordinary: a person you know only briefly but who can hit upon something that is so usable for you in giving you something within the realm of incentive.

Second questioner: **In some of the places that I go into, people have a lot of stress, scratchiness and negativity around them. In an attempt not to be affected...**

Just be happy when you go in there.

Reply: **Well, I project energy. I send love. I do whatever I can...**

I do not even try that. Just go in and be yourself. When there is no hello, say hello; when there is no good-by, say good-by; just because you do not let others change you. We have a tendency to let others change us. Do not let them change you. I am trying my best not to let others change me. It is very difficult not to have others change you because you are thinking: *Why do I have to be kind to this person?* And it is true; that is a normal reaction. But what I have been trying to do, if the other does not want a reaction, that is fine: I will say, "Good morning," and they will reply or not. If they do not, I will be outside of myself and not let it affect me. In other words, be happy and do not let others affect you.

John J. Gaudio

Third questioner: **I counsel some kids who have problems.**

You go in and do all the right things as you are doing. You put a white light around them and be kind, but being an example is the key.

Reply: **I am doing that with intent, but is that infringing upon their free will?**

No, it is not. You are there for a particular reason. You have to do it with intent because you are involved in a program where you are trying to help and your intent is to help. That is the whole idea of it and why you are there. You just keep trying; that is all.

What I do, and it is a very difficult thing to deal with, if the other person says, or does something seemingly negative, they are placed in a category where they have to win the right to move out of it. That is a natural reaction and understandable in my sense. If the person does something to me, I place whatever blocks I have around the person in order to deal with that structure in a positive way. There is a block there, and the only way that the block can be removed is for the person to initiate particular acts in order to remove the block. I also have to be solid in my conviction towards understanding what is truly right or wrong.

Now, if I really understand what is right within the structure of that, I stay outside of whatever it is within the wrath of what is coming towards the person. I try to help in some ways, such as give minor hints, but I am involved in understanding the reactions of it to the point where it might affect me within the fringes of my reactions. In other words, it would be nice if I could see and understand the density of that particular structure to the point where it does not affect me in any way whatsoever, and my total intent is to try to help that person within the reality of it, totally absent of reprisal. I have looked at it from that density so many times, but then I say: *Am I infringing upon the Laws, or the Will of God, at that particular level? Because everything the person does, they have to go through that particular structure in order to get out of the particular area. But am I within the rigid mind of what I am and seeing the essence of that particular confinement, thereby making it more of a confinement?*

Those are the things I think about lately. When I think about that, is that on the fringes of understanding the identity of how to change the Absolute Reaction, or the Law of God, at that particular level? I mean, that is an extraordinary place! Is then what I am saying: *That I can see the absolute sphere of misconception the person put self in, and I have the reality of changing the density of it within the particular reaction of their free will, not making the wrath of it so catastrophically overwhelming?*

I have been thinking about that more so, in the last week or so. My mind goes off in many different directions in understanding the absolutely correct understanding of how I can initiate it. But then the density of it becomes complacent once again, because the full reaction of it is confined to understanding the reality of what takes place in seeing it in a particular way, and how it takes place in its reaction:

Is that the place that might say, "Lord, forgive them for they know not what they do?" Does that forgiveness change the density of that sphere? Do I really mean that statement? Does it have to be a person so close to me, that I love them so much, I have to make that statement to them first, such as a child, or whomever? Let us consider the phrase, "Lord, forgive them for they know not what they do." Because way down deep inside of myself, it is very difficult to make the initial thrust of understanding that phrase in regard to a person that I know just for a brief moment, because I have to put the whole will of what I am within the structure of actually believing: *Lord, forgive them for they know not what they do.* It might be some kind of injurious act towards me, and I have to totally forgive myself of the reality of reprisal. I have to put myself in the position that puts myself outside of it through comprehension, so that it does not have any effect whatsoever on me other than understanding the reality of where that person is coming from.

In other words, maybe it is on the fringes of believing the illusion, or those grandiose moments, of understanding that I might have duality, and that the forgiveness might be a true reality. I sometimes think about that more. You know, we have those moments of thinking we are there, and those moments could be illusions just to give us the incentive of eventually thoroughly feeling whatever it is within ourselves within our convictions. It becomes a place then where I say: *Okay, if I feel and sense that to that particular structure, and see it so precise and usable, what does it do then? Does it contradict the reality of this particular structure as a usable plane of comprehension?*

Just then, something else stimulates me into the property of understanding something outside of me: something that stimulates me into a more usable area of comprehension; because for a brief moment within that structure, I say: *What could be next? Because I see all four walls in the awareness of that particular structure. Those walls seem pretty bright and comprehendible, and are pretty usable, and totally within the simplicity of the reaction of understanding the Truth of the Law of God at that level.* Within that moment there is a striking feeling within me that says: *Oh God, I have this, and it is simple and understandable and usable!* I know I do not have it totally eradicated from the realms of misconception within the awareness of it, but it is still something that makes me feel like: *Oh, boy, I have got this together now! What might be next?*

When we feel it–and somebody else had that thought–when we feel it and understand it, but to what point? Is that what we feel next? Do we feel that stimulating quality? Do we feel the extraordinary essence of something that is outside of the realm of understanding it totally, but something that is usable, like we did last week? We felt those brief moments, or extended moments, of what is going on within the realm of this information that is going forward. Those moments had something to do with the sustenance of what can be usable in a classroom.

I thought about that class all week. I said: *My God, that was totally outside of my identity; totally outside of what I normally see, understand or feel!* That information was definitely outside of what I could understand. Only for brief moments were there clinging properties to it, making me understand it for brief moments. It was staggering in its properties, staggering to the point where it did not make me burden my incentives to understand the ability of what it might be. But then I pulled myself back in and began to feel the changes that might take place within my normalcy, and there were changes. So then I interrelated the information to something that was usable in understanding the initial thrust into a new area that might become usable within the awareness of consciousness. And those "brief moments" that had the absence of comprehension were, to me, not having the identity of comprehension.

So coming back to the previous remark about it being so totally outside of my comprehension, we put it in the context of saying: *Hey, we do the best we can.* But, *"the best we can"* is the ability of showing how we look and how we react and how we are as a person. No matter what level it is, it is what we show and what we say and what we do. That is where this information all extends itself. We could be extremely extraordinary, and have the greatest knowledge in the world, but if we come into a room and are obtuse for a moment, it bends it all into something that might not be usable for anybody. On the other hand, if we come in there with a bright attitude: it is not forced, it is what we are, and we are happy... People do not understand that at times! The happiness is outside of the normalcy of what they see and understand; it is something that makes them say, "Hey! What is the matter with him? We do not know anybody who is happy all the time!" I feel that from people. They say to me, "My God, how do you get to be that happy?" I say, "You just have to work on it. I just feel happy." That is the truth. I have always been a very happy person. Sometimes I can be inward too, but most times I am pretty well balanced and happy. However, when others see it, they are saying, "What is the matter with you?"

It all stems back to the structure of the moment of what you are, in each moment of every day. Occasionally I run across brief moments where I am not happy. I have mentioned to my wife that there are certain things that I have done within the structure of my life within the past two or three years that have made me unhappy for some moments. But I have looked at them in a way where I have taken them and used them for incentive to become a better person, because when I look at the context of the reality of those things I have done, they were totally outside of what I am, normally. Then I thought about what is usable: what I have had to do in my life to make things more usable within me; then it all becomes understandable. Then everything becomes that which filters back and becomes more usable. You do not shun your responsibilities in any direction: that is the main thing in life. If you have done that, you correct whatever it is in a way where you can shine upon it more so, and make it brighter and more usable for others.

Any more questions that I cannot answer? It has been a pathway; that is for sure! I see some of the things. I can see them so clearly. Whew! My God! Some of the things I have been through! Everything has been so extraordinarily beautiful, no matter what it seemingly was as I was going through it. But, My God, what a pathway! And all of those things become so understandable when I look at them now, because no matter what they might have been, they truly have made me what I am today. That is the unique thing about comprehension. That is the unique thing about this classroom. It is an incubator of knowledge within us that stimulates us into every moment of every day. Whether another person sees the difference in me is not important in one sense, yet important in another sense that they do see the difference within self, so their capacities might change or become more usable.

If there is one thing we should get out of what we are discussing tonight, is that we use ourselves better in our tomorrows than we did the day before, and that we do not make it drudgery, but simple and usable. We know that when we do that, it truly lifts the burden of life off our shoulders. It gives us the wings of comprehension. It makes things lighter, no matter what they might be. You are doing the best you can, and if you are doing the best you can of what you are doing, tomorrow will be better. No matter what it is in your life that you are doing, it will be better, whether it is in the family structure, or whatever. It will be better if you are doing the best you can today, and what you have to show is consistency within your ability to grow or change. When you know something is right, do it and stay within it.

(There were some minutes of silence, then John continued:) Do you ever ask yourself what takes place in those brief moments when I do not say anything? What are you doing within your mind? You should be doing something within your mind when I am doing that. Within the realm of normalcy, those brief moments sometimes might be misunderstood as having nothing to say; yet those moments are very important. What they are actually doing is giving adjustments to your ability to use your mind within comprehension. They are giving you a moment to think and see what directions your thoughts might be going in.

Did I have the ability to tell you that, last week? (Class: "No.") Then I guess I did not, but when that ability hits upon that moment, it should convey it forward to do so. That is the important thing about it: sometimes there is nothing there, or nobody there, and you feel that filtering process taking place, and there might be that moment that stores it there for something that might come forward eventually. But never, never, will that filtering process become an absolute like that, once again. It will be slanted and filtered through the density of what you are, and slightly distorted within the moving comprehension of what you are, so it will never be the same again. It is not saying it will be less, or more; it will never be the same again. When you look at it within its own attitude, you can understand why, because it changes within itself as it blends within your awareness.

It has been a long pathway, hasn't it? It has been fun though. It has been. It has been different, that is for sure. And if it was not different, we put a few spikes in it to make it different, that changed it, or distorted it, or whatever, didn't we? What should be the next thing? Then will it be more different in the years to come? What happens when we make a statement like that? Does it prepare the years to come? Does it start the thrust towards the years to come? Does it start *you* on the pathway to the years to come? We shall find out. Meditate with me for a few minutes.

CHAPTER THIRTY

Using Your Mind Correctly to Achieve Balance
February 7, 2001

(John's ending comments in the guided meditation for the evening:) My strengths are your strengths. My weaknesses are mine, until I can make them into strength for you.

(Afterwards:) How many of you have ever come up from meditation and still do not feel right? Have you ever asked yourself the question why? What kind of answer do you get? You have to use your mind correctly. Meditation is like anything else: you can pick up a tennis racket, but if you do not practice, you are not going to be good at it. You can also make meditation a crutch rather than a pawn, thinking it as a cure-all for everything. You should take the information that you get from questioning the reality of what you are, and use it each and every day. If not, it leads you into an area of stagnation. It is fine to meditate and rejuvenate yourself, but when you get to that level, at least work on something. There are days when you do not have to it, but most of the time, take the opportunity to work on yourself. That is what it is all about.

First we have to have that preconceived thought within the mind that says: *There is something beyond the flesh for us.* I know that without question. Then I say: *I am meditating, and within the realm of what I am, I am becoming closer to the source that is beyond the physical sense.* When you are meditating, you are closer to the reality that has made you. There is more knowledge at a soul level than within you in the physical sense. At some point, you extend yourself so much into the esoteric quality of what you are, there is more of you within the physical sense than there is at a soul level where you originally started. But the esoteric quality extends itself further and further into the essence of the reality that made everything else, so in one sense, it is a contradiction, and in another sense, it is not. What you are trying to do is use all of the realities that you have refracted, through all of the density that made you, a particular individual within the physical sense, and make those realities usable within the framework of comprehension. If you use your mind correctly, there is not anything you cannot do to enhance the capabilities of what you are, as long as it does not extend itself into an area that infringes upon another person's free will, which is the choice of another person. For instance, tonight you chose to be in this room. Maybe next week you will not, but this week you chose to be here. Whatever it is within me that I can give you, I will give you, but it is still your choice whether to take it and make it usable within the common denominator of you in every moment of every day.

Of course, it is so necessary to rejuvenate yourself. Of course, if you use your mind correctly, it is nice to feel so good when you come up from the meditative state; but you can meditate a thousand years, and if you do not believe that you will not feel better when you return from the meditative state, you will not feel better. You have to begin to understand how the mind works. You have to begin to use those meditations in a proper way. Rejuvenate yourself and then put yourself in that plateau of comprehension to work on yourself. Set things in motion in your life. Know where you are. You are changing consciousness into energy, into matter, and are closer to the reality that can do it quickly because you make yourself transcendable. You have put yourself in that position that is closer to the source.

First questioner: **For two years I have worked to improve my programming skills and finally got to a good place in a job, only to have it taken away from me by a boss who did not seem to know what was going on. What happened there?**

What did you learn so far? What have you done since then? You do not have to tell us, but did it make you a stronger person?

Reply: **In certain ways.**

Did it give you more focus into the reality of what you should do from now on? Did it give you safeguards into how you enter into situations so when you come out, it does not hurt you? You enter with no anticipation of any rewards. You just do what you can. If you know how you entered, then are pushed back out, there is no avenue that pushes you over the cliff; there is just a natural sequence of events of going in a new direction of all that you have learned. Everything that you have participated in within the particular thing made you more than what you were before. What happened, there was a growth process that was necessary in giving you more strength in the reality of whatever might be coming next.

Reply: **Lately when I have been talking to people at work, I have been getting some tearing in my right eye.**

That is insight into self and the capability right now of feeling a little sorry for self, and sometimes it extends itself into the involuntary system that works in mysterious ways. Do not feel sorry for yourself; say: *Hey, look at all of those things that particular sequence of events gave me. Now I have all of that new information to use in whatever project comes forward.* All of that difficulty is extinguished, and through time it just forgets itself, but making these kinds of statements increase the capability of the usability of time, and it will happen quicker rather than later. You see, eventually we forget something: something negative happens to us, and a couple weeks or months from now, it refracts us out of that area. There are necessary vibrations within the laws that are written that make us participate in dissipating something that can become overwhelming even in our ignorance.

How do we more quickly eliminate that process? By understanding the usability of the mind in questioning the reality that made us feel so bad in a particular situation. When we can do that, then it extends itself out of that area in a quicker way. We do that by looking at all of the plusses within the sphere of comprehension that was seemingly overwhelming and understanding it to the best of our ability. When we do that, and dissect it to the best of our ability from where we are, it takes us out of the anguish of it and puts us into the reality of understanding some sense of how to make it usable. It gives us the opportunity not to extinguish the reality of balance, but pull a rope towards the center of it to have the reality of it stick so we can pull self out of a situation that is seemingly outside of the steadfastness of balance. So we should take the opportunity sometimes, even when it seems heavy or confusing to say: *There is a reason for it. What is it going to do for all of my strengths? What is it going to do for my tomorrows? Will it make me stronger, or do I allow it to make me weaker and go further into myself? No, I am going to make myself stronger. I am going to put my mind in the right direction. I am going to use everything for me, not against me, and that is exactly where I should be.*

Reply: You said that eventually doctors would be able to trace consciousness throughout the body. How will they be able to do that?

Eventually what we do here in this class will catch up with the normal reality of what doctors deal with. If the doctor knows what the consciousness is of a particular part of the body that the patient is working on, they will then have information pertaining how to pull the patient out of the misconception of that area through knowledge rather than just utilizing medicine or drugs. There will be a sequence of events where both avenues will be utilized. The doctor will say to the patient, "I will give you this pill which will take care of the chemical reaction within the body. As you digest the pill, it will give you some stability pertaining to a misconception that happened to you because you misused your mind within your life. You allowed a situation of consciousness to become overwhelming in a particular part of your body. That misconception became something within the chemical reaction that was not necessarily in balance. I will give you some information in order to deal with the misconception, then within the awareness of your mind, you have to correct it within that structure in order for it not to come back once again."

The person who corrects the misconception is the person who will have a healing. Suddenly they will have a total rejuvenation of the illness that was originally caused by the reality of the misconception. Some people survive and some do not. What makes one person survive over the others? The person who survives is the person who learns something about self while they are in agony, even though they might not even know they have learned something. Let us say that the person has cancer in a particular part of the body and has had a lack of human decency: if suddenly through the awareness of pain and agony, they begin to question the reality of human decency without even knowing they have done so, that helps. Also, just having a positive attitude in that direction is the person who will be pulling self out of the misconception to have a total healing.

That is what I meant by using both avenues. Eventually doctors will find that every single part of the body has a consciousness, and that consciousness interrelates to a usable vibration within the knowledge of understanding who we are at a different level. That is where medicine is going. In other words, if you have a heart attack, and eventually end up with more compassion and balance in your life, the possibility of having a second heart attack is eliminated.

Second questioner: **Some doctors are coming to the sense that people create their own illness but do not want to present it to their patients as such because the patient is already feeling vulnerable and conflicted.**

They are not entering into the conversation in a positive way. They are looking at it from a framework of understanding it as a burden to the patient. I look at it from a standpoint of understanding the reality of it and lifting the burden. I will make the ill person become involved within the structure of information. I am not talking about going forward and making the person feel guilty; I am talking about the information that comes forward within our books; it gives the person the information to lift the burden. The doctor might say, "You have problems in the heart center. You have to go forward with more balance, and if you do that, you will begin to eliminate some of the process of that misconception from your body. We are going to treat you in a very positive way from the medical perspective, but I want you to become involved in this." If the doctor is talking to the patient in that way, it gives the patient more incentive, I think, to become involved in the reality of understanding of how to eliminate the disease. Then the doctor can further add into it, "We have had patients in the past who have begun to use their minds in a very positive way in this particular way and we have had great results." That is not adding a burden. That is lifting a burden.

There has to be a basic foundation, and the structure of it is changing within the reality of medicine. The medical profession is now talking about that the individual has to have a very positive attitude, and stress is something that deteriorates the body. These are basic themes that are being laid down now in the medical profession that will eventually become common knowledge. When it becomes common knowledge within the structure of that particular thing, then something else will come forward within that structure. It takes a long time for a particular theme to be changed in the common denominator of a particular structure within humanity.

Third questioner: **If you have a genetic flaw in your heart, do you still have to deal with that?**

Yes, but that structure of misconception can be eliminated when you understand. You question: *What do my parents have? What do my sisters and brothers have? What did my grandparents have? How did they die? Where are the weaknesses within the strain of what I am?* You work on it. Every single male in my family had ulcers before age fifty. Every single male in my family has had eventual deterioration of the eyes, glaucoma and macular degeneration. What do I do? I work on those two areas. The eye problems deal with insight first into myself, then insight into whatever I am dealing with and comprehending it. In my meditation I ask: *What is going on in my third-eye center? How do I feel? Is there balance in my third-eye? Could I have more rejuvenation when I am meditating? How long does it take for the energy in that area to feel balanced? Why does it take me so long to get to that particular position? What could I do tomorrow to give myself more semblance of balance in that particular area?* Furthermore, I thank my soul, my father and my mother for the opportunity of having that weakness within that particular structure because it gives me an opportunity to question it and eliminate it from the particular strain within the genetic process of what I am.

Reply: **What about the person who does not necessarily have a genetic flaw but there is a significant lack of emotional sustenance in their family structure?**

But there is steadfastness to the comprehension when it finally hits into an area. You can take the whole family and put them all into the worse circumstances whatsoever, then there is that one child out of eight or nine whom you can look at and say: *My God, How did that child get to that particular level?* It is through the comprehension of self. The person put self in a position.

Some individuals are genetically flawed to the point where they cannot eliminate something because at an esoteric level there are some conflicts into why that particular aspect has to happen. The person is one-dimensional. They cannot go beyond a particular plane of reality. For instance, animals cannot leave a basic plane of reality because they do not have the conscious awareness to extend themselves into an esoteric quality. Certain humans are not very strong at a soul level. Maybe the particular lifetime is not that great because of having flaws within the genetic process, so the capabilities of refracting consciousness into energy, into matter within the physical sense are not at the level that is dealing with perfection. But in that lifetime, the individual has flaws in the genetic process in order to eventually have perfection within another lifetime.

Let us take a moment to question how we got to a point where we had the capability of making a human body. At first did our soul refract down and become a blade of grass? Did it then become a plant with a blossom, or tree with fruit, and it refracted to other levels? What was it doing? The soul was learning the chemical reactions within simpler life forms. Eventually the soul had the capability of going into the animal kingdom and manifesting certain refracted animals. There has to be some purpose beyond just living and living and living until we die! There has to be a purpose that clings to some portion of us once in a while, that says: *Hey, there has got to be more to me than just the flesh. There has to be something out there that is truly unique and beautiful.* Look around us! This entire planet is so unique! It is so self-sufficient! I wonder how it was ever thought to be so! Everything is usable, and if *we* become a contradiction, we will become usable in the density of fertilizer upon earth. Even within the misconception of what we are, if we are doing something wrong, we will be doing something usable even if we are extinguished. This planet earth is unbelievably beautiful if we just take the opportunity to feel, sense and use it in a proper way so we can use more. Every time you grow, hopefully you will say: *How truly unique this place is that we live in. There are things that I do not comprehend because they are seemingly bad, but when I can eventually comprehend them, I will make them understandable. I will understand why they are here.* You will say: *Everything that is seemingly bad is good, but at first I do not understand it as so because I am ignorant. When I begin to understand that, it becomes more usable in understanding how to become more evolved within the physical sense and use more of the esoteric comprehension of what I am, no matter what it might be.*

I am sure within the structure of your soul, many, many, different lifetimes ago, you were part of the animal kingdom learning how to deal with mobility upon this earth plane. When you did that, all four limbs were upon the earth and survival energies came through the limbs interrelating to survival within the physical sense. When you stood up, your feet were still within the physical sense of survival, but your hands became esoteric comprehension of survival. Your hands now interrelated to the crown center at the top of the head. That is why I tell you, when you are extremely tired and want to rejuvenate yourself in meditation, keep your hands with palms faced down in your lap, because you are interrelating to the survival center at the base of the spine. When you have rejuvenated yourself, then you can turn your palms faced up. They now interrelate to the crown center at the top of your head.

What makes us different from the animals? We will never find the missing link! Scientists will not find it! It is because the missing link is at an esoteric level. It becomes that soul that has the capacity to have the body of a human being within the physical sense that can stand up straight and deal with the reality of changing its reality. When you were a dog or cat, you were dealing with a particular level or structure that you could not go beyond. You were confined to that particular structure. It is not saying that you did not grow within that structure, but you could not become transcendable. When you got to the point where you had enough evolvement at a soul level, you were able to stand up. Those energy centers, or "chakra" areas, that were facing down towards earth now face outward towards the environment and deal with esoteric comprehension.

Remember those different layers that I mentioned to you that you refracted through in order to become an individual within the physical sense? Those different layers interrelate to different energy centers within your body. The energy centers are the vehicles that you use to comprehend each and every day, whether you know it or not. As you become involved within the structure of comprehension within the physical sense, you then have the capacity to become transcendable. When you meditate and eventually open up a channel within those structures, the energy centers eventually turn upwardly within the structure of what you are, and you make a vortex of energy within yourself that goes to the reality of what you are.

Let us say that you become evolved within the physical sense to the point within the essence of understanding the comprehension of love and survival within the first center that the first center becomes crystallined with the white vibration. As it does so, it has a vortex to it that changes all of the seven different levels that you refracted through to become an individual within the physical sense. What actually happens, one of seven layers of consciousness and energy that you refracted down becomes you within the flesh. You have now taken some of those esoteric comprehensions and made them you within the physical sense. You become more esoteric within the physical sense. The vortex within each of the energy centers has been changed.

The essence of Christ: an ordinary man became a Christ within the physical sense because he used all of those different structures and was involved in the comprehension of those different things. We do not get into religion other than to make you understand that you are on the same pathway. When I am truly being esoteric, I have abundant amounts of white energy sources within my system. If illness tries to enter my system, there is the refractability of the crown center that makes white cells, not within the physical sense but at a multi-dimensional level. Then I have survival within the red cells from the survival center, which is red. Then I questioned it beyond that: *What makes that more sensible? I have red and white blood cells within my blood, and when the red cells get into trouble, the white cells come in like white knights, surround the misconception and gobble it up to the best of their ability.* Then I question: *Does that sound logical and understandable?* I look at it within the esoteric sense and also within the physical sense. It sounds logical and becomes something that is usable in the flesh. If I am not feeling well, then I meditate and increase the velocity of what I am, I can eliminate the misconception more quickly from my body. All of the answers become that which is usable in understanding the normal reality of the sustenance of my mind and my body. I do not take anything as living proof unless it becomes living proof. That is what I mean by using your mind correctly: comprehending what is necessary to cause balance within your body

If there is no balance you are using your mind wrong! I do not care what you say or do, you can stand on your head, and do cartwheels, but if your body is not dealing with balance, you are still doing something wrong. How do you correct it? By slowing yourself down to say: *What do I have to do to correct it? What do I have to do to eliminate the confusion in my life?* You quiet yourself down. When you cause the confusion to go away, you can then do more for every other person you are trying to help. On the other hand, if there is confusion within you, there is confusion within your knowledge towards others. It is like going to a bald-headed barber to ask him how to keep from losing hair, and he is giving you information, and he does not have hair. Go to a person who has the sense and balance and reactions within the physical sense that are living proof before your eyes. If you see a person with no balance, why would you want no balance? If you see a person that has some semblance of balance, then you look at the person to say: *That looks like a very good avenue that I should go down.* Question it as you are doing so. Do not take it as the living proof. Do not take anything I say as the true reality. I know it is so. If I cannot make it logical and understandable here, then you should say: *Maybe I should go somewhere else.*

Did you listen to what I just did? I questioned it here, here, here, here and here. (John indicates a circle.) All of the answers have to be pliable in making it here: which is the center, the nucleus. All of those bits of information is not only in the orbiting qualities around the fringes of comprehension but becomes the sustenance of a true reality that does not have to be extended into anything more, at least from where I am. Maybe from where I will become, but not from where I am. It became logical, sensible and usable. How do you make it logical, sensible and usable? By not making it drudgery. By not feeling fatigue, anguish and misconception. By understanding how not to feel that. By knowing how to put yourself in a position where your mind is being used properly for you, not against you.

All situations are not exactly what we want them to be. All situations could be the best they could be, no matter what they are, if we are using this information properly. They will not become overwhelming but will become avenues of comprehension that keep us from deviating more quickly into more avenues of misconception. I do not mind being beaten over the head once or twice. Thirty or forty times become drudgery for me. I want to know why I am getting hit in the head. I want to know why I have to put on that helmet of comprehension. If my life is chaotic, it is because I am in a chaotic place. If I want to straighten it out, I have to straighten me out first. If I do not straighten me out, my perception of everything is chaotic. If that does not make sense, I do not know what does. If I have no control, everybody around me has no control. If I have control, there is a logical sequence of events in absorbing whatever it is. If I have that within me, everybody around me is given a logical sequence of events of absorbing logic. It is as simple as that, yet as profound as that. Remember, we can use the knowledge if we are ignorant, and we can really, really, really use it if we are not ignorant. And every time we know more about it, that "really" becomes another "really." That is the beautiful thing about it.

Do I feel balance in every moment of every day? Of course not. Do I have more control over balance in every day? Of course I do. Do I feel as if some days are tough and some are not? Of course I do. Do I feel as if the tough ones and the good ones are closer together? You bet your life I do. Does it seem like when there are heavy days, they are not so heavy because I have stronger shoulders through comprehension? You bet your life I do. Am I going to say that tomorrow or the next day might not be hard? Of course not. Of course I am going to have some tougher days, but if I am strong within them, I have more quiet and beautiful days, and there is more of the ability of seeking out the beauty in whatever it might be that I might once have considered as drudgery. Now it is comprehension.

You know, I never thought about it before when I said to you at the beginning of class, "I give you all of my plusses, and all of my minuses I am going to work on, so I can make them plusses so I can give them to you." I never thought of that in quite that way before. When something like that happens to me, when I hear something like that coming through me, I say it is a new place, a new consideration, a new reality. It is just that brief moment where you extend yourself into the incentive and the reality of saying: *Hey, here is something that I have hit upon, and it is usable for incentive so I may lift myself when it becomes heavy. When I feel heavy, I am going to take out some of those praises that I previously put aside when I was in balance and am going to think about them when I need them.* That is what I mean by filling that chalice with usable information pertaining to the reality of compassion and balance and love. What is it? An extended period of understanding the usability of using all of the plusses and the minuses for you, not against you. Am I perfect? Of course not. Am I extending myself closer to perfect? Of course I am. Will I ever achieve it? Eventually I will. Does it have to be tomorrow? No, it does not have to be, as long as I am on the pathway and quest of understanding that eventually there will that moment of perfection that will stimulate me once more into the confusion and re-action of chaotic situations in order to make me understand that there is more.

Then I ask myself: *What does God use chaos for?* God uses chaos right after that moment where we feel so sensational in order to stimulate us out of that into a new avenue so that we may feel it again. Chaos keeps God occupied. It keeps extending Itself into the reality of what we are. It is not saying that God is looking at us: God feels us without even knowing It feels us. It is similar to the cells in your body dividing:

you do not have to say, *cells, divide,* or, *cells, die*; they know when to do so automatically. Because the conscious awareness of you is so extraordinary, there are so many preconceived things set in motion that you do not have to think about, because you comprehended them in the genetic process of what you are and you have won the right to be here where you are now without thinking about it. If that is not so extraordinary, I do not know what is! And if you do not see that for brief moments in your meditations, you are missing something.

I know most times I am ignorant, but I know all of the time there is Something There helping me, because That Reality knows I am going to be ignorant until I can pull myself out of ignorance through comprehension. There is that chaos, or chaotic moment of stimulation, that says: *John, you felt so perfect for a moment. You saw the true reality of those words that came through you. It made you more than what you were before. Do not feel too comfortable, and stay there too long, and contradict why you are here. Stimulate yourself into new properties of that which will extend itself into more of the Reality of What is God.*

(John led the class in a second meditation:) If there is one theme that we talked about tonight, it is using your mind correctly. Remember that in your meditations this week. After you rejuvenate yourself, put yourself in that place and use your mind for you. You are doing so many things. First you are training your mind in a proper direction. It is up to you. Some of our minds are untamed. It is up to us to tame our minds and make our minds usable for us.

Let us take an opportunity for a few minutes to think about some sick people. I am getting so many people around me calling; so many people are hurting. If you know of a person who is ill, think about the person, and together we will help each other. We will help the different people that are sick. Just think about the person. See them in a better vein. What you are actually doing is truly helping that person, no matter who they are. Believe in yourself. You truly are unique. You were made in the Image of God. The Total Reality of God is within us, but how much of It are you using? We are perfect. We just do not understand that we are. Know within your mind that the people that you thought of have peace, and total stability, and the elimination of that misconception from their minds and bodies. I thank you for helping me with the people I thought of. I love you. Come next week because when I tell you, I love you, I will have a lot more love, and that feels so good. Good night, everybody.

CHAPTER THIRTY-ONE

What We Are and What We Can Become
February 14, 2001

(John's beginning words of the guided meditation for the evening:) If my voice is a little low, it is because I have a little cold, something I caught from one of my grandchildren. He was ill, and I guess I got too emotionally involved with him. He had a very high fever, so when it is somebody that close, you just slip and let everything go. There must have been a little spot within me that was dealing with some weakness in compassion and balance.

Is everybody doing well? Has life been treating you rather well? We might want to think about some of the things in our lives that we would like to make a little smoother as we enter into this meditation; it also lays some basic foundation in a direction that we should do so every time. We should have some intent as we are going into meditation. One thing that I surely do know, and I mention this so many times in the classroom, if you are sick, it is the most difficult thing to heal yourself because you are nowhere near that place that can heal. So preventive medicine is you practicing meditation with good thought patterns, preparing yourself for each time that you enter into the meditative state. It prevents germs from entering. It gives you that aura, that cushion of reality around you that is very difficult to penetrate. The deeper you go into meditation, and the more insight that you have into it, you understand that the simplicity of that statement is so correct: germs cannot enter the purity; they just cannot get through; they cannot enter into that sphere of what you are. The gravity of what you are is so dense, and the atmosphere around you so thick, nothing can penetrate it.

Therefore, as we enter meditation, if we consider that we are increasing the capability of that sphere, that energy field of what we are in that particular way, our intent compounds the reality of the usability of meditation in preventing something from happening to us. I think it is important to consider these things because we do become complacent in our reactions in meditation. Most of the time we go into meditation with the thought of rejuvenation, which is fine, but the incentive of that should be: *As I am rejuvenating myself, I am enhancing my capability to ward off whatever it might be that tries to attack my body.* There are reasons for every particular germ existing upon this earth plane. Meditation is a usable pathway of understanding self. Considering those particular things give us insight into the reality of our lives as we become people who deal with deeper and deeper meditation. So our intent tonight is to smooth the road or pathway that we walk upon in our normal lives. Yes, we want to see the flaws. Yes, we want to see the potholes. But we want to anticipate: we want to have the insight of not having something run us off the highway of life. We want to be steadfast in the capability of steering straight and comprehending whatever it might be. This gives us the ability not to deviate so far into those misconceptions that agony and illness come forward.

True love starts with self. How clever is The Wonderment of What We Are, Beyond Where We Are, to make that such a True Reality here! Even when we are selfish, it is a consideration of love of self. Within the stimulating qualities of that within its bending purification, the reality of love of self, eventually, hopefully, becomes more than that so we can give to others. But even in that which is seemingly negative, there is so much perfection going on into understanding how to make that a seat for love of self. Meditation is that cushion, that place that can correct it and make it usable forever within self. Let us find that place. Let us seek it out tonight, each one of us, in our own unique way. Consider what we are. Consider what we can become. Consider what we can do with it within the framework of helping others, and into the book of reality that helps all. Love yourself. This is your time. With all of those considerations that we mentioned before, woven into that which makes it necessary to do so, I love you. Take a nice deep breath now... (The meditation proceeded as usual.)

First questioner: **The news channel announced the other evening that scientific research shows that our thoughts and emotions become chemicals that can literally affect our health. So this is mainstream thinking now...**

(John nodded. He has been presenting this information for more than twenty-five years.)

Reply: **I felt a really amazing burning sensation in both of my feet. Subsequently I felt energy in the palms of my hands, then some activity in the crown center, then the survival center.**

Very good. It all interrelates to your survival and the aspects that you are going through lately. You have actually won the right to use more energy in those areas, so you must be doing something right. The energy flow gave you a sequence of events in understanding what happened: you felt it in your feet within the physical sense through the rewards of comprehension; you were then ignited in your hands, which is survival at an esoteric level; then you felt it in the crown center, which ignited more of the reality of it and made it usable in the survival center at the base of the spine, giving you more strength within the physical sense, pertaining to the reality of survival and love of self. That is why you are feeling good about yourself.

Reply: Last week I asked you what medicine will be like within twenty years. This week, where will psychiatry be down the road?

Psychiatry and the regular medical doctor will blend. Doctors will realize that the psychological affect has so much more to do with the illnesses within the body, so the two will actually become one. The study and whole perception of the reality of the medical doctor will change. Doctors will look at the whole body, and of course, the whole body has to include the mind and how it participates in either deteriorating or rejuvenating the body. Therefore, the two are going to start slowly coming together in the reality of it. But we have not seen anything yet; I hate to even mention that we have not yet even begun to see the total reality of disease. There are strains of disease that are, and will be coming forward, to stimulate our minds into avenues of growth. We will have to eventually understand that the psychiatrist and medical doctor becoming one is a necessary reality in slowing down the evolution of disease.

You see, most people look at disease as something we have to cure within the physical sense. Eventually we will look at disease in regard to anticipating it, rather than triggering it. We will be dealing with the realities in a balanced way where the total reality of humanity does not hit that misconception to the level that triggers a new disease coming forward, or a disease that is totally entrenched in humanity. We will be going in those directions of comprehending how to eliminate the reality of disease being triggered within the physical sense before it happens. When we hit those particular levels, a unique thing will begin to happen: the progression of diseases already here will become that which is no longer usable within the realm of comprehension because there will be such a stabilizing quality within humanity as far as knowledge is concerned. The whole reality of understanding disease and how it is usable within the consciousness of an individual growing upon this particular plane will be understood, and our whole current perspective on disease and how we treat it will be totally eradicated at this level. We will have to think about disease in a more unique way.

So medicine in the sense that we know it today will change drastically within the next twenty years. Doctors will begin to understand that medicine in the form of pills or drugs is necessary for a period of time, but the true prescription will be the reality of understanding how that misconception came into the body through the lack of the proper use of the mind within the physical sense. That will be the basic treatment. We will actually have schools on how to have more compassion or understanding about certain aspects within the reality that makes misconceptions come forward. There will be a whole new identity of treating diseases within the physical sense.

The basic foundation of that is being set in motion today in certain ways. Understanding the human genome is one of them. Scientists will find that they will be able to change the genetic process and alter it in a way where disease will not come forward; but then they are also going to find out that there are new strains of diseases that interrelate to something far beyond the genetic process. The new strains interrelate to the consciousness of understanding how the genetic process is usable in comprehension. So there are particular reasons for particular flaws and different strains within the genetic process, and that if we trigger certain processes within that, we are going to trigger certain new diseases to counteract the particular scientific discovery. If we do not get ourselves together mentally, eventually we will hit a level where the diseases will be so catastrophic that it will eliminate the species. That is a natural evolutionary process: extinguishing a particular species because it no longer becomes usable in comprehension at a certain level.

For instance, the dinosaur became extinct; it is no longer here because it was no longer usable in that process of understanding how to become more evolved at this level. Other species have become extinct, and there are reasons within the misconception within humanity that they are gone. It is not necessarily right, but there are reasons why a particular species no longer becomes usable. Will we hit a level someday where we will understand misconception in such a way that we will have the knowledge of cloning all of the extinct animals back onto earth? I am sure we will. I will have to give that some more thought though, because there are so many changes that are going to take place within the realm of that.

Now, why should we believe any of these statements? We would have to go back and understand the nature of what we spoke about twenty years ago: how the evolution of the human has just begun to participate in understanding the true realities of some of those aspects that we have mentioned in the past. That will give us incentive to understand that maybe some semblance of what we are saying today can be the truth of our tomorrows.

Reply: **What about drugs?**

We will get to a level where people will understand that they do not have to turn to drugs. I think it will be something that will become passé: either that, or it will go in a direction where a certain portion of the population will be totally overwhelmed by it. We have two distinct avenues that we can participate in going down, and one will eventually lead to a reality of knowledge from a basic level, making illness truly understandable. I do not think that we spend enough time at a basic level in the education system to have us understand what happens to the body and what physical agony truly is. I think eventually we are going to have the capability of having people feel agony at a particular level for a brief moment to make them understand how they will feel if they continue down a certain road of abusing mind and body. In other words, you are given pain for a brief moment and told, "This is what you will feel years from now if you keep going the way you are going."

CHAPTER THIRTY-TWO

Changing the Collective Consciousness of Humanity
April 11, 2001

(John's beginning words of the guided meditation for the evening:) Put some good thoughts in your mind. Do you know what those good thoughts are? I also want you to put an intent in your mind to open up a viable channel of awareness to your higher self and find out the one thing you have to work on to make you a better person, feel more secure, and have more happiness, balance and love. I want you to think about this class: that all of this is just for you. This is your time. Think about you. You are so important. That is what this whole class is about: teaching you to love yourself, so you may love another and have happiness; and beyond that, there are so many different things that you can refract through: loving many, which is helping not only within the physical sense but esoterically drawing in energy for everybody.

It is a wonderful intent when you consider yourself. When you grow, everybody grows. I want you to feel that uniqueness tonight in this room. It will be here for you to feel. I love you. I also want you to feel free to talk and ask questions. Do not hold anything in. Even if it seems silly, it is not. If there is something you want to ask, ask it. Do not be ashamed to do so in front of others. This is a place where you should feel very comfortable. The music is soothing and comforting to your mind and body. Use everything for you. Even if there is a distracting noise, use it for you.

(The meditation continued as usual. Then John came to the heart center awareness:) To help us further understand that we truly have a soul essence or an esoteric part of what we are, visualize or sense a small dot of energy within your heart center: as you do so, it begins to expand outwardly from there, touching every part of you, and cleansing and purifying you. It is an esoteric bath. You can feel it and sense it. It not only purifies you, it eliminates all misconceptions from your body. Your body has harmony and balance to it. You can feel it working perfectly. The white light totally surrounds that unique body of what you are. The security that you felt before within you becomes more usable now. For a brief moment you can feel the strength of the entire structure of what you are. It stimulates the incentive within you to understand that there is so much more that can come when you use what you have in a balanced way.

Within that white light I want you to help me help humanity to-night. You as a single cell within humanity can help. I want you to join with me as a unit in sending out that white light that you felt around you. See it going forth from here, touching everything in its pathway. It is purifying all of the vegetation upon the planet and the water. It is touching and cleansing the air, the animal kingdom and the human be-ings upon this earth plane. It is purifying and cleansing us, putting us in a proper direction. You, by using your mind correctly now are chang-ing the common denominator of humanity into a more pliable area that is more usable in comprehending the probabilities that each person sets in motion from another level. You should use this moment as incentive to know that you are unique and beautiful. In the silence of what you are, you truly do help at this moment. A unique thing takes place within you as you send it forth: more comes through you. It cleanses and changes you, and gives you more of that necessary velocity that is us-able in achieving those probabilities that you set in motion. I love you. Within the wonderment of those feelings that you have within you, within the silence of what you are, rejuvenate yourself. You truly are unique and beautiful, and you nourish that more so now. The music is usable. Each note is a suitable vibration that will help you to relax more so. You are totally relaxed, free of tension, and everything is function-ing properly within your mind and body. You are happy within your-self. (The meditation proceeded as usual.)

First questioner: **I can see that I have to become more involved in reacting towards others, rather than holding back, but while all of this is going on, I am feeling a lot of tension. Even my sleep has been somewhat restless, and I wake up and feel tension in my legs. Is it a matter of confronting the anxiety built up over the years?**

Over your whole life you never reacted in the way you should have. You were always the scientist confined to studying books and so forth, and you never went out into the field. You have to take all of that and put it back into life. You have to go into the street. You have to become usable. All that training and study was meant for one thing: for you to go forward in life. Some people read a book; then have the illusion of being that book. You have to take what is in the book, put it in your life, go forward and make yourself a better person. Now you are involved in the game. There is stress, tension and fatigue involved, but there is understanding of what is going on in your mind and body.

We can misinterpret meditation too, thinking of ourselves as going backwards, but we are not. For instance, we might be experiencing a deep meditation and suddenly all of the anguish of the day, month or year starts coming out, and we cry. Most people sit there and say: *My God, I am so sad!* It is not so. It is really a rebirth of self. We are really releasing stress and tension from the body and mind, like we have never done before. We never gave self the opportunity to slow down and allow it to happen. At first, it seems as if we have more problems than we ever did, but that is not so; now we have a tool that makes us see problems, whereas we had never seen them before. It is not that we have more problems; we have a tool now to see our problems. We can see what we have to solve in our lives to in order to become better people.

The only thing you previously got out of meditation was stress or complacency; you did not react in life. Now you are to a point where you are reacting. Go slowly. Ask questions about it. Do not make it drudgery. Do not make it like studying for the PhD. Just be relaxed. Do not be afraid to speak your piece with others. If someone tells you something about you, speak up. Do not change totally. There is a reason why you are the person you are. Do not try to be like someone else, be yourself. Be involved, but solve the different things involved in the reaction of understanding you. That is the main thing. Put it back into you to say: *Why is this particular thing bothering me?* Then you are opening up that sphere.

We are opening up that sphere of comprehension. At first, we are way out, circling the planet in an orbit. We do not know what is going on there, but are trying to find out what is going on upon the surface and within the nucleus of it. The same thing takes place with problems: at first, we are nowhere near comprehending the problem, but by eventually changing the orbit, we come closer and closer. Comprehension does that. It brings us in closer and closer to the reality of what we are trying to comprehend. We are making progress. Sometimes we have to sit there and say: *I am not going backwards; I am going forward here. This is progress.* What does that do? That gives us incentive to work on the remaining part of it, which is what we should be doing.

Most people misinterpret meditation when first starting out. All of a sudden, they are feeling so relaxed, they misinterpret it as fatigue: *My God, I am feeling all washed out after I meditate.* They are not fatigued, but are learning how to relax. They could never relax before. Some people never know what relaxation is. Learn to flow with it and make it part of your life that is so relaxing and beautiful. Just let self go and enjoy it. Some people just try to hold onto that tension and sense that they are moving forward, and they are not; what they are doing is going around in a circle very quickly, and that "very quickly" does not understand anything. By slowing self down, they think of it as fatigue or a place they should not be in. They should be in that place because that place makes them begin to see self.

Second questioner: I had an uncomfortable feeling in my neck during meditation that I normally do not have.

That interrelates to the dualities in your life: how you feel about yourself and how you are dealing with your main relationship, or whatever you are dealing with in life: maybe it is not having a relationship. You have to be involved in something that deals with duality. Sometimes you will not feel pain normally, but then suddenly in meditation you will feel something. That is a message, so you ask: *What am I feeling? What is going on?*

If you ask a question and do not get an answer, you should ask another question. Now, if you are asking a question and begin to feel some of the pain dissipating, you are asking the right question. If you feel sometimes that the pain is escalating, you are going in the wrong direction, so you stop right there, to ask: *What is going on here? What could I do now to change the reality of what is going here?* Ask another question about what direction you should be asking the question in. Sometimes you will not get any answers because you are still asking the wrong questions, so then go a little deeper to say: *Well, if I am not asking the right question, could you give me a little hint on what question I should be asking?* Sometimes you will get an answer pertaining to the particular thing. Or you might be asking too many questions; you might get the answer: *Do not ask a question. Just relax and flow through there.* Some people make it as if they are crushing a beautiful flower. They will try to comprehend it, and all of a sudden, there is no flower left because they overwhelm it. They do not even look at the beauty of it. They do not understand what is going on around them. So there are so many aspects. Sometimes you have to escalate yourself and sometimes you have to slow yourself down.

In meditation tonight I thought about what particular thing I should ask within myself regarding what I am dealing with in my life and how I can change certain things. I know I am dealing with some complacency in my reactions and in what I should be doing esoterically upon this planet. I know my potential is greater than I am using. All of us should feel that within ourselves. I also know that I still have some anger from karate days and the neighborhood where I grew up. I know I still have that edge. I do not use it in the household that much, but I have an edge if someone comes at me; I have that part of me that wants to react. So these are the things I have to work on, and I will get questions and answers pertaining to the particular reality of a problem. That is why I want you to think about what particular thing you should be working on, and you should have received a particular aspect to work on.

Third questioner: **I feel very open and receive a lot of feelings in meditation, but then I also sensed something in my left arm.**

As a matter of fact, I think you may be far too open. Too many things bother you too quickly, so slow yourself down to say: *I do not want to feel so much.* When you do that, what are you doing? You see, another thing is taking place here: too much coming in, too much clairvoyant reaction towards others and not enough reaction towards yourself. When you have too much clairvoyant reaction, what does that do? It gives you more information pertaining to something that is outside of you, and you should be dealing with what is within you. I want you to give that some thought. I do not want you to be more open; I do not want you to feel and sense more things; rather, I want you to consider slowing that down so you may see yourself.

For instance, there is a reaction within us that should be questioning self, but suddenly if we get that clairvoyant capacity–and a lot of people have that clairvoyant capacity–we are suddenly receiving information from others that is pertaining to the reality of what we are dealing with. Most clairvoyants feel and sense that, but then allow the information to affect them, not in a way of growth, but in a way that stimulates them into an area of misconception. So we want to turn that focus back on self, by saying: *I am feeling and sensing something coming at me. I do not know what it is. What could I do to slow it down?* Let us say that you feel anxiety; you ask: *Why am I feeling anxiety? Do I feel this when I meet a particular person, or am in a particular place?* Begin to be involved in changing the reality of how you digest the particular vibration coming at you. You are then giving yourself the ability of putting up the hull on that ship of reality. You are putting boards on the ship so you can put yourself afloat upon that sea of reality. That is very important to do.

We cannot move until we have enough strength within self. We have the illusion of moving, which is fine; that illusion gives us the strength so we can eventually have the reality of it. The illusion is very important because it gives us moments of grandeur, making us think we are better than we are. Those feelings that we are better than what we are give us the strength to eventually comprehend the particular things that we have erected an illusion around. The illusion gives us the ability of thinking we are there, before we are there. By having the illusion, sometimes we collect bits of information for where we should be, but while we are dealing with the illusion, we have to understand that eventually the illusion has to become that which understands the sustenance of the reality of what we are trying to comprehend. It is a very subtle thing to comprehend, but is very important. So the reality of it seems very far from where we want to comprehend, but it is not: if we just slow self down and refocus, it is right there for us.

(Addressing the questioner:) You have to begin to use your mind in the meditative state. I would trace that feeling in the arm by asking: *What is going on in my normal, daily life that is causing that reaction within the system?* There is something within your normal, daily life that is causing that particular misconception to come forward when you are in the meditative state. Why don't you feel the particular sensation in your normal, daily life? Because you did not slow yourself down enough to allow it to happen. Then you look at that pain as a triggering process within the realm of understanding that you did not have the capacity to slow yourself down to see the reality of what you should be dealing with, and you do not make it anything more than that.

There is a sequence of events within the questioning of the reality of what I just went through that is seemingly outside of the reach of all of us, but it is not. It becomes a simple fact that escalates you into the ability of comprehension. It is there within all of us. What triggers the reality of digesting all of that, which comes at you in a more balanced way, is balance within the system of what you are, so you can comprehend the balancing qualities, whatever they might be. What gives you that balancing quality? The meditative state. Sometimes it is pushes you back into a place that is seemingly going backwards. The word "seemingly" is very important because it never pushes you backwards; it puts you into a new realm of stability within the place you should be, rather than where you are, and it is within the same framework of a particular area of comprehension, never beyond, until that framework has such an absolute reality to it that it pushes you to another level.

Getting back to the original point that I am trying to make, if you truly begin to comprehend you, and ask questions about you, eventually, automatically, when the chalice of self becomes so full with information, the reality of your questions is not about you anymore, you automatically ask questions about another person. You do not even have to think about it because there is no more room within you of questioning self. Self has become so unique within the structure of what it has become, it now has questions about the reality of another person, or something else, or within the framework of humanity.

In the guided meditation tonight when you sent that white light forward with good intent, there were bits of information clinging to different areas within you. They will change you forever, whether you believe it or not. They give you the strength of that identity of yourself at a new level without even knowing it. Suddenly one day you will say to yourself: *My God, I truly have a different identity within me. I truly have more information and more energy within me pertaining not only to myself, but other people.* It happens automatically. You do not have to turn a switch; that switch is turned on automatically through comprehension.

Is it staggeringly impossible to do so? I look at it in a way that says: *It is so much easier if it does happen. If I slow myself down and see myself, I know at first I am not going to like myself. There are certain things about me that I have to work on.* But then when you begin to work on those problems, and there are new strengths within you, you begin to see the nourishment and the fruit of that practice each day. The problems that previously bothered you will bother you no more. There are new strengths there. There is no way for the previous misconception to penetrate. There is nothing there to stimulate it because there is no longer a seat for it to fester within you. You have made yourself smooth in that area; it just refracts off you.

I know sometimes it seems hard, and sometimes it seems hard within me, but the more you comprehend, it will seem less frequently hard. Does it seem like something you might not want to do? There are times when I question that too; there are times when I just say: *I am not going to do anything. I am just going to be myself, and enjoy my other pursuits.* I do that. I take brief sabbaticals from comprehending. Then suddenly there will be something that sticks up right in front of me that says: *Hey, turn it on again. Remember all of those centers you have within you? All of those different things that opened within you that you can open and make more usable?* I get little bits of information pertaining to incentives, such as people around me getting sick; or maybe I have just met a person who is sick, and I might need just a little bit more information within the realm of what I am to heal them. That will stimulate some incentives within me.

Then each time I will question the reality of myself as an individual, physically, sensually and emotionally: *What part of me am I using? What part should I be using?* Both parts of me are necessary. Both parts I can use. But what compelling factor makes me want to become more than I was before? It is unique and beautiful. It is staggering at times because I sense and feel things like I have never felt before about myself, and about others, and about the framework of humanity and its density, and the refractability of All of That Which Holds It Together. Sometimes I think I am talking to myself, because nobody else understands what I am talking about. There are times when I can feel my consciousness penetrating other people in a unique way. That compels me forward too.

Everything that happens to us happens for a reason. If we use it, and understand it, the reason is good. If we do not, it begins to club us over the head, and eventually we end up going down those streets of agony. I have been a very fortunate person in my lifetime. Even for those brief moments where I felt agony, I have had the capacity to pull myself out of it quickly. I see new realms, new avenues, that are coming forward because I am getting older. I am thinking about different things and ways of leaving the planet, such as leaving in a more peaceful, relaxed way, rather than those ways that are normally thrust upon us. The only way we can get beyond those normal ways is to be beyond the normal ways. Logic will tell you that.

Then we look at the incentives of individuals who have participated along those pathways, and think about that for a moment. Even in those brief seconds before he died, Christ was looking upon His Father and saying, "Why have you forsaken me?" A unique person like Christ makes us understand that even he believed for a brief moment that there might not be anything beyond him. So those particular pieces of information give us the necessary filtering qualities that are usable in comprehension. Certain times I think about some of those things. I am sure what I am talking about might seem heavy to some of you people, but it feels so light when I think about it, because it has an uplifting quality to it when I hit those levels. I feel it now within me. It makes everything so smooth and understandable and usable. Of course, when that total man, John, comes back from the meditative state, the total reality of all of those things that stimulate him will be refracted back into those cavities of misconception within him. The unique thing about it is, he must then take the opportunity to seek out those misconceptions and make them more usable in each moment of every day, even on those days when he looks in the mirror and thinks he looks grotesque, saying: *I should not be where I am; I should be somewhere else.* There is always pleasure within the reality of understanding that he is part of that total theme.

Fourth questioner: How do you define duality?

First there is love of self; then there is love of another, which is duality. Duality is the ability to think beyond self. Duality is everything you are involved in. Duality is male towards female; duality is male or female comprehending anything else; duality means something else other than you. Then when we refract past duality, we love at a humanitarian level where we are able to love many. We are doing acts pertaining to the reality of changing that common denominator, which is humanity, which has a consciousness. That consciousness has a collectivity to it, which we can change. That is what we did tonight in meditation when we sent the white light forward. We actually changed the awareness of the entity of earth. That is a duality within the structure of us, understanding self towards earth. We are cells upon earth, just like the cells within our bodies think of us as a universe. A single cell within our body thinks of us as being it! To that cell there is nothing beyond us. We appear to be gigantic, the total reality. We think in the same way of earth, and earth thinks in the same way of the galaxy. It is something that mushrooms out from where we are.

We mainly consider duality as one person interrelating to another. If you have the ability to love yourself, automatically there will be another person there for you to love. If not, there will be confrontations within that reality that will give you the ability to see yourself, whether it be at work, play or wherever. Certain people need the closeness of the duality of a partner, which has a confrontation within it. Then the structure of that becomes singular once again, just as the centers within your body become singular once again. There are energy sources within the body that have both male and female sides; yet in the center, it is androgynous, which is neither male nor female. The idea is to bring your consciousness towards the center and make the energy centers something that becomes a reality within the structure of humanity rather than the singular. However, your consciousness is always going back to the singular within the dualities. If you can have a confrontation of good or of something that you deal with, it gives you something that you grow from; then there is that confrontation of bringing it back to the singular once again. That is what I mean by duality. You cannot love another person unless you love yourself, because you have nothing to give. When you have love within you, then you can give.

Fifth questioner: **What is going on with England and mad cow disease?**

There is a misconception within understanding how to feed and kill animals: we have to begin to understand how to feed them correctly. We have to understand that there is a necessary reality of the food chain. We cannot slaughter a cow, then take the remains and feed it to another cow. Once a particular disease manifests, there is a triggering reality within the system that says we are misusing the particular thing. Once that disease is brought into the structure of humanity, once it is triggered, then all the rules change: then the rules are, if you are in harms way you can catch the particular disease. However, let us say a person such as a nun, priest, or rabbi goes into a plagued area. Everybody is dying, but nothing happens to the particular person. Then you think about it for a moment, and you see the purity of the person. When you think of the purity of the person, nothing can filter through that purity. By the time the disease gets to a place where it can sit, fester and become something that overwhelms the host body, there is no place for it to enter.

Why did the HIV virus come forward? We can trace this back to something I mentioned twenty or more years ago: there was a misconception within humanity. There was a reality that was taking place that was not dealing with the normal structure of reality that is usable in comprehension. When that takes place, there is a particular disease that will come forward to make us understand that we are misusing a particular vibration. What was that particular vibration? How is the HIV virus mainly transmitted? Sensually: we were getting to a place where we were misunderstanding the comprehension of beauty and sensuality within the physical sense. When we distort something so much, there will be something that is triggered within the realm of humanity that will make us begin to consider the reality within that misconception. A disease comes forward that says: *If you go and have sex with a person that you do not have a relationship with for a long time, there is going to be the possibility of you contacting that disease through that particular stimulation.*

What does that do? It changes the conscious awareness of a particular misconception within the reality of humanity. It makes us slow down to begin to see a particular thing in a more proper way. Why? Because originally we distorted it so much that it was not seen in a proper way. That is the triggering process within the realm of disease. Therefore, we can look at disease as that which is good rather than bad. If we begin to understand what disease is here for, it is telling us we are going in the wrong direction. If we slow down, it will not happen to us. When we are not achieving our probabilities properly, we are contradicting why we are here. If we are contradicting why we are here, the host body is going to die from contacting the particular misconception that overwhelms the body. Now, it does not make us a bad person, it makes us a person who is not comprehending. Doesn't that make disease seem like something that is less negative? It is useful. Then that makes us understand one more portion of God that is understandable. Before that, we did not understand it.

Reply: **I saw a movie about a famous artist. He was insecure and unhappy, also alcoholic, but was creative in his art. After he became famous there were changes in his personality where he became an egomaniac.**

He did not grow out of the same level. When you feel very secure in one place, you are there too long. If you stay there too long, you begin to feel so secure, you think you are extraordinary. That is a contradiction of growth, so you should not stay there. Eventually such a person actually goes crazy. Hitler thought he was a god after a while. It goes into a position where the person is so entrenched in that one area, they actually think they are unique and extraordinary, and it mushrooms so much that they become very secure. By becoming very secure in that place, they do not want to move, and that contradicts growth.

You want to feel secure just enough to say: *There is something beyond this.* I felt some extraordinary things as I was going through some energy changes. If I did not sit there for a moment and say: *There is something beyond this,* I would have become complacent within it. Then there is no humility within the reaction of it. You stay there so long that you really think you are profound. If you think you are profound, you become more comfortable. If you become more comfortable, you become more profound within that. Then it becomes an illusion of being profound because it scatters itself so much on the other end of the spectrum. It is a contradiction to growth, because there is never an end to it. There is always more, and that is what makes it so unique.

Have you ever hit that brief moment one time when you are enlightened? Has anybody ever felt that? Where you are stimulated to a point where it is so unique and so outside of where you were before, and when you feel that, you see an absolute? That happened when I saw the Adam and Eve story. I was meditating, and suddenly it flashed before my eyes. I saw the reality of it. When something like that happens to me, I always question the same thing: *Why didn't I see that before?* I always get the same answer: *Because you were light years away from it before. You were nowhere near comprehending it. If you were nowhere near comprehending it, it was outside of what is necessary for you, so why should you be seeing it when it contradicts you? But now that you are there, and you see it, you have won the right to see it in that way.*

That answer has an extraordinary property within it that does not condemn anything before it. That is the unique thing about it. It does not denounce the previous understanding. It says: *Where you were before, made you see where you are now.* That is good. You are no longer in the previous place, and it is no longer where you want to be, but the previous place is not negative. When I see certain people, usually religious, who condemn other religions and so forth, you know the person is nowhere near those absolute moments because those absolute moments do not contradict anything. When you see something so extraordinary like the Adam and Eve story, you understand it and see why that story was necessary.

Now, when you feel those absolutes, it is like an experience of a flash of light coming through you. I have seen that a few times. It is like being in a dark place, and suddenly a blinding searchlight is turned on. When you see that flash, it pulls you back. Some people who have had near death experiences see that flash. That flash is the refractability of the soul within the visible spectrum, changing the reality of what you are. In other words, you are going to get a flash of consciousness within the system of what you are. Usually it is white because white is the crown center, which comes through the top of your head. That is why sometimes you will feel a spinning reaction in your head when you are meditating: that is because there is a vortex of energy on the top of your head. There will be times when you are meditating where you will receive little bits of flashes, which are the rewards of your comprehension. That is the ability to escalate your ability to comprehend. Comprehension does it. By comprehending, there is more within you, and if you comprehend the next thing, there is more within you.

CHAPTER THIRTY-THREE

Meditation Changes You Forever
May 16, 2001

First questioner: **I took your advice and asked the question in meditation what I should be questioning. I started getting some interesting answers in terms of extending myself more in different directions. I will try and see what happens.**

How do you know if it starts to work?

Reply: **By the results: by how I feel, how it affects me, and if changes are made.**

Yes, and if it does not change anything, then you know you are on the wrong pathway. You are getting the wrong answers and it is important that you question the reality of it. Now, if you have a physical ailment, and are working on it, it should start dissipating. Some physical ailments are not easy to get rid of because we have a particular genetic flaw, so it takes time to eliminate the misconception from the mind and body. You have to trace the reality of what you are. That is the idea of how you become usable in meditation: you see where the misconceptions are. You take the awareness of each misconception and eliminate it from your consciousness; then you can lift yourself above the genetic process of what you are and change the density of it forever. Then you can share what you have with people around you, and it changes others forever. There is a reason for us having the particular thing within us. Isn't it amazing that we can trace everything back, and no matter what it might be, some of the genetic process of what we are is within everything? Doesn't that make you inquisitive? We should understand that no matter what life form we took down through the eons, whether it be plant, worm, or horse, we participated in that particular avenue. The capability of you upon this planet interrelates to how you become usable in understanding the chemical reactions of how the particular structure takes place.

It all comes down to that basic theme, but how do we refract that? How does it become us? How does it become usable? How do we change a misconception within self? Within modern medicine, we change ourselves in a brief time by ingesting certain medicines, drugs, or chemicals, in order to cause some stability, but if we do not change the awareness of the misconception within our minds, the illness will come back upon us again. We have to eliminate it from the source. It is like having a source within our system; then we block that source for a while with a chemical reaction gained through medical knowledge. But then when we do that, and in the process contradict the reason why we are here, that source no longer becomes usable. If we eliminate one particular disease, another disease will come forward that will be more catastrophic each time. Why? Because we are changing the basic theme of this particular life in becoming usable in achieving our probabilities.

There has to be a reason why we are here! Question it within your meditations: *Why am I here upon this planet? To make carbon dioxide for the plants?* I thought about that for a while. Another question: *Is there something beyond death?* I have questioned it. Please tell me if you come up with a better answer other than understanding that we are within the stage of life to achieve certain probabilities that we set in motion in order to become more evolved at a certain level. Some people even question: *Why we have to live life at all? If we stayed at another level, we could become anything.*

Why do we have to play tennis? Why do we have to eat? Why do we have to breathe? The reasons are the same in regard to the awareness of why: we have to become more evolved. We are only using a certain portion of what we are, and living life changes the probability of achieving something. It gives us a new slant on the capabilities of what we are in a less developed area of our awareness. It gives us the capacity, the roadway and the strands of comprehension to the Density That Made All of This. Therefore, It is at our disposal when we use the reality of That Portion in a proper way. I cannot think of anything more unique than that! And within the Uniqueness of That Structure, within the Essence of the Almighty of Whatever It Might Be, we have free will! We have the capacity within our free will to blame the Creator because we do not have the capacity to take on the blame ourselves. How unique can that possibly be, when we think about it?

Just think of moving your finger and you can move it! Just think about that one thing. Think about how you became what you are within the awareness of what you are and how unique that is! You are multi-dimensional. You have the capacity of taking the different layers and densities of you at those multi-dimensional levels and making them you, here, now, when you use what you have, here, now. Not before: no more will come unless you use what you have here within the physical reality properly. Isn't that logical and sensible? Why would your soul give you too much? Even within our desperate attempt to understand reality, *we* would not give another person a burden beyond where the person is.

There are layers of protection within the awareness of what you are, and you strip those layers away. Those layers become enlightened when you strip the knowledge of what you are down to the point where it is totally balanced here within the physical reality. You do not have to be totally balanced all of the time; only to the portion where you can lift the barometer of what you are to a certain level. I have searched the balance out so many times, in so many different directions. I have certainly distorted it within many aspects within my life, but every time I search it out, and it becomes a reality, it becomes something that is instantaneously sparking me to another level. The uniqueness of it is extraordinary.

Search it out. Question it. It changes the density of everything that you think of in a more proper way, but it never condemns anything you have ever been, or where you are going, because it makes you see that particular thing as something that was totally necessary in putting you where you are presently. It might have been a negative strain of reality for a brief moment because we are ignorant within our quest of understanding it, but it always straightens us out, it always slaps us on the hand each time. The only way we can overwhelm ourselves is by becoming so dense within our misconceptions that we become that which contradicts the reason why we are here, and then disease will come forward.

Every night in the news we hear so many different theories concerning health and disease. Now they say disease is caused by stress, or some other factor. Now scientists trace particular health factors back to whether you use your mind properly, or whether you were breastfed: that these factors impact upon your health. We hear different little things that I mentioned twenty years ago. We are just becoming usable in the normalcy of reality. We are just brushing the surface of understanding what we are and who we can become. Once I mentioned in class that maybe in a couple thousand years, the newborn comes out talking. People thought I was kidding but I was not. You can see the way things are going within the structure of the comprehension of humanity: how we are changing so drastically within our knowledge. We see the difference just within two or three generations: children nowadays are light years away from where we were at that age. It is incredible how quickly young children are going forward in knowledge and how the mind is changing.

If we look at it properly, we begin to understand the creation of this place. There are certain people that are coming to that awareness in science, now understanding that our consciousness has to deal with comprehension and awareness in order to eliminate some of the misconceptions from the planet. There are no longer any avenues beyond that. We are getting to the point now where we know the pathway of how we became human beings within the physical reality. Now we can look back upon the genetic process and fill in the information, change it, put it in the proper perspective and see where our flaws are.

On the other hand, when we get to that place that can see the flaws but treats illness instantly through the use of drugs within the normal avenue of medicine, we can no longer function here. That worries me. Anytime that we hit a unique place where we do not put consciousness into the reality of understanding something, it scares me, it frightens me. There are no safeguards. There will be something that comes forward next that will be so devastating, it is scary. It is not a disease that attacks one organ in the body but instantaneously explodes us into death. Disease becomes no longer one thing, it becomes an attack on the immune system, which is the reality that sustains and protects us. Why? Because we do not bring the two of them together: scientific medical knowledge *and* the knowledge of consciousness, and put them into the center of the attention of the ill person. It is another matter if the doctor says, "I am giving you this medicine, or pill, but you have to go back into the reality of what you are and be more compassionate, or be a person who considers another person, or have the awareness of why you have that disease." Then you can truly understand the statement, "Go and sin no more," which means, "Now that this healing has been done upon you, and you are normal, do not go and do the same thing again, or the disease will come back and afflict you again." It is as simple as that. The only way most people regard a spiritual healing now is that it is a miracle of some kind that is beyond the scope of normalcy. Rather, the spiritual healing is the reality. We must question why it took place and why Jesus made that statement. Make it logical and understandable.

Have you often wondered why one person has a disease, then suddenly is totally rejuvenated? There is no illness in the body. There is no misconception in the body. Then another person, who has the same disease, dies within a month? The dying person is a person who does not change. The person who does not seek out the particular change will never be well. When they get to the point where the illness can be terminal, and they do not change self, they can never survive! Never. Who does survive? It is the person who sees that spark, that reality, and has to change. They might say that they were "born again," or took a pill, but whatever it is, there has to be a change within the awareness of their knowledge in order for the illness to be eliminated.

It is not saying that we should shun the responsibility of going to a medical doctor. It is saying that when we go to the doctor, we must understand why we have that disease in our body. If we do not treat both of those directions, I guarantee that there is less of a chance of the reality of that disease or misconception leaving the body. If there is just a trickle into the area of misconception, the medicine or chemicals are definitely going to put a shield over it, and there will be a framework that seemingly eliminates that disease. The surgeon might even open up the body and pluck the tumor out. But somewhere along the path, there will be an ignition of misconception in another area of the body because the person did not change their mind properly within the framework of that misconception.

I can see flaws within myself that if I do not change, I will see an avenue from where I will leave. I can see it. Sometimes I am weak and do not change it within my structure. I see some genetic flaws that I am working on. I have worked on them to the point where I have perfected them more than what my parents have done, but is that enough? I do not think so. I think we have to deal with that pathway to the point where we can understand it so totally that we can lift ourselves, open up the doors of reality and the light shines upon the misconception. It no longer becomes that which is hidden within the process of what we are. We awaken ourselves to the enlightenment of how we can totally eliminate it from the process of what we are.

When you meditated tonight, you changed the chemical reactions in your body into a more profoundly beautiful, balanced way, whether you believe it or not. You prevented certain things from happening within the structure of what you are. It is called preventive medicine. When I said in the guided meditation, "Your mind will be sharp and alert," you eliminated the probability of having your mind deteriorate, as you get older. You will have a clear mind as you go through those elderly years. You are going through those different layers of probabilities that you set in motion, with the clearest mind you can possibly have. You did that for yourself if you listened. It ignites something within you. It has a penetrating quality to it. It changes you forever. There is no illusion to that.

A lot of people are frightened by meditation. When a newcomer to the class feels and senses what is going on here, they run from this place because there is no easy solution within the framework of what they are thinking of at that moment. But there is no easier solution than what we are talking about right now, because it escalates itself. The more there is within you, the less there is out there that can get you. The more there is within you, the easier it is. The more time you take to replenish the supply of energy that you have within you, the easier your entire day is. I get my daily work done so quickly because my mind is working properly and there are no false moves. When I am rushing, sometimes I have to take a deep breath, pull back and tell myself to slow down; otherwise I make it harder for myself. When you slow down, everything becomes smooth, pliable and moves in a proper direction. You eliminate those flaws within you.

That is what meditation is all about: making your life more pleasurable and achieving those probabilities with less pain and agony. You are not deviating off that main highway, that river of reality. You are not going into the tributaries of misconception and dealing with the illusions of thinking you are in the main stream. You have those capabilities, and it is simple. It is hard if you do not. Each time that I hit the place where I say, "It is hard if you do not," I tell you there will be hard days, but if you do not do what we do here, there will be days that are so hard, they will overwhelm you. If you do what we do here, it will have the capability of even grabbing those tough days and making the reality of your experiences sustainable. Seek it out. Make it you. Do not take my words as the truth. See how you feel when you meditate properly. See how you can work. See how your mind is. See if you are happier. See if there are lesser distortions within your body. It is your life. It is your tool of meditation. It is your pathway. It clears the brush of misconception so it can become clear and understandable. It eliminates the fears of misconception that you are hitting in the shallows of the river because you have eliminated the shallows from the brightness of what you are. It will happen to you tonight, whether you know it or not, but now that you know it, compound the reality of it. Even within the ignorance of what we are, we can use this place because there are so many safeguards even in the ignorance of what we are to have the capacity to use it.

I do not know Who It Was that made this place, but Whoever It Was, was Profound! The only thing that is wrong about this place is our perception of what is usable within the framework of pain and agony because we do not fully understand it. What we mention tonight gives us the enlightened avenue, which will eventually give us a bright highway. We have to seek out those different streets within the map of what we are, changing and putting streetlights on every street that we pass through with the knowledge and understanding what we are. Some of us will touch a lot of people in our lifetime. Some of us will have the capacity of being in places to really help, but if those things that we mention tonight sink in, it will not only help within the simplicity of what we are, the simplicity will grow into something that is so profound that we will touch people in a way that will change the framework that is usable upon this planet.

Years ago the U.S. Patent Office was going to close down because they thought that everything had been invented. Can you imagine that? Can you imagine what has been invented in the last five years, never mind the last thirty years? Can you imagine what it is going to be like in the next ten years? What we are going to know about the body? What are we are going to know about the mind? What we are going to know about our capabilities beyond where we are within the flesh? It is not going to be something that is hidden. We also have a strand within us that says: *Maybe that is not so.* But there is going to be an open highway of understanding of what truly happens to us after death. It is going to become something that is usable because we are going to enlighten ourselves to the point where that becomes usable. I am sure that when Christ was nailed to the cross, he could have used one sharp thought to eliminate all of the pain and agony from where he was, but he did not. He wanted to feel it and sense it within the fullest extent of what he was. He was experiencing a misconception not within the burden of what he was, but a misconception from a burden of others performing it upon him, which is totally different. He even had the capability of seeing something that was wrong within another person and having the capability of taking the blame, which is very difficult. I try to do that sometimes, but it is hard. Sometimes it happens to me for a brief moment but it never sticks totally; but each time that it happens for a brief moment, there is more of that sticking quality within me. I was not fooling when I said you are unique and beautiful, because for brief moments I could see the glow and the potential within each one of you. I am not saying that I am different or profound, but just for a brief moment I had insight into an awareness of a place and a thing that gave us the capability of seeing that moment of brilliance.

Second questioner: **You talk about the overall view of things and that there is an automatic thing going on in all of us: that in our bodies it is recorded what we need to know about ourselves. If people knew about your map of the body and really believed in it, what would that do for us all?**

Well, it would change the awareness of understanding disease and why it is here. You seek out something for a particular reason. The reason why I questioned disease to the point where I think I understand it within the framework of what I am, is because I look upon everything as being part of God; so when I do not fully understand something out there that has misconception, I see ignorance within myself. If we look at it from the piece of the pie of what we are within the physical reality, disease seems very negative, detrimental, painful and agonizing. It seems as if it is something that contradicts the true reality of understanding the Good of God, because if God is so perfect, why do we have disease? It seems as if God is not so perfect. Then when we understand it to a certain point, we understand its reason within the framework of the density of why we are here. It gives us an avenue of understanding that if we are not doing what we are supposed to be doing, we are going to be eliminated. If we look at it from the density of understanding more of the total reality of the pie, we can then understand disease as a meaningful reaction of extinguishing a particular portion of what we are because we are not functioning properly.

When we look at it in this way of understanding the reality of disease within that framework, disease is not so bad. Then misconception is not so negative anymore, because within the particular quest of understanding whatever we contact in regard to disease, we have put it in the framework of what is usable in comprehension. If we do that, then we can see it in the enlightenment of understanding the creation of this place and how unique it is. Remember, in the back of our minds, we know everything is perfect, but the comprehension of us understanding the perfection is distorted because each of us is a portion of what we should be, and it is necessary to be that because we are involved in setting those probabilities in motion and achieving them. Now, when we put that in the context of understanding the reality of what we are dealing with, and our probabilities, it makes sense. It makes it more usable. Do we know everything we should know about that density? No, we know a portion of it that puts us in an enlightened state of understanding that it is more usable in understanding that this place deals with total perfection beyond our comprehension.

Third questioner: **Some people know about the map of consciousness but cannot put it in motion.**

I know. We are clueless because we do not give ourselves the opportunity of slowing down to that point where we are not clueless. We do not seek something out from that balanced state, we try to seek it out on the subway or when somebody is clubbing us over the head. Rather, we want to say: *I am going to meditate and seek this out from a balanced state.* We want to seek it out from that vantage point of meditation that clears that velocity and makes us a sponge of reality by clearing the channel. We see it in the proper way: in that total reality of what we should be seeing. We are not the fringes of it, but taking it right into the nucleus of it and looking at it.

There are some people who are ill. The information does not say that the person is bad because they are not taking control of the disease and becoming normal again. It says that the person might be in a place of weakness, making them a person who does not have the capability of eliminating the disease within the framework of what they are. For instance, if the person has a lack of compassion towards self, and allows others to take advantage of them, there has to be the framework of understanding the reality of what that pattern of behavior is to the point where they can look at it logically. It does not make the person a bad person; it makes them a person who does not comprehend the reality of balance and compassion.

Reply: **I know people who are helping other people but not themselves.**

Why are they helping everybody else? That is another thing: some people are helping everybody else to make self look profound. That is fine if they are questioning the reality of it, so they can eventually become beyond that.

Reply: **Some of these people are like doormats because they let others walk all over them.**

Yes, so the person is contradicting the reasons why they are here and the probabilities they set in motion. If they continue to do so, they are extinguishing the reality of what they are because it is a necessary avenue that should be taking place. The person is no longer become usable in comprehension.

I cannot think of anything that is more logical about this place, and I have sought it out so many thousands of times! I wish somebody would enlighten me beyond that! I wish somebody would come up to me and tell me the reason why we are here! If the reason is that we are going to live and die and become some organic compound for a tree or something, I can understand that too, but there has to be something beyond the reality of what we are. Maybe it is that we die, and the vapor of what we are becomes that which somebody drinks in ten thousand years. Well, fine, I can understand that; I can understand a portion of that physical reality and how it works. But what I want to know is: *Why is this particular person, John, upon this planet? Why did he have those two parents? Why did he set these things in motion? What did he achieve? How did he get these answers from where he got them? Where does he refract to, that these answers came to him with no knowledge of anything else?*

There has to be something beyond the reality of what we are that has all wisdom. I did not get my information from a book; it came from the Total Conscious Awareness of God that is within each of us. But what portion of It are we using? That is the key. There is something so unique about you. There is nobody exactly like you. Don't you think the Total Reality of God is within you? I do. What portion of It you are using and distorting is another thing. I think of how unique we are, just as a snail or worm is so unique. One night I was listening to someone on television saying, "The genetic process of a worm is so similar to the human being." What does that tell you? The worm is so unique, just like you are unique. It is different. It may become usable in a different framework of understanding the chemical reactions here. Eventually it might become a more usable vehicle of comprehension that has transcendable capabilities. But right now, it is where it is, and totally unique, just like a leaf, branch, or blade of grass is totally unique. Whatever it might be is totally unique.

We have the capability of changing the level, growing within it and bringing more levels down. We are trancendable. We have properties that can change more rapidly within that system. We have hit a portion within the evolution of where we are upon this planet to have the capability of refracting to different densities and making the capability of what we are usable within our expression of comprehension. We are unique beyond the structure of a certain portion of uniqueness, but it does not make us more than the worm. It makes us different. It does not give us the capability of hating the worm, or not understanding its usability. It gives us the ability of finally getting to a point where we say: *That worm has everything that we have, but somewhere within the spark of that, we branched out into a more usable area within the framework of comprehension.* That genetic process flung itself into a new area of awareness. Where do you think that came from? That came from the knowledge of what we were before within the comprehension of humanity.

For instance, when you meditated within the density of humanity tonight, you changed the entire capability of all our probabilities, whether you know it or not. So slightly that you cannot see it, or feel it, because it should not have a capability of changing the density of you until you are ready to see it. It is just an illusion of strength in order to eventually have strength. But while you have the illusion of strength, you think you have the strength, which is necessary so you can eventually have the strength. Therefore, the illusion of strength is so usable. But when you are beyond the illusion, the reality becomes the sustenance of the strength of what you will be forever. Originally the illusion gave you the strength to make you have the eventual capability to have the strength. Now, do we look back upon that, and say the illusion is disgusting and terrible? No, the illusion is a necessary steppingstone within the avenues of comprehension that made you what you are and you cannot denounce it.

The only time you denounce something is when you go into so

much misconception within the properties of a particular level, you think you are so profound that everything around you is not usable anymore. You condemn this and that. Everything is condemned because you think that you are God at that level, or think you are profound. Hitler, Mussolini, and many other great entities have deviated into such areas of misconception that they thought they were gods upon the earth plane. When you think you are totally a god, you have gone too far within the framework of a particular level. The density of it contradicts your growth because you do not think there is something beyond where you are.

There is always something beyond where you are. That is the uniqueness of this place. When you get to that place that you think you are so profound, you contradict your growth. Always balance it and bring it back in. That is why so many great people have never thought of themselves as being profound. There is always that balance of humility within the framework of comprehension that always makes the person question the ability of what they are to the point where they never think of self as extraordinary but common and usable in the framework of what they are. If they truly understand the pathway of knowledge, they understand that if they are truly balanced where they are now, there is something that will come forward which is beyond where they are now. Each time that you feel and sense such a moment, it will make you feel so humble and so glorious, all at the same time. It is a blessing event because you will actually feel your wisdom lifted to a new area, a new enlightenment, and a new knowledge of understanding the creation of everything. For brief moments you will question the reality of: *Why have I never seen it before?* The answer will always come back: *You were never anywhere near it before to understand it, so why should you have seen it?* Now that you seen it in such a way, the simplicity of it becomes so usable without condemning anything else.

CHAPTER THIRTY-FOUR

A Different Playing Field
June 13, 2001

First questioner: **How do you focus in meditation?**

You have to train yourself going into meditation. When I lead you in the guided meditation with, "Now focus on the toes, feet and ankles," that is focus. If you teach yourself to go through that procedure thoroughly, and use concentration, then you begin to understand how the energies are flowing in your body. That procedure will teach you how to focus on anything else as well. You can literally focus on a particular thing from a particular level. Sometimes I will mention: "Think about something you want to do in life." In doing that, you are teaching yourself to focus on a particular goal and are doing it at a level where it has a penetrating quality, a staying quality, so it stays with you in your tomorrows. It may be in subtle ways but you are able to concentrate more so. When you are dropping into meditation, talk to yourself: *I would like to focus better.* See yourself in an event during your normal day that you would like to focus in on more. Then see what happens within that event tomorrow, whether it is at work or play. You do not have to go through the relaxation of the toes every time, but it is important to do so, maybe once or twice a month. That gives you the ability to focus. Then see the difference in how fast you are dropping. I would question everything I went through: *Do I drop deeper now than I did before? Where am I within the meditation? Am I at a higher threshold now than when I first started? Have I absorbed more of the essence of my soul? When I drop deeper from where I am now in the meditation, is it at a higher level because I have won the right to have more of that reality?*

There is so much to question. In the second half of class I am going to do something different: I am going to have M read a particular classroom evening to you that is going to be in the new book. (Chapter 29, The Extraordinary Umbrella Of Comprehension, 1/17/2001.) For twenty years, I have been talking about focus, and we are going to focus in on the words. When I go through the book to proofread it, M reads it to me. Then we have G and D correct some of my grammar sometimes but never the statements within it. The important thing is, while M is reading it, I am focusing in on it to make sure there are no misconceptions or something that is outside the context of what we are dealing with in this classroom. Everything has to fit. There are no contradictions. There is nothing there that says I am something that I am not. I am not going to say that I am holy, holy. Whatever you see is what you get, and all of that has to fit.

The same thing takes place when you are trying to focus. Everything has to fit. Everything has to become logical, usable and understandable within its simplicity, and not extraordinary. Make it usable. Make it something that you put within the context of the normalcy of what you are. That is the important thing about everything we do here. That is why some people leave the class: they do not think they are getting anything, but what they are getting is the reality of spontaneous reactions into the simplicity of what they are, and they do not even realize they are getting that. It is not anything that is going to push them into areas where they are going to stay for a long period of time and feel profound. Of course we are going to feel profound and extraordinary in our meditations, but the capacity within the grasp of what we are doing in this classroom gives us the ability to make it simplicity. We do not want to make something harder for ourselves; we want to make it more pliable and usable. We want life to be more pleasurable. That is what we are striving for, I hope.

So the meditation gives you that rejuvenation and relaxation, giving you the capability of keeping your body in the best shape you can. Along with that is bodily exercise and watching your balance in regard to weight or whatever fluctuation it might be. You have the ability of using that tool to help you to comprehend the particular thing you are going to achieve, and when you do it from that level, there is tremendous force behind it. It stays with you. It becomes you. You are more than you were before. I want you to know that. Sometimes you have a tool in the garage that you are not using. It is there within you. Use it.

If there is something in your body that you want to work on, understand the consciousness of that center. Understand the usability of that center and how you can increase it. Let us say that you have something wrong in the chest area: have more compassion, balance and awareness of what is usable. Focus in on you. Make sure you are in balance. Make sure nobody is taking advantage of you. Make sure you have the capacity to achieve that balance within you; then see what it does within the realm of your life. See what it does in your family. See what it does at work. See what you have to do to make yourself have more of that. Even though sometimes you are being threatened in the dualities of your life, whether it be within the family, marriage, or whatever, if you get stronger, there is less of a chance of anything out there bothering you. Logic tells you that. If there is more within you, there is less out there that can bother you.

Then if we can look at it within simplicity, and within the realm of balance and compassion, life becomes more usable and pleasurable. You are happy more than you are unhappy. You are not saying: *I am going to be happier today than yesterday.* You are striving for comprehension, and the ability to understand and absorb. When you understand and absorb, happiness comes automatically. There are lesser distortions. You have prepared yourself. There is less fear through comprehension. Also it is so important that you ask questions, because they hit exactly where you are at that point. Those questions come from where you are, and it strains all of the properties of you through you all day long. Those questions are so important because the answers stimulate the reality of what you are. You do not take the answers as the total truth; you flush them through the system of what you are and make them usable for you.

If you happen to have that capacity, your ability to absorb has been increased because of the beauty of what you have done for yourself. That is unique and beautiful, and that balance gives you the capacity to transcend. It is almost like putting down a layer of bricks: you cannot put the next layer until the first layer is there. The same thing takes place in comprehension. There is no way around it. There is no room for space in between. You always have to lay down that foundation, then the next one, and the next one, and it happens automatically. It is nothing that you have to think about. You do not have to say: *I am going to wait for that next moment or event.* You are going to make it spontaneous and simple. You are not going to make it extraordinary, like something out of the Cabbala or the Bible. You are going to make your reaction in your next moment; then you question it. When you do not feel good about a particular reaction, what does that tell you? You have to change it. I did not feel good about certain reactions that I was prone to, such as some of the anger that I had in me. I used to sit there and actually shed a tear, saying: *I have to change that! That is not right! I do not feel comfortable doing something like that!* That is change. That is the incentive to change. Use those moments. Sometimes when you are seemingly way down, those are the bright moments that give you the brightness to lift yourself.

(Second half of class:) We can stop M at any time. If there is something you want to question, that is what this is about. (M starts reading Chapter 29.)

That class was different, really different. It was the first class that I could actually say that I left, and it was beyond me. It was something that was beyond what I could cling to. I mean, there was so much going on, and I was seeing so many things, I could not grab upon a particular thing and use it instantly to say: *Yes, I know where that goes.*

In other words, I was seeing things that were not usable right then. I see different things in life that are unusual to see. I was getting some images of different things that were not usable to me instantly. Normally if I am mentally somewhere, I can take something and logically go through it, see it, sense it and make it usable instantly, but I could not do it that night because there was certain things going on that were not intended to be usable then. Certain things were going on that were refracting through the density of what I was. When I see things like that, what happens then, over the next week or two they filter through me, then certain things begin to happen to me.

I could not do that, which is fine. I could feel comfortable with that, but it did have a different effect on my ability to use my abilities, whatever they might be. The energy was awesome, but very, very balanced, very steady, and very out of the ordinary. I did have a very difficult time coming up; I know that. It was that deep and that is unusual for me because I come up very quickly most times. Since then, I have noticed a difference in my ability to drop deeper too, which is unusual because I usually drop very deep, anyway.

It is very difficult sometimes. The information that I seemingly get is so clear and so precise to me, and I have been giving it some thought about the capacity of newcomers being on the fringe of being frightened by it. I think a lot of them are frightened by it. When they are coming into the class for the first time, I think they sense and feel something, and are very frightened in the initial thrust into hearing some of the things that we say here. It has made me question the reality of why we are doing this: I suppose it is not mainly for the class; I think it is mainly for the information pertaining to some of the things that have to be said or whatever. Certain things and certain evenings: there are certain people in the classroom to interrelate to how things can be stimulated into a direction to draw in some of those energies. For instance, there might be a new person in the class one night that makes me go into a particular direction.

I had a few thoughts in the direction of trying to understand the reality of these factors and their capacities to make oneself usable in humility, which is something I have to consider. I have to consider also why it does not affect me to the point where I could have more people coming in the classroom. I know if I opened myself up more, there would be a lot more people.

Structure is the key. If we had a format or set pattern like the fourteen-week series on the energy centers and reading the energy field that we presented for so many years, we would have a lot more people coming

in. I know that. That is not what we are up to now. We are up to changing the reality of each week. We do not have a format. We do not want
a format. We want things to happen spontaneously. That is why we
have a smaller group: where we are refracting to now definitely gives
us the capacity of more written words for a particular structure within
the books.

Second questioner: **You mention people are frightened about what
they hear. Is it a matter that the person is seeing a part of self that
they have to change and is encouraged to do something about it?**

Yes, and then of course, they are going to blame me, but that is fine; I
understand that. I would not mind them blaming me if they understood
that they were blaming me, but they do not. They should be blaming
self. They should be working on self. In other words, what happens,
the balancing qualities of meditation give them that plateau of seeing
self, and when they see self, they associate it with the school. When
they associate it with the school, they say: *Why do I have these problems all of a sudden? I did not have any problems before I went to that
school.* They have been given the tools to see their problems; they could
never see their problems before; but what happens, they sort of refract
to another area and transfer that particular structure to another person.
I do not mind them doing that. Years ago, it used to happen quite frequently: I would get telephone calls in the middle of the night from
these people accusing me of all sorts of things such as, "You are flying
through my room," or, "You are doing such and such to me." You cannot believe the calls I used to get. Then certain people would pick up
on some of the awareness tools I was teaching in class and sometimes
misinterpret things, or be frightened. Sometimes I would project an
image of myself into the corner of the room using energy and thought
patterns, and two or three clairvoyant people would run out of the room,
saying: *Why is he putting himself in the corner?* I was actually teaching
what thoughts do. When you send out a thought, there is an image with
that thought. If you have a lot of energy around it, you can actually see
the outline of the particular person. That is why we see ghosts and
things like that.

Today the information has a different effect on students, although I
am sure if a newcomer was in class that night when I was seeing flash-
ing lights and people at different levels, (Chapter 29) they probably
would have said: *This guy is way out there! Let's get out of here and go
somewhere else where it is common and usable.* Maybe one day we
will go back to teaching psychometry and reading the energy field. We
actually taught people how to read a person's energy field. We do that

on the fringes now when we are talking about healing. We try to have you open yourself up to the particular structure that can scan the other person's body and see where the imperfection is.

Now, that evening (1/17/2001) did not have any particular identity to it within the framework of what I was instantaneously comprehending. What it did was refract me through different things and put them in different categories. It is just like what I did this evening when M (first questioner) asked me about focus: some of the reality of that particular evening, (1/17/2001) was in the answer that I gave her. What the information does, it encapsulates the different structures that you are dealing with in those particular areas and puts them in categories. It is hard to make us understand that we have this particular structure within us, but when I am answering a question, I am drawing from that. It is almost like a computer bank, but not like a computer bank, because it is changing so drastically when you put new information into it. When you are talking about a computer, you are talking about something that has been programmed. What we are talking about here is something that has programmable properties that change the structure of the information pertaining to the reality of answering the next question. It is not like the computer that gives you the same answer each time and is always accurate to a particular level. This is a different playing field. It changes the ability to be accurate at a particular level. It has a transcendable quality to it. It gives you the property of changing that structure. There is a different level, a different playing field. There is a different usability in answering a question. When tonight's question about focus was asked, some of the reality that was absorbed within the structure of that particular class was in the structure that helped me answer tonight's question. When the information came to me that night, it seemed to be outside of the identity of instantaneous usability, but in tonight's class I could use it. Continue, M.

I say: *Why don't I push it in that direction where I open myself up more, and have newcomers feel and sense certain things so they will come back?* Then it makes me question the reality of why we are here and why we are in this particular place: *What is happening within this particular room? Why do we continue? Why do we go in a certain direction?*

I have been giving some thought into those particular questions; but most of the information relating to last week's class was interrelated to the reality of the creation of consciousness into what is usable in the framework of humanity, and how the capacity of certain individuals within the physical sense impact upon that,

Can I stop you, M? Now, when I answered the first question tonight, we brought it down into normalcy: it was more normal in the reaction of comprehension. And when we listen to it in that paragraph, it is outside of the normalcy of comprehension, because it is new information pertaining to a reality that has to be dissected and made common: not that it is not common; it is common at a particular level, but is not usable within the simplicity of it *here* within the physical reality, even though it is absolute simplicity. When I listen to it, sometimes I say: *Where did that come from?*

and how to sway that reality in one direction or another. Those particular things have been passing through my mind over the last four or five days. It has been making me consider the reality of balance, and the utilization of thought patterns, and what an extraordinary capacity those particular factors have within the physical sense in changing our reality. It also made me see that there is so much to be done, yet it interrelates to what I can do within the framework of what can be done, and the will that I have to do so. It made me think about certain capacities of certain individuals within the physical sense who were not even known upon the planet but chose to come into the physical reality to change certain realities without being within the spotlight of the change of that reality. We could maybe consider some of the pathways that are necessary within the physical sense in that capacity.

It is very interesting: an umbrella of comprehension, a swirling pattern of chaos stimulated by the simplicity of thought patterns that cling upon it and draw upon it. It made me feel the reality of this umbrella of consciousness that is constantly moving. I had never thought of it in that way before…

Oh, I love chaos! I think chaos keeps God occupied, otherwise we would not have It around, It would be somewhere else! I think of the butterfly effect that the scientists talk about: just the flapping of the wings of a butterfly changes the entire structure of everything. It is just like when you take a deep breath, then breathe out, everything upon this planet has been changed because of that. So there is no set pattern in understanding the reality of what is truly going on around us, which is unique, because if we truly understood it, we would probably distort it so much. For instance, if we could control the ocean we would ruin this planet, and in a couple of months we would all be dead.

So the usability of understanding chaos is so important because chaos keeps God occupied in that framework, that structure. For instance, some people might believe that God knows what is going to happen. God does not know what is going to happen. God knows that when the butterfly moves, it is going to change everything. It knows that is going to happen, but It does not know what is going to happen from that change, and the reality of it is usable in understanding the free will within the structure of what was laid down at that particular level. That law is an absolute.

What is an absolute? For instance, I said to myself the other day: *God, forgive me, I do not know what I was thinking about!* Then I got the answer: *God already forgave you.* I have heard that statement, "God forgives you," from many religious people, but I never saw it from the structure that I just saw it, because it is an absolute: God already forgave you. Then another answer came along: *It is you who have to forgive yourself.* I thought about that for a moment. When you see striking moments like that... For me it was a striking moment. Then I said: *Yes, that is absolutely right! Whatever it is that I condemn myself for within the structure of what I was thinking about, I have to forgive myself. I absolutely did something within the context of what I am that does not fit and I have to change that. I have to make that pliable and fit.* If it does not fit, I have to change it and make it fit, and I have to do that within the framework of forgiveness within myself. I have to digest it and see it as something that was a reality that I had to do at that particular time in order to change the identity of what I was to a particular level, and that gave me some semblance of balance so I could move further into the property of understanding the Simplicity of That Which Made Everything, Which Is God.

I thought that was unique because sometimes we hear people say, "God forgives everything." But how does God forgive everything? The answer that I received was the structure that gave me the capacity of seeing the sphere of that: that God forgave me within the framework that was laid down by the refractability of the consciousness of that which was laid down here for us by It. But there are absolutes. There is no deviation from the absolute. So now I know that God forgave me, but it is an absolute. But within the structure of that absolute, there has to be some comprehension that gets to the particular nucleus of that particular thing that I am trying to comprehend. Then it is refracted through the density, and I have to forgive myself.

How do I do that within the Awareness of God and make it fit? How do I make it fit into that sphere of knowledge that makes me? It is like the religious person who is up on the stage preaching, while at the same time seeking out hookers on the side. That does not fit. You do not say one thing and be something else. That is why here in the classroom, what I say, is what I am. It is right there. I am not saying that I am that holy guy who does not have those other thoughts. I never say things like that, because it does not fit. If it does not fit, I will not use it. That is what we are talking about here: the ability of understanding the usable vibrations within our thoughts, as we consider how we refract the density of this particular level and keep it together.

Consciousness holds this level together, holds this earth together, in the same manner that you hold your body together. There is a total conscious awareness of you. There is a sphere; there is energy; just like there is an atmosphere around earth. Earth has an atmosphere. Earth is an entity with a great deal of energy that had the capacity of making matter so enormous within the structure of whatever scientists say that "Big Bang" was, or whatever it was that had the capacity of collecting. When I think about that, I say: *Well then, if I grow, just like a cell within my body grows...* Your cells are dividing now. Your cells are doing what they want. They are within the total conscious awareness of you. There are heart cells and lung cells. All are different. All of them have a different refractability. All of them have a different level. Some people ask, "How do we get to a point genetically where the total conscious awareness of us knows that the heart cell is different from the lung cell?" That level, that awareness: there is a triggering quality that fits, and refracts into something else, and makes it. The levels are different. They interrelate the different levels of awareness that we left for ourselves as we refracted ourselves here. Those levels fit within the framework of understanding how the genetic process takes place.

Third questioner: **How should we regard cloning and using animal cells for humans?**

It gives us the capability within the physical sense to refract ourselves within gray matter and use ourselves in that particular capacity. I looked at that, three weeks ago. I knew you were going to ask that question. In my mind while I was meditating, I saw the answer coming for that, and it is an answer that you totally did not expect. You expected me to hit upon that particular structure and see it as being outside of the context of the reality of growth, didn't you?

Reply: **Yes, because you have touched on that before.**

Yes, well, I touched on it from a place where I did not see it thoroughly. I see it more thoroughly now when we see something like that within its capabilities. It is also the awareness of growth within that structure. So in other words, when scientists get to that point where they discover a vaccine for a particular thing, like Dr Salk treating polio, in any big discovery, there are about four people in different areas of earth that are so close to getting it all at the same time. These particular people are at the cutting edge of using that information, but it takes people like you collectively with your thoughts, for the information to be drawn in, in the first place.

My wife and I were looking out at the lake tonight, and I told her that we really do not know what is going on upon this planet at all! I know I do not. I mean, I may know something, but there is so much going on that we do not know about that holds the density of this place together. Sometimes I am looking at the water, and it does things you would not believe. For instance, a single drop has the ability to collect with another drop; then all of a sudden, it will start dancing the water; then about ten minutes later, the lake is like glass. What causes that to happen? Then all of a sudden, there will be a line in the water: the line will just start moving out and is not caused by fish or anything. Then I thought for a moment: *That lake has a conscious awareness of itself.* I do not understand the properties of it. I do not understand how it does all of this collectively. I do not understand how it shivers, and how it is flat, and how it becomes weighty or choppy. I understand the wind interrelates to it, but it is something beyond that. There is something beyond the simplicity of saying: *The wind blew the surface of the water and it shimmered.* No, it is not so, because it happens sometimes when it is so absolutely still. The water was dancing.

One day we were sitting there, and when I see things like this, it just blows my mind: we have a bird feeder up for the hummingbirds. It was September, and the hummingbird came to take a drink. It came to the window right in front of me, hovered for two or three seconds–which it never does–and looked at me; then it went to the next window and looked at my wife; then it was gone for the winter. The bird actually said goodbye! It blew my mind! The bird said goodbye, and I did not see her until spring. Thank you! Then the other night I was thinking: *Where is that bird? Doesn't she like us?* Whooosh! Right there.

We really do not know anything, and if we begin to see particular things, that is what changes our entire structure of understanding the identity of what thoughts can do. We have to understand that these thoughts can and really do change the identity of what we are, and it is something that we should practice. I know I am really bad at this sometimes because I still have some anger in me, but in regard to my thought patterns, I notice today out driving, that I can really truly pull myself back from the thoughts of angry drivers more than I have ever been able to do before. I have the capacity to really be within myself sometimes. One of my phrases now is: *It is not my story. Whatever is going on is not my story.* I am trying not to make it my story, and if it becomes my story, I have all the capacity to stop it at different levels. You do not want to go down that level that takes you way back. You want to hit at those levels that stop something before it becomes catastrophic in the growth of what you are. In other words, do not deviate back into something that you were, that you changed because you did not like it.

I have never had the capacity to change the density of a particular paragraph as we are doing tonight. It is so important that we do something like this. That is why I tell you to ask questions. Go home, meditate, ask questions, come back and ask more: it is the best dialogue to learn by. The Greeks really had it right; open forum is the best dialogue because it puts you exactly where you should be in answering or asking a question.

When we see people scientifically manipulating certain things such as cloning, it takes place within the structure of comprehension that gives us the capabilities to do so. What we do not want to do is to distort something so much that it becomes a contradiction to the reality of the original thing. In other words, if we had a blight that destroyed all of the corn upon the planet right now, and we did not have the original strain of corn, we would never have corn again. That is what we have to consider. We have to consider that we should not eliminate something, we should add to it. When we make a pineapple apple, we should not eliminate the apple or the pineapple.

Reply: What about tampering with drugs to eliminate something?

We have to be very careful. We see that within the germ population: we have to understand the capacity of the refractability of germs. If we eliminate one germ, there is another germ that comes forward. The capacity of a particular thing that stops that germ, makes something beyond that germ, which makes it twice as hard to eliminate. That is what we have to really watch out for. When we look at it from that context, the particular scientific discovery becomes a contradiction to the reality of understanding disease itself. Why is disease here? It is here to eliminate us if we are not achieving our probabilities. When we contradict that reality, more disease will come. When we do not contradict that, no more disease will come. It is a catch-22 almost, but not quite.

Let us say that you were going down a pathway where you had a lack of compassion, balance and love towards others, or even of yourself: you let others take advantage of you in compassion, balance and love of self, and you start to dissipate your heart center. Then suddenly the doctor gives you something that rejuvenates that particular center. We are now getting to the point where we have drugs that can almost cure the body. Now it seems that there is not anything that we cannot cure within the body medically. Before, it was that we could not rejuvenate the heart, but now doctors are finding out that we can rejuvenate the heart. But if you do not change the misconception from your mind that is contradicting that particular capacity of compassion and balance, I do not care what they give you, down the road you will die that way, and your life will be shorter rather than longer if you do not eliminate the capacity of the misconception. Now, if you had a particular thing wrong within that structure, and the doctor gave you the pill to momentarily balance you, and you understood the misconception, that pill would be absolutely beautiful. It would give you some semblance of balance so you can question the reality of the particular misconception within consciousness, because the misconception contradicted why you are here.

Doesn't that make sense? Isn't it logical, understandable and usable? I do not know anything else that is more logical and understandable within the reasons why we are here, unless you want to go back to that theory I mentioned a week or two ago, that we are just germs here, making carbon dioxide for species on another planets. We are doing that, and they are watching us and like it because they need that carbon dioxide.

Fourth questioner: **What is self-love?**

Total security: you feel secure within any structure or situation that you deal with. There are situations that may threaten you, but you can have control over you within that structure. Love of self is survival. If you are secure within yourself within any situation that might come along, there is more of a chance of you being totally in control of that reality. If you are going to have a confrontation with another, you should have whatever capacity to have information pertaining the reality of what you are. If you and another have a confrontation, and you are totally secure within yourself, you take the other into consideration because the other does not threaten you at all. That is information pertaining to the reality of what we can become within our duality. If you are secure, it has a vibration or knowledge to it pertaining to the reality of what you can give the other so the other can become more compatible within a particular situation.

Fifth questioner: **When you are working with a really negative person and trying to keep your spirit clean, you would be so secure that you would be able to let yourself be open and try to help them?**

It all depends upon the situation. I would not shun the responsibility of a confrontation. I never shun the responsibility of a confrontation. I always say what I have to say. I was talking to my family last week: there was a controversy, and I was amazed; I have three sisters, and nieces all over the place, and we very rarely have even the slightest bit of trauma; but when I do see something going on, I always say to them, "Hey, sit down and talk. Say what you feel. Do not hold it in." When you are letting it out, find out what you feel and sense in that, and grow from that so you can let something else out the next time.

There is another avenue you can take if you have more information and balance within you: you can hit the other with contradictions to their misconceptions. For instance, if the person is just so crabby, you come in the room and say in a cheery voice, "Good morning! How are you?" You put a flower on the desk, making them understand how you feel. Some people come up to me and say, "What are you on: speed or something?" I say, "What are you talking about? What are you bothering me for? Because I am happy you think something is wrong with me? There is something wrong with you!" I will go at the person in a kidding manner, but I will say, "There is something wrong with you if you think something is wrong with me." Balance is the key. If you are balanced in that confrontation, there is less of a chance of you going up and down on that seesaw. You are in that center.

CHAPTER THIRTY-FIVE

Dealing With Detrimental Thought Patterns
June 20, 2001

First questioner: **Before you have told me when something bothers me I should take advantage of the opportunity to express myself. I had a recent situation where I fell back not reacting. It was not a big situation but I started to feel my jaw bother me. Is that a matter of not speaking when I should?**

Absolutely.

Reply: **Along those lines, there is a tooth in my lower left jaw that is moving around. The dentist is not sure what to do about it. Is this because of a lack of not expressing myself properly?**

Expressing yourself properly is very important. When you meditate, you will feel energy in those areas; if you go really deep, you can actually be rejuvenated in your teeth and gums. Listen to what your body needs and what your mind needs also. If you have a day where your memory is not that good, work on it. It is happening to me now at my age where I have to work on particular things. The same thing takes place in the body: when you feel and sense something going on in your body, work on it. If you feel pain, ask questions why you are getting that pain. If you have a problem in your normal, daily life that you want to achieve, work on it from that level in the meditative state.

Second questioner: **There may be situations where detrimental thought patterns from others might be coming at a person. In that situation what kind of effect will those thought patterns have on the person?**

It is necessary in illness: detrimental thought patterns stimulate any misconceptions in the body, so if you have a particular part of your body that you have a problem with, the detrimental thought patterns of others will stimulate the misconception more so. However, there are safeguards within the system of thoughts that protect us from misconceptions. What we have to do is become stronger in our meditations. Years ago when we had so many people in the classroom, some people

275

would try so many times to manipulate my mind and body, so I had to build up some strength. There are also cushions at other levels. For instance, there are so many thoughts going at the President of the United States. There is a structure within the system of comprehension that protects certain individuals within the realm of that, but it also gives the person an opportunity within that structure to build upon the rewards of it within their system. The more you have of purity, the more there is of protection, so when a thought comes at you, and you have that cushion, it is almost as if the arrows of misconception will glance off that armor around you. It glances off you rather than penetrating the quality of what you are.

How do you protect yourself? You grow. If you feel something coming at you, you take the opportunity within the structure of that to say: *Hey, I am feeling and sensing something. I will make it usable for me rather than have it become harmful for me.* If you take it, you will use it and refract it through you, and use it as strength. You will see certain properties coming at you, which are necessary for the reaction for you to comprehend where you are. You use everything for you, so those thought patterns are very important.

We also have some safeguards at different levels of comprehension interrelated to thought patterns, so within that structure we have some protection from the realm of those particular thoughts having such a detrimental reaction on us that they overwhelm us; they only have that stimulating quality. If you feel and sense something like that, there will be an automatic triggering process within the realm of what you are that takes you out of harms way. In other words, if you are with a certain person and see that every time you are with that person you feel certain things that you do not like, you make the decision not to be with that person. You stay outside of the sphere of that comprehension.

Then there are certain people who do not have the quality to use those thoughts at a far distance and the thought patterns become refracted within the awareness of humanity. A thought pattern is just like sound: it has a cushioning property the farther you get from it. So there are so many safeguards within the system of understanding how to use your mind correctly and how to deal with the rewards of whatever reactions coming at you from another individual within the realm of comprehension. Thought patterns are important. Thought patterns of others sometimes have a penetrating quality that only refract or reverberate whatever misconception is within your body.

Now, if a person wanted to send you hate, harm or whatever, you have to remember that they are going to end up with hate and harm within their system before the thoughts ever get to the point where they cause harm within your system. Anything that you think goes through you first. That is why I tell you to use your mind correctly. Eventually you earn the misconception within yourself before you can send it to another, especially if you are manipulating, because what you are then doing is contradicting why the other is here upon the earth. If you manipulate the other, you are contradicting the reason why the person is here.

Third questioner: **What if you are misusing your mind?**

You work on it. That is what we did tonight. I want you to work on the particular thing. I have some thoughts like that and I work on how I use my thoughts: *Why do I have that problem? What is it that I am thinking? I do not want to have that thought. I feel bad about that thought. The next time I have that thought, I will think about it and not use it again.*

You see, half of the problem is that sometimes we get to a point where we do not remember to reinforce the statement we have given self. If you have a problem but then get to the point where you have stopped the problem, then you say: *Okay, I am stopping the problem here, but when it comes again, I will have the thought once again to stop it.* It is the same thing if you want to stop smoking or any other bad habit. If you get an urge to smoke a cigarette, you will remind yourself: *I will not have that urge anymore. I will think about my fingers being yellow. I will think about my lungs dripping with nicotine.* You will think about all of the disastrous things you have to think about pertaining to the reality of how disgusting that particular habit is in order to eliminate it from the property of what you are. Also with thought patterns: when you have negativity within your mind, stop it instantly from letting it go anywhere: *Why am I having this thought pattern? How did I get to this particular point that I have to have this particular thought pattern?* Then there is a sequence of events where you can eventually shut the door on the reaction of triggering that particular thought. That is what you want to do. That is what you should have been doing tonight. Do it tomorrow in your meditations.

Not only do we work on problems of weight, smoking, over-reacting or under-reacting, we work on thought patterns. We work on the particular things that we do with our minds. If you have a lot of things going through your mind that you do not like, stop them. Stop them slowly at first. See yourself in the meditation. See yourself in your tomorrows not reacting in that very negative way. It will take a while because you have had such thoughts in your mind and body for a while. It is going to take a while, so do it slowly. Shut it off. It is like a big leak: keep tightening, tightening, tightening to shut it off.

Reply: **I tried that and felt like I was physically fighting the person, to the point where I had to stop.**

Okay, so you went too far within the realm of it. You tried to eliminate it too quickly from your system. You see, that gave me another answer to something that I have never answered quite like that before. That is interesting: not only do we have a wrong direction that we could go in, we could be going in the right direction too fast. I have seen that in other ways before but not exactly like that before. In other words, the absolute answer becomes the reaction of what you are seeing: you are going too fast so you are actually feeling ill within yourself. You have to question whether you are going in the right or the wrong direction: *Now, I know I am questioning this particular thing, but I must be questioning it too much because I have made myself ill. I am going to question it less and see if that works. If that works, then I am going down the proper pathway. If that does not work, I am going down the wrong pathway.*

Fourth questioner: **How do you explain thought patterns regarding headaches?**

Sometimes a person who has either low blood pressure or high pressure to the head will have a headache. What does that tell you? Headaches are a lack of balance within the use of the mind in a particular direction. It is a very tricky problem to heal. I am usually very good at eliminating headaches with some people, but not so good with certain people close to me: if they get reoccurring headaches, do you increase the velocity of the energy? If you do, it gives them an upset stomach. As you are projecting the energy at them, it stimulates their crown center and the third-eye center, then the third center of the solar plexus, which gives them an upset stomach.

Very rarely do I get a headache. Sometimes I get a little numb in the head and it always comes from the solar plexus. I am sure it comes from different places in different people. If I over reach or over do in some manner, such as on a rare occasion when maybe I have two or three drinks at dinner rather than one, it might bring on a headache. Then there are days where I can feel there is a misconception that is causing a foggy head, and I do not know why it is happening. I do know why it is happening, but I cannot trigger it to the point where I can say: *I can stop right here. I went too far, so I have to see where I have to stop.*

Fifth questioner: **Recently I experienced an intense circling pain in my thigh that reoccurred off and on for several nights. I questioned it and thought it had to do with somebody's negative thoughts toward me. I tried putting the white light around me, but could not seem to eliminate the pain. I finally figured out who was unhappy with me, but meantime...**

You see, I just take the responsibility of whatever it is. If it is a negative thought from someone, I do not say it is Harry, George, or whoever. Whatever the pain or discomfort is, I am going to eliminate it. I do it with strength, by saying: *It is not me. It is not my story. If there is no reason for me having this, I am not going to have it. That is it. It is not me.*

Reply: **It was not me, but I could not eliminate it.**

It is still there and interrelates to everything that you do during your normal daily life, which is enough to comprehend, so in order to stabilize it, you say: *It is not me. I do not have these thought patterns normally. If these thought patterns are coming at me, they are coming at me for a particular reason.* Whoever it is that is emanating the thought patterns, God bless them, I try to stay out of the realm of reprisal by questioning who it might be. I do not care who they are, or where it is coming from; I am going to stabilize it.

Reply: **I got upset.**

I try not to get mad anymore. I get mad at stupid little things, but I do not get mad at things like that. I just stabilize it or surround myself in the sphere. I put myself outside of it. I reacted to the point that I wanted to react within the sphere of it. If the other does not understand it, I isolate it outside of the realm of what I am and it does not affect me anymore. It is a cold attitude, but that is the way I can survive within the realm of it. I have had to do that over the years. We would have enormous classes, and the thought patterns that were going around, and what was happening, was incredible. I had to learn how to do that. I would get caught up in it and blame myself for it; then I would say: *My God, that was not me. That was someone else doing it.* Eventually you get to the point where you say: *Hey, I am not going to engage in this. It is not me.* You get to that point where you have the strength not to go there. Meantime you ride the wave of whatever it might be.

CHAPTER THIRTY-SIX

The Full Spectrum of the Healing Reality
August 1, 2001

(The guided meditation proceeded as usual; when coming to the white light, John made these remarks:) Now look or sense that white shimmering dot of energy within the heart center. It begins to expand outwardly from that point, touching every part of you, cleansing and purifying you right down to the cellular level. Believe in yourself now. Know what the statement means, "Each part of your body is being healed right down to the cellular level." I love you, God. That white light totally surrounds you. You can feel the security within it. It extends itself into the wonderment of that esoteric part of what you are and feeds upon itself within its own velocity of comprehension. It is something we do not even have to think about. It will be there, forever: a never-ending river of reality flowing from the essence of what you are and where you came from. Within the essence of the purity of that white light, knowing what it is doing for you, and its capabilities, and how it will change you into a more pliable, usable person within the physical sense, comprehend all the beauty that is upon this planet and use it for you. I love you. Within the silence of what you are, knowing without question that everything is functioning properly within your mind and body, rejuvenate yourself. Bathe yourself in that wonderment, that light. Cleanse yourself more so and more will come: a never-ending fountain of light within the essence of your soul. Feel the love within this room now.

I want you to think about your day: I want you to think about the things you thought you did right and dwell upon them to do them right tomorrow. Then I want you to think about some of the things you might have done that you did not think were necessarily right, and I want you to improve upon them in your tomorrows. I am going to look at the truth and blessings of those things within me, and dwell upon them for a few moments. I see myself in a better place for all of my tomorrows so I may touch whomever I come in contact with, especially those close to me, and truly show the love I have within me. I want you to do so within yourself also. You can feel that uniqueness now within you, and I want you never to forget it. When things seem heavy, you will feel that uniqueness, and the burden of the misconception will be lifted because you are special. I love you.

(Afterwards:) You should have felt something very special. You are going to feel a lot of changes within your life. There is a reason for you being here tonight, especially tonight.

First questioner: I have felt a lot of different energies lately: a rejuvenation process going up both sides to the lower rib cage. I felt another unusual sensation the other night when I was talking to a friend on the phone: after I finished, I started feeling a discomfort in the lower rib.

Those energies that you feel in your body are rejuvenations in different places within you. The discomfort relates to you feeling a lack of compassion, or balance, or human decency, or of understanding of what was going on within that structure.

(Addressing the class:) I know that some of the things I mention to you are seemingly way out there, and that it is hard to digest some of these things, but when you begin to feel your energy field at those levels, the reality of what I am telling you becomes so true and natural. Eventually some of you will extend yourselves into those particular areas if you meditate. When you do, then the reality of it will stick at those moments and give you an analogy of the situation that you are feeling and sensing within you. What G is feeling in his body right now are some changes within his comprehension of lower duality within the physical sense and how he can become more usable within that. There is some stress and tension within that structure, and some rigidity, and the reaction can be chaotic, stressful, or tight, or not absolutely correct at times. You will feel those things in your body and you will question it. Question it to the point where you begin to see some of those avenues within you.

Let us discuss at a basic level some of those things I was just talking about. Now, even if you do not believe me, let us think about the logic of that information pertaining to the reality of making your life better. When you look at it even at a basic level, all of those other things I mention are important within the reality of understanding that eventually you will extend yourself into those areas of awareness; but right now those areas might be less important because the logic and usable vibration of the information within the simplicity of its usability in each moment of every day are more important to you. It is as if I say to you, "If you listen to your body just as if you listen to your car, you can understand there might be something wrong with it." Just at that basic level, the information is usable; you do not have to believe that it extends itself to some other awareness. But if you begin to focus upon those particular things within the structure of what you are, then you will see the simplicity of the information and use it at that particular level. If you feel it at another level, but do not care to know where, or what particular part of your body it came from, that is fine within the structure of what you are.

The point I am trying to get across is that even at those basic levels the information is true, accurate and usable in making you a better person. So when I think about it in that way, within the simplicity of it I see the information as becoming something that is a pattern that is usable in the framework of humanity. It is just like breathing air: we do not care what portion of it is hydrogen or helium; we just want to breathe it and use it. The same thing takes place within the structure of comprehending those particular parts of your body. I hope you use this basic information. Sometimes I scare newcomers in class because I start wandering way out into some of those structures. I feel those areas refracting through me and I see where the information comes from: it comes from that esoteric part of me and it might be information that is usable in a book, maybe in one or two hundred years from now.

Reply: **I was reading about Sir Isaac Newton. He came up with a single mathematical equation that explained things so clearly about the workings of the universe. It changed all prevailing scientific concepts, but at the time he was vilified for his discovery.**

Something like that has a tremendous effect on the reality of what we are, if we can figure it out. We can go back to what we were just talking about before: do we have to know the particular equation? No, we do not have to know that. The same thing took place within that structure. There is a reason why you just mentioned that structure pertaining to the reality of Sir Isaac Newton. Am I going to answer that pertaining to what might I know about mathematics in the quest of understanding comprehension? No, I do not have an idea of what is going on within that structure. Is it necessary for any of us to know it? No, because we get back to that basic theme.

(Addressing questioner:) Now we can understand why you asked that question. You do not even know why you asked it. You asked it for one reason, and we got it for another reason. It formulates or compounds the reality of how usable that last thing is that I just mentioned to you: we do not have to understand that everything is mathematically confined to the reality of what we are; we just are what we are, and it is necessary to be so.

Reply: **You have talked a lot about feelings and how, as we grow, we gain that sensibility. I have wondered about people involved in other**

disciplines like science and music who are also healers. What part do they play in the overall scheme of healing?

Mathematics, music and other disciplines are each one finger of it. What we are doing has the entire structure of the hand: it is not one finger; it takes in the reality of everything. In other words, we are extending ourselves into comprehension. Comprehension within the essence of itself escalates the ability of a particular structure. Some people will isolate themselves within a particular square of the structure and begin to deal with the information pertaining to that reality at an extraordinary level. What we are doing here is extending ourselves within a full spectrum of that reality. When we do that, the realm of its capabilities refracts itself into the essence of understanding how to heal what we are. It takes in the visible spectrum and refracts itself through all of the different densities, sound and the capabilities of whatever it might be. But the main property within it is that it changes consciousness into energy, into matter, and stimulates matter within the physical sense to the point where it lifts it within that particular structure to a particular level and changes the density of its usability. When it does that, it gives us more of a capability of understanding the refractability of how we heal. But if you have isolated yourself within one particular structure, it does not take itself into those frameworks. It has a portion of it within it, but extends itself into sometimes isolating itself into the one particular structure and does not see the total picture. That is not what we do here, but it is understandable because it is something that the person has chosen to do.

For instance, there might be an individual who has the capability of coming upon the earth plane whose soul might have the knowledge of refracting into the physical reality but does not possess a totally sound body. Maybe you have seen a person who can sit down at the piano and play Mozart, yet has no knowledge in any other direction. That is what is called the isolation of the refractability of a particular entity within the physical sense. They are a genius only in that one spark of the essence of what they are. Then there are other people like Michelangelo, who can take their particular abilities, and use and ignite those sparks beyond the normal reality of a particular structure.

Close your eyes for a moment; I just want you to picture this: I want you to see a man and a square piece of marble about thirty feet high. As he looks at this marble, he can actually see and feel and sense the essence of what is going to be carved out, even before he starts. He knows where the first chip is going to be, the next one and the next one. He is going to have tunnel vision: that is the only thing he is going to concentrate on. He is even going to forget to eat. Friends are going to have to pull him away to sit him down and tell him to take a deep breath, look at the sky, eat and drink. Michelangelo was an individual who took something in one particular structure that had not one finger but many fingers within the structure of beauty. He could not only sculpt, he could paint, because his art was flowing. It was coming into the throat center, not the sacral center. The most gorgeous woman, totally nude, could walk by him, and he would not even see her. She could have the most fantastic perfume on, and bring in the most fantastic meals, but he would not even see her. The throat center was lifted. It was an esoteric comprehension of the throat center, which then flowed through his hands and arms right into the chisel chipping away. Have you ever had the opportunity of seeing any of his work close up? You can actually see the veins in the marble! How in God's name! His ability to understand the human anatomy was absolutely incredible: the structure of the muscle on the leg or toe. One mistake, one miscalculation of what that gigantic piece of marble had within it, and he would not have had that masterpiece. What his capabilities were! Talk about concentration and the capability of focus. Incredible!

Some people had other directions. Christ's capabilities were in the direction of making people understand that the direction they were going in was wrong and that there was freedom beyond the flesh. Think of some of his phrases and ways that he mentioned certain things to people. Think of his capabilities: how nothing he did contradicted what he did; nothing! If you search it out, nothing he did contradicted who he was. Everything had a purpose to it. Everything had a flow to it within the framework of free will within every individual. Imagine having the capability of not even having a negative thought towards another; if he did, for a brief moment, he had the capability of pulling it back. Then he had the capability of being beyond that point where he did not have to think about having a negative thought because there was no negativity within him at all.

If you really listen to what people say, you can understand where they are coming from. There are no illusions to that. For instance, a person would walk up to Christ and ask him, "Did you do a certain thing to a certain person?" He would say, "Well, ask them." They would ask again, "Didn't a certain person say this about you?" He would say, "Ask them." He could not even answer questions pertaining to another person. The person might persist, "They said you were bad and you did certain things." He could not even stick up for himself because it would contradict what the other said. He would say, "Ask the person." The person would say, "Well, we already did, and they said such and such about you." He would not say anything because he already answered that question. Then the person would say, "Aren't you going to say anything? Don't you realize what we are going to do to you?" He would say, "I have nothing to say." Then he might say a little phrase, "There is a place for you within the realm of where I go." Or, "Think about what you say and what you do." Not one word was a contradiction. He would just make a statement. The statement was within the realm of what was wrong within a theme. It had nothing to do with interfering with the person's free will, and had something to do with the choice of the person's free will, so he could make a statement like that and it did not contradict what he was doing.

Then there was Moses: his job was not in healing but to make people know what the wrath of What God Is within the realm of each individual. For instance, if you say bad things about your neighbor's child, you are saying bad things about your own child. It was emphasized to the point where the reality of it became something that was true and necessary because there was a framework that was being set down. The energy around him was intended to be so, because people have to understand what structure takes place when they make thoughts within a certain direction. Thoughts have so much power.

Therefore, now when we see within the physical sense that we have come a long way, we have to ask ourselves: *Is this the right way? Where do these new diseases come from? Were they here before? Was the structure usable?* If you had to ask me what my particular reason is upon this earth plane and why I might know about some of these other people... Anyway, why should you believe what I know or do not know? But if I have to understand what my capabilities are and what I have to bring upon this earth plane... or what you have to bring upon this earth plane: you will have to question it in meditation. I have questioned the reality of what I am. I am sure I cannot catch up to the information of what I am. There is a reason for me being here, and it is not the same as Moses. Moses had the capability of saying: "You are doing something wrong." On the other hand, *this* is something that has all the fingers. It is saying: "We are all doing something wrong; we all have different little things that unite into a gigantic consciousness and we can change the structure of all of that. There is no silent majority. There is no silence at that level. Everything has a usable vibration that is understandable in the refractability of the awareness of this density."

Is this information important? Will it be something that is knowledgeable and usable at the present time? I doubt it. Will it be something that maybe in one, two, or three hundred years from now, someone picks up a dusty blue book called "COMMON AS RAIN," looks at it and says: *My God, who was saying this, back at a time when nobody else was saying it?* Then you can understand how Sir Isaac Newton felt when he was doing something at a particular time when the conscious awareness of humanity was nowhere near there, and how so many people hated him because he was changing the structure of everything that was being believed at a particular level. With the new knowledge, people were threatened within themselves. You can search out these things within yourself. Just take the moments within your meditations to do so.

Second questioner: **Could you elaborate on " the silent majority?"**

Every thought you make affects everybody else, so if you are not saying anything, you are saying something. If I have a hateful thought—which I occasionally do, more than I would like–I try to change it. If I do a thoughtless deed, I try to change it within the awareness of what I am. But even after I change it within me, that deed becomes part of the total conscious awareness. So if that deed has hateful intent within it, it slants everybody else's perception about that particular density. It is not something that is overwhelming, but it does have a slant to it. It is like walking up on a rocky ledge, and if you have to move to the right, it is because there is no place to step. The same thing takes place here: there is no place to step because you have made a void within the structure by making misconception part of the reality of it.

Third questioner: **We hear about so many murders and violence in the news. What does that do to us?**

People are moving so fast, they cannot comprehend it. People are moving so fast, they cannot control the reality of what they are. They have to slow things down.

Reply: **Even seeing violence on television, people start thinking about these things. What does that do?**

That escalates the reality of what people think in that direction. Whatever it might be, they are seeing it. If there is a violent film, certain children go out and try to emulate those particular structures within humanity. In one sense, it is helpful because there is less fear in children, but in another sense, it is not so helpful because there is less control without the reality of fear to slow them down within that structure.

But that fast pace is understandable because there are things happening very quickly upon the earth plane now, and it is important that we get it right. If we do not, it happens so quickly. For instance, the dinosaurs disappeared so quickly. If the scientists try to trace it, they are amazed that there were so many dinosaurs; then all of a sudden they were all gone. What was the reason for it happening? There was some sort of misconception within the awareness of the property of how the dinosaurs used themselves within that structure. A level was hit within the evolution of the earth where such a gigantic animal was no longer usable. It was cumbersome within the awareness of entities that had to refract within the physical sense to make a usable vibration or body, so we might say that the reason the dinosaur is extinct is because it was not usable anymore. But there will come a time when, for our amusement if we can balance things correctly, we will be able to clone a dinosaur in order to see it; but it will not be usable once again in a soul taking its body and using it within the physical sense to become more evolved. Why would we do so when we have evolved to this point where we have made a more moveable, pliable, physical body?

Then we might ask, "What if we destroy ourselves? Where will the next awareness go?" It goes to a collective body of whatever next species upon this earth plane is lifted to a particular level that becomes usable within that physical sense as a home for the properties of extending ourselves into comprehension. Now, when you look at these aspects, you might question whether this is the absolute truth, or is there that little portion of it, even as you are seeing it as an absolute within your mind, that you say it might not be true? What makes all of that usable?

I want you to think about this for a moment–it is hard for me to think about it within my mind but I try to do so sometimes–that there are maybe two hundred people that hate you so badly. They think you are the nastiest person on earth. They take you and nail you to a cross. They use nails that are rusty old homemade spikes, two or three inches long. They nail you right through the wrists–not through the palms–on each side. You are up there bleeding to death, and you still have the capability of loving everybody down there. Then they drive spikes through both of your feet to hold you onto the cross. That is why you see the bones and how it is crushing your bones: agony like you cannot believe! Imagine taking a pin and pricking it into your wrist: now look at the veins and imagine the blood rushing out of your body, and people are rejoicing. You are half nude, dirty and tired because you are carrying this thing maybe fifty feet through the city, stumbling on the stones, cobbles, steps and different things all the way to a mound. You fall. Besides that, they put a crown of thorns on your head. Have you ever pricked yourself on a rose bush? There are spikes actually put upon your head, close to the eyes through the eyelids, and you are in agony. You are able to lift yourself above that.

I will get to my point: remember that little area I was talking about that says: *Maybe what I am doing is not true.* You turn towards the light. You see a light because you are at a level now where it is extraordinary, and you say, "God, why have You forsaken me?" Think about that for a moment; in other words: *Why have you put me in this position? Why must I be in this agony? Why must I be dying like this?* Even that individual, who had all of those extremely extraordinary properties, at that last moment, doubted whether all of those things he did were the truth. Think about that. It is just like when I mention certain things to you, there is that single strand within the structure that says: *I know it is true, but I cannot prove it because it is something beyond the realm of where I am.*

At the moment that I die upon this cross, am I immediately at the Right Hand of My Father? What does the right hand mean? Why wouldn't it be the left hand? Doesn't that tell you, when we mention that the energy of the male comes in on the right side and the energy of the female comes in on the left side, that that is a true reality? Symbolically there are so many things going on. Where did I get this information? Did I get it from the Bible? Are any of those things mentioned in the Bible exactly like that? Are there hidden phrases within the Bible that can be interpreted at many different levels?

Yes, because if you make a statement in the Bible, it is an absolute. It does not contradict any statement at any other level; it just extends the awareness of the truth of that as a basic foundation for the next truth, which does not contradict either that truth, or the previous truth. So when you are reading something at that level, that particular structure can be read and understood from wherever you are within whatever density that you are dealing with, even if the reality of it is infringing upon misconception because it is absolutely true. It extends itself beyond the awareness of that particular thing, then it extends itself in a spiral to that next level, and you can see and interpret it at a different level. Why wasn't that information in the Bible at that time? It was, but it was not said in that particular way, and it did not extend itself to the awareness of where we are today. Then if you have that capability of seeing that strand, and understand the reality of it, you can extend it to that next awareness that is readable at any level of awareness because it is an absolute. It extends itself beyond that without contradiction. Are there any questions? Let me ask a question: what do you think when I mention something like that?

Fourth questioner: **Before I started meditating, if a person said something negative to me I would be angry; I could not forgive them. But now if a person says something, I try to figure where they are coming from, and what their insecurities might be, and I can react differently.**

Very good. For instance, the next time you go to the dentist, have him drill your teeth without Novocain, and while he is doing it, and you are in pain, try to like him; then try to love him. I practice this all the time. But then one day I went beyond the barrier. The dentist told me very casually that he was going to do a root canal. I told him to go right ahead. There was no Novocain. All of a sudden, he started drilling right down through each one of the roots of the tooth. You talk about agony! Meanwhile he was just chatting about little matters, while taking these little tools: each of them had a thread on it, and he was putting them in there, and wiggling them around all away down. All of a sudden, the pain was excruciating. I said, "Hold on for a second!" I had to drop deeper and deeper. It took me about twenty minutes to get rid of the pain, which was unusual for me; I can usually get rid of pain in an instant. I will never do that again. Then he said, "We are going to the next size." I was saying: *Every time these tools are getting a little bigger, and he is putting these things all the way down and making the hole bigger each time!*

Afterwards, he said, "Were you in pain a little bit?" I said, "What? Are you out of your mind? Why didn't you tell me you were going to something like that? It is not as if you are drilling normally!" So I do not think I could love him at that moment. That is the point I am getting back to: whether it is a dentist, or whoever, it is small compared to the agony of what Christ was going through, and he still loved all of them. That is the point I am trying to get across: I do not know where that is! I have never felt any of that! I have felt certain slivers of it, but I want to know how in God's Name, he got to that level where he could have done that. That was absolutely extraordinary.

You have to understand that there was a total theme about the reality of why Christ was here. He knew why he was here and what he was set in motion to do. He could have chosen to make just one thought: *Leave me alone and don't bother me,* and everybody would have moved out of his way. He had so much power and energy around him, but he could not even infringe upon that reality. That is why everything was set in motion. Everything took itself beyond where it would normally be, and that is why it became so absolute and extraordinary. You have to remember that was two thousand years ago: where was the population back then? It was nothing, but today look at how many churches and religions and books are written about him. People are interpreting this man and what he did. It is so very extraordinary.

Reply: **If he had said something, he would have contradicted the other's free will?**

Yes. Not only that, it would have contradicted why he was here. He knew he was going to die for everybody and he could not contradict that. He could not do anything to stop that theme from going in that direction.

For instance, when M comes to the house, and we are working on another book, while she is reading, I am looking for contradictions. Sometimes she will include something in the transcript where I was kidding and that contradicts what I am doing. I will tell her to delete it because it is not pertaining to the reality of what I am dealing with; or there is a contradiction in my statement pertaining to the reality of the theme of what I am; or I am at a new level where I can see something in a different way. So we will change a phrase. Sometimes my wife will tell me that a particular word or sentence is grammatically wrong. I will look at it and say, "No, that is the right word. In English it might be the wrong word, but it is what I want in that particular structure, so leave it in." Not only that, I want the reader to know I was not the brightest guy, so everybody can do what I have done. Good night, everybody.

CHAPTER THIRTY-SEVEN

Turning The Tide
Sept 19, 2001

(Start of meditation:) Put some good thoughts in your mind. Is it hard to put some good thoughts in your mind now? You know what a good thought might be. It is so important when we gather together, whether you believe it or not. Every week when we meet, we should give some consideration to that umbrella that protects everybody. Right now, it seems as if there is going to be a concentrated effort to find and punish some of those people, (referring to the 9/11 catastrophe) but we can do things with our minds. Believe in yourself: that is the main thing. Quiet yourself down if you can.

You want to give yourself stability. You do not want anybody to change you in a negative way; you do not want anybody to infringe upon your free will; you want to feel strong and protected. When you work on yourself as you are doing now, even as you are entering the meditation, you are protecting yourself. I want you to know that within your mind. You are the person that does not walk into an area that going to go astray. You are the person that looks to the right when you should look to the right, and looks to the left when you should look to the left. You are the person that takes the extra minute and misses the accident. All of these things happen to you because you protect your-self. Meditate to put that energy around yourself: you give yourself that aura of protection within the true reality of what is going on. Little things will happen to you in a positive way rather than negative, and when there are some events that touch you that are seemingly negative, you will have the capacity and the strength within you to change them and make them usable for you.

(After the relaxation of the parts of the body:) To help us further understand that we truly have an esoteric part of what we are, I want you to either sense or visualize a small pure white dot of energy within your heart center, and it begins to expand outwardly from there. As it does so, it cleanses and purifies you right down to the cellular level. It totally surrounds you in that unique aura of white. I want you to feel and sense it, and use the balancing qualities of it for a few minutes in silence; then I am going to ask you to join with me to do something. Relax: join with me now; I want you to send that white light some-where with me. I want you to see the white light in the disaster area in

New York: see a gigantic spotlight coming down, and cleansing and purifying that area. Do the same with the Pentagon in Washington.

Now I want you to think of that white light as good: it enters into different structures, and people, and all of the vegetation and animal kingdom. I want you to see it spreading forward from this room, and as you are doing so, you know that you will replenish the supply automatically. The white light goes forward, touching everything in its pathway. It seeks out misconceptions and makes them obvious, especially in people who are hateful and wish to harm others. These people become conspicuous. It gives these people a flash of light within their minds, making them realize that they should not harm others. The white light not only touches these people, it touches certain people in power, and as it does so, it gives these people the knowledge and wisdom to cause some semblance of balance upon this earth plane. It gives everybody a new awareness of wanting to help rather than harm. The earth itself is glowing. If you were in outer space looking upon it, the earth glows in that aura of white.

With the wisdom that you have within you, you have changed the common denominator of humanity. I want you to know that. Within the silence of what you are, knowing that everything is functioning properly within your mind and body, do your own deeds, remembering that it is a sin to put energy in motion to hurt another. It is your right, your birthright, to send forth the white light within the confines of humanity in a positive way because you have chosen to be here. You give everybody upon this earth plane more love, compassion and balance. From this room tonight, we have changed this place that we live in forever, and you will see a noticeable change. It will give you incentive to want to do more so, and each time that you do, a portion of that stays with you and changes you. It makes you new. You have heard of the statement, "Born again." Each time that you meditate, you do that to yourself. Every cell within you is reborn from the structure of your knowledge from another level, utilizing your mind correctly from this level. I love you. Be safe. (The meditation proceeded as usual.)

First questioner: **We talk about terrorist groups as cells that suddenly trigger catastrophic events. In the past you have talked about harmful cells within us that do not necessarily manifest. They are sitting there, but when we go into areas of misconception, they can trigger disease within us. On a larger level as we deal with various aspects of consciousness within humanity, does a similar kind of thing happen within the collective consciousness where we have these cells that trigger catastrophic events?**

Yes, exactly in the same way: whether you believe it or not, this room tonight changed the reality of that aspect. You will see every one of those terrorist cells found and collected because you have helped. Believe me, what you did tonight will turn the tide. I want you to think about it in your meditations from now on, too. It is important that you use your mind properly when there is something catastrophic going on. If there is a hurricane coming, and it is going to hit land and cause devastation, if you have knowledge of it beforehand, get involved in it. Realize what you have within you, especially if you have been meditating for a very long time. You can hit levels of comprehension that you can filter down and change the reality of that in the same manner as working on a sick person.

Tonight we were working on the total conscious awareness of humanity, so the energies that were flowing through you were dealing with those particular realities. You not only change the entire structure of humanity, you change you forever. You have more of that humanitarian knowledge within you, and the next time you transcend to those levels, you go into higher levels because the seat of where you are has changed. Your focus has changed. You have lifted your reality to that particular level that can see more. You will get more insight into the nature of reality. You will begin to see the flow within the dimension of the common denominator. You will have the capacity in certain instances to see events before they happen and be able to help. That is the whole idea of what we did in the first meditation.

Second questioner: **In this meditation I was aware of what seemed to be lines of silver and black. I was trying to ask what that meant and just got the message not to go anyplace.**

Just use it for where it is. There are things that you do not want to delve into. You just want to send something. You do not want to use your focus in some other dimension. For instance, people ask me if I can visit the dead. You do not want your focus to be at that level. If you happen to hit upon a strain of it, and see something like that, fine; you interrelate to it for that moment, but do not change your focus from where you are here within the physical reality.

Is it possible to visit the dead? Of course, it is. Where do we go after dying? We go through all of the different levels until finally hitting the soul. If in meditation you happen to come in contact with someone who has died, they might be in one of those layers. You people who have more capacity of being transcendable will have more capacity of seeing what is going on at different levels. Sometimes you can receive such a magnificently vibrant picture of the deceased. The colors are indescribable. You will see the person in the peak of perfection within the best frame of what they were within life, but the reality of the image will be sustained at an extraordinary level. If the person had blue eyes, you will see a blue you have never seen before. Their color of hair, features and attitude will be extraordinary and indescribable, and you will know that it is not something that is within the physical sense. When you see those kinds of images, you just focus on them for a brief moment, see and help them. You learn from the particular thing; then bring your consciousness back. You do not want to seek out those images. If the image seeks you out because you happen to be in a glancing area of the particular level, that is fine; or if you need to do that to refract through that area in order to send energy to the other, fine; but do not seek out those places. If a particular image comes, ask questions and find out more what is going on, so that if it comes again, you will have more of an inside sense into the reality of what you are seeing. Then your focus can be trained on something different than the new reality of what you have just seen.

Years ago, I can remember so many things that were going on within the structure of my growth. I can remember leaving a building and flying through walls at speeds you would not believe; it was absolutely incredible; you talk about fear. I said: *What is going on?* And immediately, whish! I was right back. Then I asked a lot of questions about what was going on: *What happened there? Would I want to do that again?* You think of the possible consequences of your reality: the reactions within the structure of making that something that might become common within you and how it could change your personality: *Where would I go? Why would I seek that out? What would be my reasoning behind wanting to do something like that? Why would I change my focus from the physical reality to that reality?* The answer came back: *You do not have to go anywhere. Everything you have is within you.*

Extrasensory events like that are unnecessary. If something like that does happen, there is a reason for it happening into the reality of understanding where you are in a more digestive way, but if you seek it out, then you are changing your focus of understanding the reality you are participating in. From the vantage point that I see it, you do not want to do that. So many people get stuck in a reality within the physical sense that is seemingly extraordinary, yet the basic foundation of it becomes a contradiction to the reality and the reasons why we are here. If it does that, then it is not something that has the true sense of being something extraordinary; rather, it has the perception of being that because the person thinks they are profound, and when they think they are profound, it slows them down from becoming more of what they can become. You do not want to do that.

So when you are out in the fringes of feeling extreme, you want to bring it back into the center: if you are feeling really low, you want to bring it in; if you feel really extraordinary, you want to bring it in. You want to make it a balancing quality that makes you a moveable vehicle of comprehension. You do that by saying: *If I am feeling the wonderment of what this might be at this level and I feel so extraordinary, why wouldn't I want to feel more?* If you take it, use it and think of yourself as being so profound, no more will come. If you take it and do not use it at all, no more will come. But if you have a balancing quality between the two, and put it in the center, and it moves you into the higher essence of the reality of understanding Whatever Made This, more will come. Each time it will be so extraordinary. It will touch you and there will be a flash of intellect. It will change the reality of you forever and will give you knowledge like you have never had before. You have to digest it. You have to put it within the system of you. You have to make it something that is common.

Some of the people that have had these kinds of experiences appear to be just so ordinary. I have had the opportunity of meeting a lot of people in my life: people who run big companies and are wealthy beyond your wildest dreams. I do not know why, but I have had the capacity of being where I have met some of the highest intellects in the world. I have also had the capacity of meeting some of the people who seemingly are the most devious. I do not know why I have been put in these positions, but I have met possibly some of the highest Mafia people and such. The one quality that I have noticed in some of them is their capacity of being just so ordinary and making you feel comfortable, no matter what their level is. The people that are not like those are usually the people below them who are trying to get where the top people are: they will never get where the top people are. The people who run these big companies are extraordinary, unique and so different. They can talk to you in the same friendly manner, no matter what your station in life is. Every one of them has that quality and it takes that. They do not know why they have it. They also have the ability to delegate certain strands of what they want done. If you ask them to spell something, they would probably look at you as if you are crazy because their mind is moving so quickly in a direction of understanding the total reality of something. You can see a collective body of people behind the person that takes care of all of the details, because they know that without that spearhead moving through the traumas of life breaking up the misconceptions, there would not be any company; it would be refracted. For instance, when a great CEO of a company dies, you can see the stock drop because that tip of the spearhead, the person of innovative qualities, has been taken away.

That is what you want to become: you want to become that moveable vehicle without extending yourself into the drudgery of thinking about it for those moments. Let it happen automatically within the awareness that continuously propels you forward from the center of understanding the true speed of reality. That is what I mean by bringing yourself into the center within the meditation. It moves you, changes you, replenishes and refreshes your mind and body. It eliminates those probabilities of harm happening to you. You are special. You have never seen anybody look exactly like you. Know it.

Third questioner: **When I want be involved in healing a person, sometimes I am more aware of the flow. I am able to open my crown center and have it come through me. Other times, it is not happening.**

What is the first thing you have to do when you want to heal somebody? You have to go into a deep meditation. What are you doing? You are going closer to your soul, so logic tells you that you are going closer to the other's soul that you are trying to figure out what is going on. Then you feel and sense what is going on in your body. When somebody asks me about a particular person, I can feel and sense what is going on in their body, because I know what I feel and sense in my body. During the healing if I feel something different in my body, it is not from my body, it is from the other. Then I begin to ask questions and open up particular centers. When I am dropping off and interrelating to the other, I am doing a number of things: I am sending energy and feeling different things. I might even receive a message to give to the person. If there is something I might have to say that helps the person change the reality of what they are, I will tell them after I send them energy.

You can do other things in the healing. You can send the person color. If the ailment is within the solar plexus, send them yellow and see the vibrancy of it crystallined in white. Put a pyramid over them. Visualize the person acting better. Do everything that comes through your mind that might help them. See a pyramid of white surround their house: see one side of the pyramid going absolutely north and different colors within the pyramid. See the person getting better. Change the probabilities within whatever it might be that you are seeing. Ask questions too: *What more could I do to help this person?* If it is something beyond your comprehension, ask for help from Jesus, Moses, Buddha or whomever you want to use, or you might want to think of other people you know that might help, for instance, the collective body of people in this room. You say: *As a unit, please help me;* then learn from that. Or: *Jesus, help me, so I may learn so I can put myself there.* Years ago, I can remember sitting in front of a person, and the disease was so overwhelming that I had to say: *I need help.* The statement: *I need help,* gives you the reality of understanding that what is coming through you is not totally you. In the instance when you are working on a person who is experiencing a lot of pain, and you are feeling a lot of pain, that will tell you that there is too much of you involved in the healing, so you ask for help. On the other hand, if you feel the pain for a brief moment, that gives you the understanding of what is going on in the other's body for a brief moment so you may turn on something within your body; that is something different. But if the pain lingers within you, ask for help.

Reply: **Is there ever a time when you do not have the right to be involved in giving a healing to an ill person?**

As one human being to another, you enter into it. You do not try to infringe upon their free will; you just send them energy. When I see a person who is sick, just the thought is going to heal. Sometimes I will give the person a thought. I am constantly working on someone, somewhere. Sometimes during the day, I will have a thought, and that thought is sending energy. See the person well. See energy happening to the person.

Reply: **Tonight when I was doing that, I had the sense that the person is shut down.**

I can give you an example: I received a call from a person a couple weeks ago, asking me to work on two different people. I said, "I will work on both people, but I can really work on the one person who believes that I can do so." I can work on the other who does not believe in any of this, but not as much as I can work on that one person who opens up that channel of awareness, saying, "Help me." For instance, Jesus walked by a lot of people that were afflicted. Why didn't he just help them? Because the person had to have the free will to ask. Just by Jesus walking by, I am sure the person was better because they happened to be within his sphere. What about the person who touched his garment? What happened then? Some of the healing essence went into the person and they felt it. Jesus was extraordinary to be at that level. When you touch someone like that, you actually get a shock of consciousness. It is not something that is going to shock you in a way like electricity, but you will feel a fluttering of energy coming through you. Sometimes you might feel it in this room when we meditate at a higher level.

Reply: **So the healing might be about their receptiveness?**

Yes. It might be about whether the other wants you to enter into that space. Some people are so private; they do not want to be affected. For instance, a person will mention they have a headache, and I will tell them that I will try to send them some energy. If the person looks at me like I am a deaf-mute, I will just back right off. I still send them energy, but how much of a positive effect is it going to have upon them? It is as if you offer a glass of water to a dehydrated person coming out of the desert, and they just turn it over because they do not know that is good for them. You know that they need that sustenance within them, but whatever you give, you are not going to help them.

The same thing takes place within the system of understanding. That is why Jesus said, "Do you believe?" People can even heal in the second instance, asking the healer to heal their friend. If they ask for a healing for their friend, it ignites the awareness within that particular structure that gives the person the incentive to want to give. Usually though, it is basic human instinct to say: *If the person does not want help, I cannot give it; I cannot force it upon them.* If you are at that level, the particular thought is compounded into the free will of the other, so you pull yourself back and do not emanate.

You give the person what you can. You give them thought patterns. You wish them well. I am in a business where I often see some of the negative things that happen to people. Sometimes I consider that I might even say to a person who gives out such negativity to others that I do not want their business anymore. I came very close to that today with a person who gives me a lot of work. I am still pondering maybe telling him if he is going to continually act the way he is acting, he should not even bother calling me to do more work. I am thinking about it beyond the level where I have looked at it before. I have looked at it monetarily before and how it interrelates to the structure of my business, but now I am looking at it from a different level that says: *It is wrong to treat others that way.* The fact that this person gives me a lot of work does not mean that I should hold back from telling him he is not a nice person. I am considering it; I am weighing a lot of options within the structure of that, interrelated to what is usable in my life.

Fourth questioner: **I have a lot of anger about what happened in the terrorist attack on New York.**

Yes, I have the same thing; everybody has the same thing. What you have to do, you have to balance yourself first. That is where it starts.

Then you have to say: *What can I do?* There is absolutely nothing you can do from here other than help people out monetarily, give blood, volunteer or do whatever it might be, but if you allow that situation to give you insecurities, you are giving everybody around you insecurities. I think we have to go back to normal now. We have to begin to say: *I feel bad about this, but I have to be normal.*

CHAPTER THIRTY-EIGHT

A Planet Of Reaction
August 13, 2003

(First questioner:) **Why do terrible things happen to good people?**

People take different pathways. Just because you are going down a pathway and think you are being good, you might not be achieving those probabilities that you set in motion for this particular lifetime, so there are things that will happen to you that slow you down from going in that direction. It is very important to understand that. For example, let us say you chose a set of probabilities such as learning and understanding compassion within the physical sense, but in your daily life, even though you are good, you deviate from the pathway and are complacent within your reactions of understanding compassion. In other words, there is something in front of you that you do not confront, or there is something else that you are dealing with that does not have compassion, so you should refocus back on compassion. The point is, you set certain things in motion from another level to comprehend them, and if you do not, you deviate into misconception. The misconception causes disease, which eliminates the body so you can re-manifest another body in the next life that achieves those probabilities that you did not achieve in this lifetime.

(Reply:) **We did not achieve compassion for self, or for others?**

It does not make any difference. First you have to have compassion for self before you can have compassion for others. When I start guiding you in the meditation, I always mention self first. You cannot give something that you do not have. You can have a confrontation that will give you some information pertaining to the reality of that, but you cannot give compassion to others until you have it. So many people have confrontations with their partner because there is insecurity within both; then there is the confrontation and parting of the two. On the other hand, if there is knowledge, there is a joining of the two, and movement into comprehension. That is what I mean by "the velocity that is usable in comprehension." If you learn either to slow yourself down or speed yourself up, you give yourself balance, which then gives you insight into the reality of what you should be doing upon this planet.

(Reply:) **We can be complacent in our compassion?**

Yes. If you are being complacent or dormant, you should learn to speed up. You learn that from the balanced position of the meditative state because the information that you are getting at that level is pertaining more to the reality of understanding those probabilities. Maybe you are a baseball player out there playing soccer all of the time and you should be playing baseball. It is not that you are bad because you are playing soccer; you are just doing the wrong game. The same thing takes place within probabilities: understanding what is good is something different. Let us say you have a child in school, and the child is insecure, dealing with a lack of initiative and complacency within self. If you give them a little aggression by reprimanding them, that will give them a little anger that makes them come out of that situation. Then aggression is not bad; you are giving the child something to move them into a more pliable area. Therefore, you have to understand what good or bad is: "good" or "bad" is the perception of where it is within the reality of comprehension. Therefore, "being good" means being good within the reality of truly understanding what good is.

(Second questioner:) **I have a friend who got into a bad car accident a couple years ago and received very bad back injuries that are beginning to deteriorate him at this point.**

Yes, and you say to yourself: *If God is good, why do these things happen?* But you have to understand that we have free will within the physical sense. Have you ever noticed a person who is really ill, then there is a healing involved where they become rejuvenated, go forward with balance and no longer have the disease? What do you think happens there? While they were in the pain and agony of the disease, they begin to comprehend something, such as: *My God, I was this way. I should not have been this way. I should have been more tolerant. I should have listened to myself.* There are so many things going on, but if you do not change, it escalates the misconception and further turns off the switch within the body, because you are going in the wrong direction. The pain and agony are supposed to be the indications that slow you down from going in that direction. Disease is a tool of the soul saying: *You are not doing what you are supposed to be doing.* No matter how good you think you are, if you are going down that wrong pathway, it is something else.

We return to the perception of where we are, and what we understand as good or bad. We might think that a particular person is good.

We do not know what is going on in their reactions. We do not totally know what has happened in their life. We do not know where they are within the realm of comprehension. We do not know what probabilities were set in motion. We do not know why they were in the position of harm happening to them. We do not know why, within their own free will, they happened to be in the wrong place at the wrong time. Then there are certain people who are not in the wrong place at the wrong time, because the reaction of balance puts a filter around them. It puts a safety belt around them. It puts them in a position. There is less of a probability of harm happening to them because they have won the right to have that position. They have eliminated the storms upon that river of reality. There are just calm seas, and they are able to go forward and understand what is around them. They have eliminated the distortions within the waves. The current within that particular structure has no rapids but just peaceful moments because they have eliminated the rapids through comprehension.

(Third questioner:) **We are put here to learn and to comprehend our reactions. What would be some examples of learning compassion in our lives?**

There are many examples in your choices of compassion. Do you think before you react? Do you actually see what is going to happen to the other person after you say something? When I am dealing within a duality, there are certain things that I purposely do within the structure of balance within the participation of that particular structure of duality that changes the other person forever. Even though they might think I am mean, or whatever, I might say something that switches them suddenly to make them see self, and I have to have the strength within me then to understand compassion. What is true compassion? Should I say something because I see that person deviating into an area of misconception and drowning within the reality of it? Do I stop that person, or do I mind my own business? Could I take on the wrath of understanding that they might not like me after that? Or if I make them see self for a moment, don't you think that eventually they are going to say: *That person gave me more problems than I had before!* Actually I gave them the ability to see the perception of the reality of compassion within self, and they misinterpreted what I gave them as something destructive rather than good.

What is compassion? Compassion is the ability to understand oneself within the ability of balance; then to consider another person within the dualities of life, whether or not the other understands that that will be there forever, as a friend or whatever. You give them exactly what they need for that moment. It is similar to when you stop a child from doing something: you do not want the child to do a particular act, so you stop them. For instance, when you put a child in that playpen of life, you do not let them out of the playpen until they understand what is around them to the point where they will not get into a position of destroying self. Even though the child might be crying in the playpen, you do not let the child out of there; you just say, "You have to stay in there until you comprehend." Or when you take the child out, you take the child by the hand and show them how to cross the street. The child is crying and thinking: *What a mean person,* but you are actually teaching them how to survive. Many people come ask me about how to raise children. The main thing is that you have to teach the child is how to survive, which is learning "love of self." If you do not teach the child that, then everything around the child becomes destructive, and they cannot comprehend it. Either the child becomes so timid that they go inward and do not react, or they have so many insecurities that they try to beat others up.

We can understand the balancing qualities within the structure of the refractability within life even within the spectrum of understanding color and how color has an effect on us. Some colors are factors in slowing down aggression. For instance, in certain prisons there is a pink room where hostile people are placed to calm them down. We know that the color red is aggression, so if white is added to it, it is pink, and a pink room will relax such a person momentarily; but if you leave them in there too long, they will begin to feel insecure and become hostile again. Therefore, the reaction of understanding compassion is within what you are determining within another person and what you can deal with within yourself towards that duality to give balance and compassion to them. It might not be what the other wants. You might be strong enough at that time to give them what they truly want, by telling them to not go any further. The other might look at you and tell you they want to go further. Then you have to explain to them what is going to possibly happen, that there is something there that might come from the reality of that and take them away forever.

When I was a little boy I was involved in so many sports, but I never put myself in a position where I thought I was going to be overwhelmed by something. I never liked those positions, like hanging from a cliff where there was a possibility of death. There was always the thought: *Even though I am very strong, that rock might slip away, and I might fall.* I never willingly put myself in positions like that. If I am climbing that mountain, do I know what all those millions of years did to make that rock so insecure to the point that I might fall and be eliminated? So my awareness was: *Hey, I am going to be involved, but I am going to deal with some reaction of a filter around me so I do not get in the position to be overwhelmed.* Sometimes I did do some stupid things when I was younger, but it got to that position where I could see that I had to pull myself out of those kinds of reactions. That is dealing with compassion for self and beginning to understand the velocity of compassion.

You cannot look at another position if you do not have it within you to have the insight to see that position. For instance, if you are on the tenth rung of the ladder and need to go to the twelfth rung to look over the wall, you will never see over the wall until you get to the twelfth position. You will look at the wall and understand this side, but you will never understand what is over on the other side. By lifting yourself, you are going to understand what is on the other side. What is on the other side is another person or reaction or place or thing to comprehend. The unique thing that takes place then is that everything after that becomes more beautiful, sensible, understandable and usable. It begins to escalate your ability to comprehend because it pushes itself forward. You do not have to worry about speed then, because the reaction of comprehension escalates you perfectly within the structure of that. You begin to see things in a very fluid way. If you can begin to see things in a balanced way where you do not have to worry about things, you are moving along at a speed that is understandable. You see the roadside, the trees, the sunset and everything around you. You are not going too fast in the vehicle of comprehension. That is what it is all about: putting yourself in that position of being happy.

I often wondered years ago what the rewards of comprehension would be when I was opening up those centers within my body that interrelate to life and beyond what I had ever seen before. What it does, it increases everything: every sense you have is increased to a higher level, which makes everything more enjoyable. Do you remember that preconceived thought that I have within me? You might want to consider it putting within you: *Everything is God, so the next thing that I comprehend, more of the Essence of God is within me.* It is as simple as that. We cannot dispute that Something Unique and Beautiful made this, and that there are some factors out there that we do not understand, such as disease and children that are sick. We do not understand the full reality of all of that, but we know within the back of our minds that Whatever It Is, is Totally Unique and Beautiful. In the meantime I do not understand the full reality, so there is some trauma within me saying: *I do not want to see that little child sick.* Then information comes back to me, saying: *If you do not want to see that little child sick, John, lift the awareness of you within the structure of the common denominator of humanity that eliminates that particular vibration from*

*this physical reality so the child will no longer suffer. Lift yourself to
the point where you understand that the person does not deviate into
misconception so much that disease has to come forward. The person
can see the reality of the misconception and turn back into the flow that
is the true reality.*

When you grow, each one of you, you change all of those things
upon this planet, because you are like a cell within earth, just as there
are cells within your body that are dividing and dying right now. You
are a cell within this earth, and if you change and become more usable,
everything out there changes and becomes more usable. Everybody
out there can use that vibration because you lifted it. You gave others
another step on the ladder to see the light. Search within yourself in
your quiet moments and ask those questions, and you will see what I
mean, even sometimes when you become complacent within yourself.

Some people who meet me during the day, say, "I never knew that
you meditated." I say, "Why? Just because I am happy and balanced?"
I kid around, fool around a lot. Does that mean that I do not have any
intellect within the reality of understanding what is usable? You see,
my happy attitude is always misinterpreted. Everybody has to have
their suits on with ties, sterile, not reacting. This is a planet of reaction,
but it is also a planet of understanding your reactions each time and
making your next reaction better.

(Fourth questioner:) **How do I have compassion for myself and others?**

Compassion first with self by questioning: *What is going on within my
body? What do I have to do to slow myself down, or increase the velocity? What do I have to do to eventually just have that happen automatically, even though so many things happen automatically?* For instance,
you have won the right to have your heart beat without you thinking
about it. If you had to think about your heartbeat, you could not think
about anything else. If you had to think about everything going on in
your body, you could not think about what is coming next. So those are
all preconceived thoughts within the conscious awareness of you that
make you react, because that was something that you won the right to
have happen within your system. That balance causes all of that within
your system. The heart beats because there is a preconceived thought
that is built within you to make it happen and is triggered automatically
because you lifted yourself above that level. The same thing takes place
with the use of the mind, but where does compassion start? Where does
love start? Where does strength start? Ask: *What do I have to do to
make this body more pliable? Do I have too much anger? Do I have too
much hate? Do I go forward too boldly, or not fast enough? Do I have*

to slow myself down? Do I see some faults within me that I am not working on? These are compassion aspects for self. That is why I tell you to work on things within you within your meditative state. You are changing you. You are giving yourself more compassion and understanding about everything that is happening on this planet. You are eliminating that leg hurting, or that headache. There is something that you are doing that is causing it to happen: I do not care what anybody tells me; there is a reason.

When we look at illness in this manner, it is not negative, is it? It is slowing us down from going in the wrong direction. Compassion, love, or whatever it might be starts from within, and they all intermingle and blend together. What does compassion give you? It gives you balance. Balance gives you love of self. Love of self gives you the strength to go forward. Strength gives you comprehension of human decency, love and compassion. When we went through that sequence of events in the guided meditation, whether you believe it or not, there is a consciousness within the body that interrelates to all of those things I mentioned to you. When I mentioned survival within your feet, you could not survive on this planet without energy coming up through your feet. You would not have balance. You would not be able to walk forward. When you became a human being entering a new level, you stood up rather than having all four extensions down like an animal. Your feet interrelate to the color red within the survival center, which deals with the reality of stability within the flesh. Your hands interrelate to the crown center; esoteric comprehension comes through the hands. When you see the paintings of saints with light coming out of their hands, the value of that is to understand that the white light comes out of your hands because it interrelates to white from the soul. There are so many things going on that we do not understand. Do we ask questions within us why? We do not understand what is going on within us. How are we supposed to understand anything else outside of self? When we put that vessel upon the river of reality, we must have no flaws within it or we will sink. We will just sink into the muck of reality, and the muck is good if we look at it properly, because it tells us: *Hey, you should be filling those holes with comprehension.*

Therefore, it is important to begin to understand what is good and what is bad. If you meditate, it rejuvenates your body and puts you in a position of balance. It clears your mind and gives you focus. When you get to the point where there is balance within the system of what you are, you eliminate all the distortions and begin to work on yourself from that position. You take a deep breath and you are there: you are in a position that gives you focus. It gives you the reality of seeing some of the answers to some of the questions pertaining to the reality of what you want to comprehend.

I am dropping deeper, deeper and deeper as I am talking to you. I feel more and more balance within my body and mind. Now, logic tells you, if you look at things from this level, you have more of a chance of comprehending. You have to train yourself. You can put yourself in a position whereby even while you are talking, you can drop off deeper, deeper and deeper. You can feel your mind change. You can feel the focus within your mind change. You have more of an identity of understanding the circumstances of the questions that others might ask you. There is more information pertaining to the reality of the truth of those questions so they can grow. You are turning on more of you within a balanced state that gives you information pertaining to a balanced state. Look at it logically. Look at it uniquely. Look at it so that it is usable for you. If it is profound and beyond your reaction, you are there before you are ready, so pull yourself back. Make it simple and usable because that is what it is supposed to be. It is supposed to be a reaction that is spontaneous and usable within the realm of comprehension. It gives you a reaction of a feeling within you that is overwhelming at times, because if you are truly on the pathway, what comes next has no choice but to overwhelm you for a brief moment, because it is beyond where you are. I love you. Let us take a break.

(Second half of class:) If you are new at it, practice. Put yourself in that quiet place. Work on yourself. Train yourself. How important is focus? It is important. Work on yourself. When you become a better person, you have better things to give to others. It is as simple as that. Do not become stagnant and not react: react. If you do not like your reactions, question them. Sometimes I react where I might say something in an obnoxious way to my wife. I will just turn it around, and five minutes later, I will tell her, "I am sorry; I was wrong." Do not be afraid to change the reactions of what you are. If there is something that you did that you are ashamed of, change it. Being ashamed of something is telling you that you have to change and make yourself better.

Do not take anything I say as the truth. Work it out within yourself. What I say to you, I know is the truth within me because I have questioned it, but you have to question it. You have to put yourself in that position that moves forward. I know one thing: each time that you change, and each time that you look at everything on this planet, you will truly understand that Something Truly Unique started All of This. When you see something negative, you will look at it in a way where you say to yourself: *It seems negative because I do not understand it. I know everything is good; I just do not understand how to see everything as good because I am not there yet. But I know eventually I will be there because Something So Profound has to be Totally Good, but my perception of good is distorted within the reaction that is necessary in order to comprehend.*

It gives us that deviation within the physical sense that fluctuates us into chaos, which is so important because it becomes a reality of not knowing what is coming next. That is the true meaning of understanding how to grow, because what is coming next is a surprise, and the surprise is that position that gives us the insight to comprehend. Chaos is what keeps God involved because nobody knows what your reaction is going to be. It is like the butterfly that flies by the house, and nothing will ever be the same just because of the flapping of the wings of the butterfly, or there will never be a ripple in the lake exactly the same again. It keeps God involved. Chaos is the situation that stimulates us into a reaction of the unknown, so we can make it something that we know, which is so unique.

Thank God, we cannot control the weather. If we could control the weather, we would destroy this planet in no time. It would not take us too long. Thank God, that weather changes the reaction. It shifts us into positions that are necessary. The storm comes along and wipes everything out, and we see it as disastrous, but the storm exists because there is so much stimulation within the awareness of the conscious awareness of humanity that the destructive quality within humanity has nowhere else to go but manifest itself into something that is destructive. And if we do not change our pathway, new diseases will come forward beyond the realm of the diseases that we know presently that will slow us down from going into areas of misconception. If we do not slow down, we eventually end up in that tributary to the point where there is nowhere to go. There is nothing left. There is no place to manifest a body into the physical sense. So the whole structure has to be changed and evolved to a point.

(Fifth questioner:) **Do we have consciousness that reigns throughout the universe? In other words, what we see as air, or emptiness, is actually consciousness?**

Oh, yes, it is the extension of God's Awareness. So the universe might be a like a cell within God. The entire structure of the Milky Way universe could be just like a cell within God. Why is the universe expanding? The scientists know that it is expanding. It is because God is expanding within the structure, and the Uniqueness and Absolute of God as It refracts Itself through Itself is that It leaves particular structures that are totally absolute and balanced. So when you go through those levels, there are particular laws that are absolute. When that takes place, you can deviate within that structure, but you cannot eliminate those absolutes. You cannot get around them; you have to comprehend them. You have to make them part of you, because there is no other way that you can go past them; because they are true and necessary and totally reliable within the Absolute. So the Structure of That refracts within Self.

For instance, if you have misconception within your mind and body, there are going to be certain things that are going to be triggered within the organs that are not necessarily going to function properly. What do you do? You search out the awareness of a particular identity within the structure. The heart center deals with compassion, balance and universal love. That is why Christ used that heart center, the Sacred Heart. Why is the heart sacred? Because there are the three higher centers and three lower centers, and the constant bombardment of molecules between the higher and lower levels. Then in the middle there is a reservoir within the heart center, and that reservoir flows forward within humanity. That is why Christ used that center. It is green. That is why there is so much green upon the planet.

(Sixth questioner:) **I found myself in a very reflective place tonight, assessing where I am, and the things I am looking at and working on. I was just looking at where I was when I started here years ago and where I am now. It is interesting to look at my situation now. There is no shortage of things to work on, no shortage of challenges.**

You see, before, there was nothing to work on because you did not see anything to work on. Have fun. That is the main thing. Do not make it drudgery. Take it out, look at it, go forth and use it in your life. See how life is becoming better for you, then take it into your next meditation and grow with it. See what the sequence of events is. Remember, if you do not work on yourself, you are selfish; then you cannot work on anybody else. You can have an illusion within you of thinking you are there, which is important; it gives you a flavor of thinking you are there, so eventually you can be there. The illusion is good, but eventually you have to take that illusion and make it a reality by bringing it into the center, the nucleus, and make it part of you. That is the key. Make it part of you. Do not use the meditation as a crutch; use it as a pawn.

I can remember when I was coaching hockey. There was a young man on the team who had such tremendous potential. As a matter of fact, he was drafted by Montreal into the National Hockey League. He went to Canada, was in the Junior A's, and a top scorer in the league. Then his girl friend asked him to come home and he came home. Sometimes I look at myself and say: *John, you are sitting in a sea of stagnation. You are not doing what you are supposed to be doing.* Then there are other times when I say: *Maybe there are times when I need a rest: just pull back and allow myself to be whatever I want to be at those moments, as long as I am not hurting anybody or using the information in a bad way; as long as I have those basic laws of information pertaining to what I should be doing with the power of whatever I have within the reality of comprehension.*

There are those times when you can pull yourself out and deal with the illusions or moments of grandeur within whatever misconception that you might be involved in, but then if you truly look at it, maybe it is not misconception but a vacation. Maybe it is necessary because what might come next might be something that is so staggeringly overwhelming that you might need that basic foundation. So there are times when you should push into comprehension and there are times when you should focus more to say: *Hey, I have to comprehend these things.* Then there are times when you should refocus on yourself to say: *I am going to drive the car. I made it now. Let us go forward now and see what is out there. I will relax and allow that velocity that is usable in comprehension–that I have won the right for–to take place by itself.*

Think of those things within yourself. You will come up with one answer each time: *If what I am feeling now is so extraordinarily beautiful, what might come next? Because I know that there is something that is next. So if I take this beauty, and use it tomorrow, and the next day, and make it part of me, then that next thing that will come. If I do not, it will never come, because my soul is watching over me, and nothing will come before I am ready.* The only thing that will come is the misconception of what you are, that is overwhelming. Nothing will ever come from your soul that will be overwhelming. It is doing everything it can to make you better than you were before, because as you become better, so does it. As you become better, more of the soul becomes you within the flesh. If that is the case, more of the power that has made you will be within you; more of the understanding of how you were made will be within you; more of the healing energy to participate in giving you balance will be within you. So you go forward in life with less agony and trauma, and more comprehension and beauty, and more of those overwhelming moments that flush you forward into new areas of comprehension within the essence of what you are. You truly are unique and beautiful. You are part of God, each one of you, everybody, everywhere. If you know that, and treat everybody like that, it will definitely be a better place to live in. It will be a better place to achieve those comprehensions, those probabilities, that you set in motion. I love you. I hope I see you next month. Take care of yourselves.

CHAPTER THIRTY-NINE

Going Too Fast or Too Slow?
March 10, 2004

(First questioner:) **Just as we use only a portion of our brain matter, the same thing is true of our energy field: that most of it is not utilized?**

Yes. Every time we lift the vibration of what we are to another level, we move faster, so the level below is something that is usable within that vibration but does not have much of an effect on us. That is how a person can go into a plagued area and not be affected. If we think of it in that way, we actually put ourselves above the normal vibrations of an area where we can be outside illness for whatever period of time we want to be.

(Second questioner:) **I am realizing how difficult it is to pass on this kind of information to others.**

You have to go slowly and be involved in your daily reactions in a normal way. You cannot go out into your life and think about this every moment. You just have to fly with it. When you meditate, you are going to think about the particular things. Some people think that I must be "right on" every minute of every day. No, I try to be as normal as I can. When I need that information and energy, it is there. I can get it instantly, but I never try to dissect something or apply it in normal activities. I think about my abilities in a way where I can become that which is normal within every reaction.

Just react. Be as normal as you can. There are times when I want to do some stupid things and I do them. I do a lot of stupid things, but I try to comprehend whatever it is. Then I look at those things that are seemingly stupid, and they really are not. They are making me balanced. Whatever they might be, they help me slow down or speed up. They help me to use my mind in a normal way. They help take me out of the context of being at that other level all of the time. Your level will move, no matter what; just take your time and look at things in a proper way. I am not sitting there and saying: *Well, I am going to go to New Haven tomorrow, but my car might blow up or whatever.* As I am going through the particular sequence of events to get to New Haven, I am at the peak of my perfection in the reactions that I am dealing with. I am being normal. If something happens, I can react in a positive way. I am not on the highway saying: *I am at another level, and nothing can happen to me.* I have so many questions of people who call me, thinking I am at that level every minute of every day. I am not. It is important that you are not there all of the time.

That is one of the things that Christ had problems with. He went to the bathroom, he sneezed, he coughed, he had a blister. He had things happening to him that were as normal as would happen to anybody else, but he was able to change those reactions quickly from becoming catastrophic because he was in control of his reactions. Because he was at a higher level did not mean that he did not have any humor, or could not fool around, or not trip over something in the street. Those are normal things that happen to people. What you have to do is control your reactions within the essence of what is going on. There is a reason why I am mentioning these things now. For every one of you, there is a reason why I am mentioning it.

Look at the normalcy of what you are in the meditative state. There are certain things I mention to you each time when we meditate that will change things slightly within the essence of looking at yourself. When you are looking at yourself, you are beginning to understand the awareness of how the energy flows and where you are within the essence of it. That is important, but you do not sit there every moment. You do not want to miss those moments. They are important because they attach themselves to the next moment. For instance, I remember when I was a little boy in the field flying a kite, and I remember saying over and over: *Where are you, God? Where are you, God?* If I sat there forever, saying: *Where are You, God,* I never would have felt anything within the Essence of God.

Let it happen. Flow with it. Use your meditations. If there is something wrong with you, work on it. I have the sniffles tonight, and while I am talking to you, I just received ten answers why. One reason is the environment that I deal with at work, but there are so many different aspects that I will change within that essence in order for it not to happen. Why? You want to stay on that pathway. You want to see those moments as best as you can. You want to comprehend them so the next moment can be more pleasurable. You want to be free of pain and agony. You want to be at the peak of perfection in the particular years that you are involved in. I do not know what else you could ask for within life.

Yesterday my wife told me that she worked on a patient that is four years younger than me, looks twenty years older than me, and everything is wrong with him. I sat there for a moment, and wondered how much of it is genetics, and how much is the essence of understanding the reality of what I am and what I am doing in the participation of understanding my velocity that is usable in understanding the direction of my body and which direction I am going to be going in. Then I put them together and sift them around: a little piece here, a little piece there, and it becomes that moveable vehicle of comprehension. For instance, I use all my plusses and put them in a category. When there are too many plusses, I shut the door and open up the door to the minuses in order to see the balance. When there are two many minuses and I might need a little praise, I open up the door to the plusses and look at them. They are there for me: all of those things that make me stronger.

I have wondered about so many different things and why they are usable. I thought for a moment of being a young Catholic boy and why we hold our hands together when we pray. Have you ever asked: *Why do we put our hands together? Why do we say, The Father, the Son, the Holy Spirit?* I am not trying to be religious; I am trying to make you see that your mind has to work on things. What is the Father? The Father is the essence beyond our comprehension. What is the Son? It is the place where the Son was within the physical sense, which is the Sacred Heart. What is the Holy Ghost? Remember the balancing qualities that I mention to you all of the time: up, down, here, there? The Holy Ghost is that unseen thing that we are trying to comprehend.

Question what is going on. Do not just do something. If someone says to do such and such, question it within self. If it is within the structure of the workplace, and you have to do it, do it to the best of your ability within that structure without changing the sphere of that authority, yet changing the sphere of the authority by making them see how perfection can work within that sphere. You are not saying that your particular way is the way it should be done: do it and show how it should be done within the way you work, or how you get things done, or why you get things done faster than another person. Why? Because through comprehension you are putting yourself in that position that eliminates the false moves from your reactions. You do not even get tired when you are doing something like that because there is a natural sequence of events that takes place. If you do get tired, you are misusing your mind within whatever it is you are involved in; you have allowed yourself to deviate into an area that makes you exhausted because you do not know your velocity that is usable in comprehension.

Take the time to see who you are in the meditative state. Take the awareness of that and use it within every moment of every day. If there is something within the essence of it that bothers you, take it back into your meditative state in those quiet moments and work on it. While you are going in a direction each and every day, if there are moments that you have to consider the reality of it, the sustenance of those meditations will become usable in those moments. You have the knowledge, strength and the ability to deviate instantly into an area that is more usable when it is necessary to do so. But if you are doing this every moment, you are missing the moments. If you are missing the moments, you are not ready for the next moment. Make it simple and usable, and it becomes more comprehendible. Comprehension will automatically escalate your ability to do something. You will get things done faster with less fatigue and less of a chance of deviating into an area of misconception. There is nothing I can teach you more than that particular sentence that I just went through. If there is something wrong with you, it is because you are going into something too fast, or too slow, and you have not looked upon it. If you look upon it, you can comprehend it. If you can comprehend it, you eliminate the flaw within the essence of what you are. If that is not logical, I do not know what is! Take control of the reality of what you are. If you do, you have more control over the reality of what you are not. Eventually you can make that move through comprehension because you have control over the reality of what you are. Think about that for a moment: simple, usable and understandable. It is not drudgery, but a moveable, simple vehicle of comprehension. It is not fatigue, but a nice, neat pathway of understanding who you are. I am older than anybody in this room. That is the truth.

I thought about this today: as you are going along, you do not know what that next moment is going to be. You do not know if the body just might stop. You do not know what is going to happen to you. These thoughts came through me today for a reason, because the vehicle that I was driving just happened to stop. It just stopped for seemingly no reason, and I was going sixty m.p.h. on the highway. I was lucky enough that it stopped in a place where it was pretty safe, right in between two highways, but even in those moments I was thinking about so many different things that could have happened to me. Ten seconds later, I would have been on the Q Bridge in New Haven. Ten seconds later, I could have possibly caused a traffic jam that would have been catastrophic, or could have gotten killed, or whatever.

I had about an hour's wait for a tow truck, so I was thinking about these things. It was a rewarding time because I began to question the reality of my body and what happens to it as I am getting older. Then I thought about the rejuvenating quality each time that I meditate, and what happens to the cells within my body, and the muscles of the body and face. You can actually feel all of that when you go very deep into meditation. You can actually feel your teeth being rejuvenated and the cells dividing. I can remember one time actually seeing the cells dividing in my body. It was incredible seeing those moments, but do I sit there and say: *Next week I am going to go back to see those cells dividing?* Those are spontaneous moments that happen within a reaction of a particular time that either cause or slow down your incentive from going in a direction that might be overwhelming. Know these things. Until you can understand the true velocity that is usable in comprehension within the awareness of what you are, you will ride the waves of that particular sustenance to the best of your ability, knowing that each time that you do so, you learn from those qualities that will cause you to have more stability within the reaction of whatever it is. In other words, the more you learn, the more you have within you of the Essence of Whatever made you to comprehend the rest of the Essence of Whatever made you.

(Third questioner:) **I find my energy field is changing a lot lately. For instance, I find my eyes tearing from time to time, as if something is getting flushed out of my system.**

Very good. That happens when you are meditating too. For instance, if I am in an environment during the day that is bad for me, when I meditate, everything about that environment is going to get flushed out of my system. Normally I prepare myself before class by meditating, but tonight I did not; what happens then, my nose starts dripping. But the tears or crying are actually purifying you and getting rid of those toxins. When you truly cry over something that is truly unique and beautiful, those tears have a quality that is incredible. There are things happening to you when you are crying or laughing that are extraordinary.

(Reply:) **I felt my heart racing during meditation.**

Did you ask a question what it was? When you feel something like that, immediately say: *What am I feeling? What am I sensing? Am I going in a direction that I do not want to go in?* You slow it down. Did you get an answer on anything pertaining to it? You hit an area in meditation where you had the ability to feel your heartbeat. I know exactly what you are talking about; it happened to me, years ago. What you do then, you say: *This is a nice place to be in. I am feeling and sensing something going on.* Slow it down immediately and ask questions about what is going on. You are actually hitting a level where you have so much balance for a brief moment that you are feeling something going on in your body.

I can remember going so deep one time where I hit on a place where there was such a foul smell. I said: *Oh! Slow this down!* It was a smell like you would not even believe! I said: *What is going on?* The answer came back: *You were so dense within the quest of what you were trying to understand in meditation, the smell was there to get your attention telling you that you were going to another level.* Once I understood that, the smell changed into a fragrance you would not believe. It was so beautiful. Why did it happen? You see, I could have misinterpreted the smell by saying: *Hey, this is some sort of garbage dump, and I never want to go there again.* But when I questioned it, it was a tool telling me I was going to a new place, and I was so dense, I was not even aware of going there. Then I asked: *Am I going to have to smell this every time I enter this new level?* The answer was: *No, now you understand it, you will never have to smell it again.* I never smelled it again.

The same thing takes place when you are feeling or sensing something within your body. Always ask questions: *If I can hit a level where I can finally feel and sense something beyond normal...* Even if you are feeling tingling in your hands or feet, or a little pain somewhere, ask: *Why am I feeling it?* Begin to question the body. When we begin to question the body, we begin to question how the energy flows. If we can begin to understand how the energy flows, we can begin to understand how that next level becomes usable within the flesh. That is beautiful when it takes place. You see, when I was meditating, I could feel that I am somewhat off balance, feeling something in the throat center. The throat center interrelates to the second center of duality, so I questioned: *Am I having negative thoughts towards my wife? Am I having too many sensual thoughts towards my wife, or not enough? Why is it happening? Why was it not balanced before when it became what it is?* I will question every single thing pertaining to the throat center before this class is over, and it will not take me that long.

(Second half of class:) How many of you meditate every day? My wife and I do not know when I am under and when I am not. We are trying to figure that out. Even when I am sleeping, I do not know when I am sleeping anymore. I do not know what level I am within, lately. I do not think I do it every day, but there are moments in every day that I do not even know about the fact that I am under meditation a lot of the time. I can remember where I was in my meditations years ago and where I am now in meditation. Eventually you actually become the previous meditation in your awakened daily life. The levels that you reach presently in your meditations will actually be you in the awakened state three years from now. Three years from now, you will be so far beyond where you are today in the awakened state. You will be awake, you will be aware of what is going on, and you will be at that level.

It is amazing. Sometimes I sleep so deeply, it is incredible, and I can be so far "out there." There are times when I am not sure if I am awake or asleep. It is a unique process that I am going through right now. There are reasons for everything. Eventually if you stay on that course, you will understand those reasons, and they become a reality. You do not wish to push the reasons because it will slow the process down. I just allow the process to flow and know that if I question it in a very subtle way, eventually those particular things will become understandable to me. It is unique to see the different processes going on within the structure of that. Even though sometimes I am seemingly totally outside of the context that appears to be consciousness, I am still receiving information, even in those moments. It might not seem like I am "together," but I am.

Make it as simple as possible, and then there is more of a chance of you making that simplicity joy rather than drudgery. That is the idea. You are going to have fun. You are not going to say: *Because I am at this particular level I should be up on some mountain using mantras, being outside of the context of the physical reality in order to deal with some semblance of balance.* As those particular times happen to you within the awareness of understanding the solitude of what you are, you will have the capacity of dealing with the solitude of what you are, even within the realm of the chaotic situations of your normal, daily life. You will have that capacity to put yourself in that place of solitude even while reacting within the normalcy of your life. You do not have to put yourself on a mountain or desert. You do not have to sustain yourself somewhere outside the context of the physical reality that you are dealing with. There is a reason for that happening now, and a reason for the forty days and nights happening then. In the past, certain individuals went into the desert, confining themselves because of the usage of the power of their minds. They were teaching themselves how to become that which dealt with the normalcy of that particular quality within the normal framework of humanity. In other words, if you have that much power within your mind, you have to train your thoughts in order to not have that penetrating quality within the essence of how the thoughts can become either damaging or good to others. Those individuals needed solitude because within the awareness of the consciousness of that time, humanity was dealing more within the reality of survival.

Now humanity has refracted itself through different levels and become beyond survival, and that particular structure is within the context of normal reality within the physical sense today. Now the capacity of understanding those tranquil moments becomes that which you have to deal with within the velocity of your normal, daily life, rather than confining it within a particular situation. Does it slow you down? It slows you down slightly because those qualities have to have some constraint to them. You have to have the ability to understand that if your thoughts can heal, they can also harm. If thoughts can harm and heal, you have to find the center of that and begin to understand how to pull back the thoughts that you consider are detrimental to another person; or you have to confine your thoughts to a particular quality within the structure of that until you lay those basic foundations around a particular structure or sphere of what you are dealing with. You have to become a person who understands; who puts preconceived thoughts in motion pertaining to the reality of the usage of your mind, understanding the quality of the essence of the acceleration of your thoughts and how they can become usable in changing the density of another person, or something else. You actually change the molecular structure of things when there is a vibration.

(Fifth questioner:) **People do not have to go up on the mountain anymore?**

They had to do it back then because humanity had a different vibration of understanding how to use their thoughts. There were certain people who had to understand that they were different. They were totally different and outside of the context of where humanity was. Then they were laying down some basic foundation about a theme that was going to be set in motion as something else too. For instance: *I am going to be going through some agony here. I am going to allow that to happen to me. I could have enough power not to have it happen to me, but in order to set a theme in motion, in order to make humanity truly understand that I am giving my life up for a particular thing, I am going to have to go through a lot of agony. I am going to have to have total control over the velocity of not using myself in a way where I could sustain myself, so that I can allow myself to be involved in a particular event that is going to be agony. Because if I understand it in its proper way, the agony within the essence of it will have a more sustaining quality within the theme I am trying to set in motion.*

I understand that some of you saw the Mel Gibson movie? I have not seen it yet, but I have mentioned it many times that Jesus went through total agony. It was the scariest thing if you did not have enough power behind you to go through something like that, and the fact that he totally loved everyone as he did so, was incredible. That was an incredible feat. Two thousand years later, we are still talking about it. Most people do not realize the agony he went through.

(Reply:) **That agony was proving...**

The essence of why he was here. In other words: *If I can go through this, and allow all of this to happen to me, and still love everybody around me, I am truly beyond normal.* Don't you think he could have stopped the others? He could have stopped them. The suffering is usable if there is a particular set of probabilities that you are setting in motion in order to make something believable and change the density of the common denominator of humanity into a more usable, viable place and way. In other words, Jesus was setting a theme in motion. He knew exactly what he wanted to do. But could you imagine having all of that power? You have a fire within you, and you have a reservoir within you to put it out, but you cannot put it out. You have to allow it to burn within you. Just that particular analogy can make you understand how much he was involved in it.

There was total ridicule. It would be as if everybody around you hated you, and you have to love everybody. When you are going through change in a certain way, certain things happen in your lifetime that you would not believe happen to you. Certain things happened in my lifetime thirty years ago, I would not even have considered. But certain things happen to you for a particular reason within the quest of those probabilities that you set in motion, and they change your identity of understanding how to give whatever it is within you in a true way.

In order for you to truly love a person you do not like, or a person that does something wrong to you, you have to learn how to truly love a person who does something wrong to you. That is difficult to do, and when you are first thrust into that area, you first have to love a person close to you, such as a child or family member who does something really bad to you. It gives you more of an opportunity to understand how to say: *I love you anyway.* It is more difficult to love someone that you do not like, or someone outside the context of your family or friends. It opens up that area that says: "Forgive them for they know not what they do." For instance, if a stranger walking along the street does something to you, you can easily say: *Hey buddy, go jump in a lake!* rather than, *I cannot send that vibration out because I can hurt that person.* You have to learn to forgive someone that you truly love, before you can do it to someone you do not like at all. Then eventually it becomes, you love everybody. That is that avenue that Jesus went down. It was extraordinary. I do not know how he did it. I really do not know how he lifted himself to that level, and there was extraordinary pain. He was a young man too, to be able to put himself in that; but he had that theme set in motion within him at a very young age. He knew exactly what was going to happen. He knew what he had to do to make that happen.

(Sixth questioner:) **Some scientists would like to believe that consciousness surrounds us, and that when we send out a thought, others will receive it. Some of the scientists are worried about that, however. They do not want to believe that we send or receive thoughts because then that makes us all so vulnerable to other people's thoughts, whether positive or negative.**

Yes, well, it will get to a point where they are going to know about it, and of course, there are people in other countries now that do know about it to a certain point and do project energy all around. But it is up to the normalcy of people like you, who meditate and deal with a true vibration, that cause some stability within the essence of the common denominator of humanity. Sometimes I have questioned: Why did those nuns, priests, or rabbis sit in a place and pray for years? They know that there is an underlying property that has to be there and they sacrifice themselves within that particular realm for that particular reason. I never could understand that before, but I can understand it now. There is a basic foundation that is needed within the sustenance of humanity in order to cause some stability from the awareness of those reactions because those reactions are detrimental to humanity. There will come to a point where there will be people who truly understand how powerful thoughts are. When you hit that level when you know that, there should be some balancing qualities within the essence of it that cause you to use your thoughts for good rather than bad, because you know what the revenge of that would be within the essence of you. If you use your mind in an improper way, and you have that much power, it escalates the ability to eliminate you quickly, too. Therefore, it teaches you not to use your mind in a negative way within the essence of the consciousness of that particular level. Good night, everybody.

CHAPTER FORTY

Shaking the Thread of Humanity
January 12, 2005

(First questioner, female:) **I am feeling some new sensations in my left leg.**

That means that you are opening up some centers on the left side, which deal with survival and will help you become stronger. Energy comes in on the left side in a woman and right side on a man. You should be feeling some new strength in that direction, helping you to cope with things in your life.

(Second questioner:) **A number of weeks ago, I had a very unusual meditation where I was sensing huge vast areas of space within myself. I never really experienced that in meditation before.**

Uncharted territory.

(Reply:) **It seemed to be focused primarily in the abdominal area.**

Very good: it is opening up new centers of balance that will give you the capacity to go forward and use some of the information that you have within your mind within the realm of human decency for yourself and others, and also control over the emotional state of what you are. Sometimes complacency within the structure of that comprehension appears to be something that deals with stability, but sometimes shunning the responsibility of reacting within a particular structure is just as detrimental to you as if you were overzealous in that particular center. There is that common balance within the structure of that place that has to become usable within every day.

(Reply:) **I have been seeing so many different things within myself, uncovering misconceptions that have been there for a long time. I am struggling to deal with some of these things in various ways.**

That is good. You are involved in the ballgame; that is the important thing.

(Reply:) **Sometimes I wonder how long it really takes to turn around these longstanding misconceptions? You talk about velocity a lot.**

Velocity is so usable in everything. Then suddenly you hit a structure within the realm of comprehension within these areas that suddenly ignites you into that realm of balance. It happens so quickly, but when you really look at the meat of the structure of it, it takes you so long to get to that particular structure. When it does happen, it is almost like a bolt of lightning that happens within that structure of comprehension, which changes the shift within the realm of what you are.

I do not like focusing in on how long something takes. I try to keep myself within the best of my ability of balance, especially within the complacency of what I have been lately. I have been complacent within the realm of dealing with that structure. I have just been letting it flow. Within that realm, it is important to understand that it is time to just let some things flow and not beat something to death. But then when I look at the awareness of humanity, and where humanity is today, and how many different catastrophic things are happening, I begin to notice that within that realm, there are some safety valves that cause the structure within the system to ignite into areas of reprisal, which condition the velocity and slow everything down. When these catastrophic natural disasters take place, we become aware of this beautiful planet that we have, and how it can deal with misconceptions in an overwhelming way when it has to. We can see that, today. We have to learn more about the structure of balance within the system, because things are happening so quickly within that realm. The conscious awareness of humanity has to have some stabilizing quality. It has been unbelievable lately: the sensations I have been feeling within my crown chakra have been actually making me dizzy, so there are so many things going on. When I start feeling dizzy, I know events are going to be happening. I told my wife that something was going to be happening, and it is always something very catastrophic that happens.

(Reply:) **You are referring to the (Asian) tsunami, of course.**

Yes, I have been getting very dizzy lately, which is unusual for me. Normally I can control it, but some of this stuff is really, really "way out there."

(Reply:) **What was behind the tsunami?**

There is a general misconception within humanity about the structure of balance within the realm within human decency, so what happens, the tsunami shakes the thread of that, which then causes some reaction within humanity where there is an outcry of compassion and balance in order to interrelate it to that structure of balance so it can cause some semblance of balance within the system. On the surface the disaster seems very detrimental because life is lost and everything changes within the structure of the realm of comprehension that will never be the same again because of it. Yet on the other end, the balancing quality of the compassion within the realm of thoughts towards that structure causes some semblance of balance within it. It is a readjustment of the realm of consciousness within the system of balance within the realm of human decency. We see that within our own country now: we have to slow down our outward projection and pull ourselves back in a little bit within the realm of our country, because we can see so many things happening within our country too.

(Reply:) **There was an interesting thing I was reading in regard to different religions and the tsunami. The Buddhists have an interesting reaction: that when something like this happens, they ask what they did individually and collectively to cause the particular disaster.**

That is what we were just talking about.

(Reply:) **Then their main goal is to generate what they call "good merit" that can be transferred to the deceased as a positive force in their next lifetime. They use their monks as intermediaries for prayers or special ceremonies to transfer the merit, as they call it.**

An interesting concept. A transfer of that power can take place within some semblance of the structure of the transition period from this realm to the next. But the essence of the first concept is more within the realm of the truth of what is going on than the second concept you are speaking of. There is no harm in what the monks are doing in their belief, and it is an outpouring of compassion that interrelates to the total conscious awareness of humanity. Even in our ignorance sometimes—and there is a lot of ignorance within the realm of our thoughts—there is sustenance for the realm of humanity. Even though we do not know what is going on, there are certain things going on within our system that cause some semblance of balance even within our ignorance, which is unique and beautiful. So we might be making a statement about a particular structure or event that interrelates to some of the things that we believe are going on within that structure: even if we are not within the nucleus of it, or understanding the total structure of it, even within the realm of misconception, there are some thoughts that enter into the structure from ignorance that cause some semblance of balance and of something that can project forward that can correct it within the system of misconception. That is unique and beautiful.

For instance, we do not have to understand what is going on within our body when we take a deep breath. Even when we are ignorant to that fact, there are tremendous things going on within that structure, dealing with the sustenance of what we are. Now, as we interrelate that particular statement into the realm of the conscious awareness of humanity, we can begin to understand that within the ignorance of what we think, the same particular properties take place within the realm of eliminating the structure of misconception, which can give us good thoughts in the direction of understanding, even within our ignorance, we really help.

(Reply:) **How does God react to this process?**

Well, I would imagine that God would react to an event like this as we would when a few cells die in our body. So there is a reaction within the system of the realm of balance and comprehension that takes place automatically, without the total conscious awareness of you knowing something has happened. It is like getting a needle prick in your body: you feel it and sense it; you do not know the total awareness of what is really happening, but you say: *Okay,* and flush it through your system. I would imagine it would be the same thing with God's reaction. We as individuals can interrelate to this planet as single cells within God, so what is taking place within the structure of this planet within the tsunami is not any different.

(Editor: Apropos to the subject matter is part of the class evening of April 12, 2006.)

(First questioner:) **What is the significance of the bird flu?**

We trigger the diseases. For instance, why did the AIDS virus come forward? Let us use that as an example of reasoning why the bird flu came forward. It came forward – and we mentioned this many years ago - it came from one sentence, "Your place or mine?" We were not looking at sensuality as beauty; as two people mating and becoming one; but as a distortion of something that is not usable in love. You meet someone at a bar and say, "Oh, come on, we will just go and do this." This was totally distorting the reality of sensuality. So a disease comes along which is a particular structure within the reality of humanity that slows the conscious awareness of humanity down. It is a disease in a form that slows people down from thinking of the awesome beauty of sensuality in a way where it is distorted. Consequently, certain people will get it even though they do not deserve it, because once the disease comes into the realm of whatever we are dealing with, if we are not prepared for it, it will hit us and change the reality of what we are.

Therefore, that disease was put in motion to slow down the reality of sensuality in the form that the misconception made it. Now, why would it break out in that form? Would that particular form be something that we spot and say: *Okay, we are going to have to slow down sensuality. We are going to have to be more readily balanced in that area.* It did slow the reality of that disease down. It did put it into a more balanced state. Then what happens, if that takes place, the structure of the nature of that disease within the physical sense will be controlled through a sequence of events called drugs, seemingly discovered within the physical sense; but it is really an esoteric triggering quality that gives us those drugs that slow down the nature of that disease. However, in order to do that, we have to change the structure of the conscious awareness of humanity into a more balanced state. If not, that disease will run through humanity and kill everybody.

Now, the bird flu is the same thing but deals with a higher level of misconception that will give us catastrophic results within misconception within the physical sense. If this takes place, and we do not change the balance of compassion within the physical sense, we will see millions of people die. In order to slow the bird flu down, in order for it not to mutate into the human structure, we have to pull ourselves back. Therefore, when you meditate, think of balance, think of compassion, think of human decency, because those are the structures that are distorted. Nobody has any human decency anymore! Nations, leaders, anybody! People who are supposed to be in high positions, people who are leading countries, do not have any understanding of balance and compassion for anybody, or other nations, or whatever. If we do not slow that down... If a few people who can hit esoteric comprehension cannot send the vibration out there to slow that down to make people see where the distortion is, eventually there will be diseases that will eliminate most of humanity. Why? Because having that distortion eliminates the reason why we are here, which is to become better people and grow. So when we look at it in that sense... and it is the only logical way to look at it.

You see, when I see something that is totally wrong, I say: *The only reason why it seems totally wrong is because I really do not understand it.* Then I say: *Why do I say that? I will say that because everything on this earth is good; it is just that my comprehension is not high enough to see it as good.* Every time you change a little bit, you see a different slant towards a particular structure from a different level that makes the reality more understandable within the quest of what you are trying to achieve at a soul essence. Therefore, it is important that we see it as so.

(Second questioner:) **Could it be that the bird flu is supposed to wipe out humanity? That is what is supposed to happen: that the nature of the earth is supposed to cleanse itself?**

Yes, that is exactly what I am talking about. However, it will not happen because there are cleansing properties within the essence of the reality of the total conscious awareness that will change the structure of it into a more positive way. So we will never get to a point where we totally eliminate the structure as it did with the ancient dinosaurs. It will never hit to that point where we will be totally destroyed from the structure of it, because when we got to a particular point in the awareness, that missing link is not here, it is at another level. Therefore, the structure of comprehension of the common denominator of humanity is so well built within the framework of understanding distortions that it has a fail-safe system that will trigger at a certain point. It is not saying we will not lose a lot of people, but what will happen, it will build a ring around the noose of the misconception through the realm of eliminating the probability.

Let me give you an example. When I mentioned to you tonight in meditation about visualizing that white light in your heart center–or you felt it go through you, or you sensed it, or maybe you did not even sense it–when that white energy field was around you, that white light, whether you believe it or not, gave you more protection from disease upon this earth. For any disease, anywhere, it gave you more protection. For instance, certain people can go into a plagued area and nothing happens to them. Everybody is dying, but nothing happens to these certain people because they are at a different level than that particular strain of disease is within the framework of humanity. It is like being on a ladder above the floodwaters. Everyone else is dying within that structure, but even though you are within that realm, you have a different focus, a different insight into the reality. You have lifted yourself out of that particular thing that could overwhelm you. It gave you the capability of being within the structure, yet having the overwhelming effect of that protection around you.

CHAPTER FORTY-ONE

Becoming Closer to That Structure That Made You
May 11, 2005

Is everybody feeling good? Questions? Then I will ask a few. Are you practicing in meditation? You should, everyday. You can skip every now and then. When you get to that plateau, that balanced place, you get answers; then you question the answers. You ask them at that level because you can retain them at that level. You can have a funnel of reality and actually absorb whatever it is that you are working on to become a better person. Everything in this classroom is interrelated to you becoming a better person and feeling better about yourself, and it all interrelates to the free will within you. Free will is what makes you strong in your meditations and free will is what makes you strong in your normal, daily life. I want you to begin to ask questions about your normal daily events, but begin to feel and sense the body. All of the information that you get in this classroom does not come from a book, but from me questioning the reality of what I feel, and how it interrelates to my normal, daily life, and how I can esoterically pull down things to balance those particular structures and make my life better. If you ask a question about a particular thing, your soul is now involved with the interrelationship of you here within the physical sense and it. There is a constant bombardment that interrelates between you and your higher essence.

You might have questions regarding the first level that you are dealing with, which is survival, or it might be about levels beyond that. We are talking about survival right now. If I feel tingling in my toe, I ask the question in meditation: *Why I am feeling tingling in my toe?* And the answer comes back: *Your toe interrelates to survival within the physical sense and survival within the feet.* Then I ask another question: *Do you expect me to believe that?*

I want the answer to become sensible and logical within the framework of what is usable within the context of humanity. The answer comes back: *Aren't you walking upon this earth? Aren't there centers of energy at the bottom of your feet? Doesn't the toe interrelate to you dealing with survival, because that is the first level that interrelates to the particular structure of earth that you are upon?* That seems sensible and logical within the physical sense, that the feet and toes could interrelate to a particular level. What does that particular level deal with? It deals with survival energies, which means dealing with the comprehension of "love of self." What do feet and toes interrelate to within the major centers of my body? They interrelate to the survival center at the base of my spine, which deals with survival and "love of self," and the vibration of it is red.

Then I have further questions about survival and the red vibration, and I begin to interrelate it to a sensible, logical sequence of events that happens within my body: *The blood runs through the system of what I am. When it is in contact with oxygen, it is red. Logic tells me that the red and white cells are in constant bombardment: if the red cells get in trouble, the white cells actually surround the misconception within my body and try to flush it from the system.* I am interrelating that physical knowledge into consciousness now: *This makes sense not only what is being said to me because I am tapping into it, but I am also giving myself a chance to begin to understand my body beyond the normal flow of reality within the physical sense to lift myself to a place to begin to understand the sequence of events that causes damage within my body or mind.* So it is not only teaching me about consciousness, it is teaching me how to interrelate feelings within my body to a situation of balance that I can interrelate to, as something that is usable in deviating out of misconception. In other words, within the consciousness of my feet, if I am feeling very fatigued in that area, it interrelates to survival energies at the base of the spine, telling me that I should slow down and begin to question the reality of survival: how I am surviving within the physical sense and how I think about myself.

If I begin to do that, and question it in a proper way, I am now increasing the capability of that particular secondary center as it interrelates to the major survival center within my body. If I am beginning to stimulate that center, logic then tells me that I have more energy and information pertaining to the reality of survival, and less of a chance of anything out there interfering with that particular structure within me. If I am constantly within that particular structure, then I can begin to interrelate it to particular aspects in my meditation that can begin to change the reality of how I feel about myself forever! When I can begin to do that, the structure of red becomes crystallined; it becomes refractable within the essence of light and becomes that which deals more with the structure of white. I am now actually changing consciousness into energy, into matter, and taking more of the essence of my soul and making it me within the flesh.

Let us think for a moment about that particular statement, and how it interrelates to growth and is so extraordinary. I know that nothing new will come unless I understand what I have, because I know there is more within the soul level than there is here within the physical reality.

I am hoping that eventually there is more here that will give me the essence of balance, but as I am going through that comprehension here, I am extending my soul further within the Essence of God. Now, the balancing qualities, or the separation, is still the same. The separation is still the same, but my comprehension of the separation has changed: my soul has become more refractable within the structure of where it is, because the capabilities of the flesh have changed that structure: ignited some of it and brought it down. I have now won the right to have more information pertaining to the reality of the Essence of Whatever This Is, because I am closer to the Structure that has made me.

To make it simple and logical and more understandable within the flesh, I want you to think about the little boy Jesus. We do not get into religion too much, but I am just using him as an entity of understanding the refractability of the essence of the soul within the flesh. If Jesus fell on his knee, he bled and cried. If he did something wrong in the neighborhood, people yelled at him, just as they would with you. His mother spanked him a few times, I am sure. He experienced all of those little things that we have had done to us in a loving, caring way. Then certain things began to happen within his structure. Even though there was a gigantic system above, and certain probabilities were set in motion, there were certain things within the physical sense that Jesus had to achieve: certain things within those structures of energy within him had to change the physical body into the vessel of what he left there at other levels that could become him within the flesh. Each time that he comprehended, each time he became more usable within the structure of understanding that, more of his soul became him within the flesh.

Then you can understand that if he had more of the soul within the flesh, he had more knowledge of healing within the essence of what he was. Let us make it sensible and logical: it is just as if we had a ten-foot ladder to scale a nine-foot wall to see over the wall. If we had a six-foot ladder, we could not see over it. That structure is an analogy of understanding how we become more usable within the structure of the framework of what we have within the physical sense. This is not hard. This is not something out of our reach. This is something in every moment of every day. I mentioned something like this to a person the other night, and they looked at me as if I was on another planet. When you think about that structure, when you think about that information, and the pathway that individual laid down for us, it becomes logical and understandable that each one of us can do it. Jesus even said, "Everything I can do, you can do, and more," the word "more" meaning, if you grow past that particular area.

I do have some thoughts sometimes. The other day I was eating a French fry at a restaurant. I thought about it for a while, then I said:

Jesus never had a French fry. Jesus was never in a car. All of the things that we have at our disposal are so far out of the framework of the particular structure that people dealt with at that time. For instance, there is so much information at present pertaining to reactions of anger. You can look at where the consciousness was then, and how difficult it is was, and how people would even hate others who even mentioned that there was a God within the physical sense. How strong of an individual it took for Jesus to lift himself above that framework as it interrelated to survival and mainly survival energies, because that is where the particular structure of consciousness of humanity, the common denominator of humanity, was at that time.

I thought about how truly unique and strong Jesus was. Then I saw some of the probabilities and questioning processes that he went through, and how unique these probabilities and processes were, and how he had to struggle within himself sometimes. Even though he had more of the essence of his soul within the physical sense–and in his case he had most or almost all of the essence of his soul–what happens next, there is that little series of doubts that takes place within the structure of comprehension. It is necessary for us to have doubt. If we did not have doubt, we would leave and not come back; we would just kill ourselves, saying: *Hey, I have all of this up there, so why should I stay here?* So there is always a little doubt, that little structure, that is put in motion. Each one of us gets these little keys into certain things that Jesus said that give us information pertaining to the reality of how we can grow and become more of God. We are sons and daughters of God.

Jesus was no different, but he became an individual who dealt with more of the essence of the soul within the flesh. Was he at the right hand of God? Yes. Doesn't "the right hand of God" make sense? Energies come in on the right side in a male, the left side on a female. If it is in the center, it is neither; it is androgynous; which is God; which is All of the Essence of Everything. You think about those particular structures. Each one of them becomes a string of comprehension within the essence of the belief that there is something more than you within the flesh, and that key, within the simplicity of it, is meditation. It is slowing you down, so you may see where you are, and if you can see where you are, you can have the balance to see where you can become. It is unique and not difficult. It is a matter of slowing yourself down and seeing what is right for you.

It is not saying you are not going to have struggles. I have struggles. I feel anguish. I feel pain and anger sometimes where I would like to react, but each time I can control those things. Each time that you can deal with them in a proper way, it becomes easier. Each time that you do, there is a new thread, new basic information, that is set there for you that will never be taken away from you. Never. It will always be there forever. Everything that you comprehend after that will have a flavor of it within it. Perhaps it is a piece of music that changes you: you will never be the same again, even though it is so subtle that you cannot see, feel, or sense it. Whatever feelings you experience, they change you forever. If you can be that person who is in tune with whatever you are, you can begin to see those subtle changes, and if you can see those subtle changes, you can see subtle reactions within the realm of misconception. If you can see a subtle reaction within the realm of misconception, you can slow it down before it happens. You do not deviate off that highway of comprehension; you stay in the center of it. Every time there is a little bump in the road, you are able to control it. It is not that you will not feel the bump; it is that you will not react to the bump in the same way. It will not have the exciting feeling of stimulating you into an area of misconception; you will have the capability of bringing yourself back in and staying on the center of the highway to enjoy all of those things that are coming forth.

That is what meditation is all about, and that is why you should be practicing every day, putting it in motion for you. Some people say, "Well, I do not have the time." When I come up from the meditative state, whatever I was involved in before, I can do ten times faster. It gives you the capability of seeing things in such a balanced way that you eliminate all of those false moves. You do not have fatigue because you have rejuvenated yourself, so you will see joy in everything that you deal with, whatever process it might be. You are not draining yourself, you are escalating yourself into the realm of balance, and that realm of balance gives you the capability of seeing what is coming next. If you can see what is coming next, you have more of a chance of comprehending it.

Sometimes I know I get carried away here in the classroom, and it does not seem as if some of you new people are going to retain all of this; but you do. In its simplest form, you use meditation to slow yourself down. You see who you are and begin to comprehend how to make life better for you. As you do so, it gives you more balance, more capability of less deviation into miscomprehension and more into the reality of comprehension. If there is more within you, there is more within you to comprehend whatever is coming next. There is more strength and more basic foundation. When those hurricanes of misconception hit you, you will not be overwhelmed. You will have the capability of being steadfast within the realm of the security of your comprehension as it relates to the stability of what you are.

Questions? You should be asking hundreds of questions within you. Do not make it drudgery. Once in a while, you just stop. I can remember when I first started in meditation, I had so many questions it was unbelievable; but then I would meditate and get the answers. I knew others did not have the answers for what was happening to me. When you are on that pathway, things become more suitable to the comprehension. When you achieve balance, it becomes so extraordinary. It is overwhelming because you have new love coming in, and that new love has an overwhelming quality to it sometimes. As the initial thrust of it comes forth, it is more than you can comprehend for brief moments, and it is supposed to stimulate you into those brief moments of escalation; but then you take it, balance it and make it usable. That is what it is all about.

It is not about just sitting there in the dormant state. In the guided meditation when I mention your knees, and the compassion and balance as it interrelates to self, it is because the consciousness in your knees interrelates to that! When I mention relaxing the base of the spine and "love of self," it is because the base of the spine interrelates to "love of self!" Now if you have a pain there, what do you question in your normal daily life? You question the reality of "love of self." It gives you an unfair advantage to comprehend what is wrong within your body before you can deteriorate it into misconception that will overwhelm you and eliminate your body. We will get into what implications that practice has for illness another day: illness has an extraordinarily beautiful wonderment within its essence as we interrelate illness to healing and understand why it is necessary for it to happen. It looks grotesque and unnecessary within the physical level, but when you are looking at it from another level, you begin to see the refractability and usability of it as it pertains to the growth of you and all of those levels that you left there for you, right up to the soul essence. Any questions?

(First questioner, female:) **I sprained my left foot recently. I don't usually have something like that happen to me. I interrelated the injury to my survival and duality, and thought about some misconceptions I might have. Around the same time though, there was a serious incident within my family of origin regarding their survival.**

That is survival, and the family might be drawing from your essence. You would be surprised how those around you affect you. Most of the time, we do not realize how the family might be affecting us. For instance, once a week, my wife and I will go to my father's for dinner, and all of my sisters and brothers-in-law are there. On the way home in the car recently, my wife told me that she felt drained by everybody. I said, "Well, how do you think I feel? I am close to that seed-atom; there is my ninety-three-year old father sitting there; of course he is going to draw from me." Others can have such an effect on you, you cannot imagine.

I just lost a cousin in Philadelphia where I was born, and he was very close to my age. At the funeral, one of the cousins said, "This is our generation that is dying now; we are looking at us next." I felt that essence in a different way than they did. I did not feel the aspect of death in the threatening way as some of them did; the cousin that mentioned it to me was really very threatened by it. Then I thought about it for a moment: you can actually feel the essence of the particular structure leaving, because there is a blood tie there, and when that blood tie leaves, you can actually feel it in your energy field. It is not necessarily in a negative way, either. Sometimes you are getting information pertaining to the reality of that genetic structure or process of what you are, which is unique and beautiful, even though you are sad within the essence of losing that person close to you. There is so much to learn at different levels pertaining to the strength of what you are here.

You learned something from that, which is good.

(Reply:) **I thought the foot injury was partly a message to pay more attention to my family there.**

That is good, so you used the information in a positive way even though there was an injury.

(Reply:) **Okay, it was caused by my own misconception, but might there be some kind of unique dynamic going on there?**

You always bring it back to self, no matter what it is. Many times I feel a drain in my body from someone around me going through something. I do not even want to know what or who it is. Years ago, I used to go and find out mentally who it was. I do not want to know anymore; I do not want to feel and sense who it is; I just do what I have to do to replenish the supply of whatever I am, regardless of whoever is drawing from me. That is what I do now. Years ago, when I was young and eager and doing things, I had a lot of aspects interrelated to ego as I was involved in my growth. That was good; I had to be very strong at those levels because I had to face certain things within the structure of myself and needed that strength. But it changes. Everything changes.

(Reply:) **You seem to receive inner answers very easily. It seems though, that most of us are not going to get immediate answers. We**

might get something the next day, but there is just not going to be that inner dialogue. You seem to experience some kind of dialogue...

In one sense, yes, and in another sense, no. I used to receive answers the next day too. I would say: *Oh, I know what that is involved from: that questioning process that I dealt with last night.* Sometimes I had to shut that off, too. It was unique having Dr. Gregory Blosick by my side, because he was so brilliant within knowledge of books. If I was going through energy changes, I could turn to him to ask him questions. I would describe such things as, "I am feeling and sensing this, this, and this, and I think it is this," and he would say, "Oh, I read about that in the Cabala or the Sanskrit." If there is something that you are going through pertaining to the reality of understanding something regarding your growth, someone will be there for you to give you information pertaining to the reality of the structure of what is usable in comprehension.

When I was going through the initial thrust of energies beyond normal, Dr. Blosick and I would be lying on my living room rug meditating, and at a certain point, I would say: *Okay! That is it! I am shutting this off! I cannot take any more today. There is enough energy flowing through me to light New York City right now. I do not want any more. I am all done for today.* He would look at me and say, "Okay, let's have a cup of tea." It was different, unusual; I mean, there were some energy sources going through me at the time that were extraordinary. I was seeing past lives and other things you would not believe. I am the type of guy that never read anything. My physical knowledge of books, or anything else, was nothing.

All of this started when I attended a hypnosis class one evening many years ago. Beforehand, I read about ten pages of a self-hypnosis book and then stopped; I just wanted to have some information pertaining to the reality of what I was getting involved in. As it turned out, I guess I really did not know what I was getting involved in, and nobody else did either. The energy was awesome. That first evening was incredible. The teacher did not know what was going on, either. I was hearing things I had never even heard before. I was feeling the raindrops outside being absorbed into the ground. I was vaulting out of my chair at other levels. It was incredible. That was something I will remember for the rest of my life; that is for sure.

After that, certain things happened that were so extraordinary: things that an individual like me who had just a basic education would not even consider. I was reciting poetry to myself, totally outside the realm of what I was. I was experiencing previous lives. I asked why I was receiving all of this, and the answer came back: *We did not want you to have a preconceived thought of what was going to happen to you, because if you had, you would have distorted it.* It was absolutely logical and understandable and sensible. The energy was like the Empire State Building coming up through the soles of my feet and out through the top of my head. At the bottom of my feet, it felt like a vacuum cleaner: you could put your hands in front of my feet at the time and feel the air just shooting right up through them. It was unique, and I was not frightened, but certain thoughts were changing within my mind, and the capability of answering questions and even asking questions was changing.

(Reply.) **There was a book published about twenty-five years ago by a person who experienced kundalini changes by meditating for long periods of time and focusing energy through the third-eye center. When the massive energies went through him, he reported that he almost died.** (Gopi Krishna, "Living With Kundalini,")

He did not win the right; he stole it.

(Reply.) **He had a frightening time. He could not find anyone to help him. He finally calmed himself down, but lived a very vulnerable life from then on. He just could not make much sense of what happened to him.**

You see, I was able to stop it; I was able to willfully say: *I have had enough for today.* I would be lying on the rug, and my legs would be lifting right off the ground, going straight up in the air. I thought I was going to go straight up, so I said, *Whoa!*

(Reply.) **The individual is now deceased. In his book he said he thought the energies had great evolutionary promise for human beings and that the phenomenon should be studied. I sent several chapters of this book to the press that published his book, assuming that they might be interested. I said in my letter, "Your author was asking for answers." I received no response.**

I can understand that. That does not make any difference to me. I wish it really did. I wish I could use whatever business sense I have, or send energies forward, or whatever. I have the capability of the information becoming well known, but the way I figure it, if it is usable, people will read it. If it is not usable, the only thing I am displeasured by, M, is the work you put in on it, and you are not getting the fruits back. That is the only thing I get displeasure from. As far as my thinking about the books, or whatever, I wish I could have more incentive, but I think I am going to have to be dead before people start reading it. That is something I do not want to think about. But if we are truly on the pathway of understanding the essence of it, and it is truly something new and significant, we have to understand sometimes it is going to take some time for it to catch up. We have to understand that within us, and it really does not really mean anything. I cannot explain it to you. I think all of you understand what I mean, though.

Practice. It is not something that is difficult. It is not anything that is going to overwhelm you. It is something that is going to take you into a new place and make you a better person. I can honestly and truly say that it has made me a better person. I am not saying that I am extraordinary. I am not saying anything like that. I am saying it has made me a better person, and I know from the knowledge that I have within me that there is a universal consciousness, because there is no way on this God's Earth that I would have known all of these things if there was not something that I tapped into. There is no way on earth that I would know all of these things from anything I read, because I never read anything like this.

So when you go through certain things like that, it sort of makes you understand that what you are going through is truly unique and beautiful, but it is something that does not make you feel that. It has a humbling quality to it that is hard to understand. Then there is always that thought that is in your mind: *If I am feeling and sensing this–which is so extraordinary–what might come next, if I understand this?* I always have that in the back of my mind. If I take this unique thing that I have that I felt today, whatever it might be–and most times when I feel something, I feel blessed–if I take it and make it more usable within me, then more will come, and this is what it is all about.

Do we make it usable? Do we make it something that deals with the classroom? Do we conduct it like we did before where we had classes three times a week with eighty and hundred people in the class, and we could not deal with it? The classes were getting bigger and bigger. All of that had to be slowed down for many reasons. I had to slow it down within myself. Too many people were coming at me. Too many things were coming at me. There was a time when I could have said, "We are going up to that mountain over there," and a couple hundred would have followed me up to the mountain. There would have been some nutty things going on. There *were* some nutty things going on. A lot of people were hallucinating about certain things. I had to slow that structure down in order to make that a true reality, and it made my life in a more balanced way. I have shut myself down a lot, but it is usable. It is usable because I am sitting here and thinking about it and making it me. What you feel and sense in this room is a true reality. What you see and hear is the absolute truth. There is no nonsense about it. That is the unique thing about it. We can make something within the physical sense. We can make a classroom with a format that has a structure to it. Then we can talk about it drawing in thousands of people. But I do not want to do that. I want to keep it simple. I want to make it something that is usable and understandable, and keep it within the context of the truth of the reality of it.

Any questions? Do you have to believe any of that? Do you have to believe anything? Do you want to sit for a while to meditate and then leave? I love you.